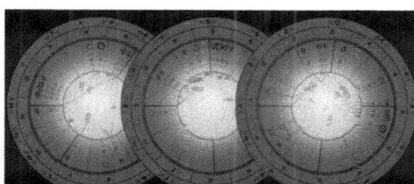

By Frank Clifford:
   Birth Charts (Flare, due 2019)
   Palm Reading (Hamlyn, 2004, Flare new edition due 2018)
   The Solar Arc Handbook (2018)
   Horoscope Snapshots: Essays in Modern Astrology (Flare, 2014)
   Getting to the Heart of Your Chart: Playing Astrological Detective (Flare, 2012)
   The Astrologer's Book of Charts (Flare, 2009)
   Palmistry 4 Today (Rider 2002, Flare expanded edition, 2009)
   British Entertainers: The Astrological Profiles (Flare, 1997, 2003)

Mini-books by Frank Clifford:
   Dialogues: Tools for the Working Astrologer (with Mark Jones, 2016)
   The Midheaven: Spotlight on Success (2016)
   The Astrology of Love, Sex and Attraction (with Fiona Graham, 2015)
   Humour in the Horoscope: The Astrology of Comedy (2015)
   Solar Arc Directions (2011)
   Venus: Your Key to Love (2000)
   Mars: Your Burning Desires (2000)
   The Essentials of Hand Analysis (1999)

Published by Flare Publications & The London School of Astrology:
   The Horary Process (Richard Swatton, 2018)
   Vocational Astrology: Finding the Right Career Direction (Faye Blake, 2017)
   From Symbol to Substance: Training the Astrological Intuition
    (Richard Swatton, mini-book, 2012)
   Astrology The New Generation (various contributors, 2012)
   Jane Struthers' 101 Astrology Questions for the Student Astrologer
    (Jane Struthers, mini-book, 2010)
   Kim Farley's Astro Mind Maps (Kim Farley, mini-book, 2010)
   The Twelve Houses (Howard Sasportas, 2007)
   The Contemporary Astrologer's Handbook (Sue Tompkins, 2006)
   Jupiter and Mercury: An A to Z (Paul Wright, 2006)
   Astrology in the Year Zero (Garry Phillipson, 2000)
   The Sun Sign Reader (Joan Revill, 2000)
   Shorthand of the Soul: The Quotable Horoscope (David Hayward, 1999)

All titles are available online and through the following websites:
   www.frankclifford.co.uk
   www.flareuk.com
   www.londonschoolofastrology.co.uk

The London School of Astrology

— *the students' choice in contemporary astrological education* —

- Accredited Foundation courses for beginners in central London
- Accredited Diploma courses for those with more experience
- Saturday seminars, Summer School courses and other events
- Short courses in tarot and palmistry (modern hand analysis)

- **New online astrology and palmistry courses for all levels**

Learn astrology, palmistry and tarot in a fun, supportive environment with the UK's most experienced, professional astrologers/tutors/writers

To find out more
Visit our website
www.londonschoolofastrology.co.uk
Email: admin@londonschoolofastrology.co.uk

Telephone: +44 (0)20 8402 7772

Self-knowledge, spiritual development, vocational training

– To all music lovers who have ever looked heavenwards –

Compilation copyright © Frank C. Clifford 2018

All rights reserved. No part of this publication may be reproduced, stored in a retrieval system, or transmitted in any form or by any means, electronic, mechanical, photocopying, recording or otherwise, without the prior permission of the copyright owner.

Frank C. Clifford has asserted his right to be identified as the author of this Work.

Each of the contributors retains the rights to their essays.

First edition published in 2018 by Flare Publications
in conjunction with the London School of Astrology, BCM Planets, London WC1N 3XX, England, UK

www.flareuk.com and www.londonschoolofastrology.co.uk
email: admin@londonschoolofastrology.co.uk

A CIP catalogue record for this book is available from the British Library

ISBN: 978-1-903353-53-0 (softcover)
978-1-903353-54-7 (ebook)

To contact Frank Clifford, please email him at info@flareuk.com or visit www.frankclifford.co.uk

My sincere thanks to Diana McMahon-Collis for project managing,
Jane Struthers for proofing the essays in this book,
Sy Scholfield for checking all the data, charts and sources,
Clifford Hayes (www.hayesdesign.co.uk) for the beautiful cover,
Barry Street of The Astrology Shop in Covent Garden for his continued support
and to Mario Trevino and Dan Nasir-Hill for helping with data entry.
A big thanks to all the data collectors for their dedication and energy over many years
and to all the wonderful astrology writers who contributed to this fundraising project.

Some of the text was first published in issues of *The Mountain Astrologer* (USA). My thanks to Tem Tarriktar, Nan Geary, Jan de Prosse who edited, proofed and published these original pieces.

THE BOOK OF
MUSIC HOROSCOPES

Flare Publications
The London School of Astrology

CONTENTS

Contributors' Biographies	6
The Harmony of the Celestial Spheres *Frank C Clifford*	12
The Astrology of Pop *Neil Spencer*	14
Charts: Jazz	22
Creativity and Diversity *Alexander Graf von Schlieffen*	27
Dave Grohl, Congo Square and New Orleans Jazz *Michelle Young*	30
Charts: R&B and Hip Hop	33
Music, Magic and Mishaps *Stefanie James*	43
Neptune Rules the Playlist *Steven Forrest*	46
Neptune *Frank Clifford*	49
Charts: Pop Idols & Pin-ups	50
Fame *Frank Clifford*	56
Venus *Frank Clifford*	62
The X Factor *Hannah Glover*	66
Charts: Country & Singer–Songwriters	68
The Moon, the Musician and the Listening Public *Lynn Bell*	80
Whole Lotta Love *Mark Jones*	85
Charts: Music Royalty	93
George Harrison *Pete Watson*	96
Good Vibrations *Paul F Newman*	103
The Wild Mercury Musical Journey of Bob Dylan *Sue Farebrother*	107
Dance Me to the End of Love *Brian Clark*	109
Dwelling with the Devil in the 8th House *Mandi Lockley*	114
Sphinxes of the Music World *Victor Olliver*	116
Lust for Life *Diana McMahon-Collis*	121
Michael Jackson *Glenn Perry*	125
Neptune and the Search for Nirvana *Carole Bone*	128

'I know that deep blue sea will soon be calling me' *Fernanda Paiva*	133
It's All About the Performance *Michele Finey*	139
'All you need is your own imagination...' *Deborah Perera*	140
Rock Rebels *Kim Farley*	143

Music and the Saturn–Neptune Cycle *Bruce Scofield*   148

Chart Data & Sources   150
(Includes an index of all the musicians)

Charts: Easy Listening Vocalists   163
Mercury and the Moon *Frank Clifford*   169

Charts: Disco, Dance & Electronic   170
Music Television *Emily Chow-Kambitsch*   175

Charts: Latin Stars & Euro Pop   178
Global Reach *Franco*   186
Mercury: The Transgender Singer *Sy Scholfield*   188

Charts: Rock   191
Signatures of Rock *Frank Clifford*   191
Women Who Rock *Tony Howard*   195
The Aquarian, Uranian Nature of Progressive Rock *Tim Burness*   209
Last Style: The Fender Stratocaster *Armand Diaz*   211

Charts: Duos, Groups & Band Members   213
Portrait of a Jam Band: Phish *Kathy Rose*   220
Further Observations *Frank Clifford*   223

Charts: Stage & Screen   224
Sarah Brightman: An Eclectic Angel *Shawn Nygaard*   231
The Voice: Julie Andrews *Mari Garcia*   236

CONTRIBUTORS' BIOGRAPHIES

LYNN BELL   www.lynnbellastrologer.com
Lynn has been a consulting astrologer for more than thirty years and travels widely as a speaker and teacher. She lives in Paris and taught at the Centre for Psychological Astrology for many years. She now teaches online for MISPA, Astrology University and in person at The London School of Astrology. *Planetary Threads*, her book on family patterns, was reissued by Ibis Press in 2013, and she is also the author of *Cycles of Light*. Lynn was honoured with the prestigious Charles Harvey Award in 2016. She can be reached at lynnbell@mac.com

CAROLE BONE
Carole has been studying astrology for almost twenty years, gaining her FAS Certificate in May 2001. She studied with renowned Glasgow astrologer and author Anne Whitaker for two years before becoming first librarian then Secretary of Aquarius Rising, an astrological association based in Glasgow. She also enjoys writing and photography and has had several poems printed both online and by United Press. Her poem 'Stardancing' won the 2011 National Poetry Anthology and is one of two to have been published in *The Mountain Astrologer*.

TIM BURNESS   https://timburness.wordpress.com
Tim has run a busy astrological consultation and teaching practice at several points over the last thirty years, working with people from all walks of life. He has been featured in *The Independent*, on local radio stations and he has also contributed to *The Astrological Journal*. Tim is interested in raising the profile of accessible and intelligent astrology as a tool for self-awareness and healing. He lives in Brighton, UK, and can be contacted through his blog at https://timburness.wordpress.com, which features a range of astrology articles.

EMILY CHOW-KAMBITSCH
Emily has been exploring astrology since January 2009, when she first learned approaches to psychological astrology from Dr Jennifer Freed in Santa Barbara, California. She began study at the London School of Astrology in 2012 and later received its Certificate in Astrology. Emily holds a Masters in Classical Language and Literature from the University of Oxford, and a PhD in Classics from University College London, and enjoys applying the rigour of academic research and knowledge of Greco-Roman myth to her study of astrology.

BRIAN CLARK   www.astrosynthesis.com.au
Brian has been a consulting astrologer and educator for most of his adult life. He also is the creator of the Astro*Synthesis distance learning program, which has been shaped from his experience as an astrological educator over the past forty years. He is the author of three new volumes: *From the Moment We Met*, *Vocation* and *The Family Legacy*. Brian has been honoured with Life Membership in the Federation of Australian Astrologers and the Association of Professional Astrologers for his contributions to the discipline of astrology.

FRANK C CLIFFORD
www.frankclifford.co.uk

Frank has built an eclectic career as the writer of a dozen books (including *Getting to the Heart of Your Chart* and *Palmistry 4 Today*), a consultant astrologer and palmist, a researcher of birth data, and the Principal of the London School of Astrology. In 2012, Frank was the youngest recipient of a lifetime award from the Astrological Association, and a writing honour from ISAR and a Regulus Award nomination have since followed. Frank has written for *The Mountain Astrologer* since 2008 and guest edited the magazine a number of times.

ARMAND DIAZ, Ph.D.
www.integralastrology.net

Armand is an NCGR–PAA certified astrologer with a practice based in New York and a worldwide clientele. He lectures nationally and internationally. In 2012, he published *Integral Astrology: Understanding the Ancient Discipline in the Contemporary World*. The following year, he co-produced and co-edited *Transpersonal Astrology*. His most recent book, *Separating Aspects*, is on relationship astrology. Armand's writings have appeared in *The Mountain Astrologer* and *The Astrological Journal*. He is Books and Articles Editor for Astrology News Service.

SUE FAREBROTHER
www.suemerlyn.com

Sue has been a professional astrologer, lecturer and tutor for more than twenty-five years. She teaches at beginners' and advanced astrology levels for the FAS and the London School of Astrology, where she also teaches tarot. Sue gained a distinction in 2007 from the Sophia Centre for her Cultural Astronomy and Astrology MA dissertation on the links between astrology and tarot in the 19th century. Her beginners' book, *Astrology Decoded*, was published by Rider/Random House to critical acclaim. She is currently writing her second astrology book.

KIM FARLEY

Kim discovered astrology at the end of the 1980s and since then it has enhanced her life in countless ways. She loves the intensity and connection of private consultation work as well as the joy of shared vision experienced in live classes at the LSA and FAS, and over the years she has introduced the subject to a generation of students. She has a second more recent vocation as a funeral celebrant. Music has always played a huge part in her life, from early reel-to-reel recordings of the Top 20 to her current involvement in co-hosting Vinyl Therapy events.

MICHELE FINEY
www.celestialinsight.com.au

Michele is an astrologer based in Melbourne. Michele began studying astrology in 1980, later going on to train as a hypnotherapist. Her astrological interests include mundane and medical astrology, as well as planetary cycles. Michele has presented her astrological research throughout Australia and in the USA. Michele produces a beautiful 32-page astrology calendar and she is the author of Solar Fire's *Health and Wellbeing Report*. Her books include, *Secrets of the Zodiac* and *The Sacred Dance of Venus and Mars*. Email: mfiney@cinsight.com.au

STEVEN FORREST
www.forrestastrology.com

Steven is the author of several best sellers including *The Inner Sky*, *The Changing Sky*, *The Book of the Moon* and most recently *The Book of Neptune*. His work has been translated into a dozen languages. He travels world-wide teaching his brand of choice-centred evolutionary astrology – an astrology that integrates free will, grounded humanistic psychology and ancient metaphysics. Over a thousand people have passed through his Astrological Apprenticeship program since its inception in 1998, with chapters meeting in America, Italy, Australia and China.

FRANCO   www.soulbody.ca

Franco is somewhat of a Renaissance Man: a mechanical engineer, astrologer, musician, runner, energy worker, Wiccan priest and an overall ham. He realized that he had gift for divination in the late 1990s and soon discovered astrology, engaging in intensive study and coaching under Toronto astrologer, Julie Simmons. He has served as the secretary and vice-president of Astrology Toronto and is currently co-director of Alphee Lavoie's Astrological Investigators as research astrologer. His astro-detective articles have been featured in *The Mountain Astrologer*.

MARI GARCIA   http://mgarcia550.wixsite.com/mari-garcia

Mari is a consulting astrologer who has been involved with astrology since 1990. She has lectured widely both in Australia and the USA and has published articles both online and in print. She is co-author of *Scala Coeli: A Collection of Astrological Essays*. She edited the compilation *An Ancient Art in the Modern World: Australis 97 Congress Papers* and was also a contributor to the anthology. Mari is also co-principal of the Astro Mundi school of astrology. For consultations, contact her at mgarcia550@bigpond.com

HANNAH GLOVER

Hannah discovered a passion for astrology in 2011 and studied with The London School of Astrology. She works as a welfare rights adviser in London and lives in Kent with her daughter. She can be contacted at hannahrglover@hotmail.com

TONY HOWARD   www.astroraven.com

Tony graduated summa cum laude from the University of Colorado with a B.A. in History and Film Theory. His writing has been featured in *The Mountain Astrologer* and in Donna Cunningham's 2010 Astrology Blog-A-Thon. He is a featured contributor to *Astrology, the Next Generation* (2012). Tony is the creator of FindAnAstrologer.com and AstrologyUniversity.com, and is the managing director of Steven Forrest's publishing company Seven Paws Press. Readers may e-mail Tony at tony@astroraven.com. Tony currently resides in Portland, Oregon.

STEFANIE JAMES   www.stelliumastrology.com

Stefanie signed up to the London School of Astrology at her Saturn Return and has since travelled around the UK and abroad talking, teaching and writing about astrology. Alongside running her website and seeing clients, she co-founded and hosts the transatlantic podcast HIJAC Radio, exploring mysteries, current affairs and alternative perspectives through the lens of astrology.

MARK JONES   www.plutoschool.com

Mark is an astrologer, psychosynthesis therapist and hypnotherapist based in Wales, and working with clients and students all over the world. Mark is a regular speaker and workshop leader in Europe and North America. Mark's first book, *Healing the Soul: Pluto, Uranus and the Lunar Nodes*, explains his approach, while his second, *The Soul Speaks: the Therapeutic Power of Astrology*, explores the transformative power of the natal chart reading. His third book will be on the planetary nodes.

Contributors' Biographies

MANDI LOCKLEY　　　　　　　　　　　　　　　　　　　　　　　　www.mandilockley.blogspot.co.uk
Mandi has written for *The Astrological Journal* as well as for numerous websites, including her own Astroair blog. She published the e-book *Saturn in Scorpio: Your Guide Through the Dark* in 2012 and in 2010 worked with Donna Cunningham and C.J. Wright as Saturn Editor for the International Astrology Day Blogathon. Mandi also writes dark fiction and has had numerous short stories published. She attained her Diploma in Astrology from The London School of Astrology and now teaches at The Academy of Astrology.

DIANA MCMAHON-COLLIS　　　　　　　　　　　　　　　　　　　　　　　　　　　www.mindbliss.co.uk
Diana has written for thirty years on astrology, tarot and health, and is a non-fiction editor/mentor of Mind, Body, Spirit titles at JerichoWriters.com. In 2001 she co-founded the tarot association TABI.org.uk. She has worked as the in-house astrologer for *Easy Jet* and *Spa World* magazines and as a regular speaker and consultant at Champneys Forest Mere health resort. She is currently writing for *The Mountain Astrologer* and holds the Company of Astrologers' Advanced Horoscopy Certificate. Blog: https://celestialspot.blogspot.co.uk

PAUL F NEWMAN
Paul is a professional astrologer with over 300 articles on the subject published in magazines throughout the world. He is also a freelance copy writer and editor of fiction and non-fiction work for dozens of authors. His published books include *Luna: The Astrological Moon*, *Declination in Astrology: The Steps of the Sun* and *You're not a Person – Just a Birthchart*, as well as the fictional work *Guardians of the Stellar Grael* and the annual *Glastonbury Wonky Broomstick* diaries. You can contact him at pneuma@live.co.uk

SHAWN NYGAARD　　　　　　　　　　　　　　　　　　　　　　　　　　　　www.imagineastrology.com
Shawn has been an astrologer for sixteen years. In addition to private readings, Shawn has created and taught astrology classes in Minneapolis, focusing particularly on the in-depth meanings of the astrological symbols. He hosted the popular archetypal astrology radio show *Imagine That!* and has been an annual guest speaker at the Minnesota Jung Association. Shawn holds a degree in music production, and is a graduate of the CMED Institute in Chicago, where he studied archetypes and symbolism with Caroline Myss. He now teaches online for MISPA.

VICTOR OLLIVER　　　　　　　　　　　　　　　　　　　　　　　　　　　　　　　www.victorolliver.com
Victor is the editor of *The Astrological Journal*, the Media Officer of the Association of Professional Astrologers International and is *The Lady* magazine's first-ever star-gazer. Before obtaining a Diploma (with distinction) from The Mayo School of Astrology, he occupied a number of senior editorial posts in the UK media and won two PPA awards for his feature writing. He originally trained to be a barrister but says, 'I took a dislike to the Old Bailey's décor.' His sphinx essay is adapted from his book *Lifesurfing: Your Horoscope Forecast Guide 2015*.

FERNANDA PAIVA　　　　　　　　　　　　　　　　　　　　　　　　www.hitchhikingstars.wordpress.com
Fernanda earned a degree in history from the PUC Sao Paulo in 2007 and moved to London shortly after, where she became interested in psychology and taught herself tarot and astrology. In 2011 Fernanda got both Reiki degrees one and two, and it was only in 2012, during her Saturn Return, that she decided to take her passion for astrology more seriously and enrolled at The London School of Astrology. In early 2015 she got her certificate with distinction. Fernanda is currently living in the Forest of Dean where she also teaches astrology and sees clients.

DEBORAH PERERA
Deborah has had a lifelong interest in astrology and metaphysics. She began studying astrology seriously in her early twenties, gaining a certificate from the FAS. She also has a keen interest in yoga, and has a teaching qualification after studying in the USA and Canada. She is currently teaching art to people with special needs, and recently completed The London School of Astrology's Diploma in Astrology. She lives in Surrey with her husband and daughter.

GLENN PERRY, Ph.D. — www.aaperry.com
Glenn is an astrologer and psychotherapist in Haddam Neck, Connecticut. He received his doctorate in psychology from Saybrook Institute in San Francisco. In addition to private practice, Dr Perry is director of The Academy of AstroPsychology, an online school that offers certificate and diploma programs in psychological astrology. Glenn has written eight books on astrology, including *An Introduction to AstroPsychology*. He lectures internationally, teaches courses at the Nodoor Academy in Beijing, China, and served on the board of ISAR for many years.

KATHY ROSE — www.roseastrology.com
Kathy began her study of astrology at the age of eight. She opened her private practice in Denver when she was twenty-four, and has been offering professional astrology consultations ever since. Currently a resident of Virginia Beach, VA, Kathy has built a thriving astrological practice with an international clientele. She is a Highest Honors Graduate of the Noel Tyl Master's Certification Course and serves as Tyl's Teaching Associate. Published frequently in *The Mountain Astrologer*, Kathy has a very popular YouTube channel: roseastrology.

ALEXANDER GRAF VON SCHLIEFFEN — www.schlieffen-astrologie.de
Alexander is a painter and astrologer and has been teaching and lecturing on astrology worldwide since 1996. From 2003–4 he had his own astrology show on German TV. He has released over a dozen audio books and was a columnist for the German edition of *Vanity Fair*. His first book, *When Chimpanzees Dream Astrology*, was published in 2003 by the CPA Press. In 2013, his second book, *Im Netz der Beziehungen*, was published by the Chiron Press in Germany. In both books he displays a new and refreshing perspective on the astrological quadrants.

SY SCHOLFIELD — www.syscholfield.com
Sy is an Australian astro-data collector, astrologer and scholar writing extensively on sexuality in the horoscope, visual art, film, the media and popular culture. He is credited as data editor of various astrology books including Frank Clifford's *Astrologer's Book of Charts* (2009) and *Horoscope Snapshots* (2014). Since 2013 he has been an editor at Astrodatabank and has contributed almost 10,000 of his timed research data to the late Lois Rodden's collection. He is currently writing a book on the planetary archetypes of sex, gender and sexuality.

BRUCE SCOFIELD — www.onereed.com
Bruce began a lifelong study of astrology in 1967 and has been a consultant specializing in psychological analysis, relationships and electional astrology since the mid 1970s. He has authored seven books and numerous articles on astrology and has served on the education committee of NCGR since 1979. He has Level 4 certification from NCGR-PAA, holds an M.A. in history, a Ph.D. in geoscience, has taught science at the University of Massachusetts and currently teaches for Kepler College. His website contains info on Mesoamerican astrology and other topics.

NEIL SPENCER www.neilspencer.com

Celebrated for his pioneering writing on Bob Marley, reggae and punk, Neil was the editor of *New Musical Express* between 1978 and 1985, when the paper was at the height of its influence. He has also written for *The Observer*, *Mojo* and *Uncut*. A self-taught astrologer, Neil contributed a Sun sign column to *The Observer* for many years and his monthly forecasts can be found at his website. He is the author of *True as the Stars Above: Adventures in Modern Astrology* (Gollancz, 2000), which will be re-issued in expanded form as an e-book in 2018.

PETE WATSON www.starscan.plus.com

Pete is an experienced, self-taught astrologer who has lectured around the UK and been published in various magazines, including *The Astrological Journal* and *The Mountain Astrologer*. Pete's specialisms include locational and midpoint astrology, and his website offers articles on both subjects including a list of delineations for each astrogeography line.

MICHELLE YOUNG www.michelle-young-astrology.net

Michelle, the Pisces daughter of a concert pianist, was born in the theatre. Beginning her own performing career at 8, Michelle sang in several languages, played several instruments and danced. Grant Lewi's books hooked her on astrology. Earning her college education with her voice, she wrote a monthly column as Scorpion Starr for the campus paper. She freelanced with *Dell Horoscope* as a cover features writer and monthly columnist for nine years and returned to *Horoscope* in 2014. Her first book on multiculturalism won a national and two state awards.

The Harmony of the Celestial Spheres

An Introduction by Frank Clifford

A study of music and astrology reveals some interesting parallels. Both are, in essence, languages. Whether looking at sheet music or the horoscope, we read, interpret and articulate the symbols and phrases, and listen for major themes and refrains. In popular song, a composition may have subplots but it tells a main story, much like the natal chart with its signatures and key aspects.

With both music and astrology, our goal is to translate and convey the mood and timbre of the composition. Both are structured by time and their own distinct rhythms; some phrases/notes/aspects are more harmonious – others less so, expressing and presenting certain disc(h)ord. Music leaves room for improvisation, for the listener or musician to make a personal connection or to stamp their own personality onto the piece. In a similar vein, for a horoscope to be brought to life, it requires context from its owner and is styled by the interpretive approach of the astrologer.

Both are chronometers that mark time on both personal and generational levels. Our musical preferences form an auditory spine of our history, reflecting the values and attitudes of ourselves and our peer group at any given time, while our chart speaks of our early experiences and the times into which we've been born. Both are forms of personal and social identity, and can be a means of self-definition. But whereas Tolstoy tells us that music is 'the shorthand of emotion', surely then astrology is (to quote David Hayward's book of astro-quotations) 'the shorthand of the soul'.

It is rare to find an astrologer who doesn't have music, in some way, directly linked to their life or livelihood. The two subjects have had mirroring histories. Most memorably, the Pluto in Leo Baby Boomers sparked a global explosion of music in the 1960s (from the Beatles to mainstream folk music and protest songs). The same self-help generation ushered in an 'Aquarian Age' of spiritual and metaphysical exploration in pursuit of an 'individual, unique destiny'. And who can forget that the most successful astrology book of all time – *Linda Goodman's Sun Signs* – was written during this time and then published in 1968?

For this volume, I reached out to dozens of astrologers asking for essays on an area of music. The plan was (and is) to use monies generated from this project to help astrologers in need of financial assistance to attend astrology conferences around the world. What follows are over thirty essays that examine the associations between the creative arts of music and astrology, or that look at specific musical genres or astrological epochs, as well as some astro-biographies that demonstrate how we encounter the musical personality as a direct expression of the chart's major themes. I've also added a handful of musical observations from an article I wrote for *The Mountain Astrologer* in 2014. And, scattered throughout the book, you'll find over 500 birth charts of the most influential musicians of the past century (for whom we have birth times).

For the Chart Data & Sources section of this book, it would have been simpler (and far less work) to have listed everyone alphabetically, but then some fun would have been lost for those wanting to study a particular genre or compare the charts of musicians who worked together. Of course, many artists could qualify for inclusion into more than one category but I've made a number of choices along the way that reflect the purpose of this book and also attempted to simply matters (alphabetically, by era or by group). And there are dozens of artists I would love to have included but had to leave out because I don't yet have access to accurate data with confirmed sources for them. You'll find an invitation to contribute data to future editions of this book on page 150, where you'll also find the start of **a complete index with birth data (and sources) for those included in this book.**

Enjoy the book and thanks for helping to raise funds. Here's a quick run-down of each chapter (you'll notice that each of the twelve chapters begins with the constellation of a sign of the zodiac, starting with Aries and ending with Pisces – the natural zodiacal order):

1. **Jazz** • the charts of jazz singers and musicians
2. **R&B & Hip Hop** • the charts of artists whose work could be categorized under the soul, rhythm and blues, urban, hip hop or rap genres
3. **Pop Idols and Pin-ups** • here, you'll find horoscopes of those who have made contributions to pop music and pop culture, including the pop sensations and heart-throbs of their day, as well as those who featured in music TV competitions like *The X Factor* and *Idol* franchises
4. **Country & Singer-Songwriters** • a selection of country and western performers, which is followed by many notable singer-songwriters
5. **Music Royalty** • this large chapter contains charts of a group of global artists and bands whose voices and names are instantly recognizable. You'll find some of the most famous singer-songwriters, rock, pop, soul, country and jazz stars here rather than in their own categories in other chapters. On occasion (in sections on The Beatles, The Doors and Elvis Presley, for instance), you'll notice a + symbol, which indicates that I've included charts of related people who are associated with the artist(s)
6. **Chart Data and Sources** • this chapter contains all the birth data of everyone included in this book, and an index of all the charts presented
7. **Easy Listening Vocalists** • a small selection of charts of popular MOR singers and balladeers
8. **Disco, Dance & Electronic** • a chapter of charts on some of the key players in dance music
9. **Latin Stars & Euro Pop** • a selection of music stars from Latin countries and the Continent
10. **Rock** • this chapter includes horoscopes of the women and men who fall under the broad umbrella of rock music
11. **Duos, Groups & Bands** • a chapter dedicated to chart comparison of some of the most famous acts of the pop era and their members
12. **Stage & Screen** • a horoscopic tour through a variety of artists, including film score composers, opera singers, Broadway Babies, stage singers, chanteuses and film musical stars

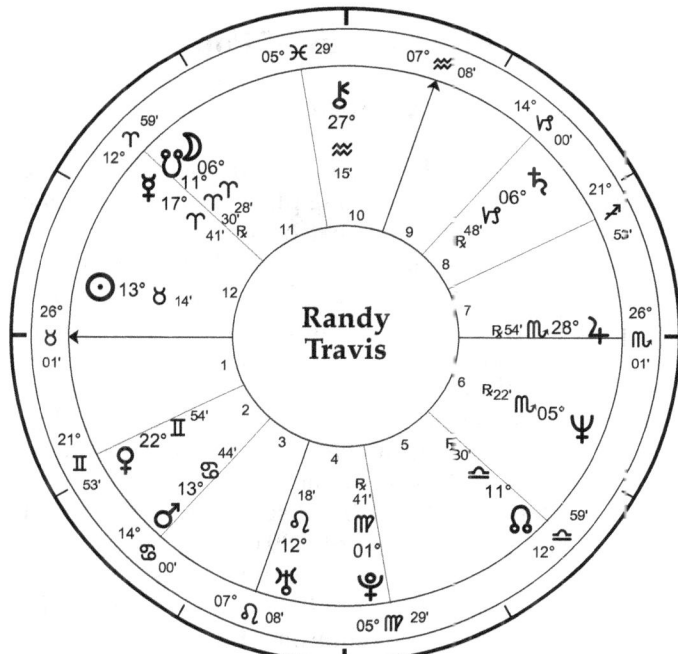

The chart wheels have been calculated using Placidus houses but I've added another feature (the outermost grid) for those of you who prefer Equal. See the chart above of Country singer Randy Travis. I've also added Chiron and the Mean Nodes of the Moon. All charts have been calculated using Solar Fire software.

There's more info about where to find data online on page 150, but for those interested in data books (people, events and countries), I would recommend:

- *The Gauquelin Book of American Charts* by Michel and Françoise Gauquelin
- *A Multitude of Lives* by Paul Wright
- *The Canadian Astrology Collection* by John McKay-Clements
- *American Histrology* by Ronald Howland
- *The Book of World Horoscopes* by Nick Campion

I've also compiled two volumes of my own: *British Entertainers: The Astrological Profiles* (2003 edition) and *The Astrologer's Book of Charts* (2009).

The Astrology of Pop

Neil Spencer

The modern world arrived bang on astrological schedule in 1891, when the two far-flung planets of Neptune and Pluto met – a conjunction that only occurs every 500 years. Here was the seed moment of today's global culture; the next few years saw the arrival of the motor car, the safety bicycle, the phonograph, the gramophone disc, the jukebox, a telephone system, the radio, the cinema and, a little later, the aeroplane. On that list are most of the media that fuel a major rock band today, though it would be half a century before the arrival of the electric guitar (1933) and the arena gig (1965).

Since Pluto wouldn't be discovered for another forty years, the astrologers of 1891 had no idea of its convergence with Neptune in Gemini's skies, nor of the similarly loaded oppositions of Uranus and Pluto in 1901 and 1902. However, adventurous Edwardians might have associated the political and cultural upheavals of the era with the 1900 meeting of Jupiter and Uranus, the latter planet already being associated with revolution and technological innovation.

By contrast, today's mundane astrologers are privy to a range of cycles to calibrate the longer and shorter epochs of history. Jupiter, Saturn, Uranus, Neptune and Pluto provide ten such cycles (trans-Plutonians can wait), several of which prove to be startlingly synchronous with the evolution of popular music. As we shall see, the Promethean energies of Uranus have an especially important place in pop.

Not all planetary cycles are equal. Writing in the 1980s, Leyla Raël Rudhyar divided them into an 'A-list' of cycles that 'sound the low-frequency tones of evolutionary epochs' (Neptune–Pluto, Uranus–Pluto, Uranus–Neptune), while the rest modify the transformative themes of these three cycles. In particular, Rudhyar associates the four Jupiter cycles with 'discoveries, ideals, visions and social trends', an insight that chimes well with pop music's growth and its characteristic fads, fashions, and genre-mutation.[1]

As the art form quickest to respond to social trends and political events, pop surely reflects all the major cycles, yet it's the 13.8-year Jupiter–Uranus cycle that proves most illuminating. For the late Charles Harvey, this duo's conjunctions and oppositions 'encourage the Promethean spirit of rebellion and self-will, and a spirit of individual and collective optimism and enterprise.'[2] Harvey's words perfectly describe the pop convulsions of 1900, 1955 and 1969, to name but three. Richard Tarnas has also pointed to 'a tendency in culture for events and figures that played roles in Jupiter–Uranus alignments to possess a mythologized, legendary aura … evoked to the point where they became iconic.'[3] This, too, proves perfectly apt for the gaudier stitches in rock's rich tapestry.

The Jupiter–Uranus conjunction of 1900, which occurred close to a Uranus–Pluto opposition, brought not just the technology to record and distribute music on a mass scale for the first time,[4] but also a revolution in music itself. America was its crucible, the nation's troubled racial plurality bringing a fertile cross-pollination between African-American and European tropes, where polyrhythms and call-and-response vocals met formal orchestral settings.

The outcome took over the world, with ragtime becoming first a national craze – the appearance of pianist Scott Joplin at the Chicago World's Fair in 1893 was an emblematic moment – and then an international sensation. Jazz, 'the first American art form', would shortly follow the same arc of insurrection, influence and international popularity. Later, rock 'n' roll and hip hop would repeat the pattern.

A New Music for the Modern Age

The date singled out by New Orleans pianist Jelly Roll Morton as the birth year of jazz is 1902, when the Crescent City's ragtime, blues and marching songs crystallized into a new music. A self-proclaimed 'inventor of jazz' (a title too grand for any individual), Morton was born, like many early jazz and movie stars, under the Neptune–Pluto conjunction of 1891 (and with a Sun–Uranus conjunction). From a distinguished Creole dynasty, Morton and his family were forced to

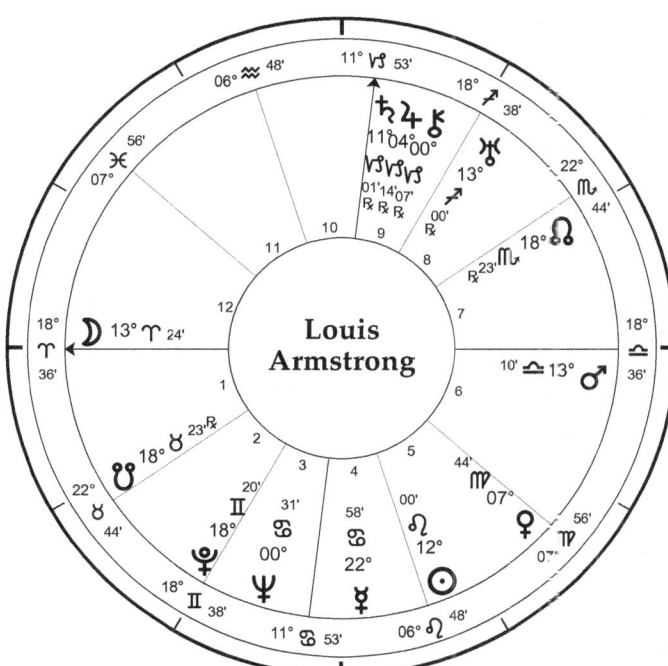

the 'American' side of New Orleans under an odious 1894 act of racial cleansing, thus ensuring that the Creole's conservatoire-trained music rubbed shoulders with that played in the brothels of Storyville.

This was a microcosm of a culture clash happening across the country, as America's cities took shape and Italian, Russian, Irish and other immigrants rubbed together with white and black Americans. To say that the resulting mélange spawned modern pop is no revelation – though astrologers can appreciate the symbolism of jittery Gemini in play, this being the sign of novelty, media, entertainment and diversity. The very concept of 'ragged time' is Geminian, played by the right hand while the left keeps regular rhythm. Look, Ma, Twin hands!

Louis Armstrong, jazz's first great innovator and ambassador, was fittingly born in 1901, with the planetary cycles of the time powerful in his natal chart. Armstrong's horoscope is dominated by a Grand Trine in Fire, tying Uranus, the innovator, to his grandstanding Leo Sun and Aries Moon (his public).

Uranus opposes Pluto, a generational signature. Saturn on the Midheaven adds stability and longevity to a career that started at age fourteen, at his first half-Saturn Return.

The cycle of Jupiter–Uranus between 1914 and 1927 is synchronous with the rise of jazz and Tin Pan Alley. The year 1914 itself holds few symbolic moments for pop (and the onset of World War I is better described by the conjunction of Saturn and Pluto), but jazz records (the word first appeared in print in 1913) arrived in 1917, leading to the blossoming of the 'jazz age' in the 1920s.

Indeed, at the next Jupiter–Uranus conjunction in 1927 – appropriately in the start-up sign of Aries – came *The Jazz Singer*, the first sound-synchronized film ('talkie') and the first movie musical. Hugely popular, *The Jazz Singer* was no great shakes, its 'blackface' minstrelsy already an anachronism, but it begat the form that dominated cinema and pop until World War II: the Hollywood musical, whose canons of song were the concept albums of their day. Pop and cinema have remained close siblings.

Since World War II overshadows the Jupiter–Uranus conjunction of 1941, one would not expect much musical revolution, yet that year saw the birth of bebop, spearheaded by trumpeter Dizzy Gillespie and alto saxophonist Charlie Parker, whose solos were the jazz equivalent of Kandinsky's abstract paintings: challenging and touched by genius.[5] Again, we see the Uranian 'shock of the new' character at work; the planet is also powerfully placed in Parker's horoscope, conjunct his natal Moon and opposite Jupiter. (Bob Dylan, born in 1941, has the Jupiter–Uranus conjunction next to his Moon.)

The year 1941 further witnessed the emergence of Frank Sinatra as a solo star, becoming more important than the bands that employed him. Although no great musical innovator, Sinatra, with his loyal army of bobby-soxers, became the template for every subsequent teen idol, from Elvis Presley and the Beatles to Justin Bieber and Lady Gaga.

The Rise of Rock

The significance of the three-time conjunction of Jupiter and Uranus during 1954–5 – the dawn of rock 'n' roll – is more blatant. Entire books have been written to establish claims on the first rock 'n' roll record.[6] However, while singles by Ike Turner, Arthur Crudup and others are contenders, the popularly understood meaning of rock 'n' roll arrived with Elvis Presley, the at-once and future King.

One facet of rock 'n' roll was that it was neither black nor white but both – the cause of a huge fracas in the still-segregated United States and an example of Uranus's role as leveller and troublemaker. Musically, rock borrowed from R&B (rhythm and blues), 'hillbilly' country and smart urban pop.[7]

Presley cut 'That's All Right', his first commercial single, on 5 July 1954 at Sun Studios in Memphis, and it was first played two days later by local radio celebrity Dewey Phillips on his daily WHBQ show. Phillips played his acetate copy repeatedly from 21:30, getting an instant, fevered response from his listeners.[8] This chart certainly signifies uproar and enchantment, with the Sun and Mercury placed between the closing Jupiter–Uranus conjunction, and Uranus square to a dreamy Moon–Neptune conjunction.

One year later, Presley was an international star, his ascent concurrent with the emergence of the 'teenager', a phenomenon that took off just as Uranus arrived in the exhibitionist, youth-orientated sign of Leo in August 1955, where Pluto already resided (thus marking out an entire generation of Baby Boomers born between 1939 and 1956; more on this later). 'Teenage' turned into an international moral panic, heralded by the delirium that greeted the movie *Blackboard Jungle* (released on 25 March 1955), whose theme song, Bill Haley's 'Rock Around the Clock', became a worldwide hit, and by James Dean's film *Rebel Without a Cause* (27 October 1955).

The incendiary nature of the time – which witnessed the first records from Chuck Berry, Johnny Cash, Jerry Lee Lewis, Little Richard and more (not forgetting the first 'soul' record, 'I Got a Woman' by Ray Charles) – is written in the astrological sky. Jazz celebrated its long haul to respectability with the first Newport Festival in 1954, just as the US Supreme Court ruled against racial segregation in schools. Note, too, the arrival of pop's most iconic instrument, the Fender Stratocaster, in October 1954. The first electric guitars had been marketed in the 1930s by Rickenbacker and Gibson, with the first solid-body prototype ('The Log') made by Les Paul in 1941 (!). The Fender Broadcaster became the first commercial solid guitar in 1950, but it was the 'Strat', in all its curvaceous, phallic, sci-fi glory, that became pop's go-to instrument.

The Jupiter–Uranus cycle between 1954 and 1969 has become the acknowledged Golden Age of Pop (if only because Pluto in Leo Boomers insist, while their performers persist). Incontestable is that the era saw pop's ascent into an unprecedented cultural force, the universal solvent of international youth and an industry that shipped discs in previously unthinkable quantities. Pop's expanding canon of stars soon eclipsed even cinema's heart-throbs, becoming not just pin-ups but guru-esque figures with real cultural and political clout. Witness the furore in 1966 when John Lennon flippantly said the Beatles were 'more popular than Jesus'.

Aesthetically, pop underwent a profound transformation during these fifteen years. The bland niceties of Tin Pan Alley didn't disappear (the big sentimental ballad remains a regular chart topper), but the distance between Pat Boone crooning 'Apple Blossom Time' and the Beatles wandering through the psych-rock pastures of 'Strawberry Fields' is immense.

To understand changes of such magnitude requires another of Rudhyar's A-list cycles, that of Uranus–Pluto. To do so, let's consider the extraordinary planetary picture of February 1962, when the seven 'inner' planets formed a stellium in Aquarius at the time of a total solar eclipse – an event rare and weird enough to send more excitable New Agers scurrying to the hills to await The End, while for others it proclaimed the dawning of the Age of Aquarius, a notion that would soon fascinate pop itself.

Of Aquarius there is certainly no shortage in this chart. Opposite the stellium lies Uranus, approaching its half-cycle with Jupiter (exact on 14 March that year),

The Astrology of Pop

accentuating the axis in which Leo's Golden Child complements the well organized society of Aquarius. The rock 'n' roll revolution of 1955 augured by Uranus in Leo had by now petered out, the teenage animal neutered. The post-army Elvis was a balladeer, Little Richard had gone to gospel, Jerry Lee was blacklisted, Chuck Berry was in jail, Buddy Holly and Eddie Cochran were dead. Pop's future was, apparently, boys next door called Bobby. At least, such was the hope of the music industry.

It hadn't reckoned with this eclipse, where something special is clearly being born. The New Moon of the stellium is square Neptune in Scorpio, signalling that whatever is arriving includes mysticism, escapism and transgressive sex – qualities that would not be in short supply over the coming years. Aquarian demands for social justice were also in the air; JFK's Camelot was in its pomp, while pop's front line had shifted to protest and the folkie coffee houses of Bleecker Street; Bob Dylan released his first album on 19 March 1962. Representing another strand of liberation and social levelling came the Beatles, who released their first single on 5 October 1962, three days before the second Jupiter–Uranus opposition, which was in early Virgo, and close to the third opposition on 7 December.

Soul music, the other eminence of the 1960s, has a more cloudy origin. Mention has been made of Ray Charles's fusion of R&B and gospel in 1955, but talk of 'soul' music only came in 1961–2, with Solomon Burke and Sam Cooke in particular. Before that, black America's music was either called 'race music' or R&B, or considered, like Cooke's early hits, as pop.

Uranus–Pluto and Psychedelia
From here onwards, pop – and, indeed, the rest of culture and politics – is in the grip of the incoming conjunctions of Uranus and Pluto during 1965 and 1966. In his books, *Prometheus the Awakener* and *Cosmos and Psyche*, Richard Tarnas has explored the correlations of this conjunction in depth, pointing to the growth of radical politics, national independence movements, the rebirth of esoteric ideas (including astrology), scientific

advances (especially microprocessors) and the era's 'spectacular musical creativity'.

For pop, one meaning of the conjunction lies in a simple four-letter word: acid. The arrival of LSD is a before-and-after moment. For Bob Dylan, who took the drug in 1964, the acid experience resulted in *Bringing It All Back Home* (released in March 1965), with its torrential, apocalyptic imagery and totemic song 'Mr Tambourine Man'. The Beatles would follow with tracks like 'The Word' and 'Rain' and their masterpiece album *Revolver* (5 August 1966). On the US West Coast, the nascent Grateful Dead were playing Ken Kesey's 'Acid Tests' and – along with the Doors, the Charlatans, the Byrds, the 13th Floor Elevators and others – were creating what quickly became known as 'psychedelic rock'.[9]

Although psychedelia became thought of as a paisley-patterned, patchouli-scented reverie, the early manifestations of acid pop bear a distinctly dark hue. The Rolling Stones' 'Paint It Black' is a case in point, reflecting the archetypes of the Uranus–Pluto conjunction: the Promethean urge to 'break on through to the other side', as the Doors put it, but also a Plutonic Underworld where one might 'take the highway to the End of the Night'. The so-called Summer of Love in 1967 was likewise not so lovely; by the end of the summer, the hippie paradise of Haight Ashbury had become a squalid, drug-sodden quagmire from which George Harrison fled in horror. Pluto is not so easily overcome.

With psychedelia, pop also embraced 'cosmic' themes, as in Pink Floyd's 'Interstellar Overdrive', John Coltrane's *Ascension*, Jimi Hendrix's 'Third Stone from the Sun', and the astrologically themed *The Zodiac: Cosmic Sounds* (sample quote: '4,000 dreams may decay into indigo dust that cover Aquarius ...').

It is difficult to distinguish between the aftermath of the Uranus–Pluto conjunction and the three conjunctions of Jupiter and Uranus (in December 1968, March 1969 and July 1969), which were arguably still within orb of Pluto. Socially and politically, this was the age of revolution across the globe.[10] However, 1969 clearly began a new cycle in pop, marking the ascent of the singer–songwriter, with debut albums from Joni Mitchell, Neil Young, James Taylor and Van Morrison, and the onset of country rock via the Byrds and Crosby, Stills & Nash.

The origins of heavy metal are also in the late 60s stew, depending on at whose feet one wishes to lay the blame. Iron Butterfly's *In-A-Gadda-Da-Vida* (14 June 1968) is one contender for metal's birth; the formation of Led Zeppelin in 1968 and their eponymous debut album (12 January 1969) is another, though singer Robert Plant refutes the connection: 'That particular indignity belongs to Black Sabbath,' he told this author, though a chart for Sabbath's first album (13 February 1970) is short of metal's *sturm und drang*.

Black America, too, made a decisive shift at the end of the 1960s, with the harder rhythms of funk; the term 'funk' was first used by James Brown, one of its architects, in 1969, which also saw groundbreaking records by Tower of Power and Funkadelic. By 1970, soul and funk had become the music of outright protest as Curtis Mayfield, the Temptations, Edwin Starr and Marvin Gaye changed tack from romantic balladry.

Nor can we leave 1969 without mention of the much mythologized Woodstock Festival of 15–17 August (along with its evil twin, Altamont, on 6 December). Despite the Monterey Pop Festival of 1967, it was Woodstock that became the template for subsequent gatherings and, indeed, for the arena rock gig (the first example of which must be the Beatles at Shea Stadium on 15 August 1965, curiously with the Sun in the same degree of Leo as Woodstock's). A chart for Woodstock has the Jupiter–Uranus conjunction writ large and with airy ideals in Libra. Its Sun–Neptune square is both idealistic and druggy. Its Venus, conjunct the US Sun (4 July 1776), focuses on national identity (Hendrix's explosive 'Star-Spangled Banner' included). Yet, despite wishful thinking about 'the Woodstock nation', it's an Earthy chart. Declared impresario Bill Graham, 'The real thing Woodstock accomplished was that it told people rock was big business.'

Ah, yes, the money! For pop's new commercial clout, we might look at another A-list cycle, Neptune–Pluto, whose 1891 conjunction had, by 1951, widened

The Astrology of Pop 19

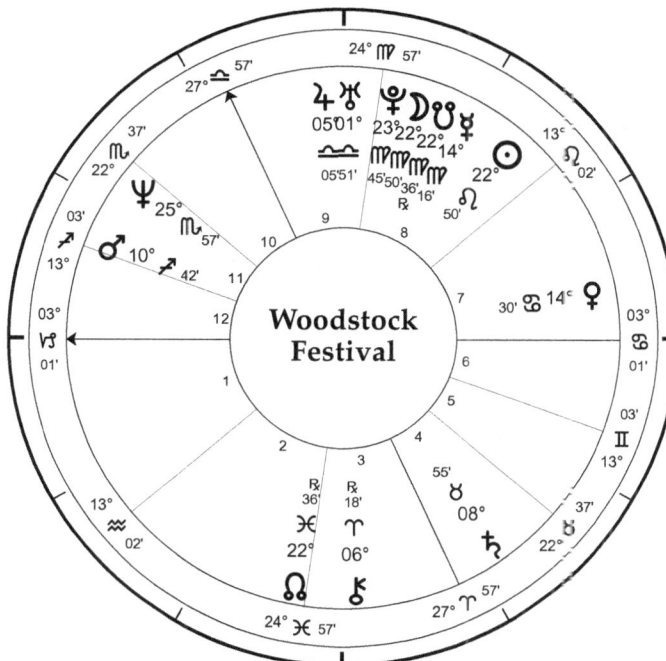

to a sextile, an aspect that held sway for most of the following two decades – years when Plutonic power and money cooperated with Neptune's creative imagination (and even its drug habits). The sextile flickered to exactitude thirteen times between 1951 and 1956, and eighteen times between November 1975 and July 1984.

New Revolutions

The early 1970s deepened and expanded 1969's agenda. There were micro-genres (metal, glam, progressive), more singer–songwriters, more cocaine cowboys, bigger arenas, larger record sales, but the Sixties 'rockocracy' was secure. However, that status quo was challenged by the punk insurrection that arrived on both sides of the Atlantic at the Jupiter–Uranus opposition of April 1976. The Ramones' back-to-basics rock 'n' roll, the Sex Pistols's cheerful outrage, the Slits' feminist provocation – punk was the Promethean spirit incarnate. With Uranus in Scorpio (from September 1975), punk's imagery was steeped in destruction, confrontation and a subterranea of rats, garbage and taboo sex. It

was cultural warfare, a Year Zero moment possessing Tarnas's 'mythologized, legendary aura'. The year 1975 also saw the first openly gay commercial pop song, Valentino's 'I Was Born This Way'.[1]

Concurrent with the ascent of punk and 'new wave' acts was the triumph of reggae, led by Bob Marley,[12] and the rise of disco. Both forms had been in play for some years, but came to global prominence under the Jupiter–Uranus opposition of 1976. Hip hop likewise reached a mutational tipping point at the Jupiter–Uranus conjunction of 1983 (in February, May and September), when Run DMC, Grandmaster Flash, and Double D and Steinski released groundbreaking hits. Hip hop and House music[13] – which also arrived under this conjunction – remain among Planet Earth's most popular pop genres.

Simultaneously, Michael Jackson's 'Billie Jean' marked a peak moment, its creator becoming the first black artist to receive heavy rotation on MTV,[14] alongside Prince with 'Little Red Corvette'. The year 1983 also saw the arrival of Madonna's first album and the recording of Bruce Springsteen's *Born in the USA*. Here, effectively, is the birth of corporate pop. With it came a new piece of tech, the CD. Now you had to buy all your old records all over again. Less corporate but equally important were the 1983 debuts by indie trailblazers R.E.M. and the Smiths.

Can Jupiter's oppositions to Saturn, Uranus, and Neptune in 1989 provide anything as earth-shaking? A glance at three acts is illuminating. This was the year that Senegal's Youssou N'Dour made his breakthrough to international stardom, cementing the era of 'world' music; N'Dour is now one of the planet's most famous voices. The UK's Stone Roses can't boast as much, but their 1989 debut became a mythic moment in Blighty and launched a generation of 'Britpop' rockers.

Washington State's Kurt Cobain also started his journey to mythic status with *Bleach* (15 June 1989), Nirvana's first album. Kurt's horoscope is startling, with 1967's Uranus–Pluto conjunction seared onto his Virgo Ascendant opposite the loose conjunction of Mercury, Chiron, Venus and Saturn. A natal chart dominated by outer planets is challenging, and 'owning' the psych-rock signature of Uranus–Pluto (back when a different band called Nirvana were playing), proved impossible for Kurt, a 'sad little sensitive, unappreciative, Pisces, Jesus man', as he called himself in his suicide note.[15]

At this point, pop's twitchy Jupiter–Uranus cycle becomes entangled in the A-list cycle of Uranus–Neptune, whose conjunction rolls around every 170 years, and which was in a 5° orb from 1989 to 1995, with Jupiter in opposition to both planets in 1989–90. André Barbault associates this cycle with 'historical renewal', and the collapse of the USSR and the end of apartheid surely fit – but Barbault also talks of the 'grip of unprecedented globalization' arriving under this configuration.[16]

Barbault's international currents certainly apply to pop, with an upsurge of interest in global folk and pop, though Neptune's dissolution of barriers worked on several levels. After 1990, pop lost a focal point. The hegemony of 'rock' that had started in 1954 began to ebb. Emerging nations, previously described as 'third world', were more interested in hip hop and reggae (the forms pop up everywhere, from Aborigine reggae bands to São Paolo rappers).

Pop in the Digital Age
From here on, western pop is increasingly modelled on manufactured boy and girl bands with anodyne songs (a phenomenon for which Japan had previously been mocked), with the template acts Take That and Destiny's Child arriving in 1990. The cutting edge of the 90s came not from rock (*pace* Radiohead) but from maverick fusioneers such as Massive Attack and Björk.

The atomization of pop would be accelerated by the digital revolution in progress at the start of the 90s (with the 'bedroom studio' now a reality, it had never been easier to make a record) and by the advent of the Internet and the MP3. Music became detached from any physical artefact – it no longer needed shellac, vinyl or CD – while the release of almost everything from pop history (including out-takes, oddities and out-of-print cult items) blurred historical fault lines. Swing, psychedelia and punk had equal availability and value in the MP3 postmodern era. By the end of the decade, the very idea of paying for music would be waning as file-sharing and disc-ripping began their relentless drain of pop's commercial power.

Such changes overshadow the 1997 Jupiter–Uranus conjunction, though this year marks the pinnacle of the UK as 'Cool Britannia' and the improbable success of Cuba's Buena Vista Social Club – salsa lessons start in earnest. Nor is there much to excite at the 2003 opposition, by which time the music industry somehow finds its products being sold down a telephone line by the computer industry (though the horoscope of iTunes belongs to 2001).

The decline in pop's status and creativity is apparent in the success of *American Idol* (debuting on 11 June 2002), which in 2003 tops the TV ratings (where it will stay for another seven years). Reality TV stars are now as important as rock gods and R&B divas, while the very concept of the pop or film star has been subsumed within a nebulous Neptunian sphere of 'celebrity', in which people are famous simply for being famous.

Music itself is more ubiquitous than ever, but its primacy in youth and the mainstream is no longer assured. The growing popularity of roots music and Americana, most obviously but not exclusively in the US, is perhaps a symptom of dissatisfaction, a return to the wellspring of authenticity: the success of the *O Brother, Where Art Thou?* soundtrack, a Grammy winner in 2002, is a sign of the times.

This returns us to the music existing prior to our entry point of 1891, and the role of tradition in pop. Clearly, songs and numbers that have evolved over decades and, indeed, centuries are astrologically off limits. There can be no chart for antique English or Irish ballads, or for the 19th-century cowboy songs. There are no horoscopes for the blues or for country music.[17]

In the 21st century, traditional music has made a grand comeback. America hasn't seen so many beards and banjos since the days of the travelling medicine show, or at least since Pete Seeger and the folk boom of the 1950s. By the 2010 conjunction of Jupiter and Uranus, one of the biggest bands on both sides of the Atlantic was a bunch of upper-class Englishmen playing faux Americana (Mumford and Sons).

Today, we are under the ongoing spell of the Uranus–Pluto square. It's thus a quarter past 1966, though so far there's little sign of the youthful revolt against the status quo promised by Uranus in Aries (the 'Me, Me, Me' of Aries Sun Lady Gaga hardly qualifies). Rather, the corporate might of Pluto in Capricorn prevails; witness the many lists of 'wealthiest pop stars' – not the most talented nor most influential nor even the best-selling, but the richest. Bling is the thing.

Can astrology help to rescue pop from the Plutonic corporate stranglehold? We could at least stop referring to 'Uranus', whose mythology is utterly contrary to the planet's astrological meaning, and instead talk of 'Prometheus'. That way, someone might write a song to go with 'Moon River', 'Lucky Old Sun', 'Venus in Blue Jeans', 'Breakfast on Pluto' and the rest. But a ditty about Uranus? Dream on.

1 Michael Baigent, Nicholas Campion, and Charles Harvey, *Mundane Astrology*, 1984, p. 177
2 Ibid., p. 186
3 Richard Tarnas, *Cosmos and Psyche: Intimations of a New World View*, 2006, p. 326
4 Emile Berliner's Gramophone Company was born in 1895, the disc soon displacing the phonograph cylinder
5 Gillespie, Parker, Thelonious Monk and others created bebop on 'guest Mondays' at Minton's Playhouse in Harlem, New York in 1941. See Donald Clarke, *The Rise and Fall of Popular Music*, 1995.
6 Jim Dawson and Steve Propes, *What Was the First Rock 'n' Roll Record?* 1992
7 For example, Presley's bestseller, 'Hound Dog', was first recorded by Big Mama Thornton, but written by two Jewish college kids, Mike Lieber and Jerry Stoller
8 Peter Guralnick, *Last Train to Memphis*, 1995, p. 101
9 For a detailed timeline, see www.lysergia.com
10 Mark Kurlansky, *1968: The Year that Rocked the World*, 2010
11 Gay songs had been sung by Ma Rainey in the 1920s, but Valentino's was the first mainstream record. Tom Robinson wrote the anthemic 'Glad to Be Gay' in 1976
12 A possible chart for reggae is that for Jamaican independence on 6 August 1962, shortly after the Jupiter–Uranus opposition. This reflects reggae's Leonine imagery and knots closely with Marley's natal chart
13 'House' electro-dance music was spawned in Chicago in 1984
14 MTV was first broadcast on 1 August 1981, at 'just after midnight', 12:01 EST; source: Wikipedia
15 Cobain died in April 1994 as Saturn transited his natal Sun
16 André Barbault, *Les Astres et l'Histoire*, cited in Baigent et al., Mundane Astrology, op. cit.
17 The founding of the Grand Ole Opry on 28 November 1925 is a possible 'birth' moment for country. The genre's godparents, the Carter family, started recording in 1927, as did 'singing brakeman' Jimmie Rodgers. The building that housed the Opry was erected in 1892.

This article first appeared in the April–May 2014 issue of The Mountain Astrologer.

JAZZ
Julie London
Ian Shaw
Peggy Lee
Miles Davis
Billy Strayhorn
John Coltrane
Thelonius Monk
Al Jarreau
Chet Baker
Sonny Rollins
Herbie Hancock

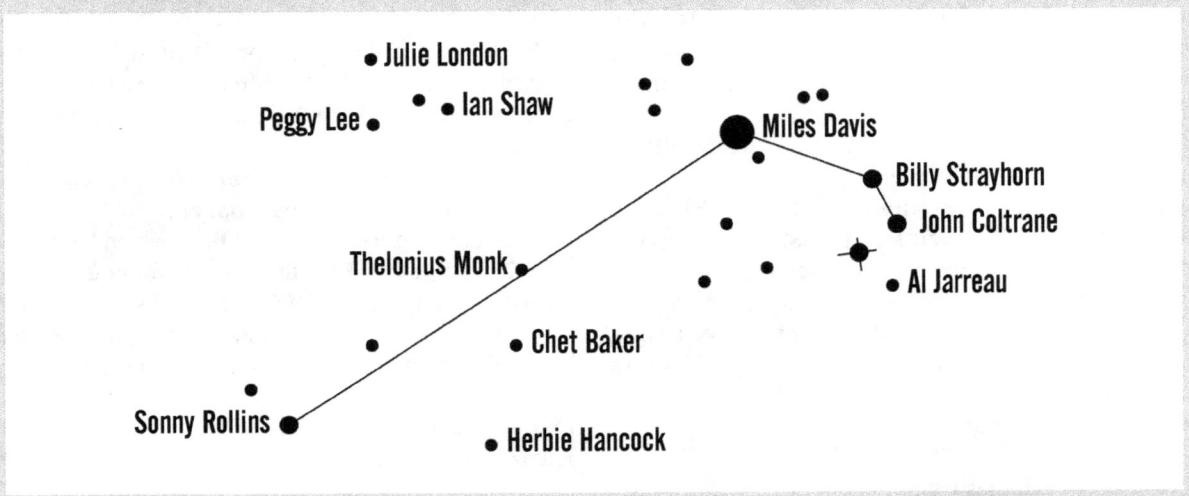

Jazz

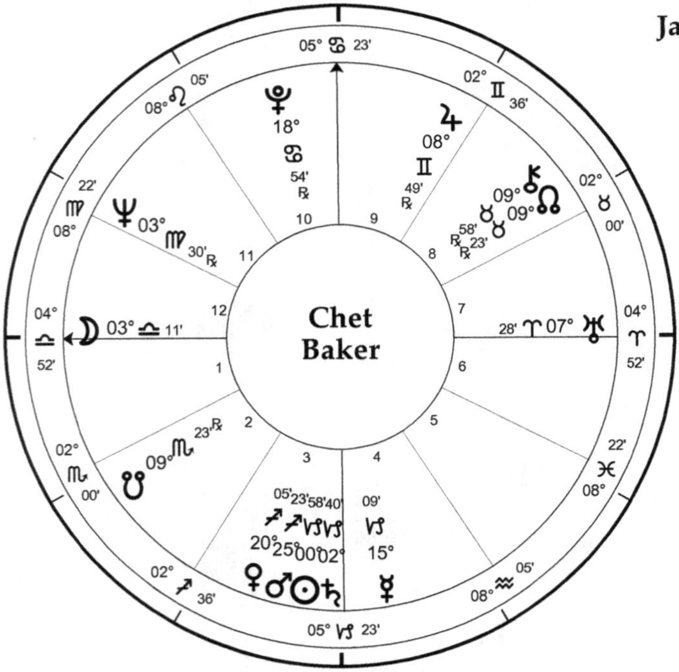

Chet Baker

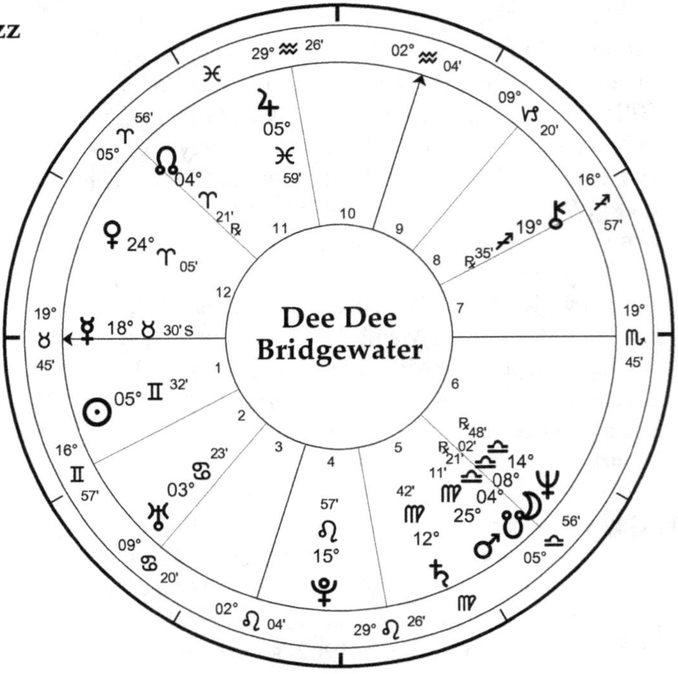

Dee Dee Bridgewater

Jazz

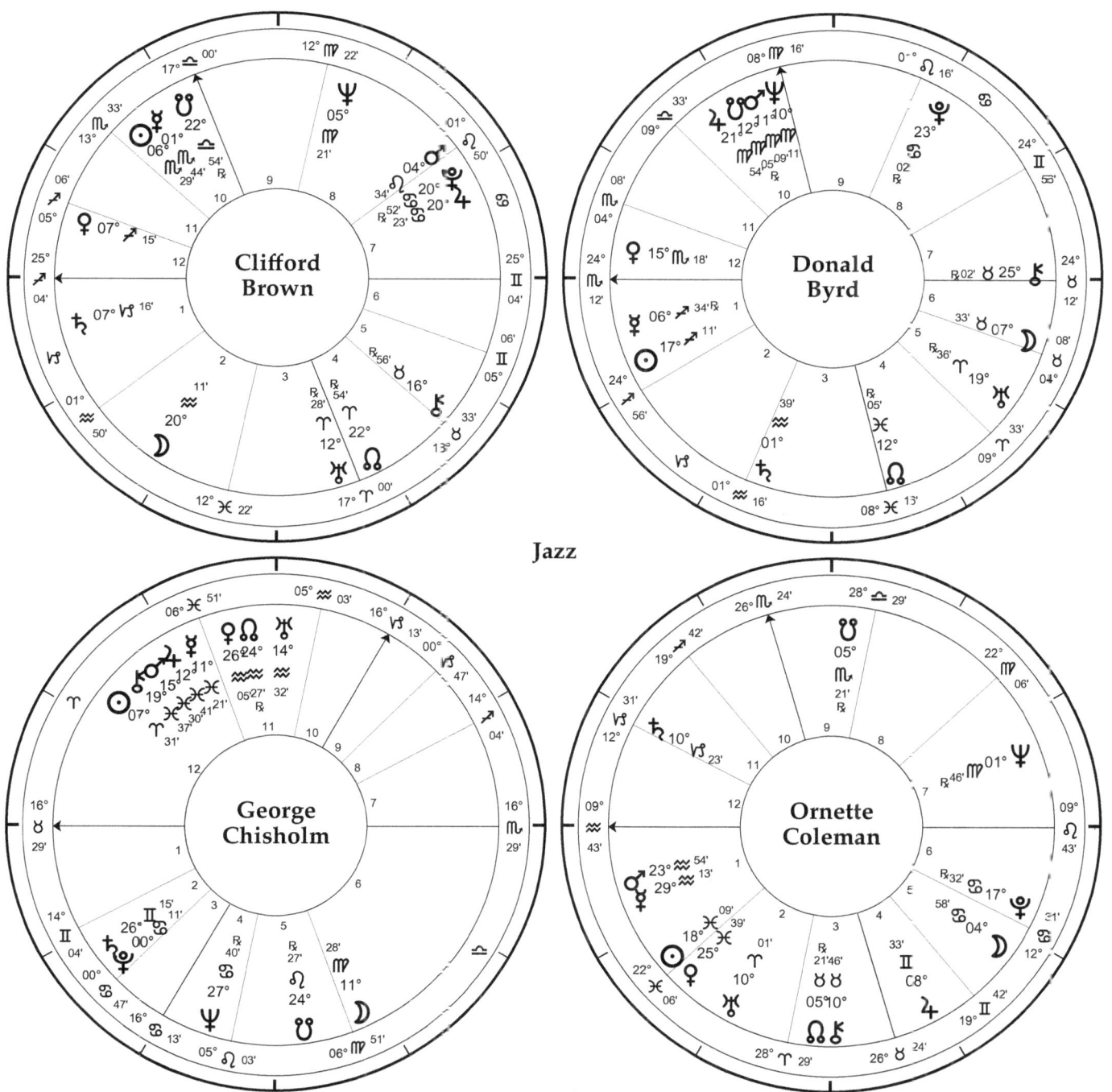

24 *The Book of Music Horoscopes*

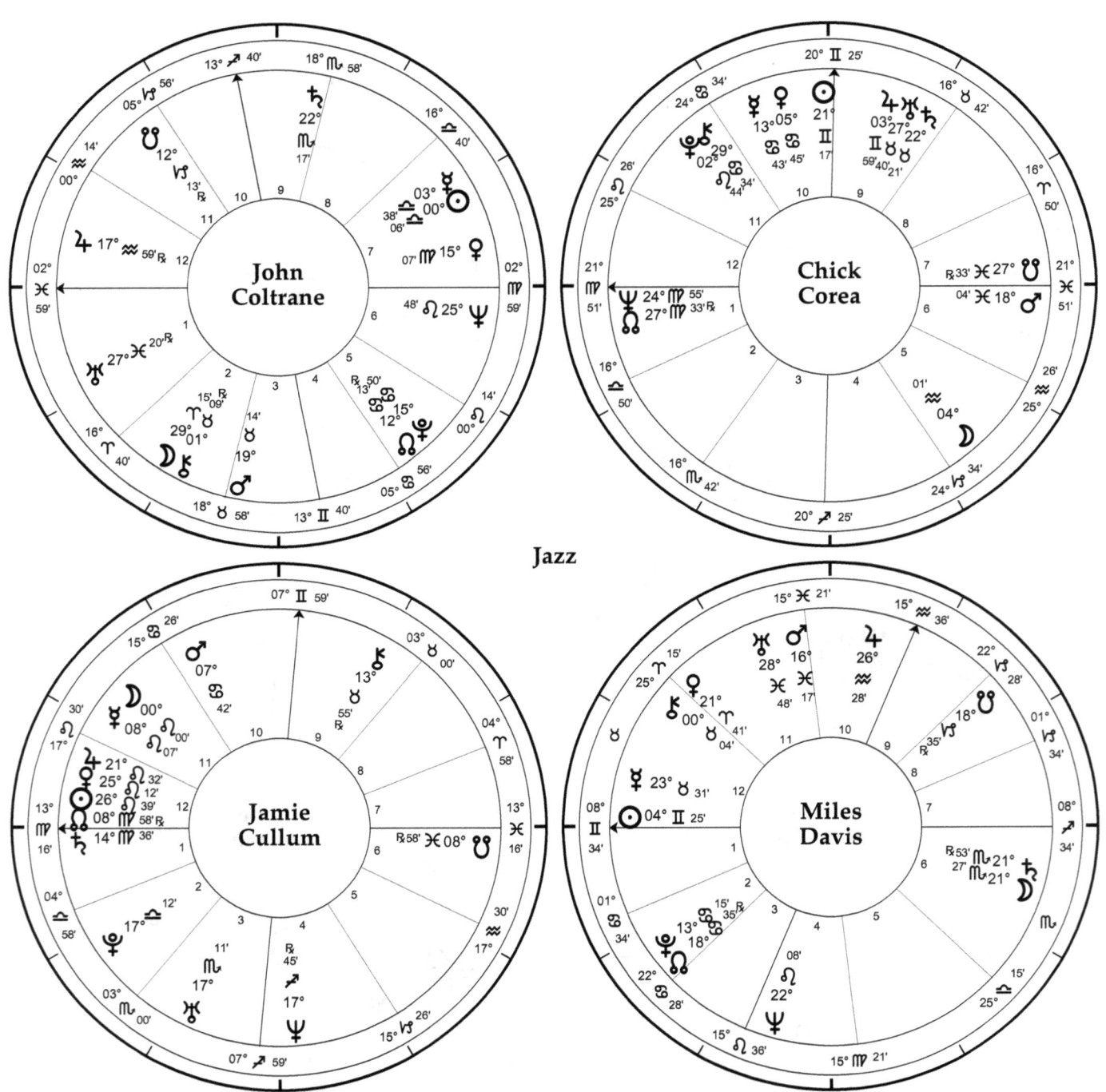

Jazz

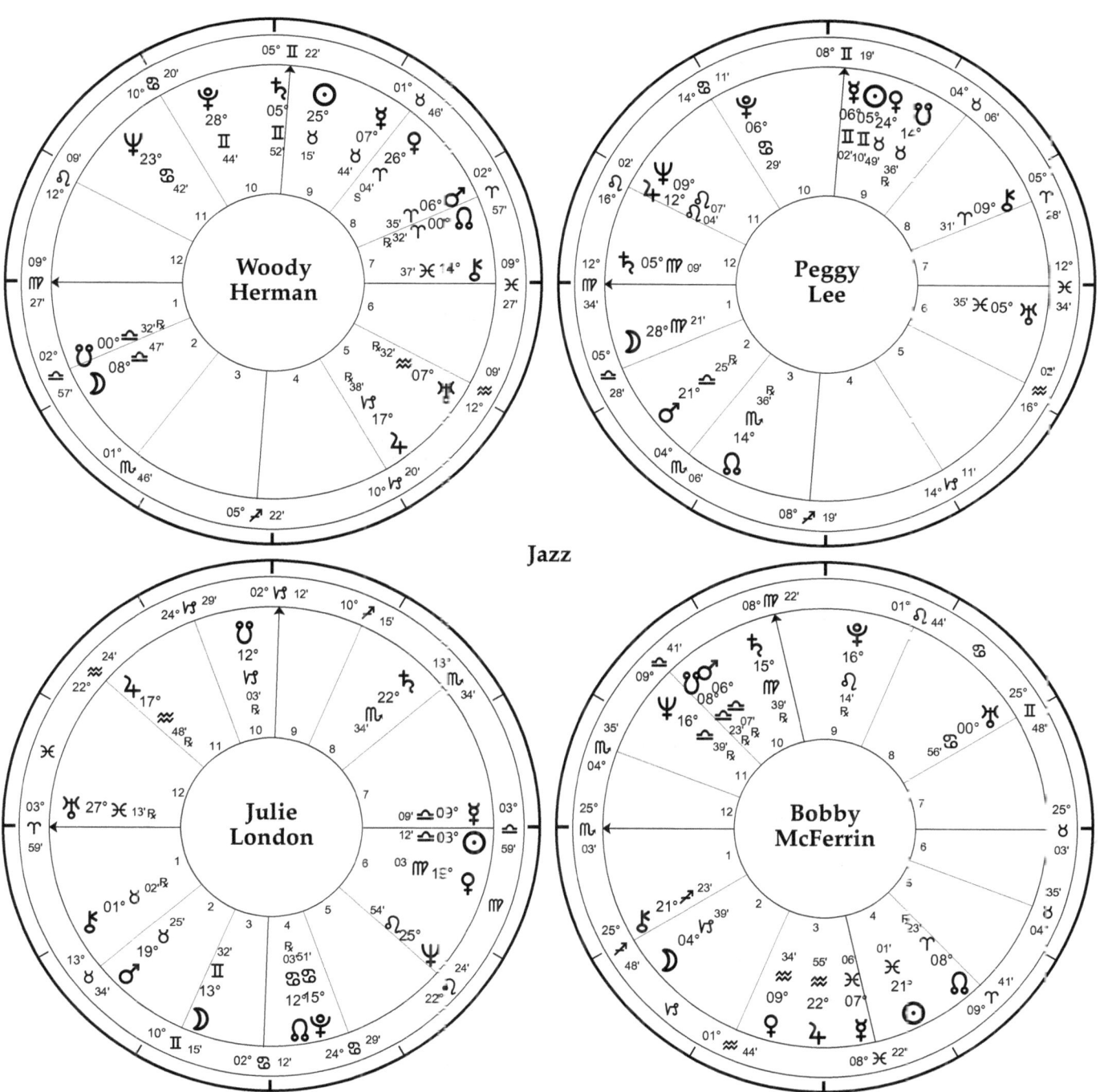

26 *The Book of Music Horoscopes*

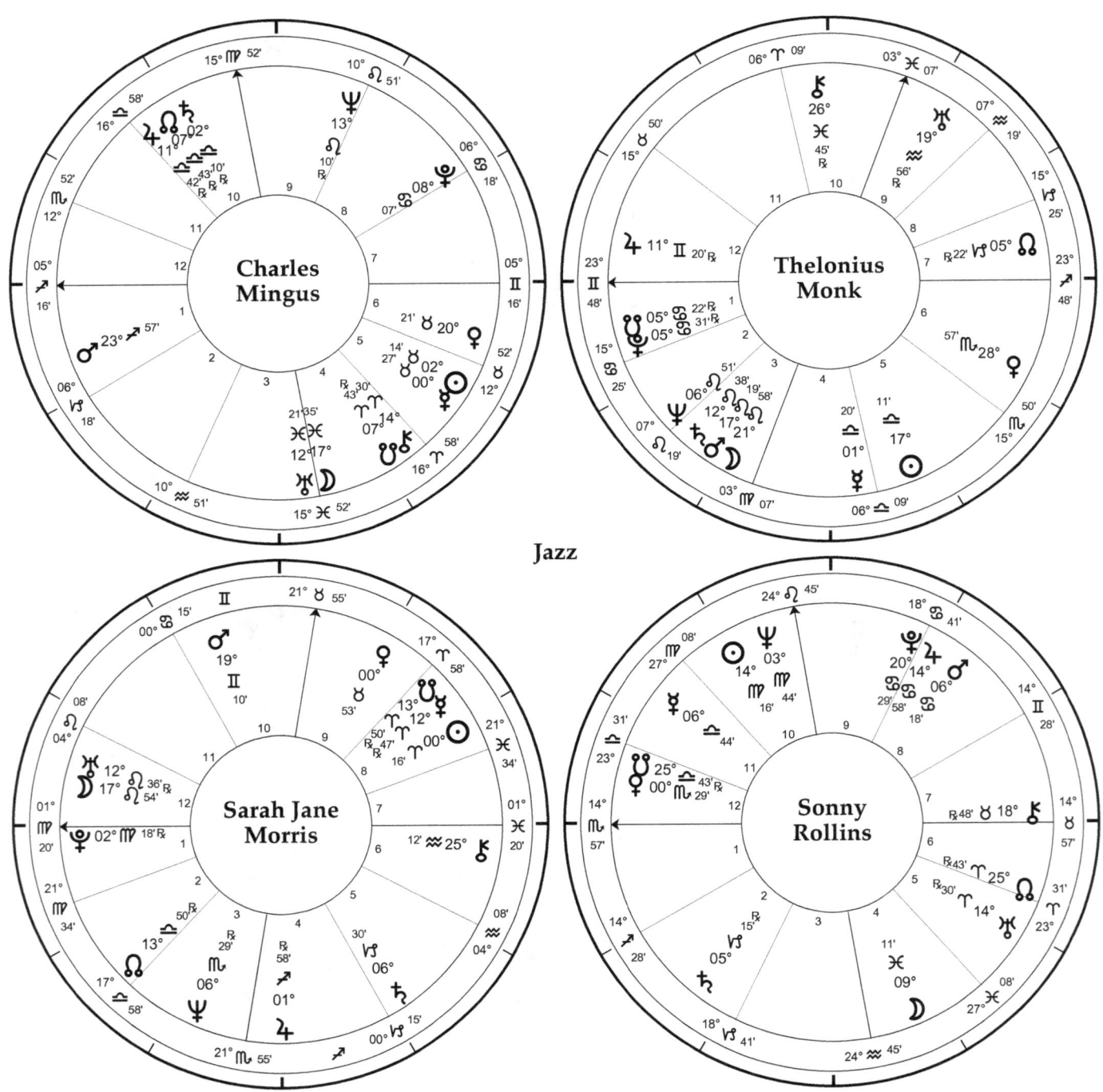

Jazz

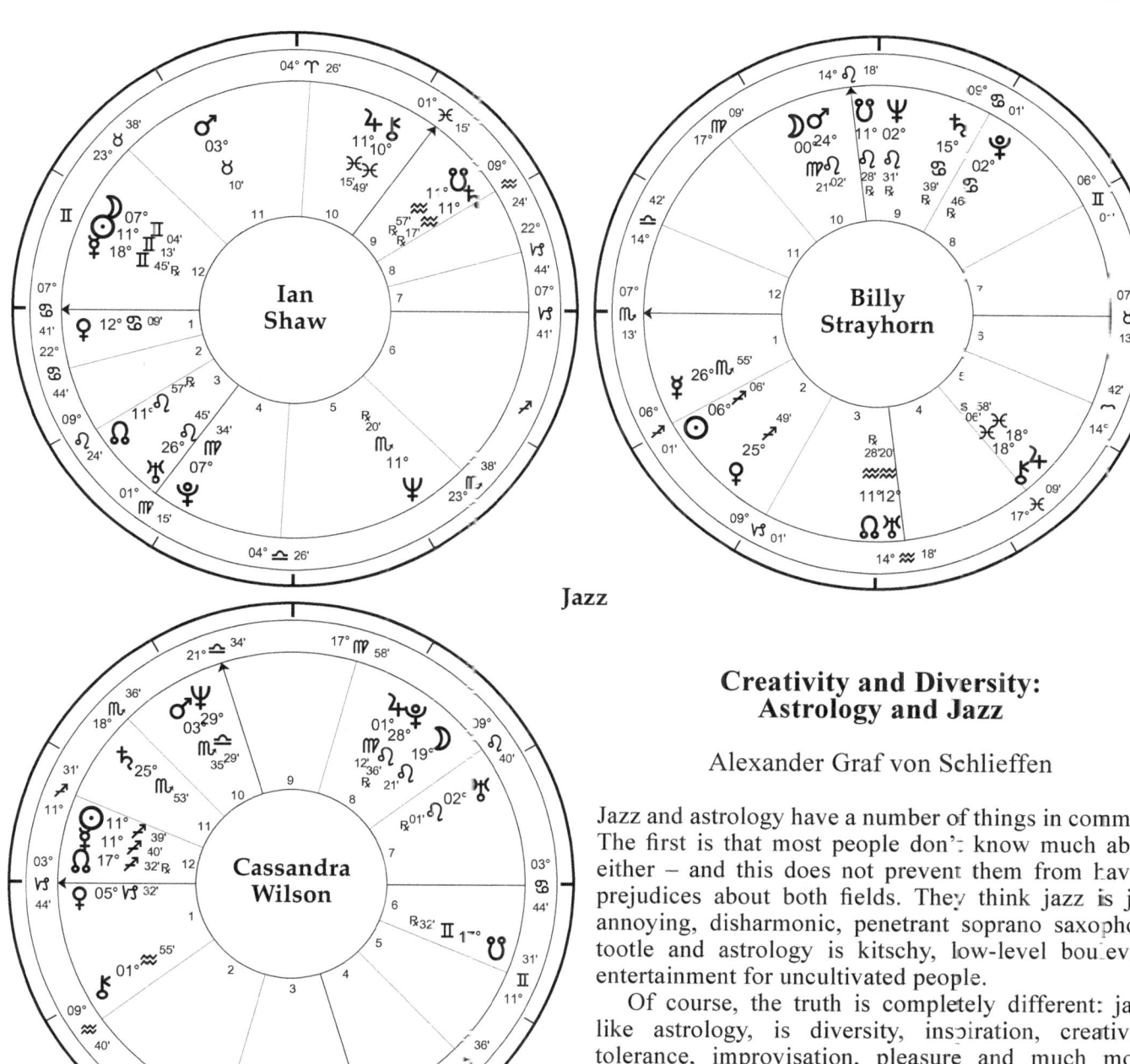

Creativity and Diversity: Astrology and Jazz

Alexander Graf von Schlieffen

Jazz and astrology have a number of things in common. The first is that most people don't know much about either – and this does not prevent them from having prejudices about both fields. They think jazz is just annoying, disharmonic, penetrant soprano saxophone tootle and astrology is kitschy, low-level boulevard entertainment for uncultivated people.

Of course, the truth is completely different: jazz, like astrology, is diversity, inspiration, creativity, tolerance, improvisation, pleasure and much more. Improvisation is a highly creative way to explore unknown musical territories and new sounds – and all while playing with other musicians. To quote Marcus Miller:

Jazz is a beautiful, democratic music. It encourages musicians with very strong, and many times, very different points of view to work together as a team while, at the same time, giving them the space to express their individuality. It's a very important art form and can be used as a model for different cultures to work together.

I cannot think of a musical genre that did not have an impact on the development of jazz. It is so rich and includes elements of funk, soul, rock, pop, Indian traditional, Japanese, African and Brazilian music.

The interpretation of a horoscope itself is a wonderful, creative adventure, too. A chart might look very simple, but it is as complex as a symphony. Every chart is an individual composition.

In astrology, the leitmotif is the rising sign and its ruler. The individual significance of the planets in signs and houses and their aspects depends on their relation to the leitmotif, just like in music (except for minimal music and punk).

Saturn–Uranus
Saturn–Uranus combinations can be found in the horoscopes of some of the most important jazz musicians, such as the innovative pianist and composer Chick Corea (conjunction), saxophone player and composer John Coltrane (trine), pianist and composer Herbie Hancock (Saturn and Uranus in the same sign and house) and the legend Miles Davis (trine).

This combination suggests: living between extremes; tradition and innovation; rules and improvisation; homogeneity and diversity; past and future; simplicity and complexity; the known and the unknown. This combination might be stressful for one's private life, but it is essential for a creative jazz musician.

When Mars is in aspect with Saturn and Uranus, the rhythmic pulsation is torn between these extremes. No wonder we find a relationship between these three planets in the charts of famous rhythm section players such as bass player Jaco Pastorius and the three drummers Art Blakey, Elvin Jones and Jack de Johnette.

Let us take a short look at the astrological analogies for musical skills:

4th Quadrant (10th, 11th, 12th Houses – Significance)
- Saturn (10th): the practical and theoretical musical knowledge and experience
- Uranus (11th): the experimental spirit
- Neptune (12th): the musical vision

Without the structural abilities of Saturn, there is no creative freedom for Uranus and no space for Neptune's musical visions.

3rd Quadrant (7th, 8th, 9th Houses – Entertainment)
- Venus (7th): the ability to create harmony between the individual elements, to make the music sound pleasant, familiar and beautiful (or just boring)
- Pluto (8th): the ability to make the music sound intense through suggestive elements
- Jupiter (9th): the desire to expand the possibilities of either the instrument and/or the music through the integration of 'foreign' elements

In the 3rd Quadrant, we entertain, communicate with and bridge (cultural) worlds.

2nd Quadrant (4th, 5th, 6th Houses – Soul)
- Moon (4th): either the ability to touch the soul or its simulation (kitsch)
- Sun (5th): the personal voice and its intensity
- Mercury (6th): technical precision, exercise, practice and adjustment of the voice to the environment

This is the inner source of the music.

1st Quadrant (1st, 2nd, 3rd Houses – Physical Basis)
- Mars (1st): the type of physical rhythm and its energy
- Venus (2nd): the physical substance of the sound of the music or the instrument/voice
- Mercury (3rd): skills and technique

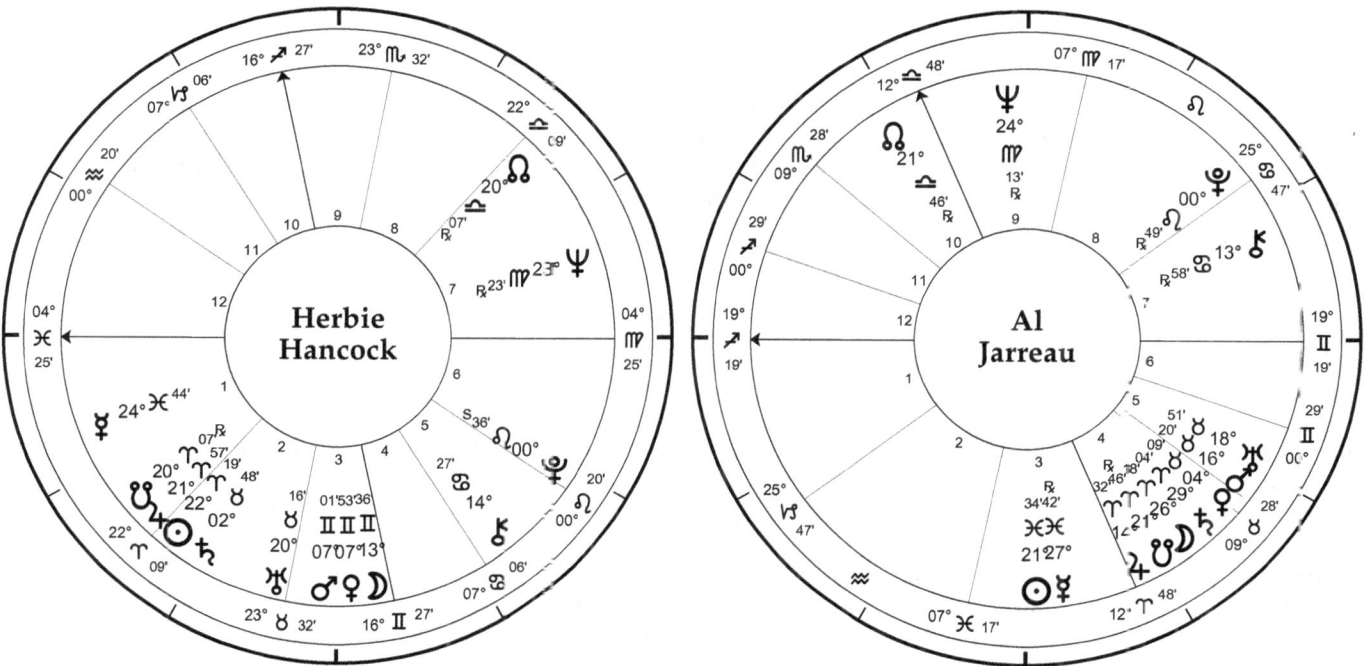

Here is the physical and practical foundation of the music or the musician.

Examples

Herbie Hancock is an outstanding master of creative diversity, innovation and inspiration. In his music, he combines many influences and yet one can always recognize his unique 'voice' below the multiple layers of musical model.

For the albums *Possibilities* (2005) and *The Joni Letters* (2007), he collaborated with Christina Aguilera, Damien Rice, Norah Jones, Joss Stone, John Mayer, Leonard Cohen and Sting. They are masterworks of musical diversity based on the rules of jazz. He made some of the invited musicians sound better than on their own records because he inspired them to trespass the boundaries of their style and reach a new level of intensity.

From the very early years of his career, Hancock experimented with a variety of styles, being an extraordinarily brilliant piano player at the same time. He has released groundbreaking albums and has worked with numerous wonderful musicians. There seems to be no limit to his creativity.

In his natal chart, his Sun–Jupiter conjunction in Aries reflects his incredible drive to keep heading for new artistic horizons and inspire other people to follow him. His task is not his ego. He has Pisces rising, so he is deeply identified with a bigger vision of something. Neptune, his chart ruler, is in the 7th House, so he needs partners to realize his visions.

A Venus–Mars conjunction in playful Gemini in the 3rd House shows a highly flirty and agile person. With Uranus on the cusp of the 3rd House, his mental as well as his physical reachability is enormous. The musical equivalent of this 3rd House is funk music. Funk is a sexy, moving, percussive, light-hearted, syncopated, groovy rhythm.

Hancock's incredible versatility is a profound need of his soul – it is shown by his Moon in Gemini on the 4th House cusp. His inner home is not a homogeneous but a heterogeneous place; so is his music.

Mercury in the 1st House is sometimes found in the charts of highly intelligent people because they have an instinctive and existential necessity to understand the world and to be able to develop their proper skills. Since Neptune, the ruler of Hancock's chart, is opposing this Mercury, he could either have become a mad scientist or a brilliant musician. In some ways, he has become both.

Saturn in Taurus in the 2nd is the solid basis for any activity. It helps to ground Mercury's talents. Hancock has been working on his basic education and has become one of the most skilled piano players in his field.

With Sun–Jupiter in an applying square to Pluto, everything Hancock does must be intense. Since he is a profoundly creative personality, it is his intention to open people to connect with their inner creative source rather than being in control of them, which would be the non-creative, shadow side of this Pluto aspect. Creativity and control do not match; creativity emerges out of these holy moments when we let go of control.

Al Jarreau is quite well known in the world of pop but he was originally a jazz singer. His Ascendant and Sun are in mutable signs, which makes him very flexible and open to different influences. In his music he melts down the boundaries between different musical and cultural worlds and speaks directly to the soul of the listener. The Sun and Mercury in the 3rd House are ruled by Neptune, which is also in opposition to the two. They are the physical (1st Quadrant) communicative expression of Neptune's vision. What does he want to express?

Jupiter, the chart ruler of his Sagittarius Ascendant, is on the IC: his main life intention is the emotional (2nd Quadrant) expression of inner joy. Funnily enough, one of his most recent albums is called *Accentuate the Positive*. His music can be very light-hearted without ever being superficial.

A unique emotional (2nd Quadrant) characteristic of his creativity is a percussive way of using his voice, which is derived from scat singing. Mars is in Taurus in the 5th House: his inner rhythm is earthbound and stable. The conjunction with Uranus adds eccentricity.

Venus, the ruler of the Libra Midheaven, is in Taurus on the cusp of his 5th House. His professional intention is the personal and physical expression of something pleasant. Since the chart ruler is on the IC, it must be something deeply emotional, and which language is more emotional than music?

Dave Grohl, Congo Square and New Orleans Jazz

Michelle Young

If you've ever visited New Orleans, striking shades of springtime blooms may pepper your memories of the French Quarter's wrought-iron balconies and the unmistakable sounds of jazz, of the kind only heard in these parts around Rampart and Basin Streets. North Rampart Street borders one side of now-legendary Congo Square, and Basin Street comes in at another. Here in the heart of the city lies a pocket of history where New Orleans jazz began.

As part of the Louisiana Purchase (1803), the city now stood 'at the center of American history ... as an essential wellspring of its culture.'[1] Jazz was already evolving in this diverse community of about 8000 people. But the culture of the city itself had been altered by the territorial purchase, and now slaves no longer had the same freedoms they'd enjoyed under French and Spanish rule. The New Orleans City Council apparently took this history into consideration and, on 28 November 1817,[2] the city fathers approved legislation for slaves to meet and dance in Congo Square on Sunday afternoons, as they had done for nearly 100 years. It was a momentous occasion. Long drums, gourds, sounding boxes, the jawbone and banjo-like instruments created the hypnotic, pulsing African bamboula rhythms to which slaves in brightly coloured clothes danced. Not just a dance, bamboula[3] served as the cultural tradition linking slaves to their home and roots.

No one actually knows when jazz began but Congo Square is where the magic came to life, paving the way for ragtime, blues and that sensual, soulful syncopation blended with brass. As the years passed, other groups including the Creoles and Italians lent cultural twists for even newer beats.

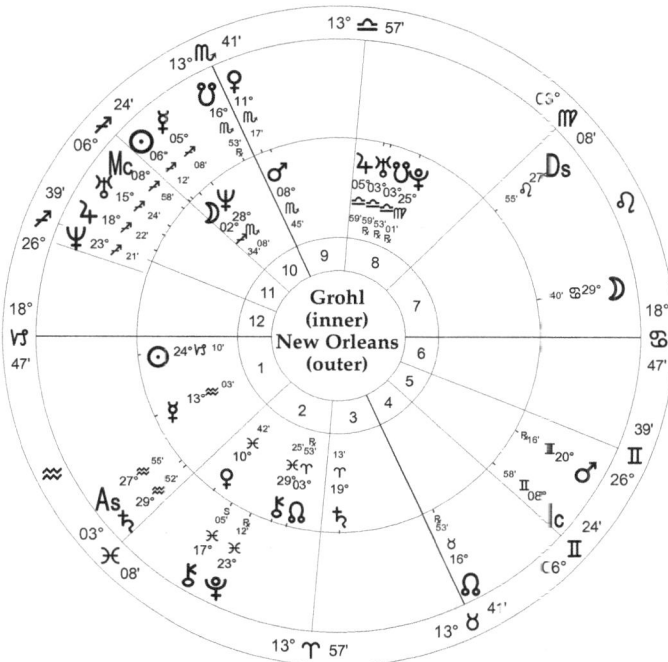

Anderson Cooper interviewed Dave Grohl of the Foo Fighters for the CBS-TV show *60 Minutes*[4] when the band was in New Orleans for a week in May 2014. The trip was part of a tour of eight American cities for an HBO Special. Delighting fans one night at Preservation Hall, the band and jazz musicians such as Troy 'Trombone Shorty' Andrews performed a surprise, free concert through open windows in the French Quarter, near Congo Square.

Although the legislation chart for Congo Square is untimed, both Grohl's general feelings and the broader perspective of the period can be examined with Grohl's chart as the inner wheel of a bi-wheel chart.

Approaching the trip like a historic exploration of music and the city, Grohl developed a sense of the heritage of each place. With his natal 9th house Mars in Pluto-ruled Scorpio, the love of learning is as much a part of him as the process of discovering the ordinary and making it extraordinary. Grohl dropped out of school at the age of seventeen, but music stirred him. Money, he says, had never been his motivation for playing music.

'I was doing it because I loved it.' To Grohl, jazz is 'musical gumbo, a beautiful blend of sounds and styles, a true celebration of what American music is all about.'

Grohl's sense of each city's heritage formed the Foo Fighters' framework for their November 2014 album *Sonic Highways*. 'If music were more a part of our daily lives, this country would be a better place,' he says. Ninth House Mars forms a quadranovile (160°) and 8th House Jupiter a single undecaquartisextile (165°) to 3rd House Mars-ruled Saturn. Yet this duo establishes a semisextile (30°, 2°45' orb), the midpoint of which resolves at Saturn in an interactive Blooming Undecaquartisextile aspect pattern (165°, 3°09' orb). Here is the lower level of the heartbeat of Grohl's chart: chart ruler Saturn in the house of daily affairs while Mars adds the passion for learning and expression of what's out there through the music he and other band members bring to life. His Eastern hemispheric, above-the-horizon dominance offers a dual quadrant emphasis with the first quadrant (Self) in contrast to the third (Others), enabling him to consider his and others' thoughts and feelings as well as their interpersonal relationship.

With Capricorn on the Ascendant, how he behaves with others is a matter of responsibility and the role he plays in that partnership with the rest of the band. What is being shared through communication and mutual action in this way becomes a part of the creative process. Pluto rules the Scorpio Midheaven, and the intense need for both the drive and the passion is evident. This kind of passion must come from within, the kind that allows deep emotion bordering on intoxication to be expressed. The passion both in his performances and in his behind-the-scenes work must be there. The broader heartbeat of the chart lying in the interactive connections between Venus, Neptune (the higher octave of Venus) and Pluto must also be present: to create the music, Grohl must feel it, hear it in his heart, and it must evoke passion.

Grohl's entry into the top rock music scene came through Nirvana. Devastated at losing Kurt Cobain, he said, '... if I heard a song that even touched on an emotion in me, I would turn it off. I was just so terrified. Because to me, that's what music always was. It was a direct connection to my heart.'[5]

The tour, however, made a significant difference. 'That week we had in New Orleans totally changed my life. It made me fall head over heels in love with music all over again,' he said. In fact, Grohl recorded a song one hour after writing it without worrying about the traffic outside. Cooper said Grohl had wanted it to be part of the music.[6] By placing the untimed legislation chart in the outer wheel, against Grohl's natal chart, we can avoid the concern about the outer chart's Ascendant, Moon or houses while still considering the aspects playing out in his chart.

Grohl's out-of-sign Moon–Neptune conjunction in the 10th House of career is conjunct the legislation chart's Sun–Mercury conjunction in Sagittarius. Carrying through this theme, Grohl's Jupiter–Uranus conjunction in Libra sextiles that conjunction in Sagittarius. His 1st House Mercury in Uranus-ruled Aquarius squares his Mars in Scorpio, which is conjunct the legislation chart's Venus.

We often see repeated patterns in synastry that have deeper meaning than we initially think, and this event chart tends to hold true to these patterns. Like Grohl's natal Jupiter–Uranus 2° orb conjunction, the event chart possesses a 3° orb conjunction between Jupiter and Uranus in Sagittarius, this time in the 11th. The band brings the New Orleans episode with these roots linked to Congo Square together as a joint project, fulfilling the 11th House need for such a connection.

Beyond what many may see as the Wounded Healer qualities of Chiron, it's possible that Chiron – through our wounding – enables us to reach new heights and to bring out new, even more refined talents than we had before we went through the process of that healing. If that's true, then certainly Dave Grohl has found it in New Orleans. His natal chart shows Chiron in trine to Neptune. Perhaps the Congo Square Moon is sitting on the anaretic degree of Cancer and in trine to his Neptune as well. That would create the ease of intuitive knowledge about the magic needing to happen in New Orleans in May 2014.

But magic and intuition seem to be working in tandem for Dave Grohl. Saturn in Aries as the ruler of his natal chart can become the restrained artist frustrated by his struggle to perform. For Grohl, this process of harnessing his energy through writing music and lyrics can tame the wildest horse inside him, even if he feels as if he's been tied to the hitching post. The need for order can become so restrictive in Aries that one might wish to achieve some independent desire, but Grohl has an eastern hemisphere dominance and is already independent. Yet perhaps he has a fear or misplaced belief that might otherwise have him setting aside his goals.

That's not likely for Dave Grohl, however – not with Mars in Scorpio serving as a kind of balancing act to deliver spurts of passionate energy, enabling him to produce the right material he's seeking in the shortest amount of time. Saturn may be sitting in the 3rd House, but Mars – eager to finish – sits in the 9th conjunct the Midheaven and also conjunct the Congo Square's Venus–South Node conjunction. Because we don't know the actual time when the legislation was enacted, we have no way of knowing whether that Venus–South Node conjunction that tends natives to loneliness and isolation is also conjunct the legislation chart's MC. But because it is conjunct Dave Grohl's MC, there just might have been a karmic sense of justice working with Grohl at the helm to bring this historic period to a rewarding sense of fulfilment by the time *Sonic Highways* was released.

1 In Congo Square: Colonial New Orleans: http://www.thenation.com/article/congo-square-colonial-new-orleans?page=0,0
2 African American Registry: http://www.aaregistry.org/historic_events/view/congo-square-soul-new-orleans
3 Both the drums and the dance were known as bamboula. Pancocojams: http://pancocojams.blogspot.com/2012/01/bamboula-dance-and-music-then-now.html
4 CBS-TV: http://www.cbsnews.com/videos/foo-fighters-celebrates-american-music/
5 Ibid
6 http://www.cbsnews.com/videos/composing-with-dave-grohl-and-the-foo-fighters/

R&B & HIP HOP

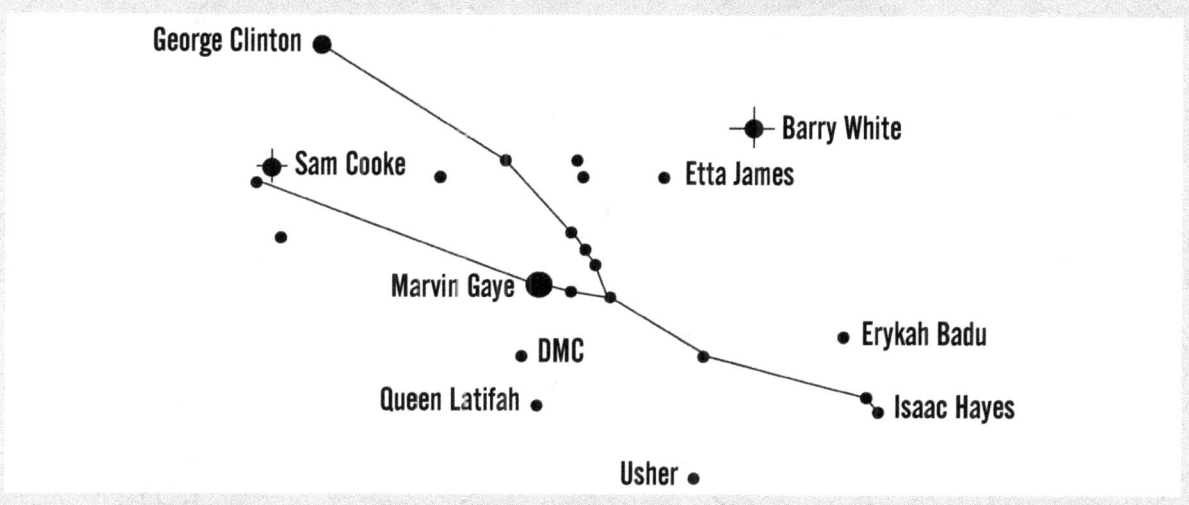

Soul and R&B

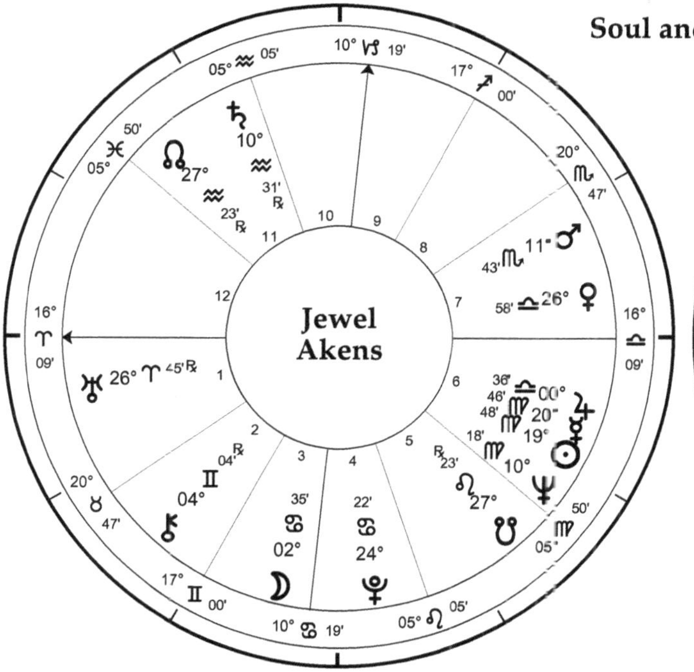

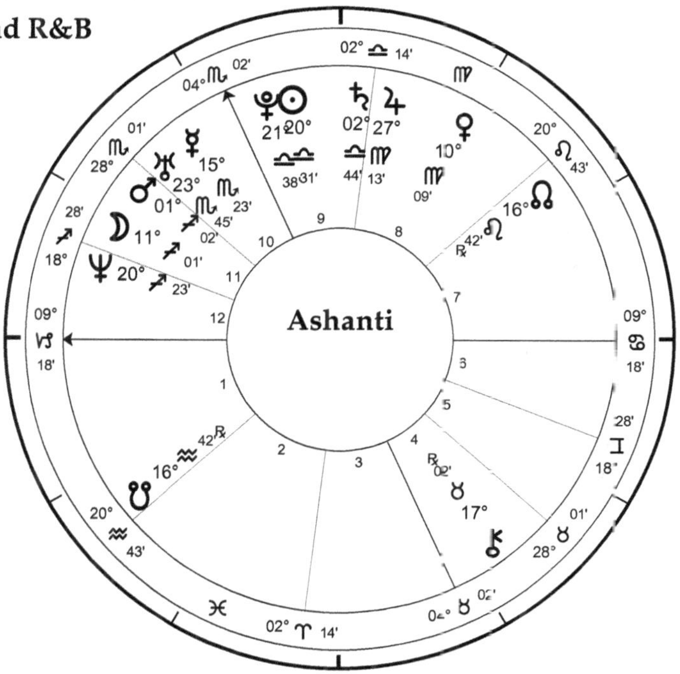

34 The Book of Music Horoscopes

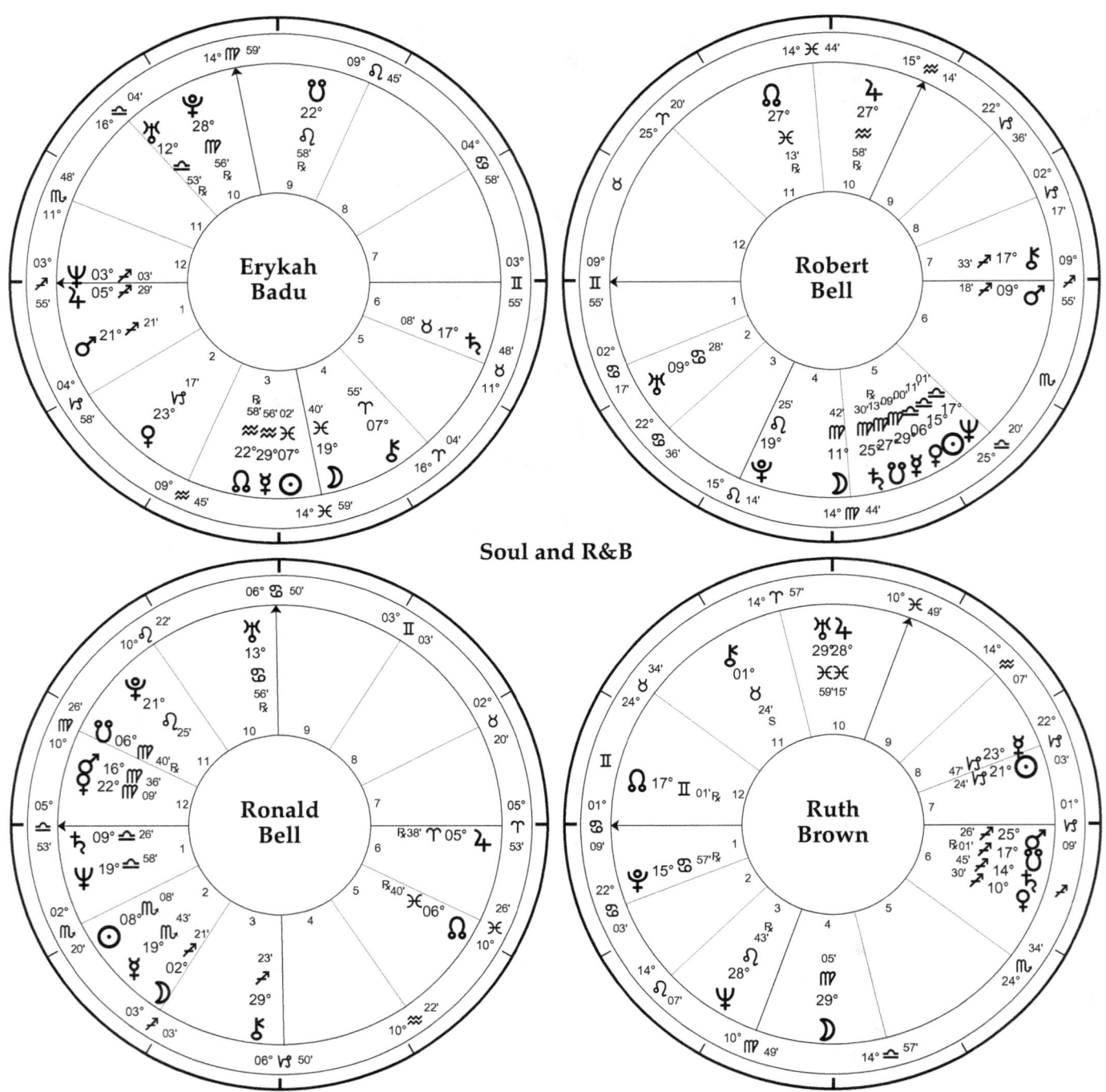

Soul and R&B

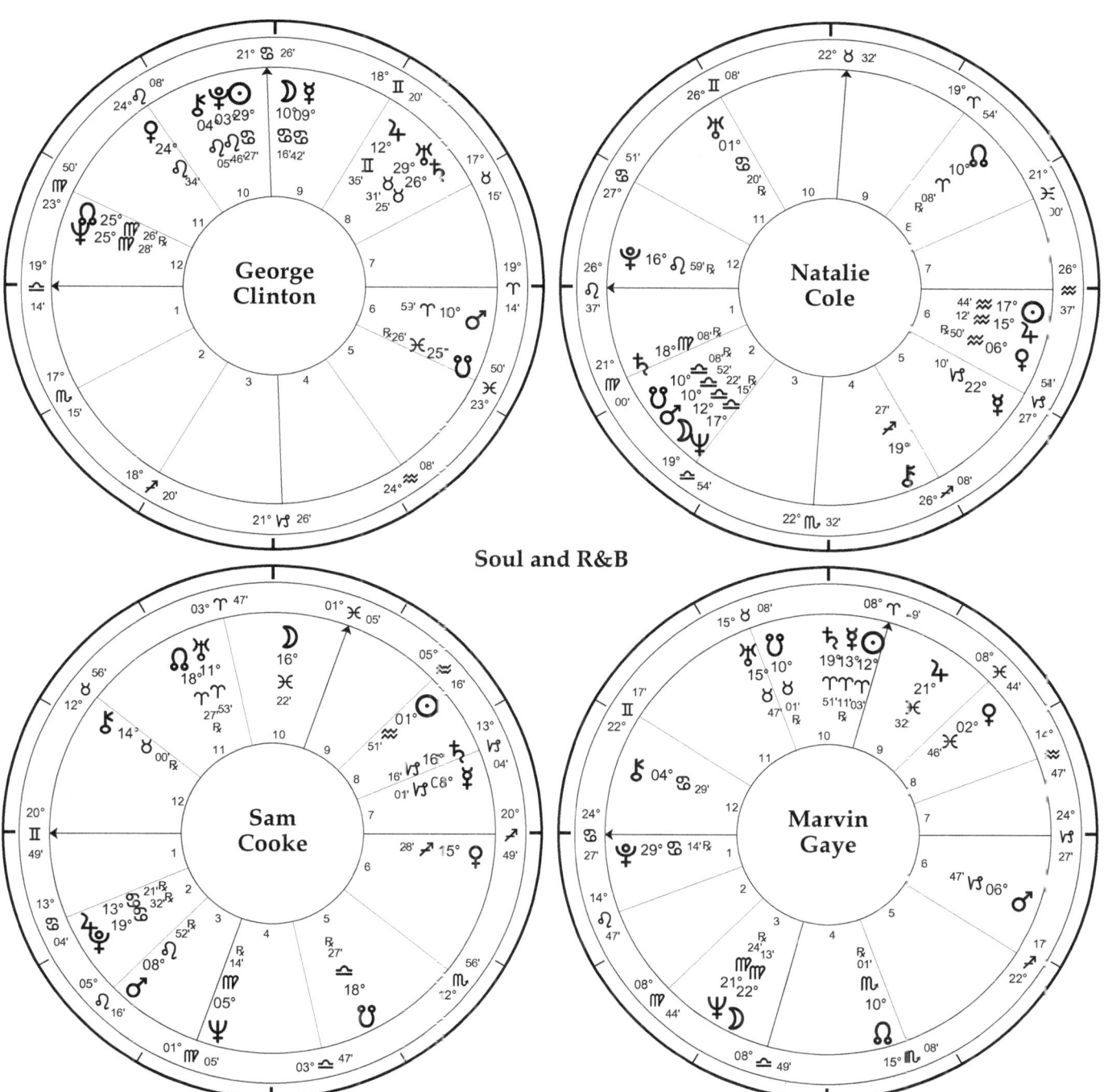

Soul and R&B

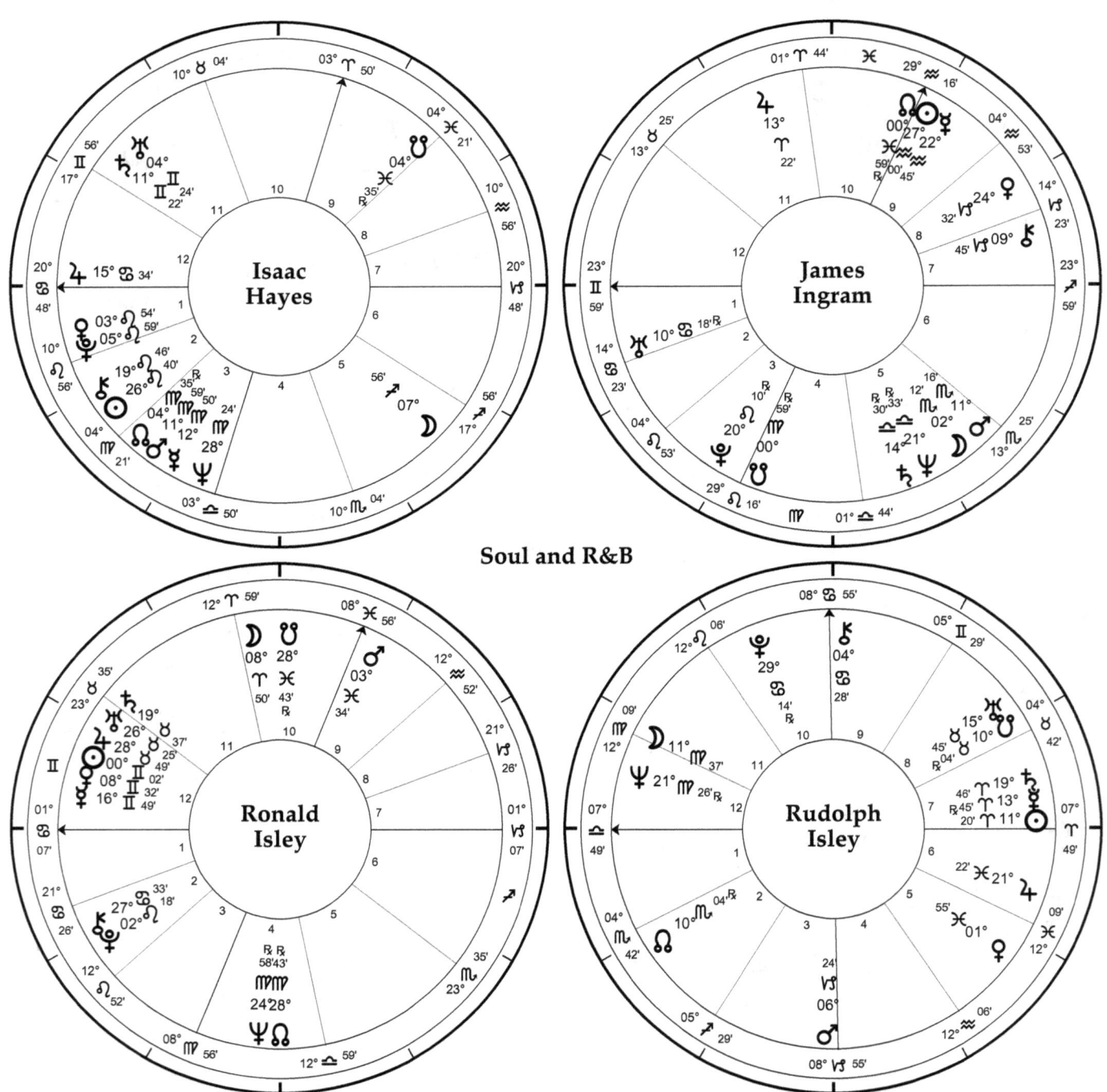

Soul and R&B

R&B & Hip Hop 37

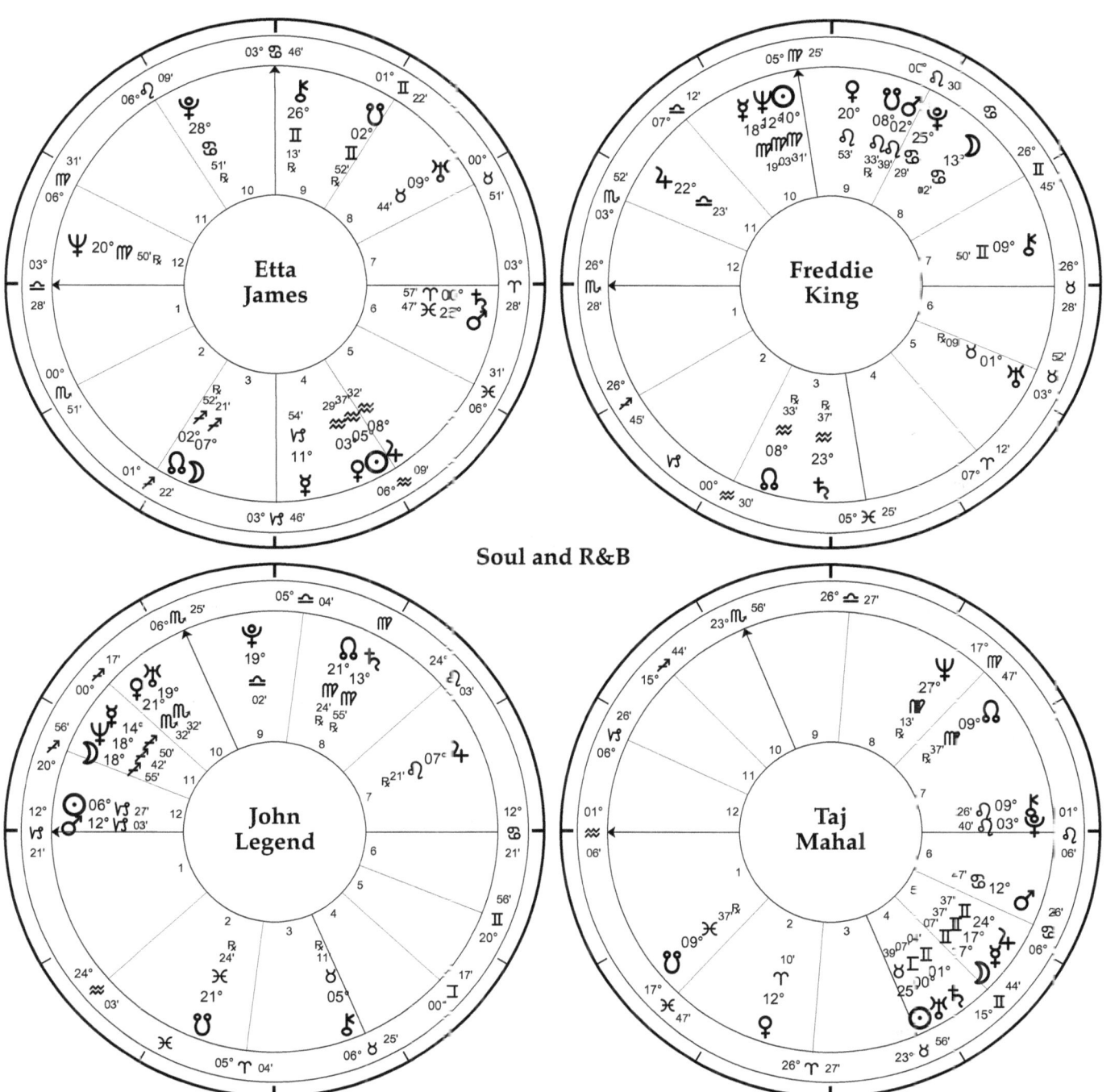

Soul and R&B

Soul and R&B

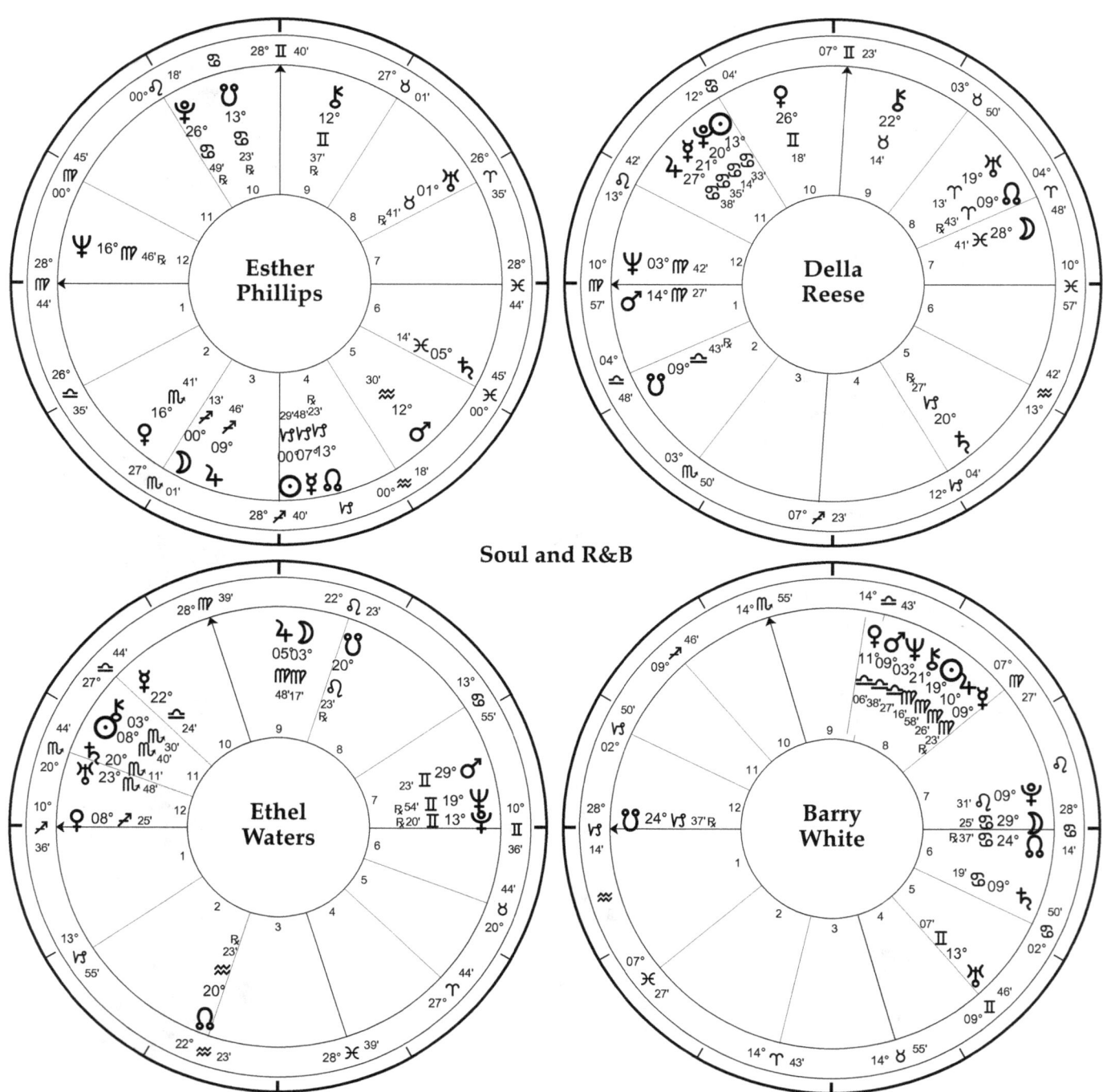

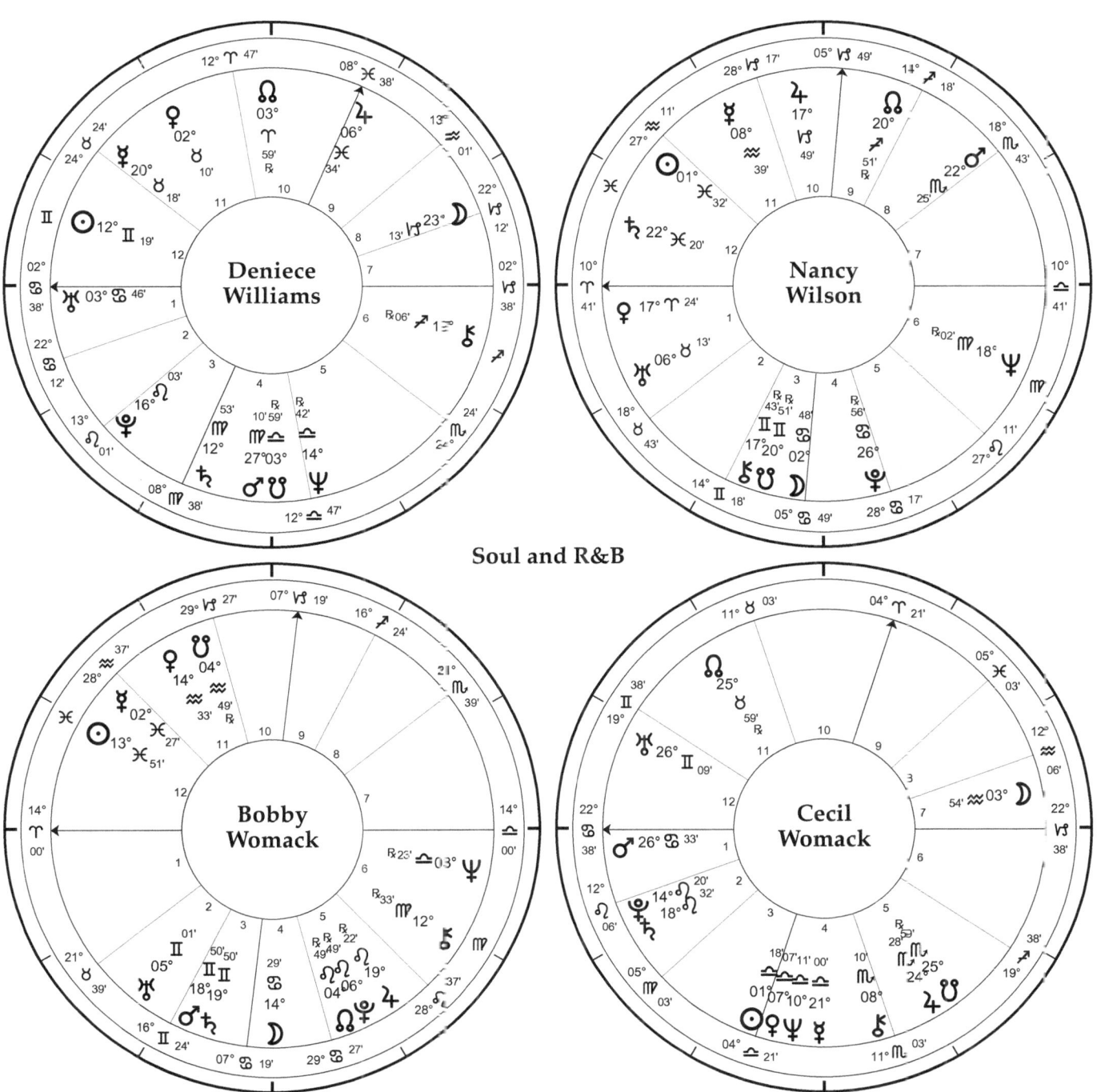

Soul and R&B

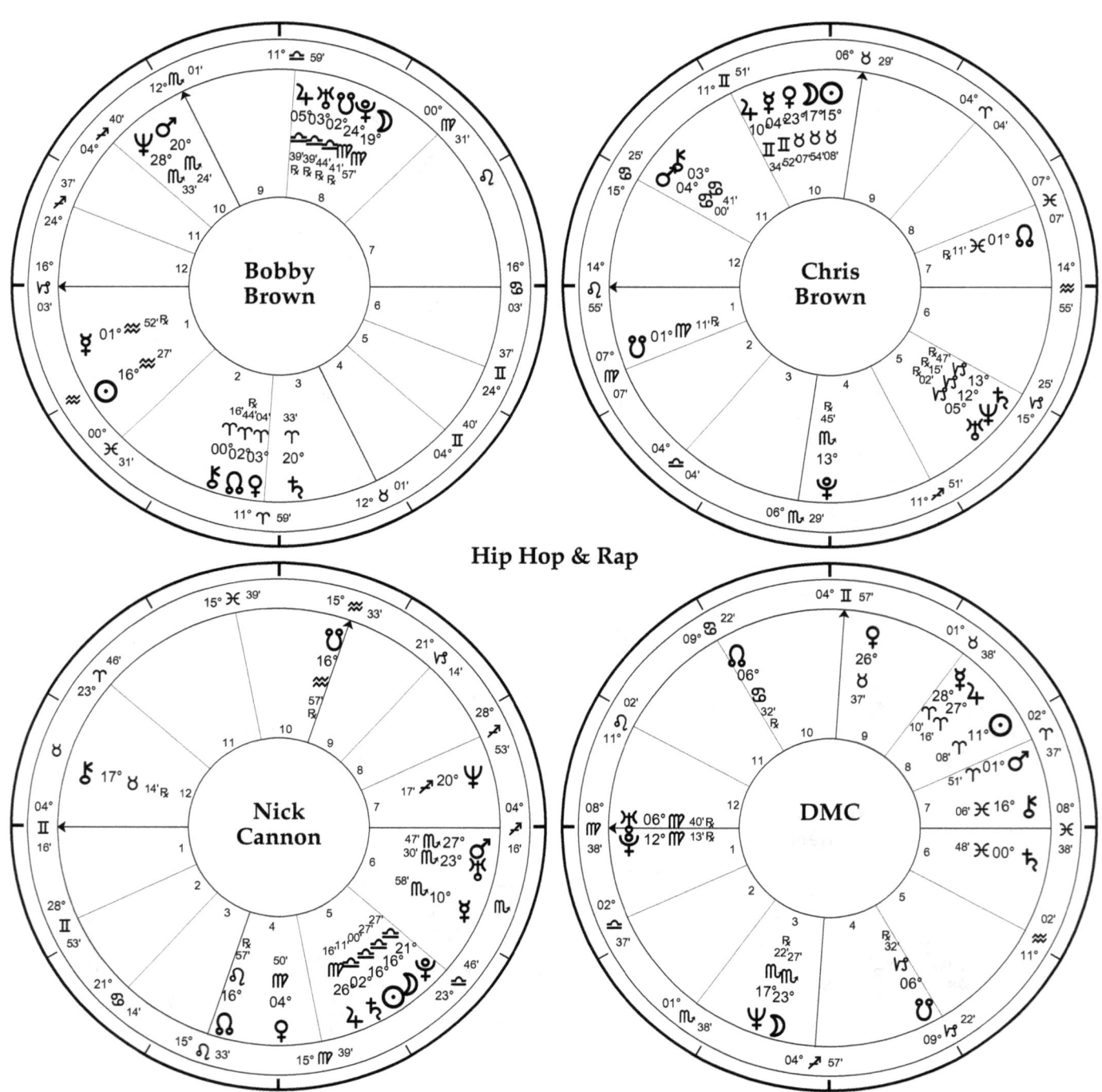

Hip Hop & Rap

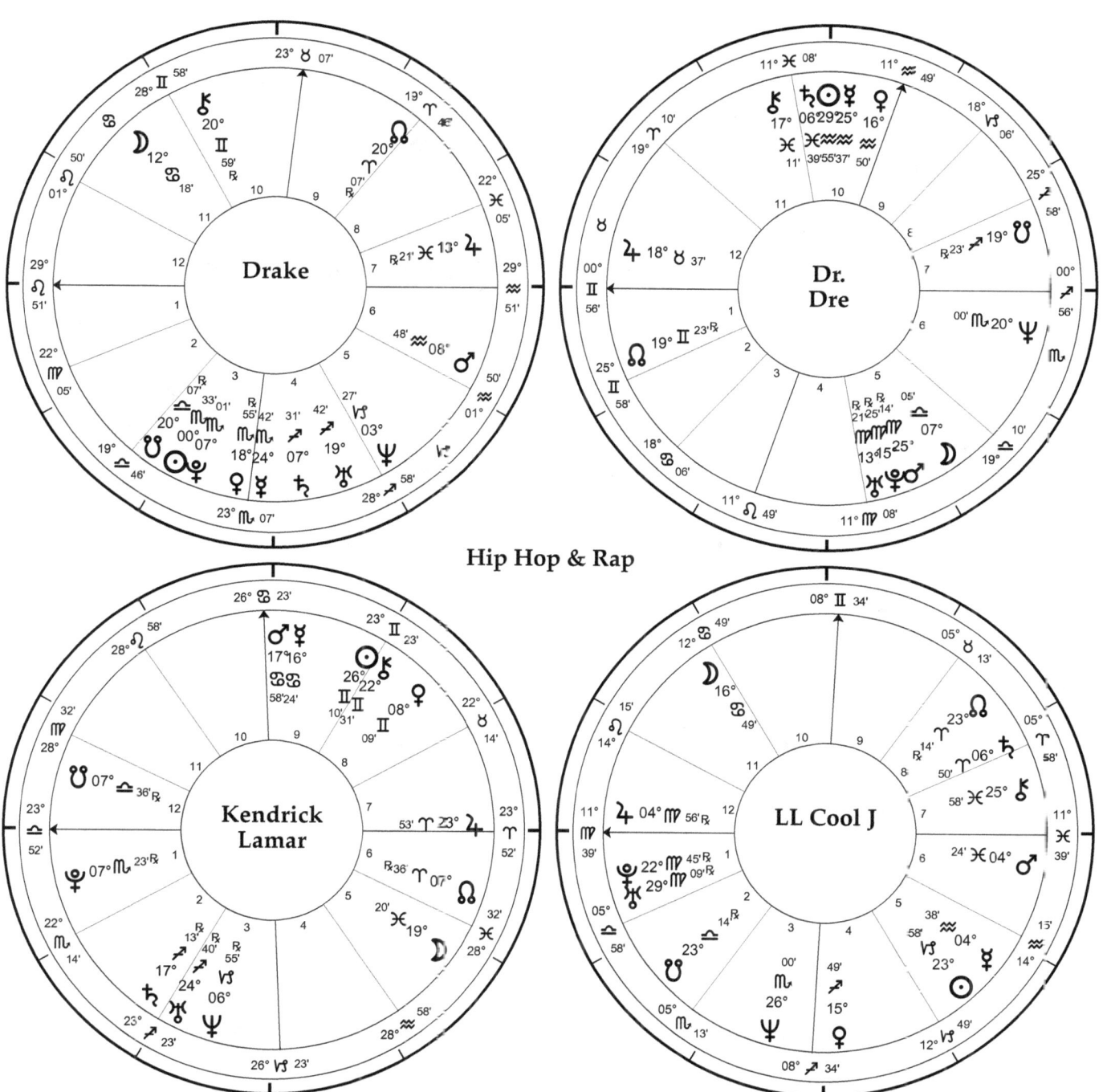

Hip Hop & Rap

42 *The Book of Music Horoscopes*

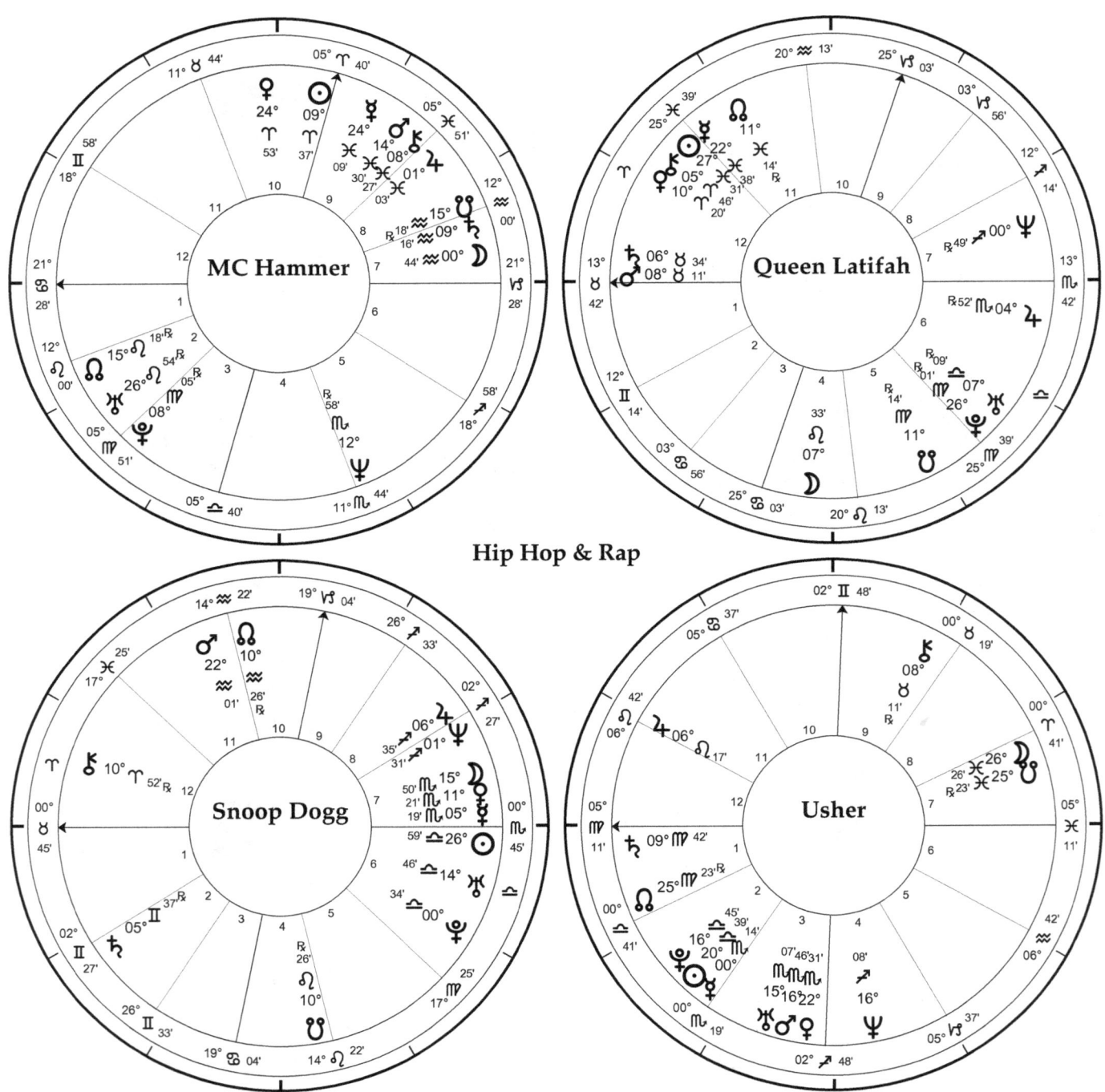

Hip Hop & Rap

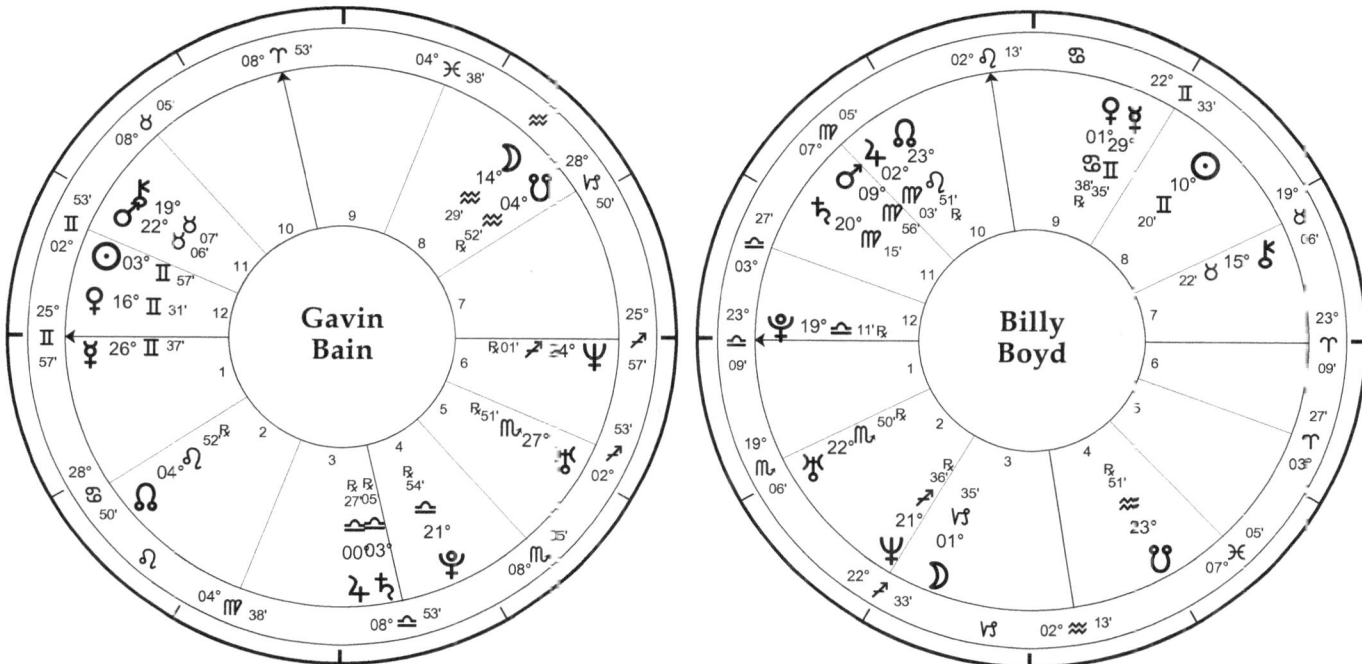

Music, Magic and Mishaps: Mercury, Neptune and Pluto in the Charts of Silibil N' Brains

Stefanie James

After a humiliating rejection by music chiefs for sounding like 'rapping Proclaimers', performers Gavin Bain and Billy Boyd were out to prove themselves. They decided the only way to have success as hip-hop artists was to tell a simple lie to cover up their Scottish roots. As Gavin said, 'The key to being a good liar is being a great listener – we were fantastic listeners.'

The boys had met at Dundee Art College in 1998. With natal Mercurys conjunct, Gavin felt drawn to sit with Billy. 'We had so much in common, as if we were the other's mirror image,' he said. Billy adds, 'We were a comedy duo, we were always together, we were always getting in trouble, we were always having a laugh … I felt like I'd known him all my life, we were best friends, we were brothers.'

Performance-enhancing Rejection

Fast-forward to London 2001 and the boys' first audition. Having travelled from Dundee by coach, they stood in front of a panel of record company judges. This was the moment Billy Boyd and Gavin Bain had been waiting for. They broke into a performance to showcase their talents, rapping with Scottish accents over a backing track they had written. To their horror, the judges laughed and talked to one another – and the boys were dismissed. Heading back to Dundee, they were devastated, their dreams in tatters. This was the catalyst which prompted them to reinvent themselves and become other people.

Gavin has a Gemini Sun opposite Uranus in Scorpio, while Billy has a Gemini Sun and Pluto rising. 'We decided to develop these characters and that's when Silibil N' Brains were really born,' recalls Billy on their transformation. Re-recording their tracks with American accents, they studied American film and TV, memorized online street layouts of California and fully immersed themselves in their new identities, refusing to break character at any point.

A series of successful gigs in London led to a lucrative management deal, which earned them unlimited access to a recording studio in Brixton, an all-expenses paid flat in London and living expenses. Gavin and Billy began living through the lens of a video camera, documenting their antics wherever they went and making comedy sketches for their website. They signed their recording contract at 13:30 on Friday 13 February 2004, with Sony UK promising to spend at least £1 million on Silibil N' Brains. With emotions running high and the champagne flowing, fictitious stories about 'old friends' Eminem and rap supergroup D12 circulated the room. Billy recalls, 'We'd always add arms and legs to this huge body of a story.'

Tongue Kung-Fu
From the song 'Tongue Kung-Fu', the lyrics 'I act the fool so well, I should win an Oscar' conjure an image of the interplay between light-hearted joker Mercury and glamorous yet deceptive Neptune. Both guys are Gemini Suns (within conjunction of each other), and each has a natal Mercury–Neptune opposition (Gemini to Sagittarius). Each of them also has an extremely persuasive Mercury–Pluto trine, adding a spell-like quality to their linguistic abilities and modus operandi. Perhaps more compelling is Gavin's Mercury conjunct his Gemini Ascendant and Billy's Pluto conjunct his Ascendant in Libra.

Billy's choice of name for his alter ego (Silibil) implies a Plutonian quality, emphasizing the hypnotic persuasion of rhythmic speech: 'I think about syllables when I'm writing and obviously my name's Billy – it was a play on words.' And Gavin (Brains) describes the Mercurial camaraderie in his choice of name: 'You put Silibil and Brains together and it's like "Pinky and the Brain" or comic book villains or heroes.'

On the day the recording contract was signed, Gavin's Solar Arc Sun was about to cross his Ascendant, propelling him from the darkness and confinement of the 12th House into the spotlight of the 1st. This encouraged the sacrifice of his true identity, reinforcing his belief in his alter ego: 'Brains – not Gavin Bain – was the person I was born to be.' Soon after, transiting Uranus would square his Sun, further detaching (Uranus) Gavin from his identity (Sun), so he validated himself only through others' belief in him. In approximately one year, Gavin's SA Sun would reach his 1st House Mercury, shining a spotlight on the lie he was living.

In Billy's chart, progressed Mars applied to a conjunction with his natal Saturn in Virgo forming a square to his natal Neptune, highlighting a need to pay serious attention to the many constantly changing details about his new identity (Virgo) while drawing on inner strength and self-discipline (Saturn). Neptune's diffusing effect on Mars may have initially hidden the risks involved, which became more apparent as time passed. Though his dreams were being realized, Billy's restricted self-expression would prove more oppressive than enjoyable.

During the hoax, Billy and Gavin had Pluto transiting their natal Mercury–Neptune oppositions, creating considerable mental tension for them both. The secret information they were guarding was highly volatile and threatened to burst at any moment like water through a crack in a dam. Problems did occur, as Gavin recalls. 'We spent so much on our look and getting our accents perfect, we didn't do any research into American culture.' When situations arose that they hadn't researched, they would create a distraction and quickly change the subject to avoid being caught out. Improvising was instinctive and intuitive between them both, suggested by the heavily emphasized mutability and Air in their charts.

Magicians
A few months after signing up Silibil N' Brains, the record company lined up a TV appearance on a popular show on MTV called *TRL*. As exciting a prospect as this was, it had the potential to blow their cover. Their appearance on the show went well but, as feared, comments from old acquaintances started appearing on forums and revealing the boys to be Scottish. No serious repercussions emerged from this event, though it exposed the enormous flaw in their story.

One morning in September 2004, Gavin received a phone call informing him that Silibil N' Brains were going to support 'old friends' D12 on stage that evening. A lie they had told repeatedly – embellished when signing their recording contract – had come back to haunt them. What should have been a career-defining moment was now tarnished by the fear of being exposed as imposters. On arrival at the venue, they nervously rushed to greet their 'old friends', enthusiastically hugging and high-fiving them. D12 were naturally confused. They had no idea who Silibil N' Brains were, but Billy improvised and came up with a story about how they had met at a venue they both played in Scotland. Seduced by Billy's magnetic charm (Pluto rising in Libra paired with his chart ruler Venus conjunct Mercury), D12 became warm and friendly, seeming to recall the fictitious meeting. The boys ended up at a post-gig party in D12's dressing room and no one had suspected a thing. Gavin commented, 'That's when it became clear to me. Bill and I were magicians, pure and simple, capable of magic, of opening every door, turning every situation to our advantage and imprinting our larger-than-life characters on to anyone we met, no matter how illustrious.'

The End of the Road
Living with the lie began to take its toll. Gavin was having dreams about his fabricated past in California. 'We completely forgot at one point that we were Scottish. I'd created such a good lie I could actually see where I lived, in my head.' Worrying about the lies they had told, tensions ran high and excessive lifestyles consumed them both. Gavin and Billy soon became addicted to a daily cocktail of substances that helped them function on an even keel. However, the cracks started to appear.

Billy got married in Scotland in December 2004 and by this point his wife was pregnant with their first child. He was tired of the charade, longing to meet his responsibilities as a husband and father. The lie had driven a wedge between Billy and Gavin, and their initial ire with the music industry became a deep-rooted anger with one another. It didn't help that the release date for the first single was repeatedly postponed. Sony was merging with BMG and began axing artists that weren't bringing in revenue. Following their worst fight, Gavin woke up to find Billy gone. Eventually the management company stopped returning Gavin's calls.

Though it was the end of the road for Silibil N' Brains, Gavin (with Mercury rising opposite Neptune) continued to identify with his alter ego, long after the partnership dissolved, not knowing who he was or which persona he should live by.

The final twist of this tale is that Gavin was born in Durban, South Africa. Looking at his astrocartography map, Gavin's Mercury–Ascendant line runs close by. He has recalled that his time living under his Mercury line was his happiest, finding his move to Scotland at the age of ten incredibly disruptive – it triggered insomnia, anxiety and depression. Adapting his communication style to suit his environment was something Gavin had learned at an early age. 'My parents were speaking to each other in a Scottish accent but then they would speak to their friends in a South African accent.' Described in his chart by his 1st House Mercury in Gemini opposite Neptune, he has said, 'If I lived with you for a week, I'd probably start morphing into your voice. Mimicking. I'm phenomenal at mimicking.'

Neptune Rules the Playlist

Steven Forrest

Neptune's reputation among astrologers generally triangulates between mysticism, inebriation and general flakiness. None of that is wrong. But we can make a case that Neptune actually defines reality as we experience it. We might call it our 'dream of the way things are'. How does a tree look to a Navajo shaman compared to a Harvard botanist? How does a woman's body look to an 11th century monk – or to a modern feminist? Recognize it or not, half of what we think we see 'out there' is in fact the mythic belief system that we carry between our ears. And that is Neptunian territory.

As Neptune changes signs, the underlying tone of our communal reality-dream changes. With its 165-year orbit, the planet spends an average of about 14 years in a sign, although that varies a bit. With each new sign Neptune enters, the collective mood shifts. There is nothing subtle about it. The implications are vast and they cover a wide spectrum of cultural tastes, attitudes and fascinations. But there is no barometer more sensitive to the whimsies of these Neptunian sea-changes than popular music. The songs we hear on the radio, in the clubs or just walking down the street reflect nothing less than the soul of the times. They mirror our collective heart. They are the dream we are dreaming. And Neptune's sign changes illuminate the story.

In common with the rest of the planets, Neptune's path through the zodiac advances and then loops back in retrograde motion. Usually that means that its entry into a new sign is a bit complicated – it crosses the boundary, retreats, re-enters, sometimes touching the cusp as often as five times. To avoid bogging this short article down with a long list of dates, I will simply state the year in which Neptune first touched a new sign and the year in which it was last found there. You will see some overlap and apparent contradiction in the dates. For example, Neptune first touched the Scorpio cusp in December 1955, but then twice threaded back into Libra, at last exiting Libra and entering Scorpio solidly in early August 1957.

Neptune in Libra: 1942–1957
Courtesy, civilized behaviour and simple decency of conduct are in the domain of Libra. The sign is ruled by Venus, the goddess of grace. We are talking about Romance – from the waist up. We are talking about character, poise and the basis of respectful, warm harmony between people. The symbol of the Balance-Scale suggests opposites in perfect equilibrium: an ounce of lead and an ounce of gold. Or male and female. Or Jack and Jill.

Against the backdrop of the sheer Plutonian horror of the Second World War, the gauzy romanticism of the period's music stood in sharp contrast. Cole Porter's composition, 'You'd Be So Nice to Come Home To', struck a resonant note – especially as we realize that many couples were physically separated by the war and haunted by the knowledge that they might very well never see each other again.

Romantic projection thrives on separation. Lonely hunger – and its comforting amatory delusions – carried poignant meaning during that nightmare time. Then the soldiers came marching home from war, hungry for the comforts of marriage, home and family – and for songs that harmonized with their Libran mood. It was the age of the great love-struck crooner. Frank Sinatra. Tony Bennett. Patti Page. Nat King Cole. Perry Como. Dinah Shore. Bing Crosby. Rosemary Clooney. Dean Martin. Peggy Lee. Eddie Fisher. Doris Day.

The tune that topped Billboard's Top 100 in 1952 epitomizes it all. It was Jo Stafford's 'You Belong To Me'. Times have changed, as has the syntax of love. Notice how nowadays simply telling someone that he or she 'belongs to you' feels anachronistic and vaguely suspect. Not with Neptune in Libra!

Neptune in Scorpio: 1955–1970
Out went the crooners and in came rock 'n' roll. Paraphrasing a line from the previous paragraph, we are now talking about Romance – from the waist down. Debates rage about the timing of the birth of rock 'n'

roll. Clearly it owes a vast debt to Afro-American blues artists and to white Europeans displaced into Appalachia. But our subject here is not the question of where or how rock 'n' roll originated. Our subject is the Neptunian mood of culture as reflected in popular tastes.

Neptune hit the passionate, uninhibited, frankly erotic sign of the Scorpion in 1955, the year which saw the chart debuts of Elvis Presley, Little Richard and Chuck Berry. Muddy Waters arrived in England in 1958, carrying the black yeast of the electric blues into the very white flour of the UK's war-children. That bread was served to a waiting world a few years later.

What was the first rock 'n' roll record? You can start fist fights among musicologists with that question. A strong contender is and the Comets' 'Rock Around the Clock'. The lynchpin of the argument for that particular song is simply that it was the first rock 'n' roll single to rise to the number one position on the Billboard charts. It did that in the summer of 1955, keyed perfectly to Neptune's Scorpionic signal.

I watched a video once that showed the very white crooner Pat Boone singing Little Richard's 'Tutti Frutti' in a very white nightclub. I almost felt sorry for the man. 'A whop bopaalu, a whop bam bam, tutti frutti, oh rooty, tutti frutti, oh rooty . . . Got a gal named Sue, she knows just what to do …' Poor Pat looked to me like an embarrassed Sunday School teacher. Then the videographer cut to Little Richard singing the song himself and the raw, strange and distinctly single entendre sexuality of the tune blasted right through Pat Boone's attempt to confine it to a polite Libran cage. The repressed Libran libido had given way to the Scorpionic roar of sheer, enthusiastic hunger – from the waist down. We now had the soundtrack for the sexual revolution.

Neptune in Sagittarius: 1970–1984
Suddenly rock 'n' roll became 'Rock'. Sagittarius is of course ruled by Jupiter, the expansive king of the gods. As Neptune entered that sign, bigger became better and nothing succeeded like excess. The music got louder. The hair got bigger. Ticket prices soared. People wanted to dance, so disco arose and took over. Sequins replaced blue jeans. Performance moved from concert halls to stadiums. Woodstock happened in 1969 with Neptune still in Scorpio, but soon the outdoor music festival, attracting populations of attendees the size of small cities, became the dominant cultural form. Bands that made their mark in the 1960s became huge businesses – think of the marketing of The Rolling Stones, The Who, Led Zeppelin, the Bee Gees, Stevie Wonder, Crosby, Stills and Nash, Earth Wind & Fire. New 'supergroups' arose: Boston, The Jackson 5, Foreigner, Styx, Electric Light Orchestra.

Sagittarius is the great Traveller, and its cross-cultural fascinations made themselves felt in the music. Reggae came out of Jamaica and left fingerprints on popular sensibilities that one still hears today. The huge success of The Police was based partly on the savvy marketing of their reggae-tinged music to the non-English-speaking world. Led Zeppelin began using the drum rhythms of northern Africa.

Sagittarius carries the archetype of the Philosopher and the music became 'big' in concept as well as volume. Think of the metaphysical ambitions, both musically and lyrically, of the 'prog rock' bands of that era: Genesis, Yes, Pink Floyd, The Moody Blues. Nothing less than albums that fully addressed 'the meaning of life' were enough.

Neptune in Capricorn: 1984–1998
Neptune's passage through Capricorn, a sign ruled by mechanical, conservative Saturn, manifested musically in two very different ways. One was in the explosion of the popularity of country and western music. The other was the dominant position achieved by hip hop or rap.

Capricorn carries a great respect for tradition; country is a very traditional musical form. Musicologically, it is typically structured in conventional verse–chorus–bridge format. Often the chords are simple. And of course in content it tends to reflect traditional values: true love, marriage, family, church and patriotism. As Neptune entered Capricorn there was a great hunger for a return to values opposed to the perceived excesses of Neptune in Scorpio and Sagittarius. Epitomizing this trend, Garth Brooks released his first album in 1989. He is the second best-selling solo artist in history, after Elvis Presley. By January 2012, his sales had surpassed those of The Beatles.

Capricorn correlates with a fascination with tools and all things mechanical. It is fitting that reliance upon drum machines, such as the Oberheim DMX and Roland 808, was typical of many hit songs from the period in all popular genres. This was especially true of hip hop, which could not have existed without the drum machine – nor without the existence of another machine, a device called a sampler, which extracts beats and musical phrases from existing recordings. Following this machine-dominated pattern, sequencers came to be an essential recording tool as well. Who needs a musician when a computer can play the whole string section for free?

In 1983–84 came the early rise of rap icons Run–D.M.C. and LL Cool J. In 1986, The Beastie Boys' album *Licensed to Ill* was the first rap album to reach number one on the Billboard charts. Generally the 'golden age of Hip Hop' is seen to run from the mid-1980s through the early 1990s. Billboard editor Paul Grein called 1990 'the year that rap exploded', based significantly on the huge success of Public Enemy's album *Fear of a Black Planet*.

Machines on one hand and conservative social values on the other – that is the signature of Neptune's tenure in Capricorn.

Neptune in Aquarius: 1998–2012
Keywords for Aquarius: innovation, diversity, shock, independence, technology, revolution. When Neptune entered Aquarius, the impact upon music was immediate and profound. MP3 coding, which reduced the size of digital music files to manageable proportions, had been standardized in 1991, but by the late 1990s its use was widespread. In 1998, right on Neptune's Aquarian schedule, MP3.com was launched. The Digital Millennium Copyright Act was enacted. And, most critically, the first MP3 players hit the market. On 9 January 2001, Apple released Version 1.0 of iTunes and the world of music was changed forever. Napster, starting in 1999, basically made music free – and, naturally, this was a total calamity for the music business. Napster was shut down a couple of years later for pirating the intellectual property of recording artists – an Aquarian battle that is still being fought all over the world.

These distinctly Aquarian technological developments created enormous changes in the mood, place and nature of music in society. They virtually destroyed the monolithic 'music industry' in its previous form. The big labels shrank, laying off vast hordes of employees. Meanwhile, small-time artists were often able to thrive, finding digital niches, fans and outlets for their music. MySpace and Facebook, launched in 2003 and 2004 respectively, created Aquarian mechanisms for outreach and contact. Streaming Internet radio took off. With its countless 'boutique' channels, it created an unprecedented – and very Aquarian – diversity of ever more isolated styles.

Successful artists, as ever, abounded – Eminem, Usher, Beyonce, Alicia Keyes, Nickelback, Destiny's Child – but the real musical news with Neptune in Aquarius was simply Future Shock. There was no longer a single popular music as there had been for many decades. That unity was gone, for better or for worse. Aquarian fashion, everyone had his or her own channel now.

Neptune in Pisces: 2011–2026
For the previous five signs, we have the great advantage of hindsight. Neptune only first touched Pisces in 2011. Whatever music its return to its own sign will bring is still mostly unrecorded – and perhaps unimagined. I suspect it will be magnificent. Somewhere there is a five-year-old genius sitting down at a musical keyboard for the first time. One might envision a music of entrancement, its notes hypnotizing us into attunement to the next dimension. That would be utterly Neptunian. Jimi Hendrix, shortly before he died, was asked about his next project. He spoke of 'sweet opium music'. Well, maybe Jimi is now that five-year-old I just mentioned.

Keith Richards once said something to the effect that 90 per cent of popular music is dreck. And of course he is right. Works of true genius are precious for their rarity. Think of Neptune in Libra and all the sappy, forgettable love songs it generated. Think of Neptune in Scorpio and the plague of recordings it spawned that reduced human intimacy to a transaction of the genitals. Consider Neptune in Sagittarius and its crop of pretentious, self-glorifying rock anthems. Think of Neptune in Capricorn and how it cranked out music so utterly boring and predictable that only a machine could have accomplished it – and often did! We might add that Neptune in Capricorn brought a resurgence of the idea of male control and domination of women, which is often evident in both rap and country music. Think of Neptune in Aquarius and how it shattered the power of music to be a unifying cultural force by seducing us into boutique genres and categories, meanwhile putting earbuds between us and the rest of the human community.

Neptune in Pisces will surely not be immune to its own dark side. We will get – evidence suggests that perhaps we already are getting – saccharine, puerile 'spectacles' and 'entertainment' which will not be remembered beyond the life span of a guppy. That's the sugary, escapist side of Pisces.

But somewhere Jimi is sitting down at that keyboard to take us further into the Piscean ethers. Maybe Claude Debussy has been attracted back into the flesh by inaudible angels in the air. Perhaps a fresh audience has been reborn, an audience that is worthy of Beethoven's 10th symphony – the one left unfinished at the time of his death. Perhaps we will attract him, too. Perhaps we have earned that. Perhaps we humans are spiritually hungry enough for that kind of music.

Hidden in the sugar bowl, behind the perfumed clouds of improbable light, beyond the empty howling hype, I believe that the power of Neptune's return to its own sign heralds a musical renaissance.

Neptune

Notes by Frank Clifford

Neptune has links to career longevity and the 'comeback kid'; timeless music; nostalgia, yearning for yesteryear; enigmatic performers who define a gentler era but are gone too soon (e.g. Buddy Holly: Sun–Neptune square Moon); fan mania, mass adulation; glamour; accessible, genre-crossing artists – that transcendent, indefinable 'something' that can be embraced by all; seduction, romance and 'swooners' (e.g. Julio Iglesias: Neptune conjunct Sun–Mercury; and Barry White: Neptune conjunct Venus–Mars in Libra); scandal, deception and bootlegging in the industry; chameleons and musical shape-shifters; androgyny in men (Virgo seems the key to androgyny in women); and gender ambiguity (e.g., Prince and 'drag addict' Boy George: both with Venus opposite Neptune; David Bowie: Sun–Mars and Mercury square Neptune; Marc Bolan: Sun–Venus–Neptune opposite the Moon).

Alongside Uranus's instinct to wake people up to social causes, and Jupiter's flair for promotion and lobbying the influential, Neptune's function is to induce an emotional response to environmental issues and the plight of the needy. Bob Geldof (Sun–Neptune in Libra, and Mercury opposite Jupiter in Aries, the signature of the inspirational fundraiser) and Midge Ure (Sun–Neptune in Libra) gathered pop and rock royalty to record 'Do They Know It's Christmas?' four days after Neptune made its final ingress into business-minded Capricorn in November 1984. The song raised millions for famine relief in Ethiopia and was the start of numerous celebrity efforts to bring salvation to the forgotten and disenfranchised (Neptune), to tackle broader human rights issues (Libra) and to address the imbalances (Libra) of power and wealth. Another Libra Sun, Sting (with Moon conjunct Neptune in Libra, and Jupiter–MC in Aries), actively supported Amnesty International and launched a foundation in 1989 to preserve the rainforests.

POP IDOLS & PIN-UPS

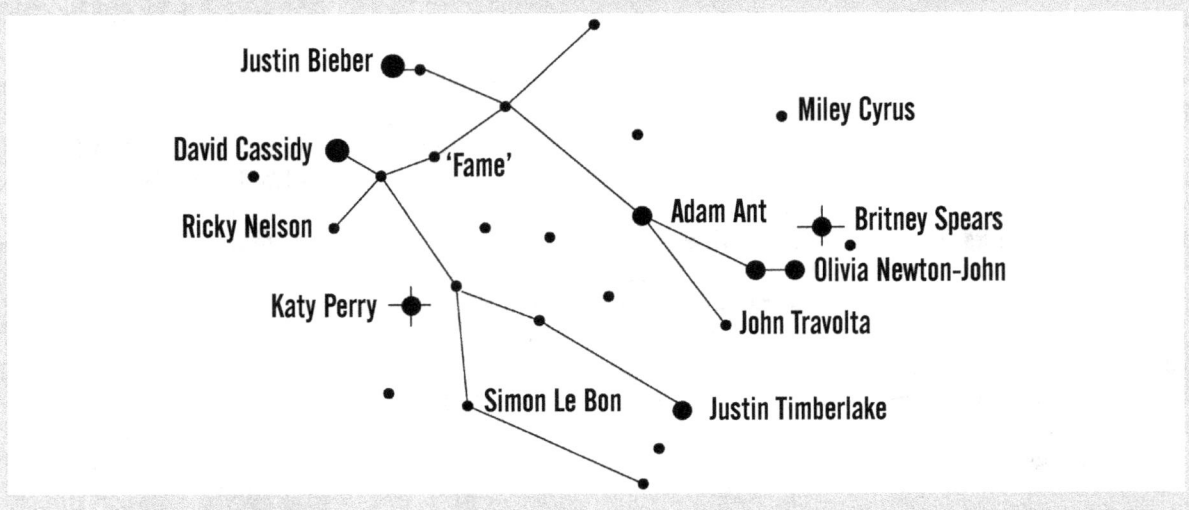

1950s–1960s

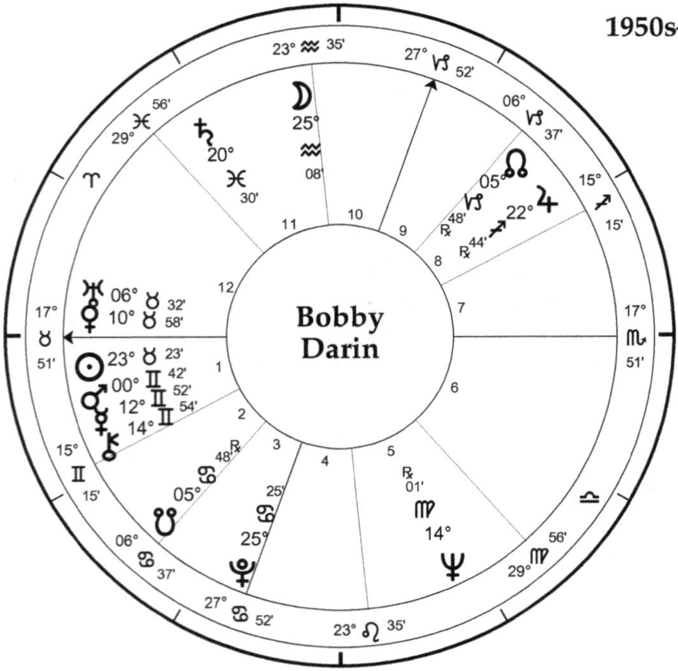

Bobby Darin

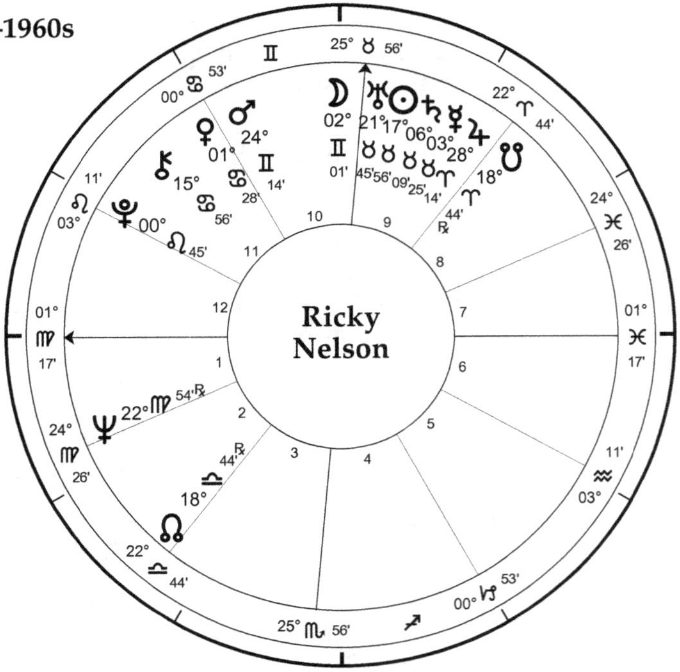

Ricky Nelson

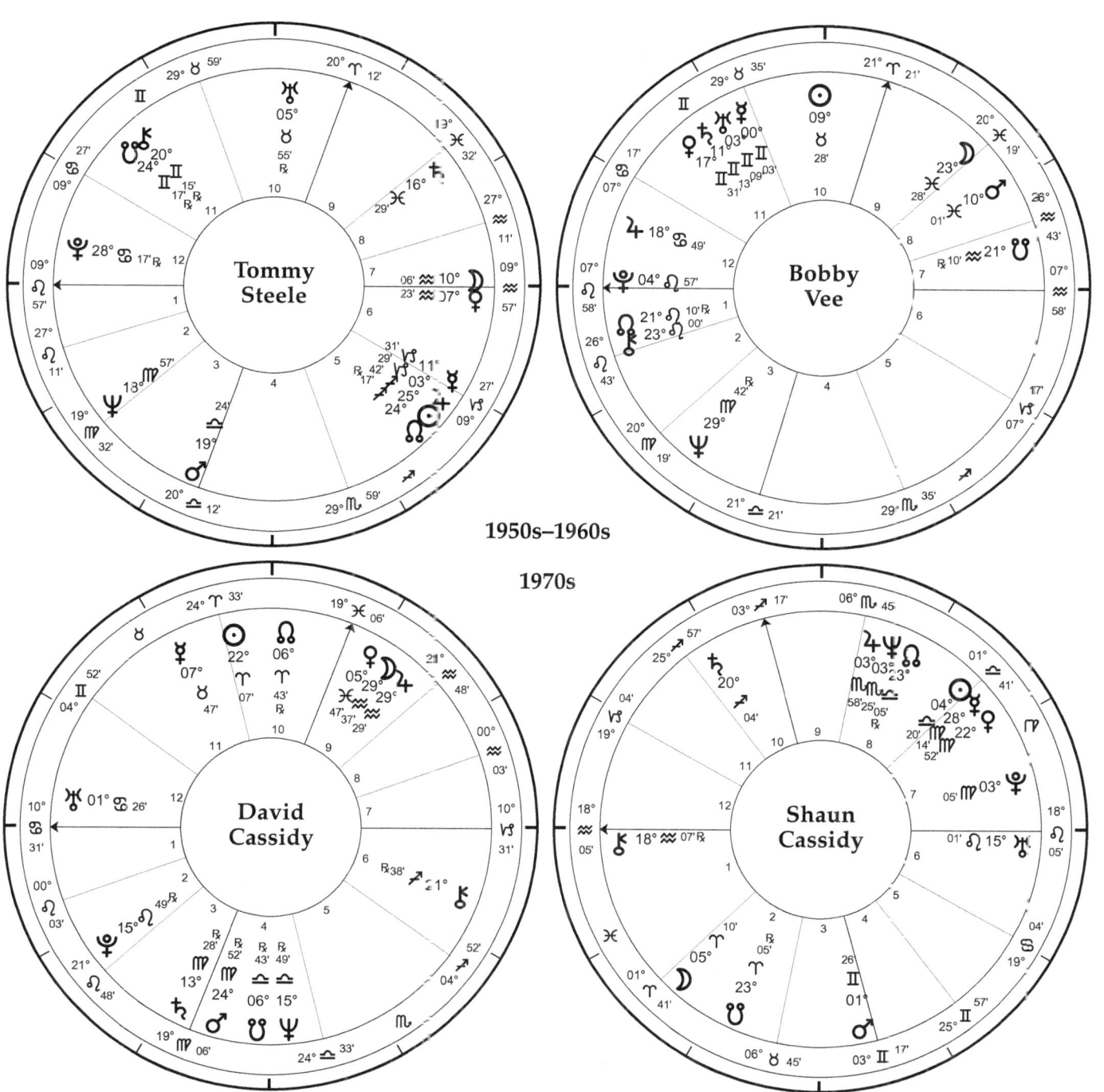

Pop Idols & Pin-Ups

1950s–1960s

1970s

52 *The Book of Music Horoscopes*

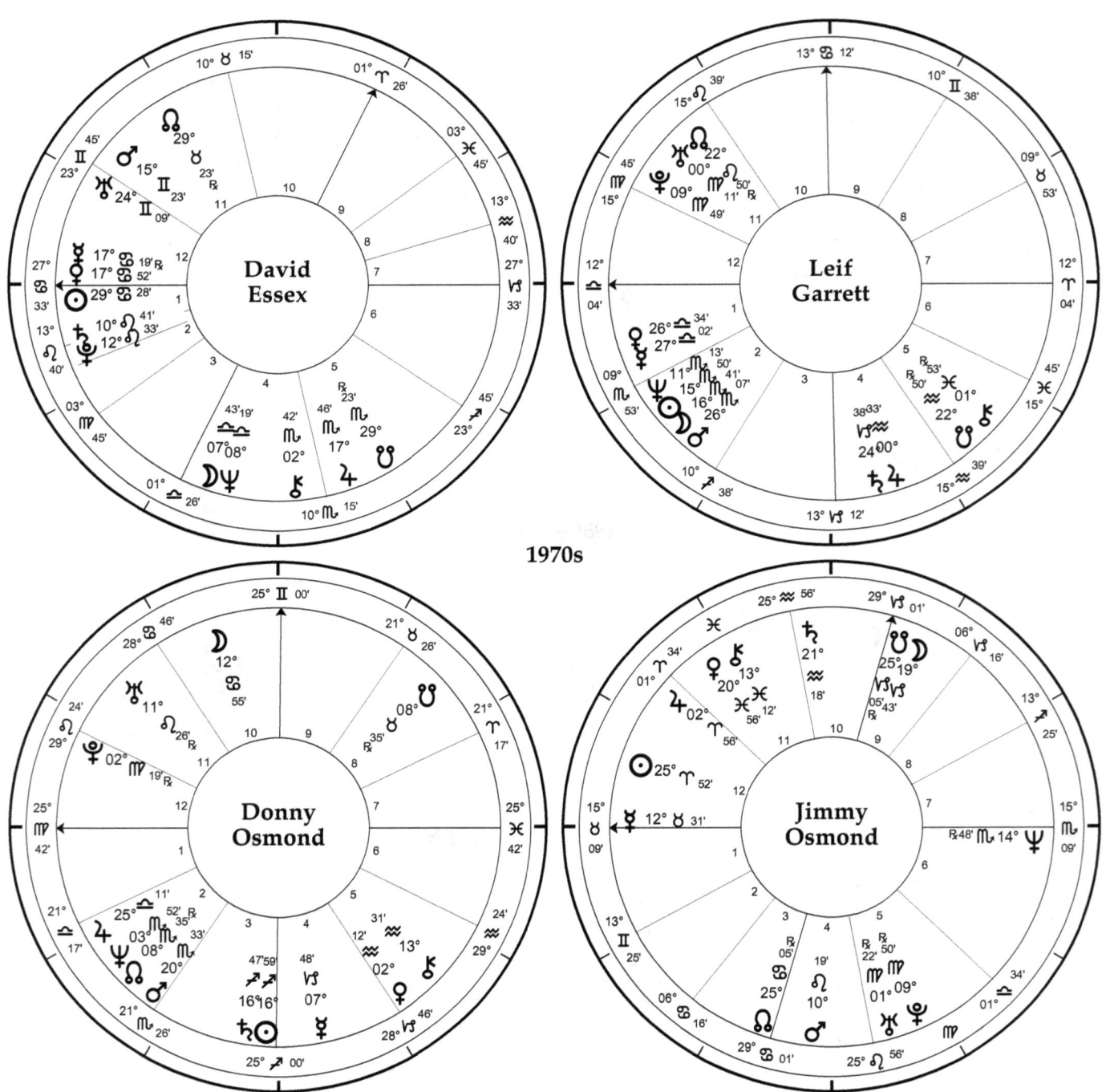

1970s

Pop Idols & Pin-Ups

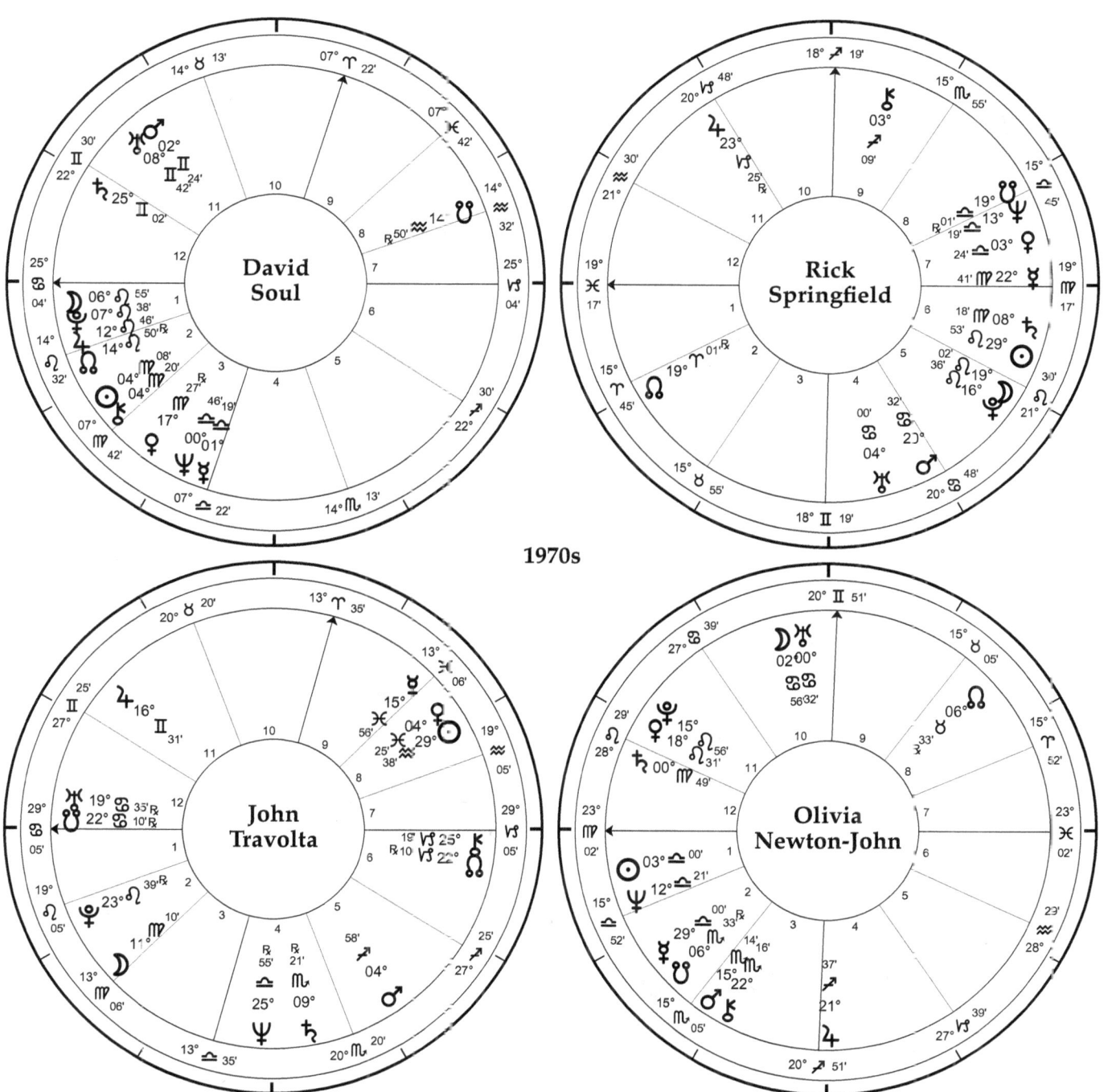

1970s

54 The Book of Music Horoscopes

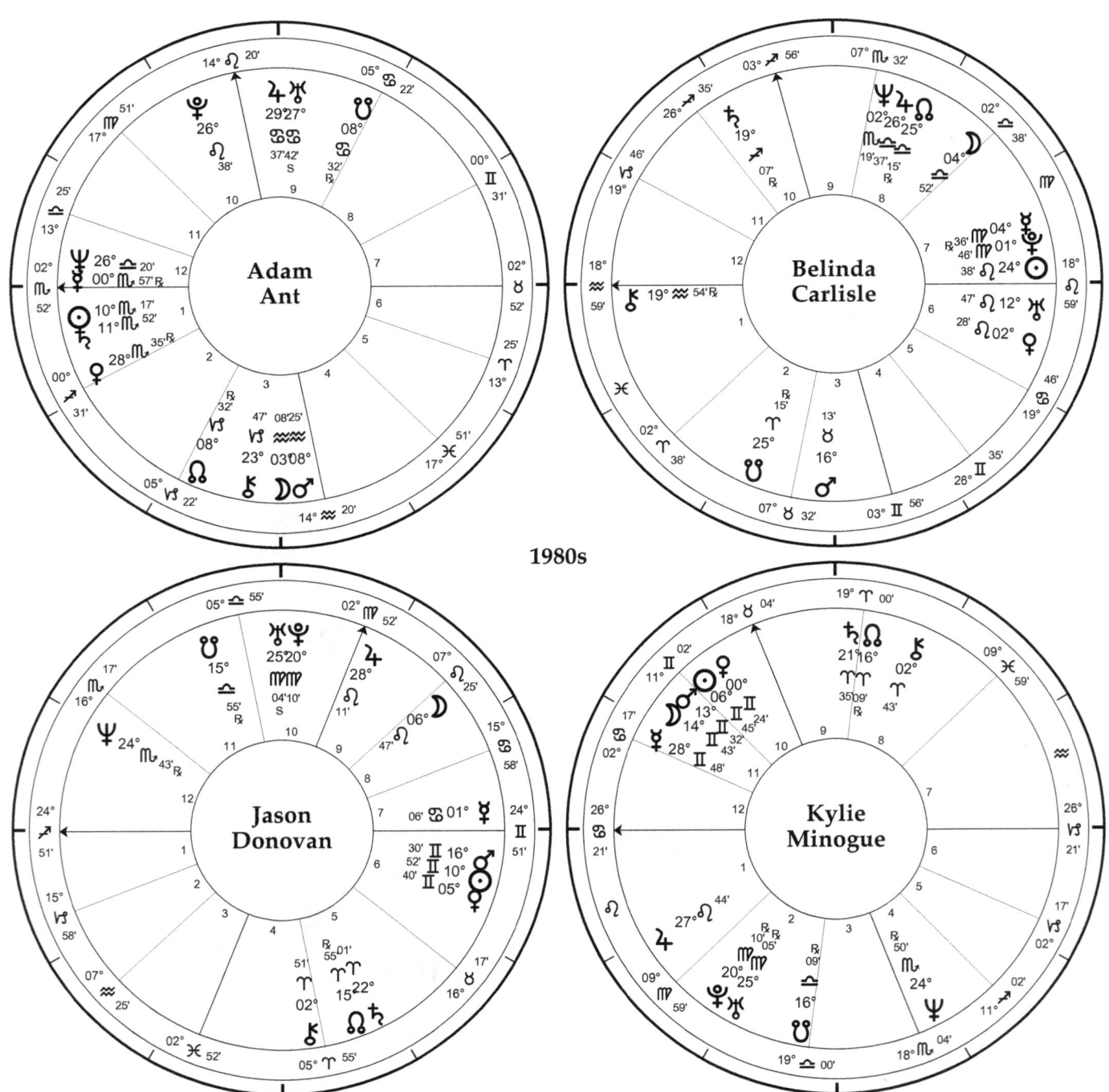

1980s

Pop Idols & Pin-Ups 55

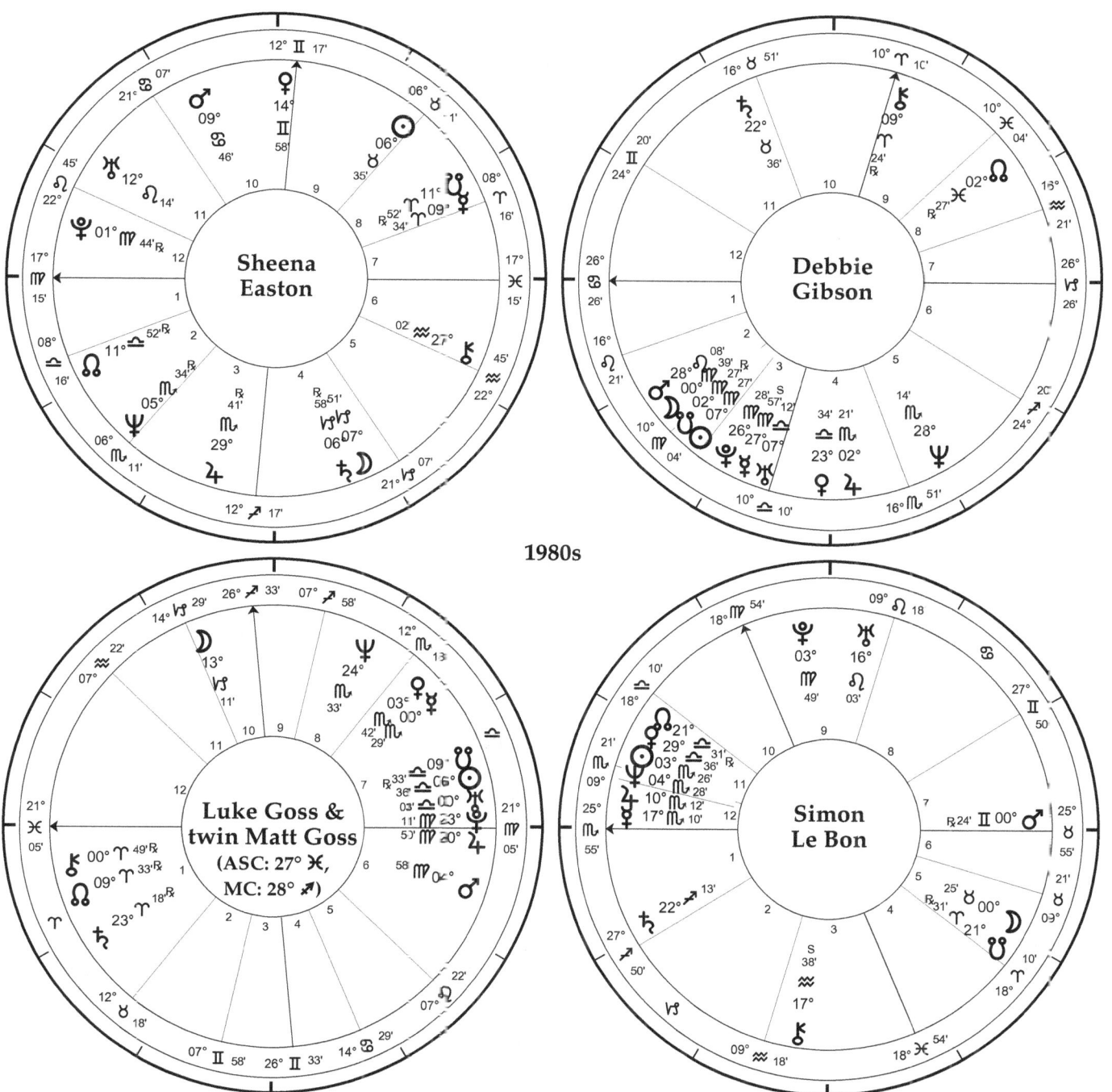

1980s

56 The Book of Music Horoscopes

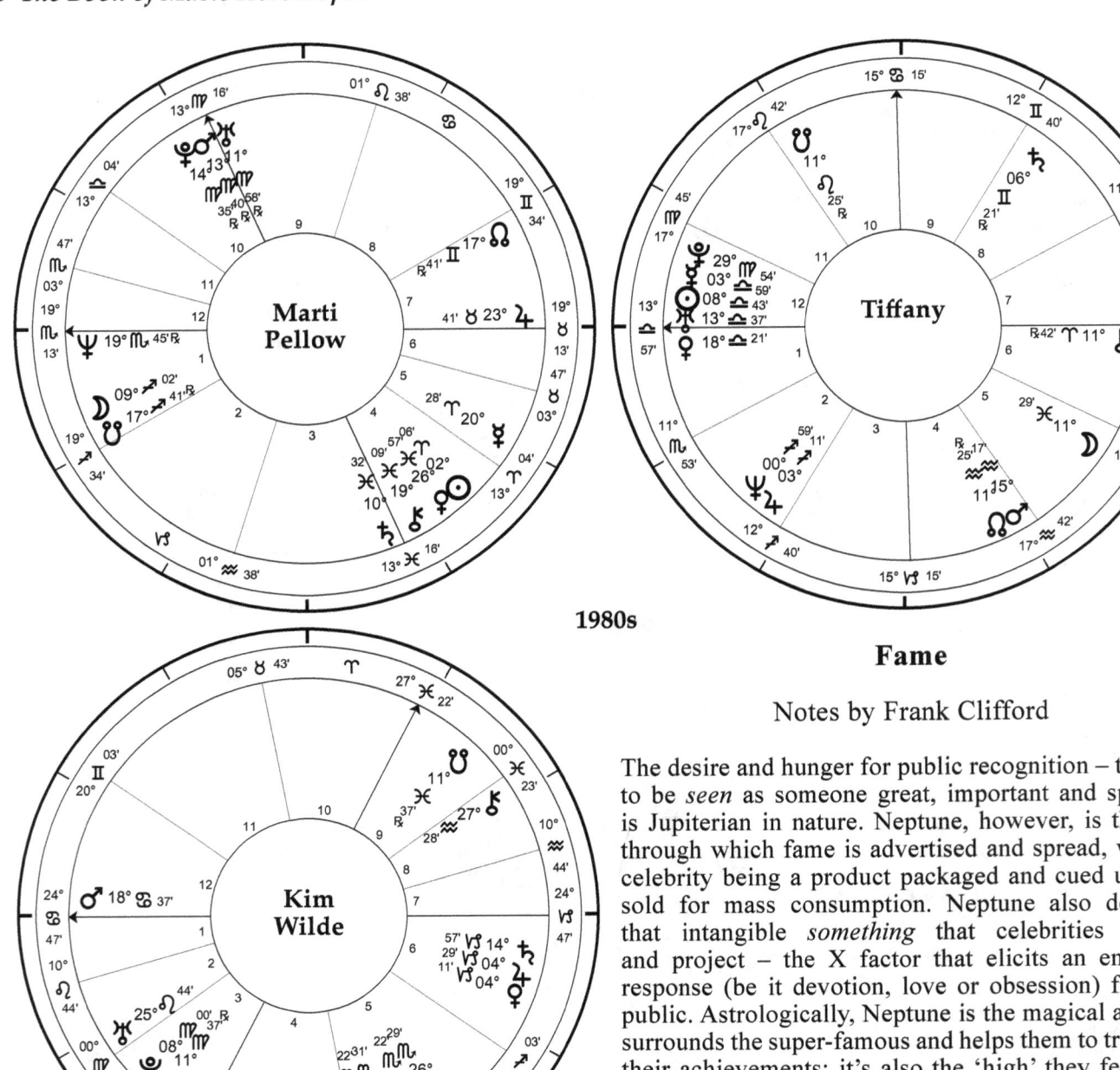

1980s

Fame

Notes by Frank Clifford

The desire and hunger for public recognition – the need to be *seen* as someone great, important and special – is Jupiterian in nature. Neptune, however, is the filter through which fame is advertised and spread, with the celebrity being a product packaged and cued up to be sold for mass consumption. Neptune also describes that intangible *something* that celebrities possess and project – the X factor that elicits an emotional response (be it devotion, love or obsession) from the public. Astrologically, Neptune is the magical aura that surrounds the super-famous and helps them to transcend their achievements; it's also the 'high' they feel when receiving applause. (For more, see 'Fame and Celebrity: The Addictive Commodities of Our Times' in *The Solar Arc Handbook*, Flare, 2018)

Pop Idols & Pin-Ups

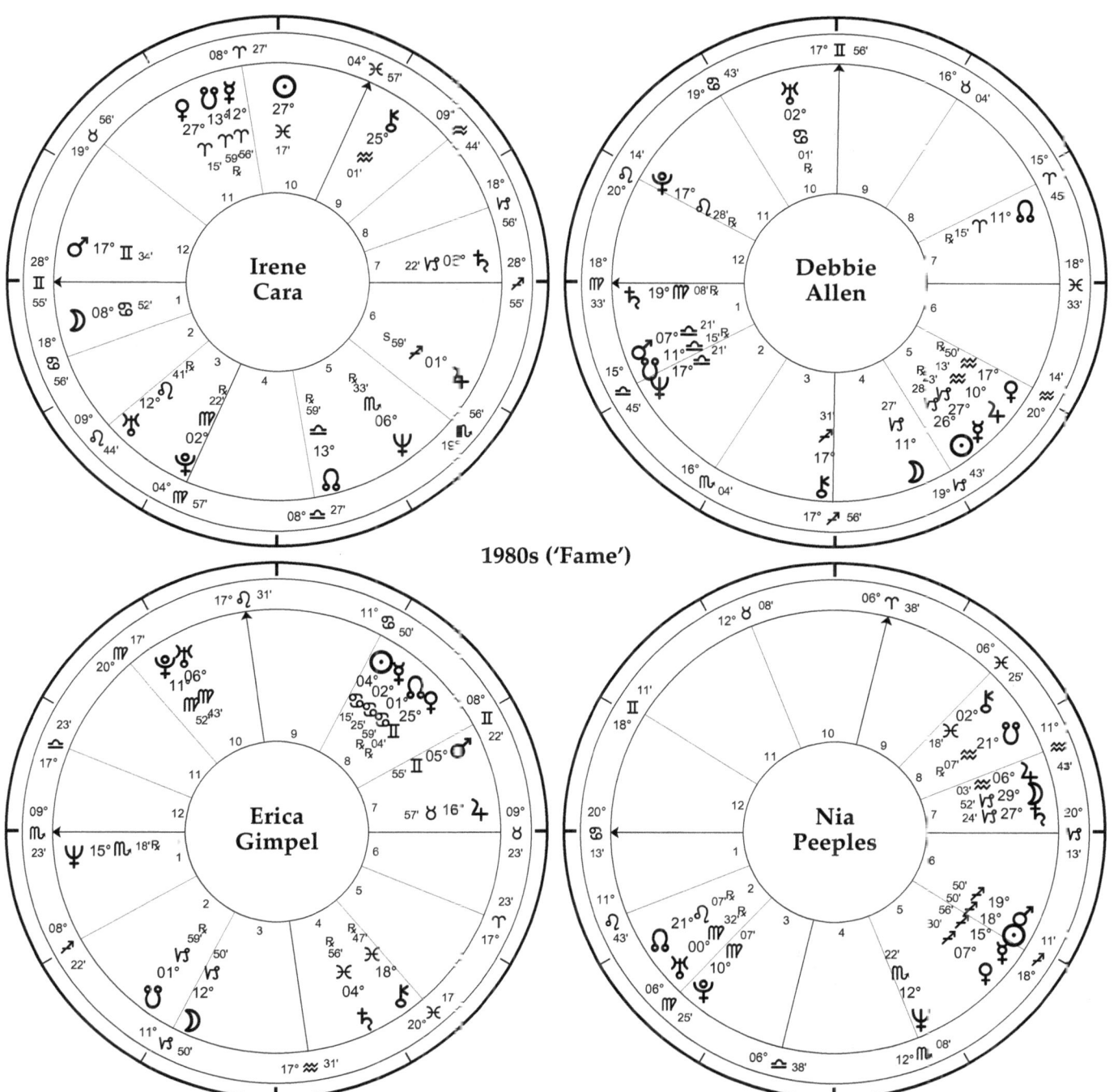

1980s ('Fame')

58 *The Book of Music Horoscopes*

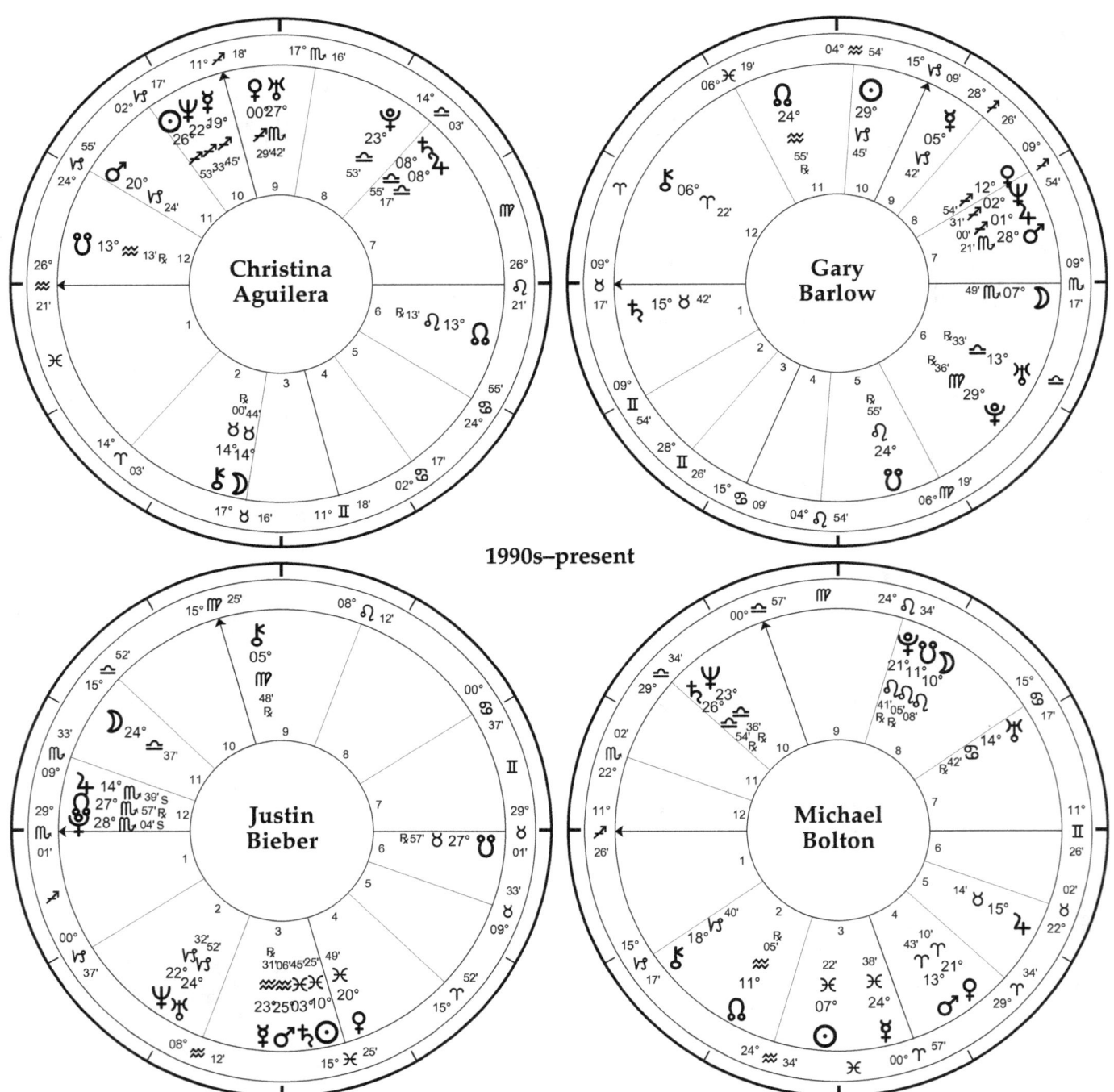

1990s–present

Pop Idols & Pin-Ups 59

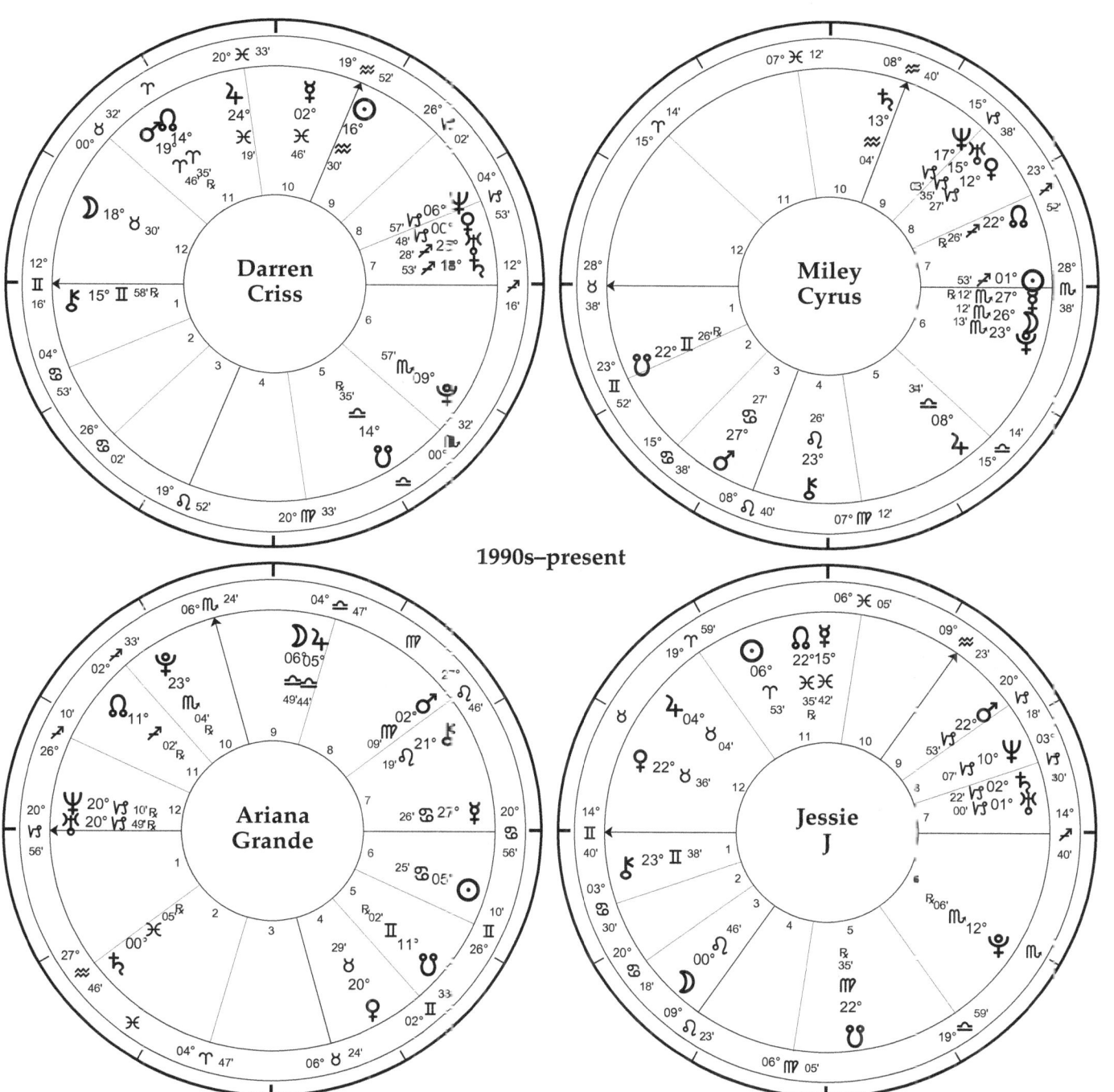

1990s–present

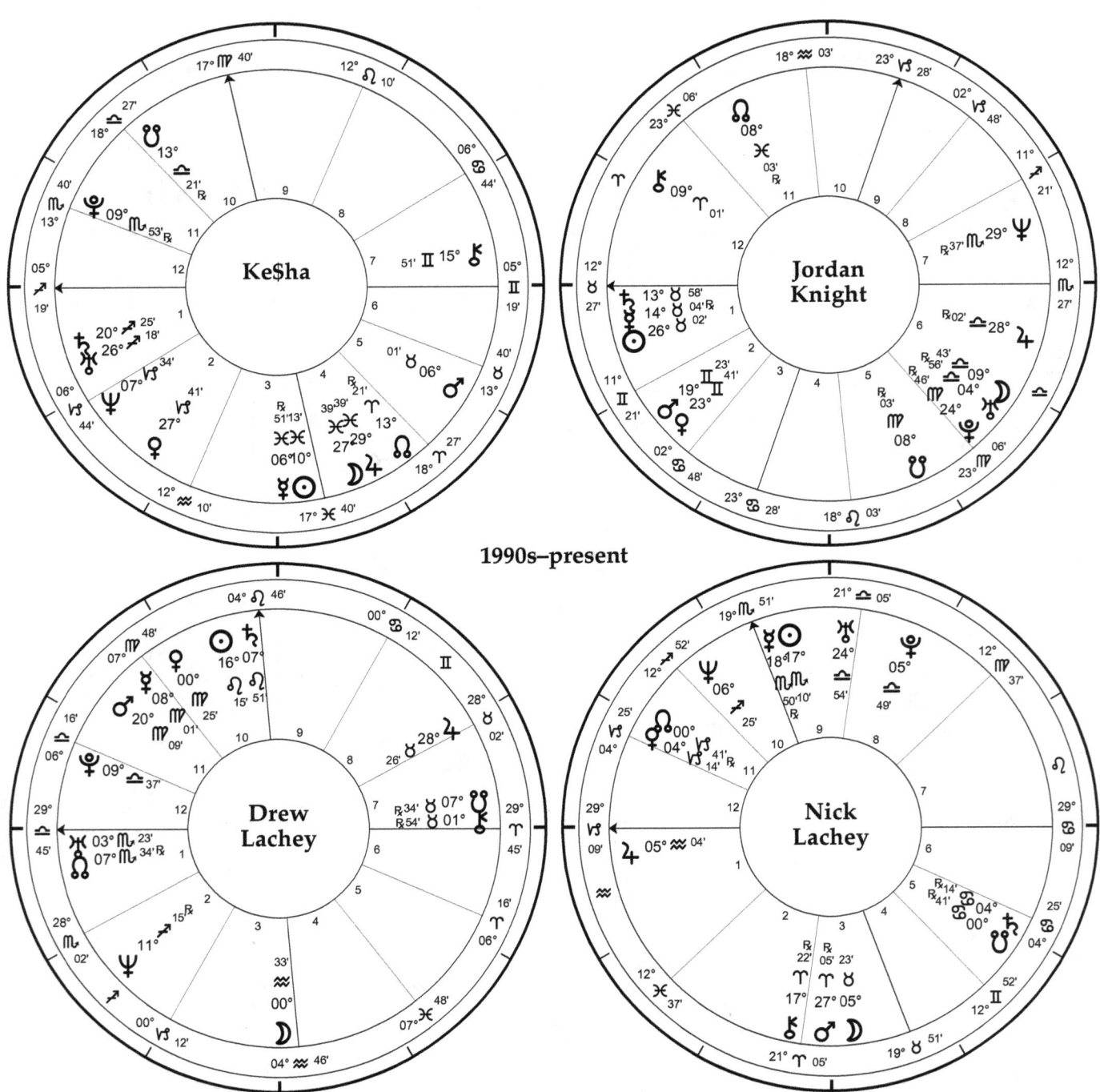

1990s–present

Pop Idols & Pin-Ups 61

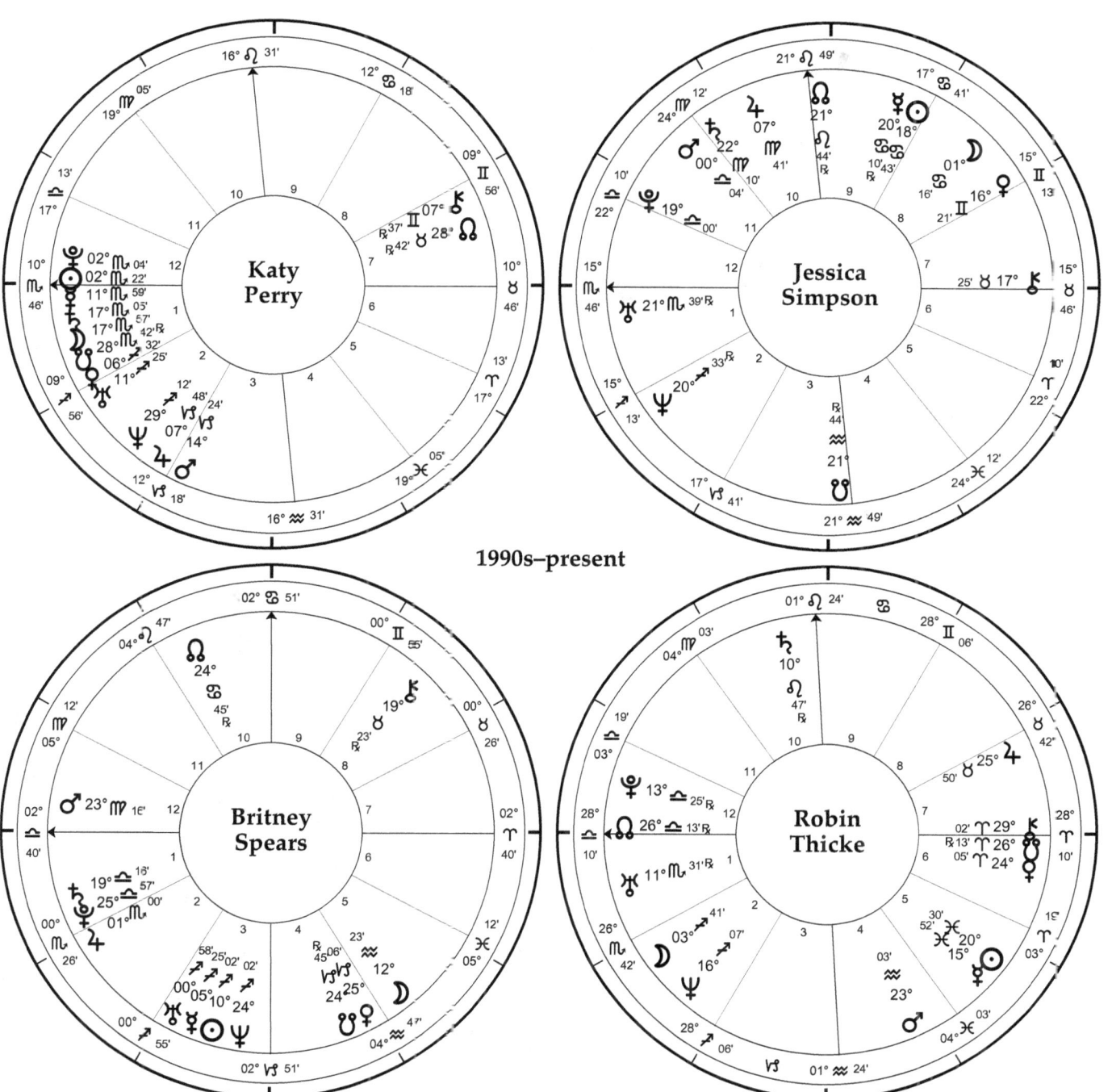

1990s–present

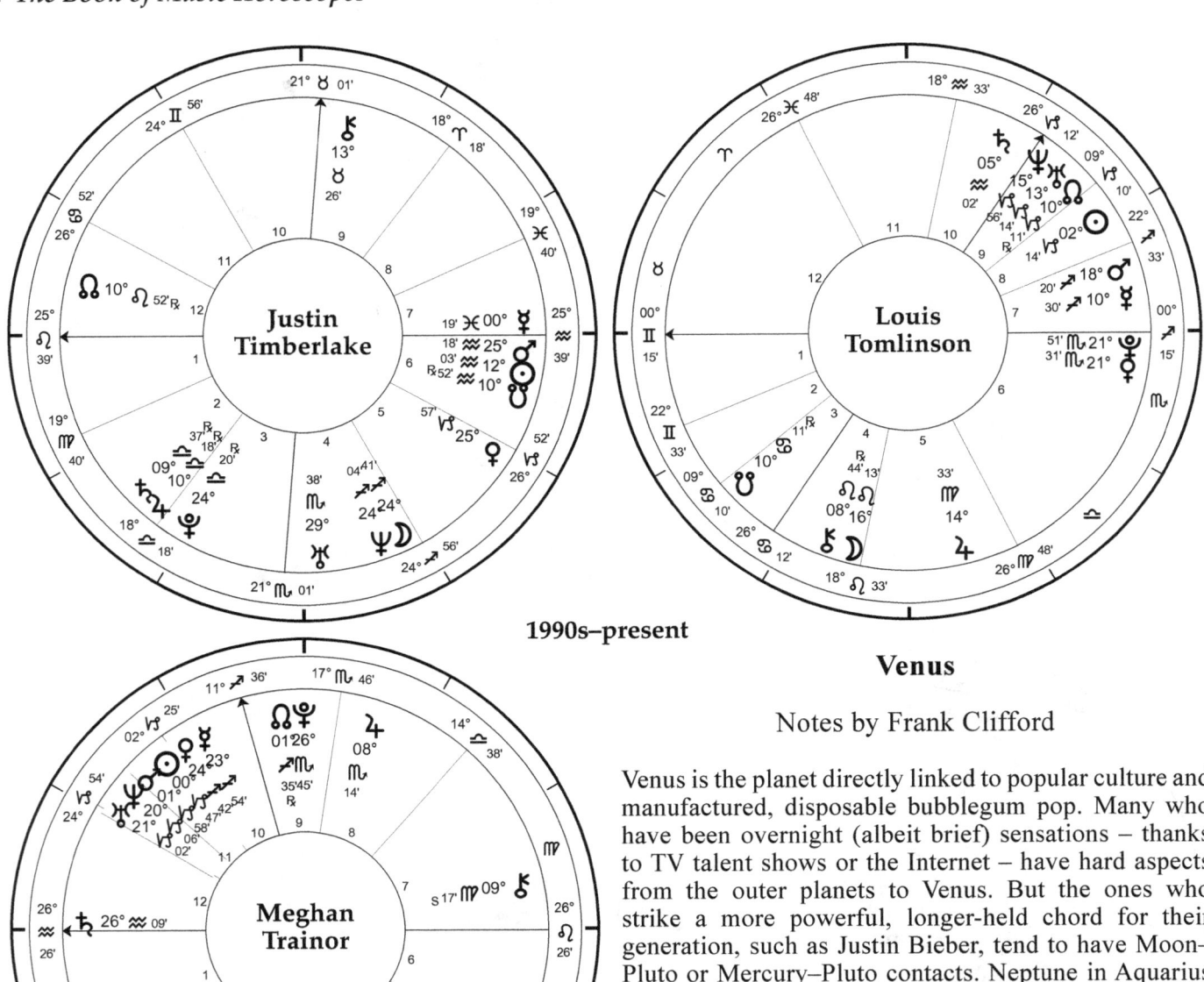

1990s–present

Venus

Notes by Frank Clifford

Venus is the planet directly linked to popular culture and manufactured, disposable bubblegum pop. Many who have been overnight (albeit brief) sensations – thanks to TV talent shows or the Internet – have hard aspects from the outer planets to Venus. But the ones who strike a more powerful, longer-held chord for their generation, such as Justin Bieber, tend to have Moon–Pluto or Mercury–Pluto contacts. Neptune in Aquarius brought us a wash of talent shows where ordinary people (Aquarius) could have a shot at fulfilling their dreams of musical fame (Neptune). *American Idol* and *The X Factor* impresario Simon Cowell is a Libran with the 'pop mogul' signature: Venus conjunct Pluto. This is an aspect shared by reality judge and *American Idol* producer Nigel Lythgoe, who was born with Venus conjunct Pluto in Leo.

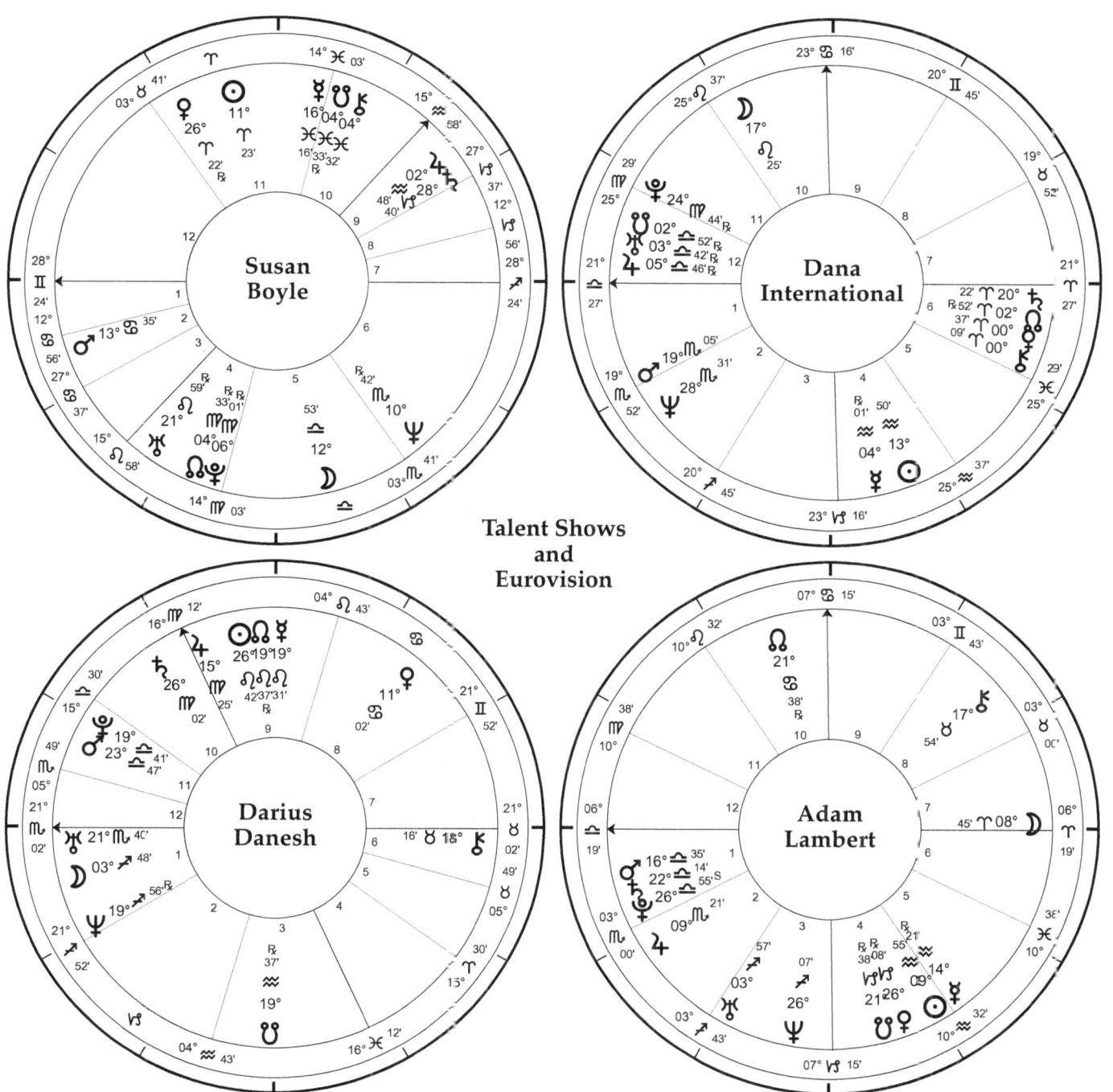

Talent Shows and Eurovision

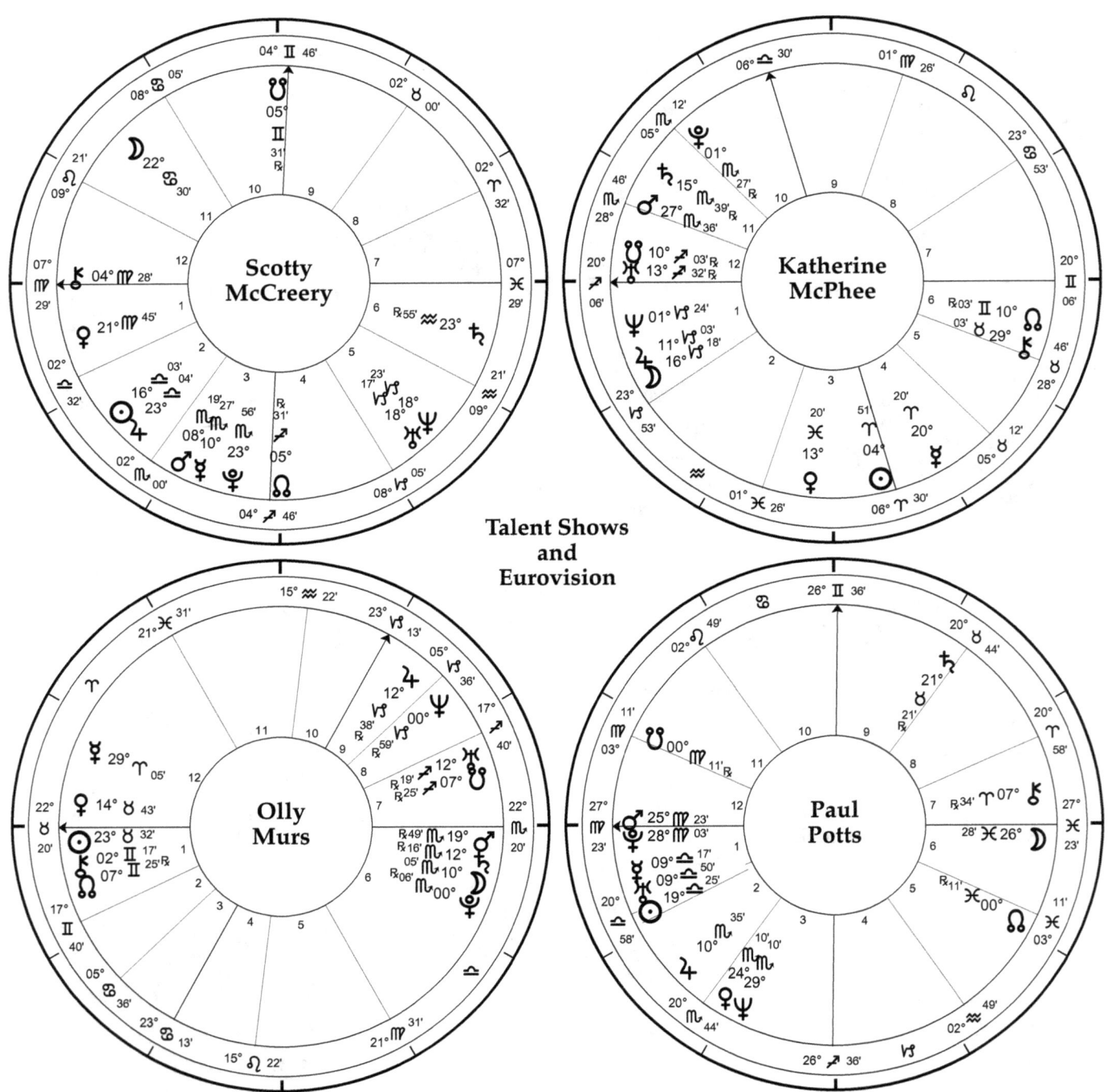

Talent Shows and Eurovision

Pop Idols & Pin-Ups

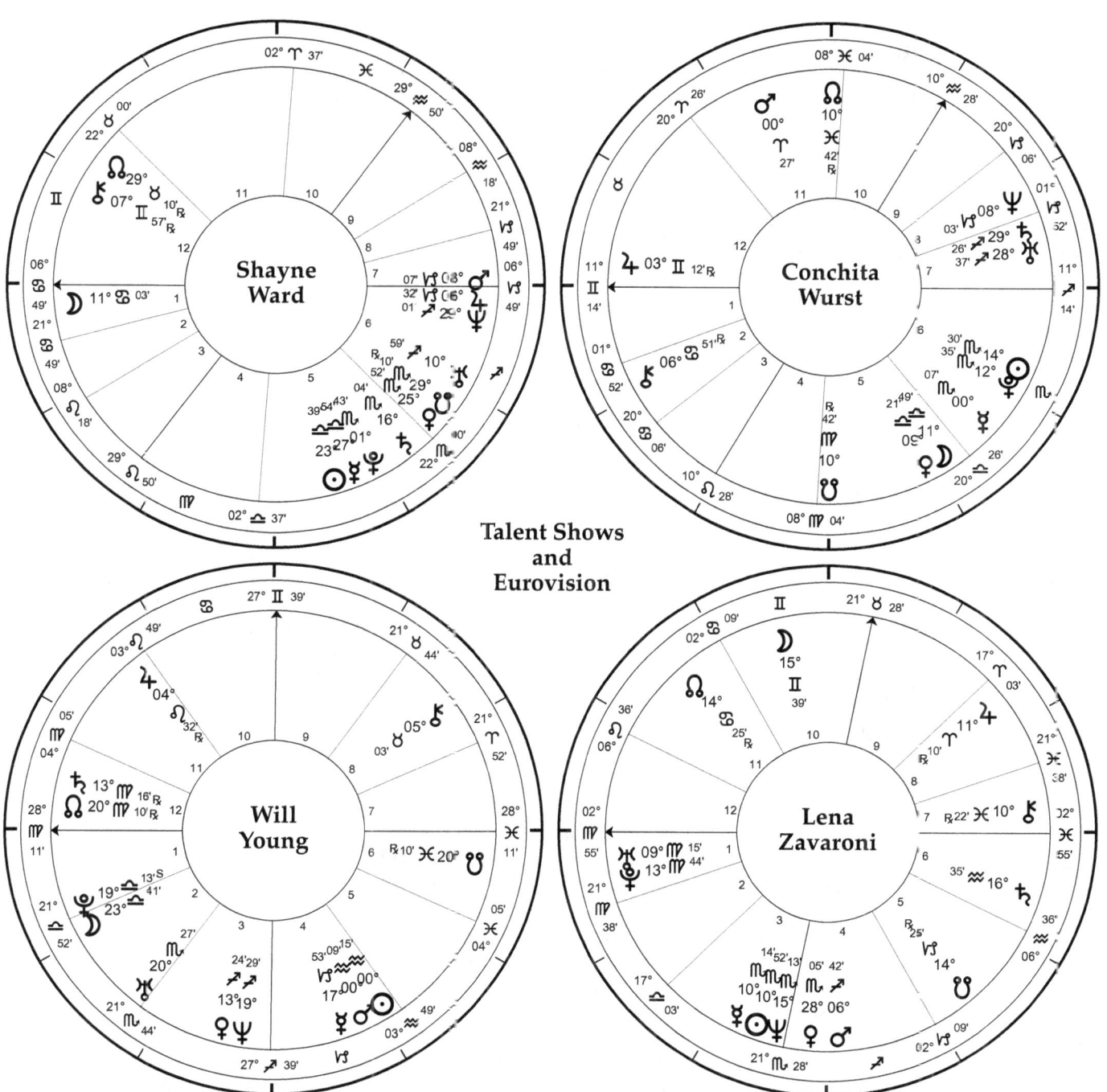

Talent Shows and Eurovision

Neptune and Reality TV

Hannah Glover

The Italian composer Luciano Berio defined music as 'everything that one listens to with the intention of listening to music.' This reveals the subjective nature of musical appreciation and allows the boundary between noise and music to change over time, and to vary from person to person depending on their own experience or predisposition.

Neptune is an outer planet and takes about 14 years to pass through each zodiac sign. Those of us born within that 14-year generation will share the essence of that Neptune sign. Neptune's themes include transcendence, the dissolution of boundaries, loss, sacrifice, escape, compassion, yearning, dreaming and the imagination. Music is one way we can experience our Neptune because music takes us out of the mundane; it allows us to escape, transcend and dissolve boundaries with others, and to dream. Interestingly, the Old English definition of the word 'dream', a word synonymous with Neptune, also meant 'to make music'. Each 14-year Neptune generation will therefore appreciate music in a different way, and in turn particular types of music will allow them to experience their Neptune.

As Neptune entered Aquarius, 'ordinary people' were transported to celebrity status thanks to the rise of reality TV. *Pop Idol* was born, hotly followed in 2004 by *The X Factor*. The idea that we would have to be special to be a star (Leo, the opposite sign of Aquarius) disappeared. Of course, music talent shows are not a new phenomena at all. Forty years ago we had *Opportunity Knocks*, where viewing audiences voted for a host of variety acts. What's different nowadays is the inclusion of judges.

By looking at the natal chart of *Pop Idol*, it's clear how important the judges are. The T-square of Jupiter, Mars and the Sun as the focal planet has a very judicial air. The Sun is in Libra, the sign associated with justice – the scales weighing up opposing sides and coming to a decision – and Jupiter is the planet associated with wisdom, which is required by any 'judge'. In addition, the Sun is exactly conjunct the Sun of head judge Simon Cowell (he was born on 7 October 1959). Finally, Mars adds the aggressive element, with the assertive judging bringing many contestants to tears. The T-square is also a reflection of the contestants' journeys in these shows. They are mentored (Jupiter in Cancer), then put out in the public eye to fight for votes and ultimately their place in the music business (Mars in Capricorn at the Midheaven) and then judged each week (the Sun in Libra). In the UK, *Pop Idol* survived two series before Cowell left to create *The X Factor*, although *Pop Idol* is an international franchise and has spawned multiple *Idol* series worldwide.

So who has been watching and voting for contestants in the UK's *Pop Idol* and *The X Factor*? According to market research, it's predominantly the under 35s. So in Neptune generations, that's from Neptune in Sagittarius onwards. The Neptune in Sagittarius generation grew up watching films such as *ET*, *Star Wars*, *Jaws*. They like action, fun, exploration and expanding their horizons. At that time, the world was becoming ever more accessible with the development of air travel, and politically more liberal – so why can't an ordinary person be a star? Many of this generation have been hooked on watching contestants through their journey (Sagittarius) and have the faith and vision (Sagittarius) to imagine that anyone can make it. The elemental combination of the show's Neptune in airy Aquarius fanning the fiery flames of the Neptune in Sagittarius generation is evident when viewing figures of *The X Factor* soared to their highest level in 2010.

But then splash! Neptune entered Pisces. The fiery enthusiasm waned as Neptune in Pisces brought in the vote-fixing scandal, followed by an increase in the 'sob factor', in which the 2012 finalists were known more for their panic attacks and abused pasts than their singing ability. On 6 November 2012, *The Guardian* newspaper reported that each *X Factor* show audience was down by a million viewers. All this was accompanied by an increase in cruel, surprise twists on the show, and proved a turn-off for the disillusioned Neptune in Sagittarius generation. We needn't turn to Neptune in Capricorn to increase the viewing figures

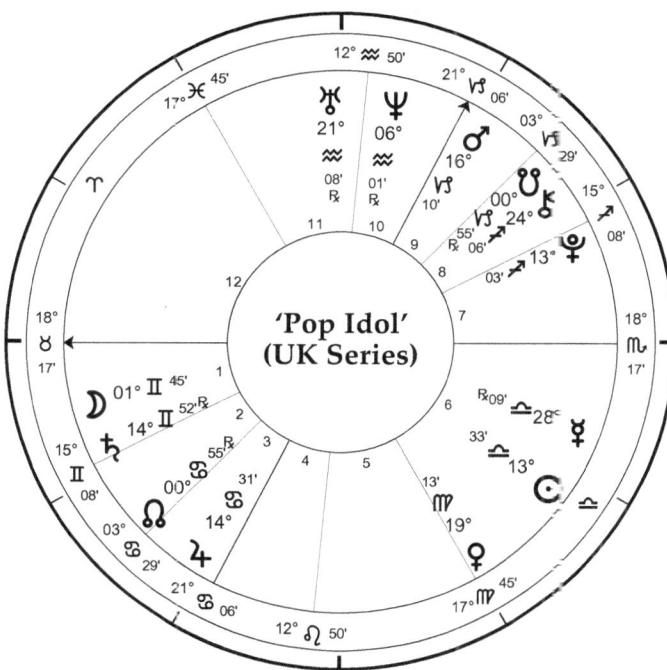

as this generation knows that visions and dreams need to be real and made through hard work; they are not believers in overnight success.

So with *The X Factor's* audience levels down, what will the future hold? 'X factor' is defined as 'an unexplained element that makes something more interesting or valuable', so it's an ineffable, mysterious element; this just speaks of astrological Neptune itself. We would think that a show with a Neptunian feel would fare well while Neptune transits its own sign of Pisces.

Neptune takes 164.8 years to pass through the zodiac and Neptune last entered in Pisces in 1847. What was successful in music during that period? Opera was important, in particular the composer Wagner, who from 1849 to 1852 produced his *Gesamtkunstwerk* (a total work of art or universal artwork), which speaks of Neptune in boundary-less and interconnected Pisces. It was a synthesis of the poetic, the visual, musical and dramatic. We can imagine how this would have captured the interest of the previous Neptune in Sagittarius and Neptune in Capricorn generations, as it has the drama and vision of Sagittarius and was the product of the sort of hard work that Capricorn admires. Despite being a controversial figure, Wagner's music stood the test of time. It's hard to imagine people listening to *The X Factor*'s JLS or One Direction 165 years from now!

What possible form could *The X Factor* take as Neptune heads into Aries? What could the start of a new cycle hold? According to Reuters (30 June 2014), by 2025, when Neptune enters Aries, we won't be signing on to the Internet – we will already be logged on. Media (Neptune) will be instantaneous. If we go back in time to when Neptune was last in Aries (during the 1860s and 1870s), we can see the rise of an interest in musical theatre and burlesque, and pioneering performances by women, and innovative creative arenas in which a great number of the public could access music. When Neptune enters Aries this time around, we would expect the same pioneering, fresh creative ideas. If still on air, *The X Factor* will need to encompass this pioneering spirit. The main audience will be those with Neptune natally in Capricorn and Aquarius. If these new ideas are born of new technology and put the 'real' back into reality, these two generations may well watch and the show may continue. But with Neptune's love of ambiguity, it may be hard to predict.

COUNTRY & SINGER-SONGWRITERS

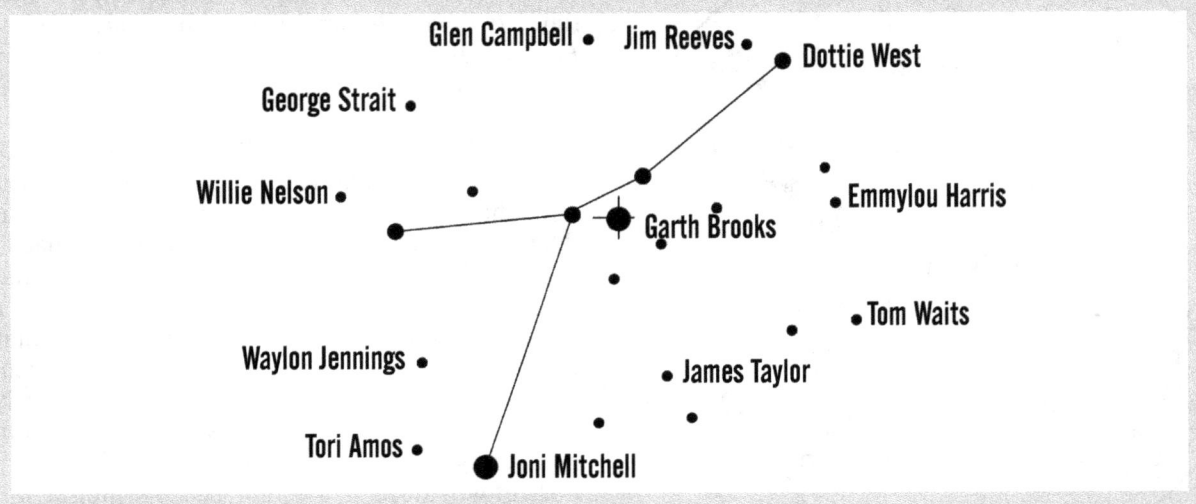

Country

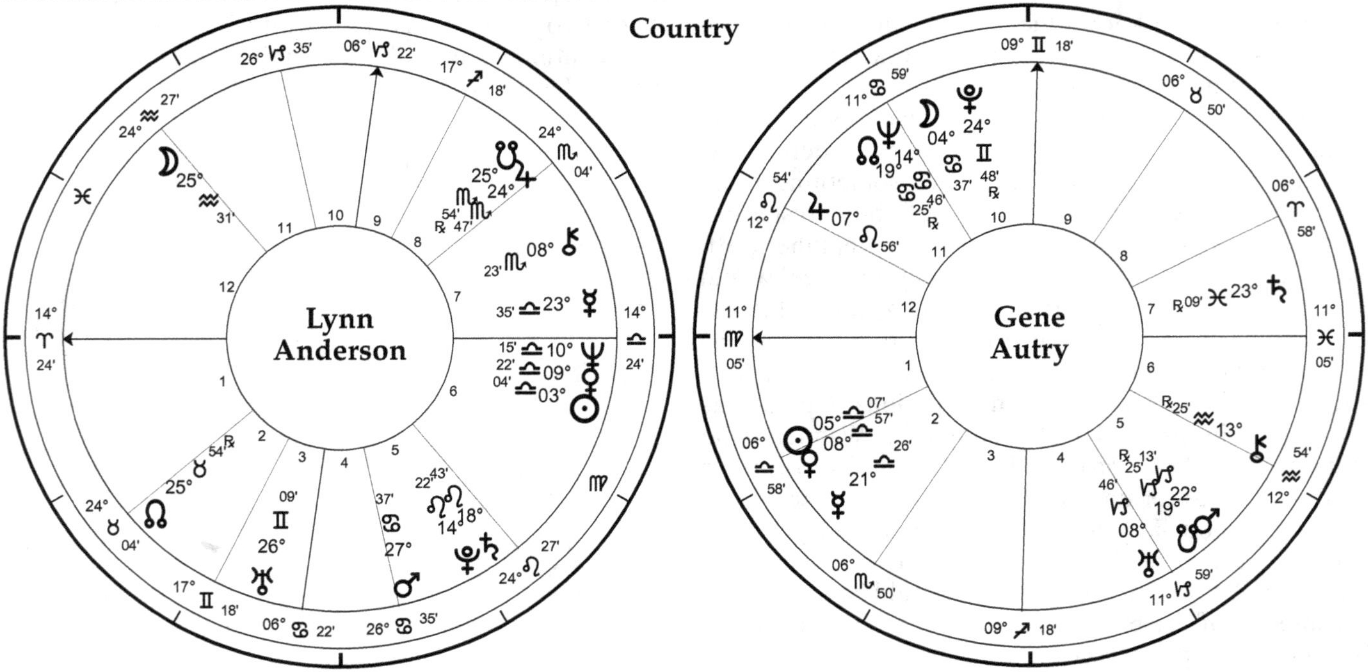

Lynn Anderson

Gene Autry

Country & Singer–Songwriters

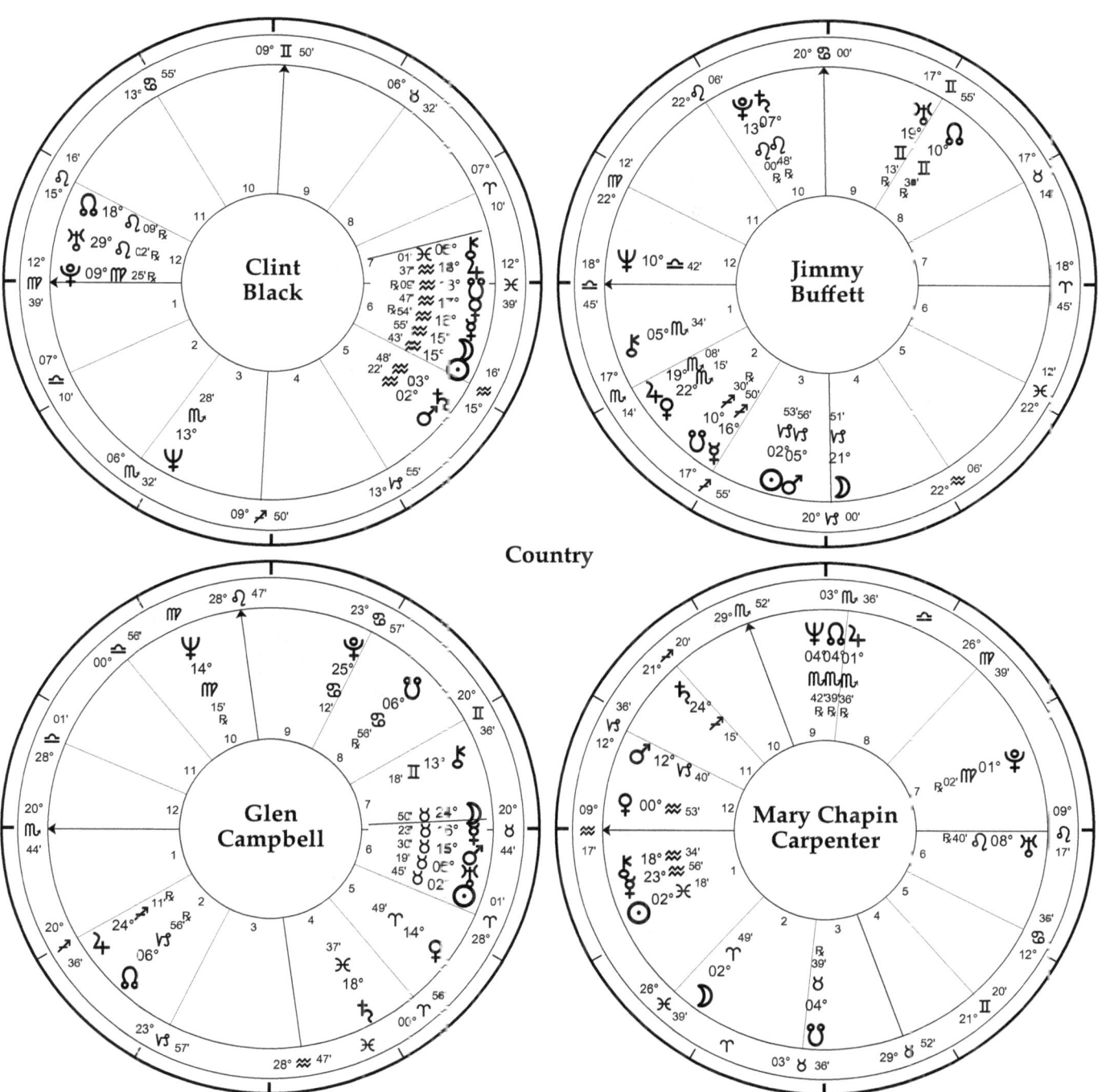

Country

70 The Book of Music Horoscopes

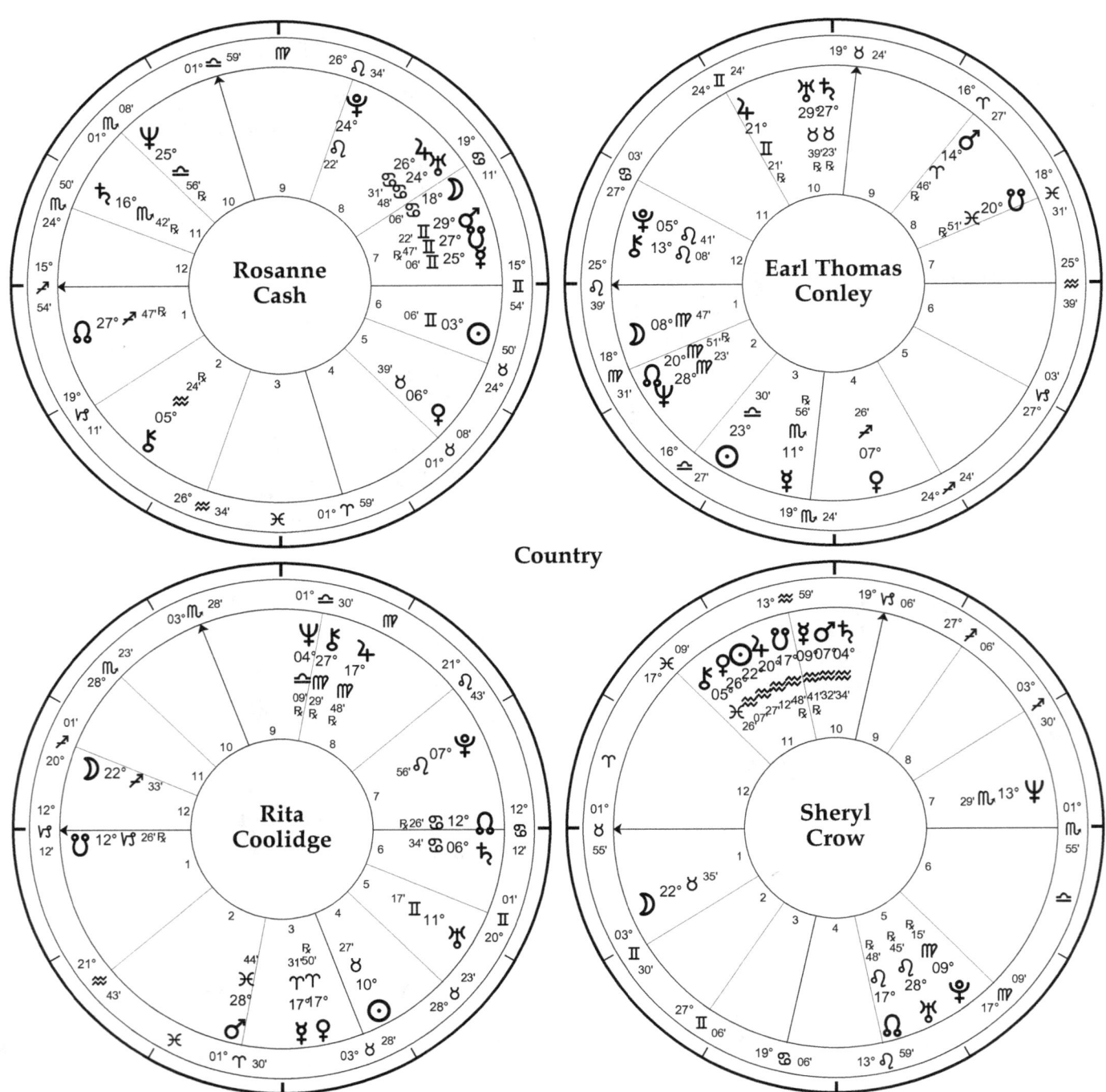

Country

Country & Singer–Songwriters 71

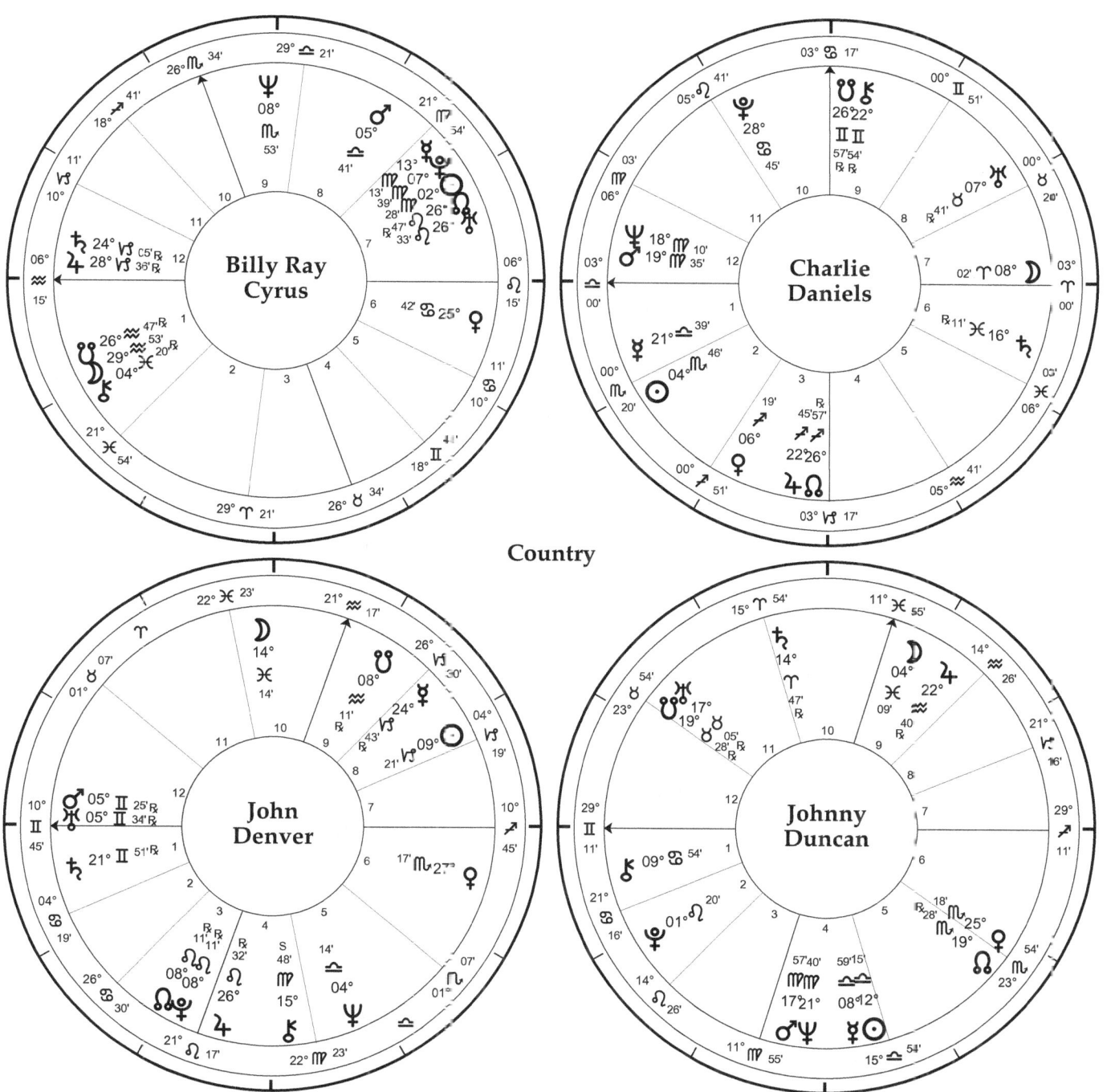

Country

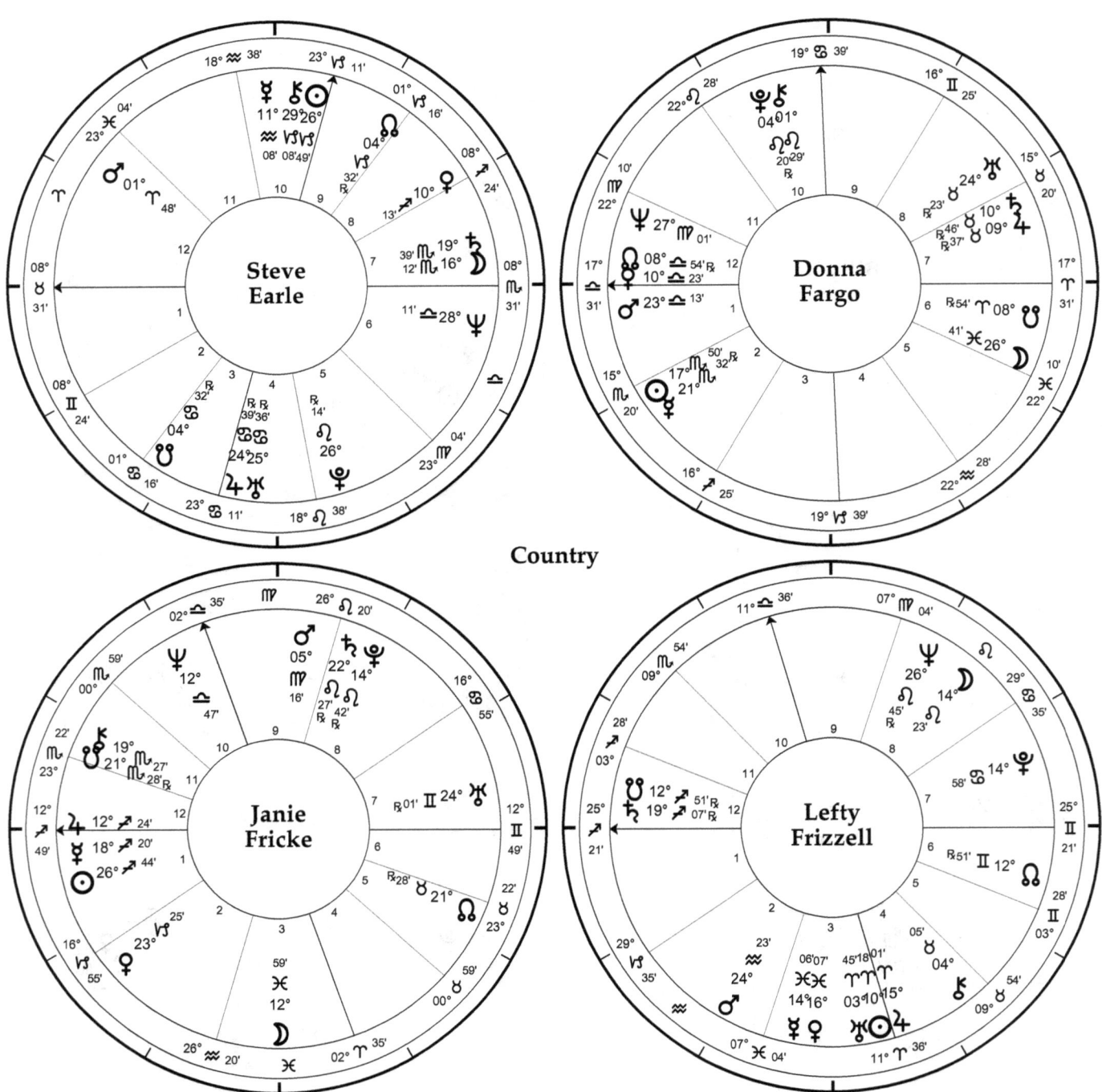

Country

Country & Singer–Songwriters

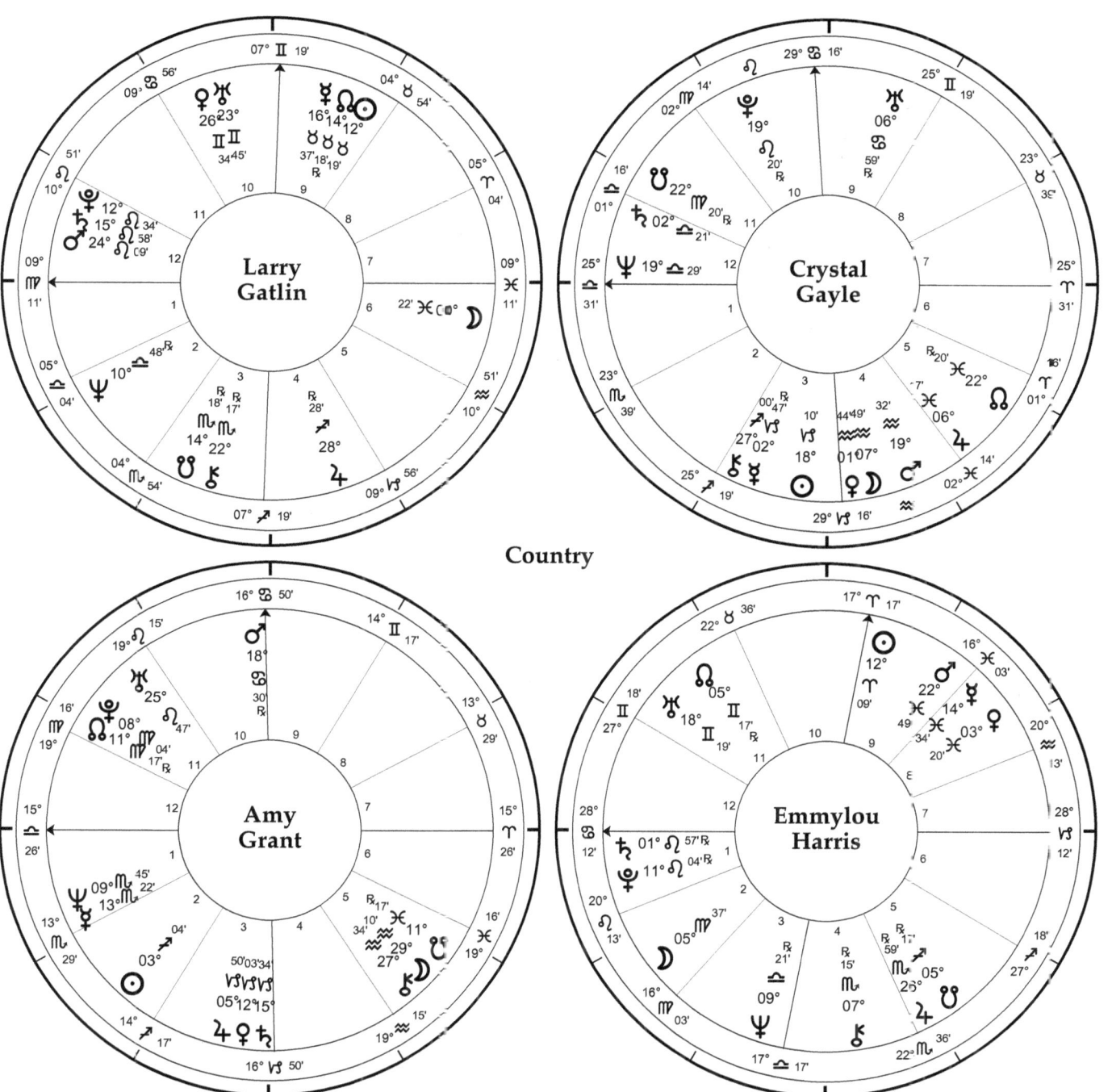

Country

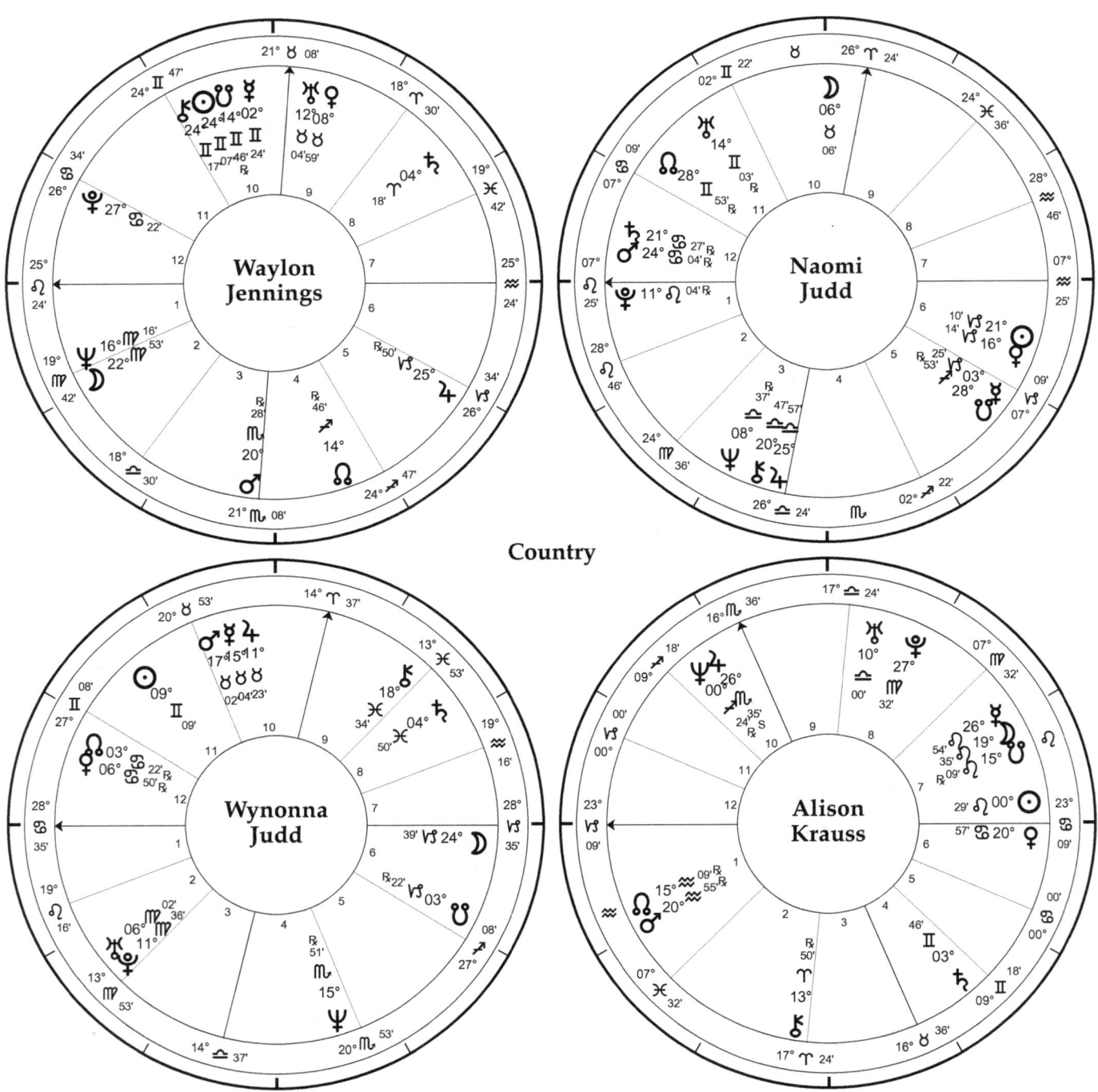

Country

Country & Singer–Songwriters

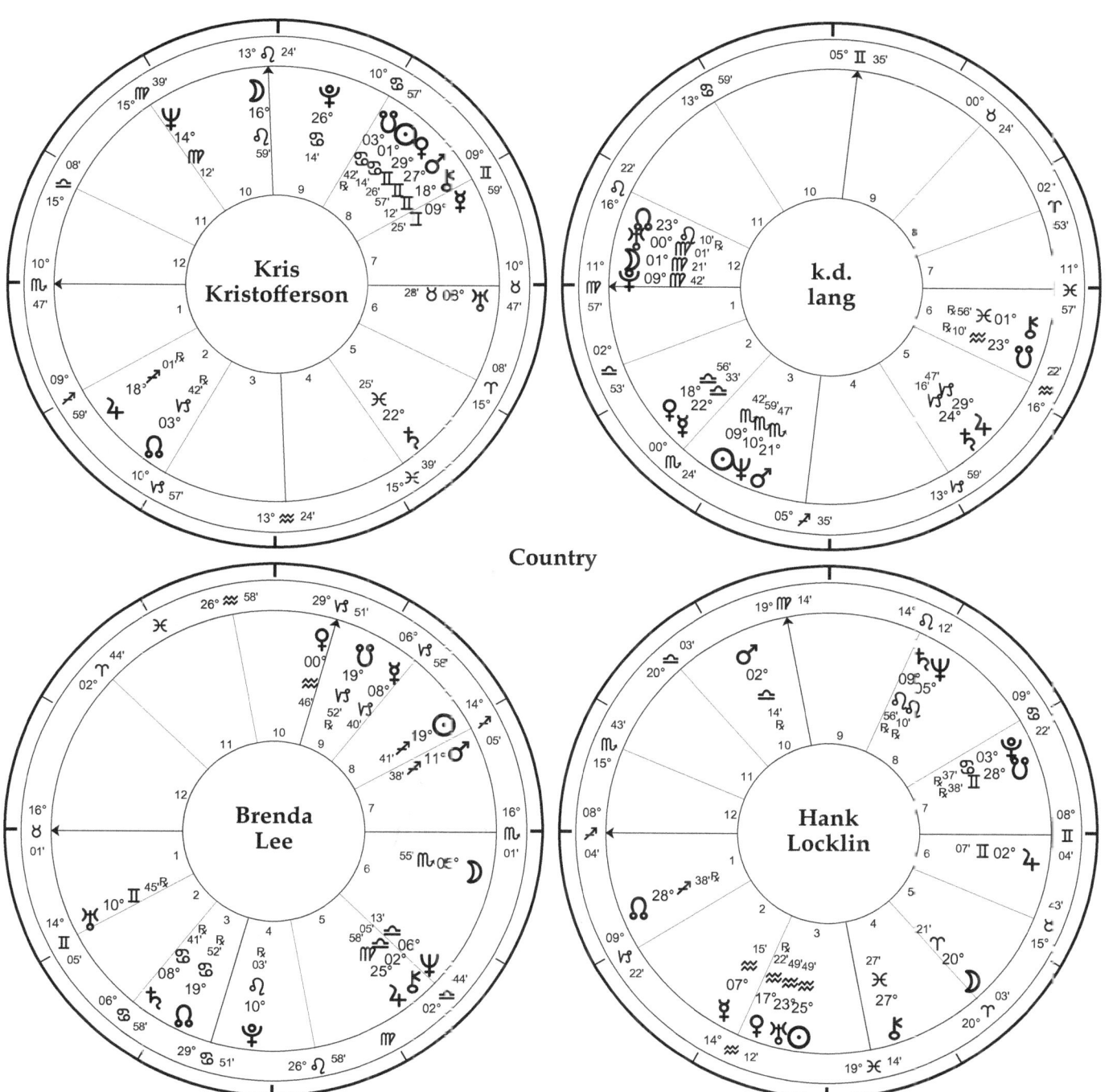

Country

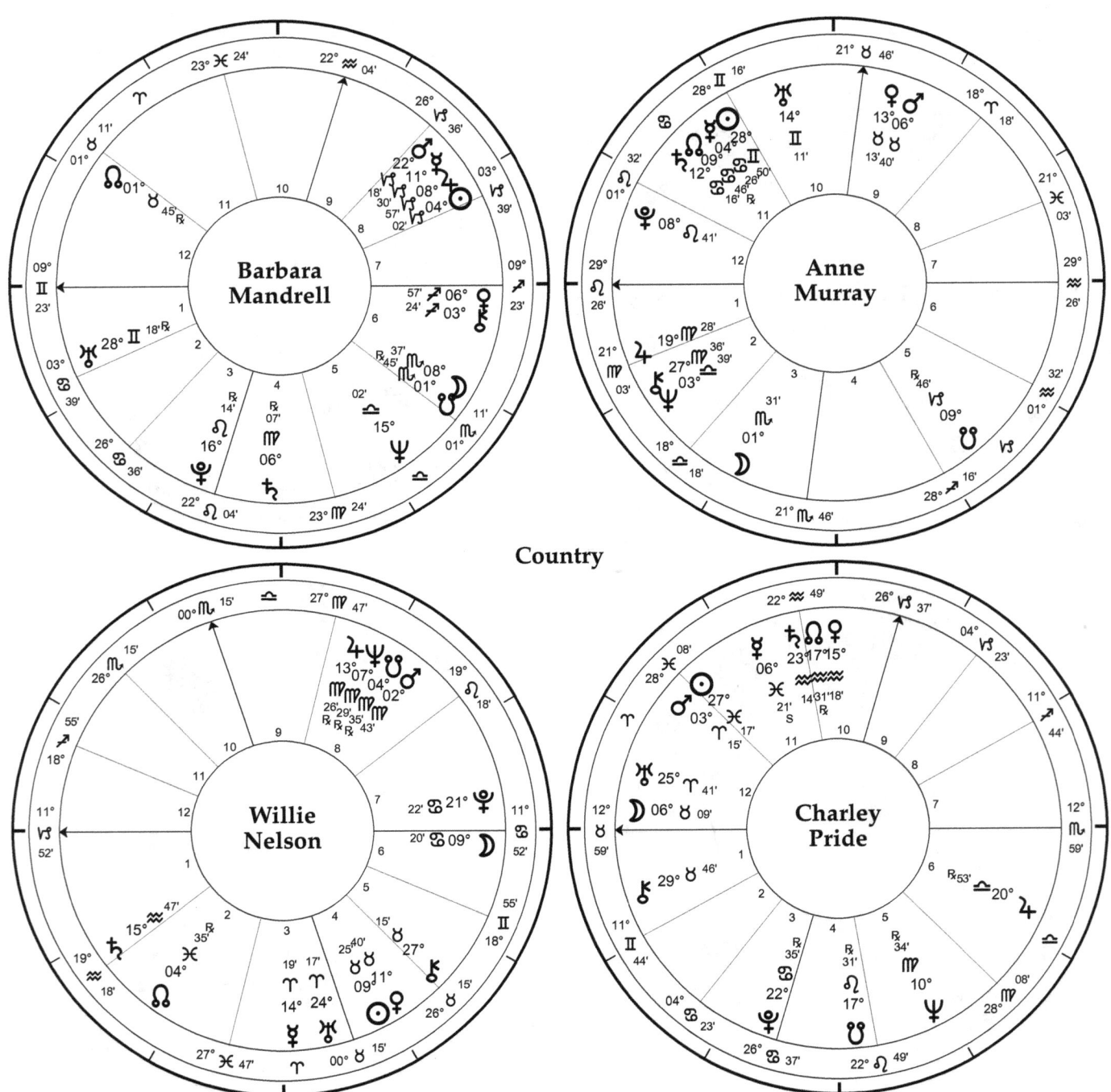

Country

Country & Singer–Songwriters

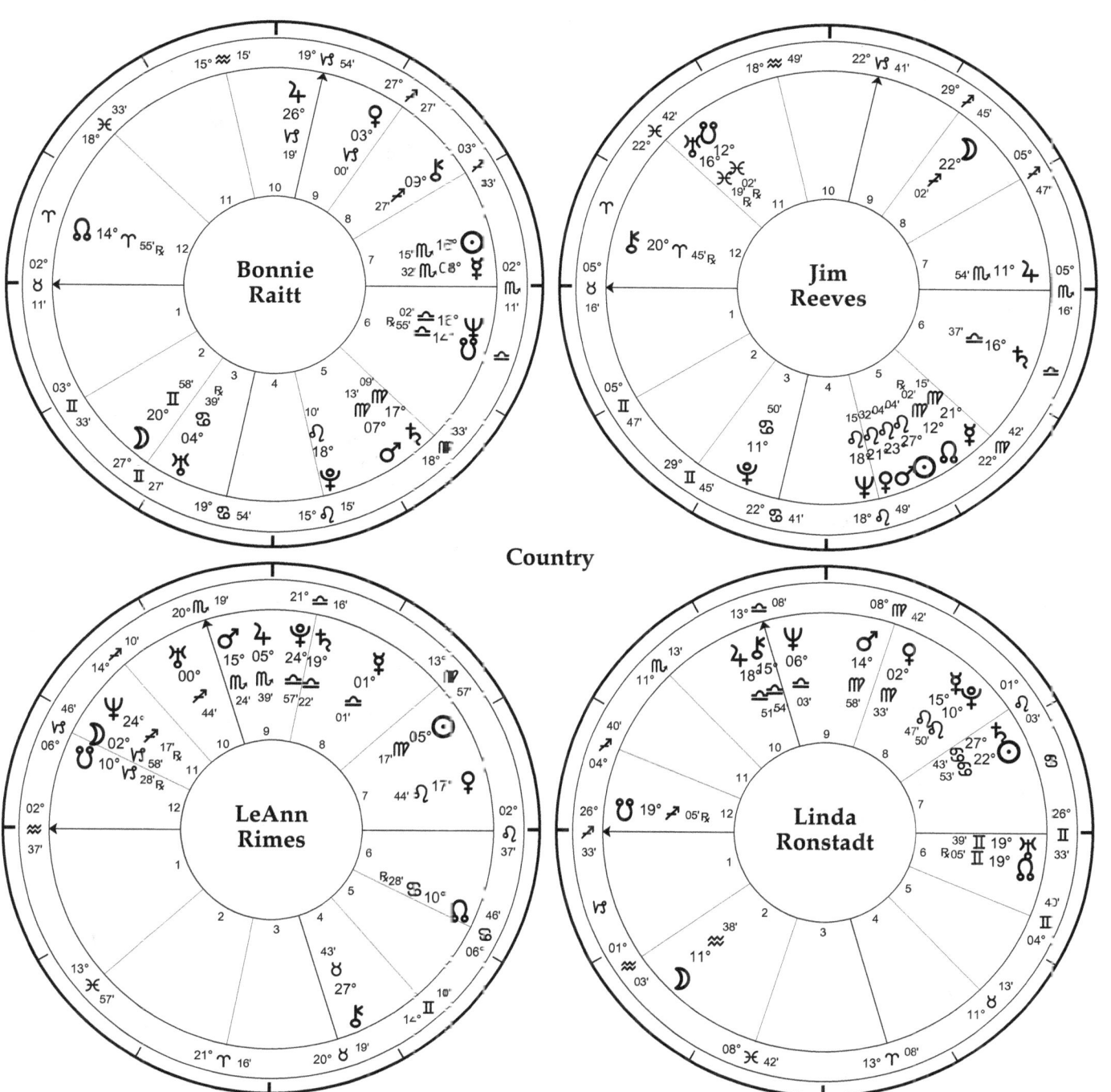

Country

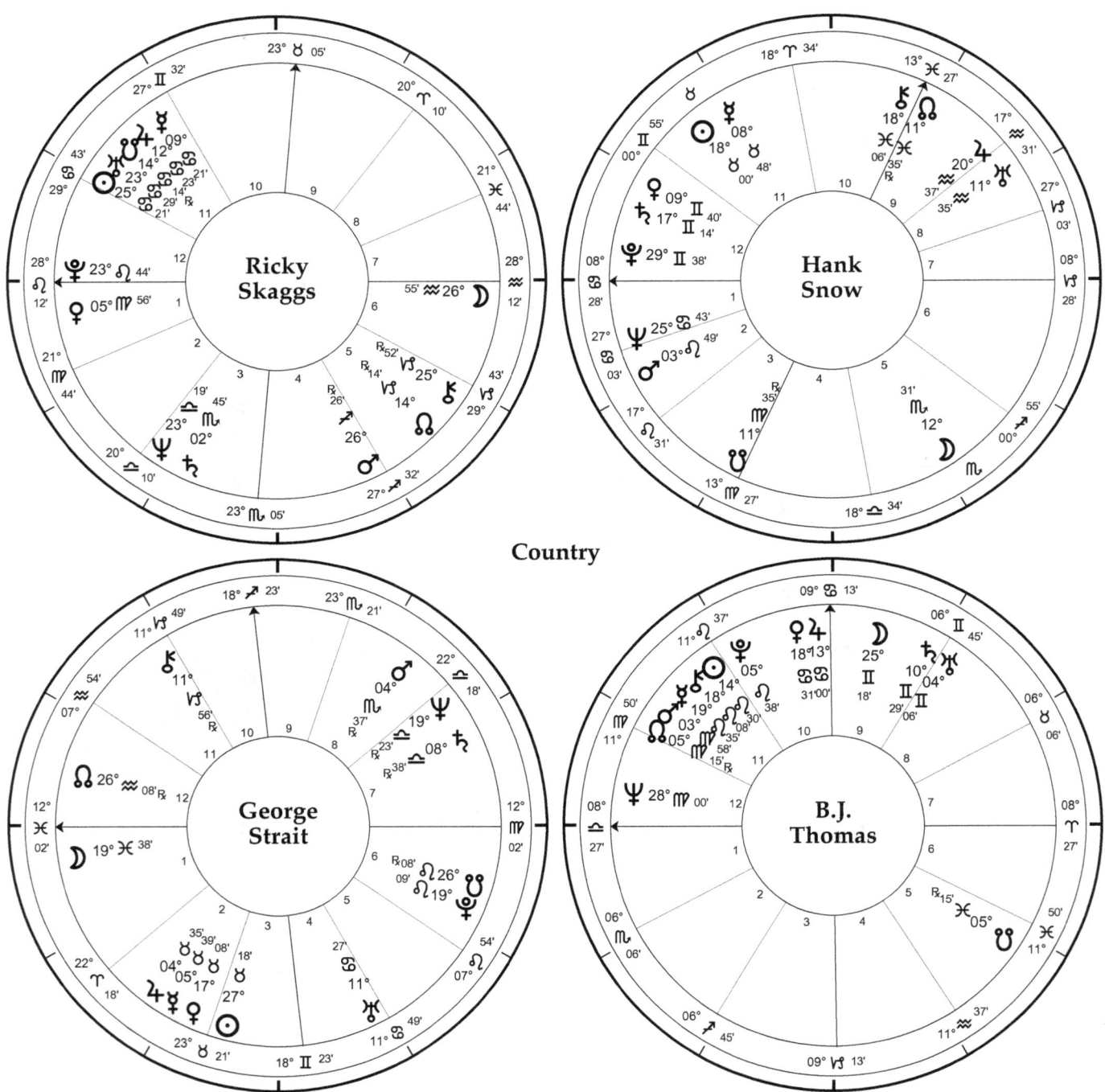

Country

Country & Singer–Songwriters

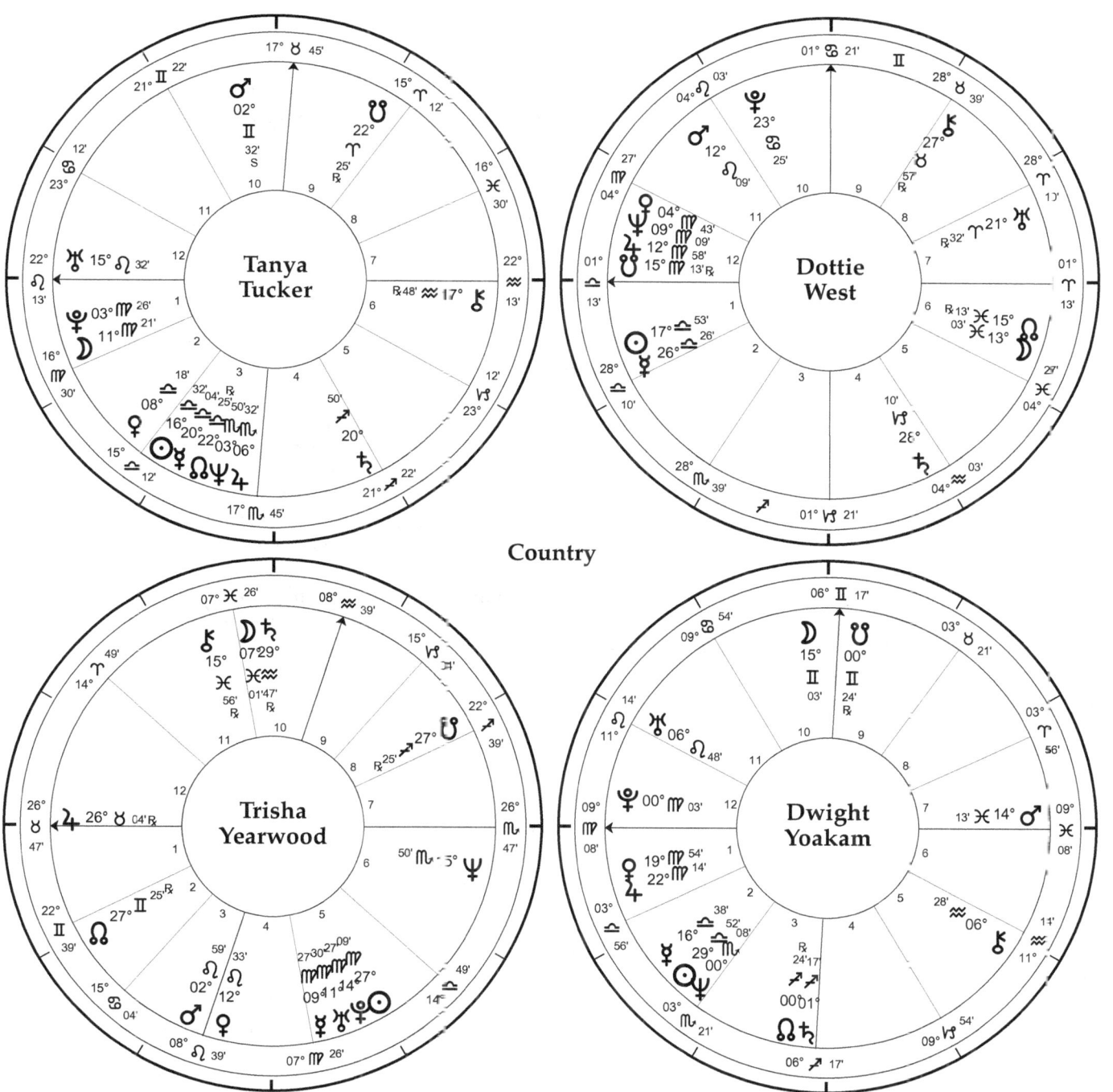

The Moon, the Musician and the Listening Public

Lynn Bell

The Sun and the 5th House are connected to the making of music, to dance, to pleasure. Music in this sense brings us to life; it enlivens and electrifies. Our feet tap, our bodies move; we may be silly, sexy, inspired. At a concert with thousands, we may roar and dance until we reach a state of frenzy and, with or without the help of mind-altering substances, enter the Dionysian dimension of music carried by Neptune and the other outer planets. Yet, there is another aspect to the experience of music, the music that stirs our inner tides for weeks, months or a lifetime. Some songs are played again and again. Some music is listened to for what it touches in the listener and, in this sense, music is connected to the Moon.

Our moods and feelings all link to the Moon in the birth chart. The Moon makes memories as well. A song that gets everyone up and dancing at a party, decades after its release, will also have this lunar dimension. As we dance, we remember dancing another time. We remember another self and the feelings of that time. Some years ago, I was at a party in Dali in southwestern China. As the night wore on, we gathered on the rooftop around a musician who began to play, and as he sang, the others listened and then began to join in. The music wove me into the feelings of the group, even without understanding the words. It strengthened my emotional connection to that place and its people.

Musical memory is one of the last faculties to be extinguished in patients who have lost everything else, and some researchers believe that it works on a unique circuit in the brain.[1] The mind has elements of Mercury, the rational and logical, but is also a lunar terrain of images, dreams, reflections. The Moon helps to connect the work of a performing artist with both the hearts and minds of the listeners and, in this way, may be the key to popularity. It is also a planet of the inner life. So, how does this dual nature of the lunar archetype, the personal and the public, express itself in the charts of musicians?

The All-embracing Pisces Moon

Certain singers become synonymous with the spirit of their age and remain popular for a lifetime. For the generation that fought in World War II, the 'Voice' was Frank Sinatra. With Jupiter-ruled signs holding the luminaries, and an angular Neptune on the Midheaven, Sinatra's talent and reach are clear, especially given a generous 5th House Jupiter in its own sign of Pisces. The Moon in Pisces near the cusp of that 5th House adds an intimacy, a longing that reaches inside the listener and evokes a response. One writer describes his voice this way: 'the intangible, mystical alchemy of sound, technique, and emotion that fused when the skinny young Sinatra murmured tender endearments into a microphone.'[2]

From 1941, Sinatra was the idol of teenage women who screamed and fainted at his concerts. A Dionysian wave ran through his mostly female audiences. When a psychiatrist was asked to explain the phenomenon at the time, he said the music was 'a sort of melodic striptease in which he lays bare his soul'.[3] This laying bare of the soul is a deeply Piscean quality. It feels intensely personal, while not being personal at all.

Pisces is a boundless sign, and a Pisces Moon reaches right inside us, rolls past individual boundaries, awakening feelings we didn't know we had. Perhaps that explains why the three biggest-selling solo artists of all time – Elvis Presley, Frank Sinatra and Michael Jackson – were all born with the Moon in this sign. These men got under the skin of their listeners, whether it was to swoon, to dance or to twist. The sensual Elvis Presley of 1955–6 thrilled his listeners when transiting Uranus conjoined his natal Pluto, activating Pluto's opposition to his personal trio of the Sun, Mercury and Venus in Capricorn. Michael Jackson's charismatic dancing and sound and his innovative videos captured millions of fans from the late 70s into the 90s.

These artists imprinted a long arc of popular culture. Even after their deaths, the Pisces Moon lingers on. Elvis was rumoured to still be alive after his untimely

Country & Singer–Songwriters 81

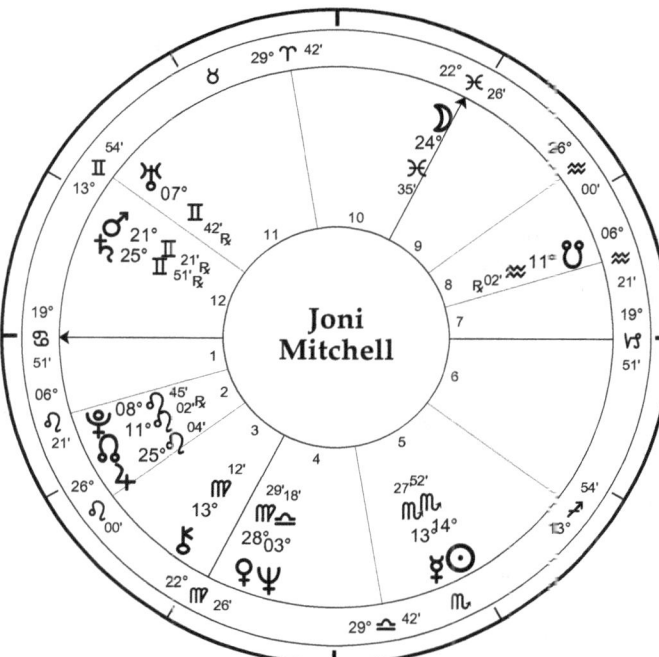

passing at age 42, and sightings were regularly reported. Sinatra's voice still haunts bars and restaurants around the world. Michael Jackson became a ghost in his own lifetime, slipping between worlds while on propofol. The vulnerability of a Pisces Moon, its inability to stay shielded from the exaltation and descent of fame, probably contributed to the unfortunate deaths of both Presley and Jackson – the phantasmagoria, the drugs and alcohol. Both men also had powerful Sun–Pluto aspects – a conjunction for Jackson and the opposition in Presley's chart – which drove the downward spiral. The very gifts that a Pisces Moon may gather through its sensitivity can turn corrosive if there is no way to find an inner skin, a personal boundary.

Individuals with a Pisces Moon often have a fragile romanticism, a lost poet's flair for impossible causes. This is clear in another Pisces Moon singer and poet, whose career stretched over many decades: Leonard Cohen. His long search for spiritual direction spilt into his lyrics and music. For those drawn to his particular gravitas, his music awakens great longing. Cohen songs are reflections, enigmas, celebrations. Poems lodged in the heart. Piscean themes of loss and heartbreak, of sacrifice and redemption. In his final years, his raspy septuagenarian voice roughened the lyrics, gravely expressive of exquisite remembrance.

Joni Mitchell, Water Child

The Pisces longing for transcendence, its embrace and recognition of pain, can be uncomfortable for many. At the same time, it is very difficult to ignore. In a piece for *The New Yorker*, the young British novelist Zadie Smith (born 25 October 1975) wrote about her antipathy to Joni Mitchell (Moon in Pisces), saying, 'The first time I heard her, I didn't hear her at all.'[4] Immersed in the joyous rhythms of black music, Smith found that she disliked what she didn't even recognize as music. Even a decade later, driving across the British countryside, she recalls the sense of annoyance this music brought up in her: '… I focused in on it and realized it was that bloody piping again, ranging over octaves, ignoring the natural divisions between musical bars, and generally annoying the hell out of me, like a bee caught in a wing mirror.'[5]

Joni Mitchell is in her mid-70s and, while her voice is now a smoky alto, her creative genius remains vibrant through painting, her first love. In the early days, her singing ranged over three octaves, and the silvery heights of her voice, her idiosyncratic phrasing and an intensely personal vision penetrated the mind/feeling barrier of the listener. Mitchell's Moon is at 24° Pisces on her MC and opposing an out-of-sign conjunction of Venus and Neptune. Here, we have an almost pure Pisces Moon, an artist who was willing to offer her inner life and feelings in a way that had not been done before in popular music. When Kris Kristofferson first heard her 1971 album *Blue*, he said, 'Jeez, Joni, save something for yourself.'

Later, after Zadie Smith began listening to Mitchell's music, she wrote:

This is the effect that listening to Joni Mitchell has on me these days: uncontrollable tears. An emotional overcoming, disconcertingly distant from happiness, more like joy – if joy is the recognition of an almost intolerable beauty. It's not a very civilized emotion. I can't listen to Joni Mitchell in a room with other people, or on an iPod, walking the streets. Too risky. I can never guarantee that I'm going to be able to get through the song without being made transparent – to anybody and everything, to the whole world. A mortifying sense of porousness. Although it's comforting to learn that the feeling I have listening to these songs is the same feeling the artist had while creating them: 'At that period of my life, I had no personal defenses. I felt like a cellophane wrapper on a pack of cigarettes.' That's Mitchell, speaking of the fruitful years ... when her classic album Blue was released.[6]

The powerful emotions of Mitchell's music are reflected in the primary signature of her chart: Scorpio Sun, Pisces Moon and Cancer rising. They were also sourced in a series of painful events. Her unusual open guitar tunings came from the adaptation of a weak left hand, a sequela of her childhood polio. She has a difficult conjunction of Mars and Saturn in Gemini in the 12th House as the apex in a tight T-square to the Moon and Venus–Neptune. Planets in the 12th, the house of the unfortunate *daimon*, often bring testing experiences of a physical or psychological nature. This T-square describes a pattern of difficulty followed by intense creative output as a composer, songwriter and painter. By the time Mitchell made her first album, she had already composed more songs than many artists would write in an entire career.

In 1995, it was revealed that Joni Mitchell had had a child out of wedlock – a child eventually given up for adoption, and one of the reasons she dropped out of art school. She has said that she began writing songs because she was so unhappy. Like many individuals with a difficult *daimon*, she was directed to a path through a series of painful experiences: her early polio; a brief, painful marriage to Chuck Mitchell, who dashed her hope that he would help raise her child and, instead, pushed her to perform with him – all these led her away from the painting she'd always wanted to do.

Even in small ways, the *daimon* can be seen at work. She missed the Woodstock Festival and stayed in New York City for *The Dick Cavett Show* on her manager's advice. Learning of the concert on the news, she composed the song that has been associated with the event ever since. David Crosby said that her song 'Woodstock' did more to give people the feeling of what had happened there than anything else. Mitchell was able to transform the frustration of Mars–Saturn into artistry, a gift for the listener.

Singing a Powerful Self
Musicians with other lunar signatures may touch their audience through a very different conduit. A quick glance at three Fire Sun women – Madonna (Leo), Lady Gaga (Aries), and Miley Cyrus (Sagittarius) – reveals the power of a Moon–Pluto conjunction.

The most successful woman in music entertainment, Madonna took the icons of religious culture, turned them upside down and made them her own. Her influence, both artistic and archetypal, is huge. It is no wonder that young women born in the 1970s cite her as a powerful role model. Madonna's chart is well known: her Moon is on the Ascendant conjunct a 12th House Mercury–Pluto in Virgo, with the Sun in Leo just behind. Madonna owns the stage and uses it in highly personal ways. More than any other female artist, she stepped into her power, offering fans an archetype for self-transformation. Her material girl, the sexy dominant dancer, still sells well into her fifties.

Lady Gaga's true birth time is in question, but there is a good chance that she has a Moon–Pluto conjunction in Scorpio trine Jupiter in Pisces. Her experiments with identity and her excesses in self-presentation have amassed millions of ardent fans. Lady Gaga changes wigs and fashions almost as fast as a Chinese mask dancer. Both Madonna and Lady Gaga break out of conventional images of the feminine; they are not afraid of being labelled bad girls. They offer their fans the possibility of self-transmutation.

Miley Cyrus is the latest to claim the bad girl crown. With a waning Moon conjunct Pluto in Scorpio in the 6th House, it may be that she has work to do around her representations of sexuality. There was a great outcry after her graphic sexual mime on stage at the VMA awards. Shorn of her luxuriant brown locks, bent over like an animal in rut, poking Robin Thicke's genitals with a foam finger, tongue lolling out, Miley provoked almost everyone. Naturally, her songs have sold extremely well as a result.

It is probably too soon to tell whether Miley is 'being abused' by the music industry or is simply 'making history', as she claimed was her intention. Her videos are overtly sexual, playful, highly eroticized. It's interesting that she has the same grouping of four planets as Madonna – Sun, Moon, Mercury, Pluto – but in the opposite part of the chart. While Miley has a waning Moon, Madonna, who represented something entirely new for a female artist, was born under a waxing New Moon. Miley, born in the dark of the Moon, might be identified with a different kind of archetypal energy, embodying the extremes of the Pluto in Scorpio generation. In the same way, Gaga, under Saturn transits to her Moon–Pluto, had a hip injury and surgery in early 2013, which may suggest that she has taken on something greater than she can handle.

Miley Cyrus became one of the wealthiest teen stars ever, thanks to her role in Disney's *Hannah Montana*. In the series, she lived a double life: ordinary, dark-haired Miley and the blonde-wigged rock star Hannah. It seems that Miley felt compelled to kill off her own alter ego. Her Sun square Black Moon Lilith is also a significant aspect in her chart.[7] Just as Lilith turned her back on paradise and was then demonized, so Miley chose to walk away from the Disney paradise. Her talent is clear on songs like 'We Can't Stop', and the video manages to be erotic and tongue-in-cheek at the same time. Her videos portray her less as a powerful woman than a naughty girl grabbing the freedom to break all the rules (in keeping with her natal Venus–Uranus conjunction). Perhaps this is a step towards claiming her power. Moon–Pluto plays on both sides of the power spectrum; it can also be overpowered, enslaved, captive. It will be interesting to see how Miley evolves, whether Moon–Pluto controls her or whether she is the one who directs its energy.

Our own Moon affects the field of others, just as the Earth's Moon creates the waves in the sea. In a musician's chart, the watery Moons, and those ruled by Venus and Jupiter, seem to have the greatest impact on others, along with aspects to Jupiter and the outer planets. In the chart of a musician, the Moon draws people to the music; it affects the tide of popular feeling. Perhaps a musician's popularity is linked to this ability to enter into our inner landscape, to move currents both individual and collective, whether in revolt, affirmation, joy or longing.

1 www.huffingtonpost.com/rita-altman-rn/music-and-memory_b_3639805.html
2 www.nytimes.com/2010/11/29/arts/music/29sinatra.html
3 Thomas M. Pryor, 'Rise, Fall, and Rise of Sinatra', *The New York Times Magazine*, 10 February 1957
4 Zadie Smith, 'Some Notes on Attunement: A Voyage around Joni Mitchell', in *The New Yorker*, 17 December 2012, reproduced at http://jonimitchell.com/library/view.cfm?id=2543
5 Ibid
6 Ibid
7 Note that Joni Mitchell also has the Sun square Black Moon Lilith. She walked away from Laurel Canyon and Graham Nash's proposal of marriage, as she did from her first husband, then walked away from the folk style she had originated.

This article first appeared in the April–May 2014 issue of The Mountain Astrologer.

84 The Book of Music Horoscopes

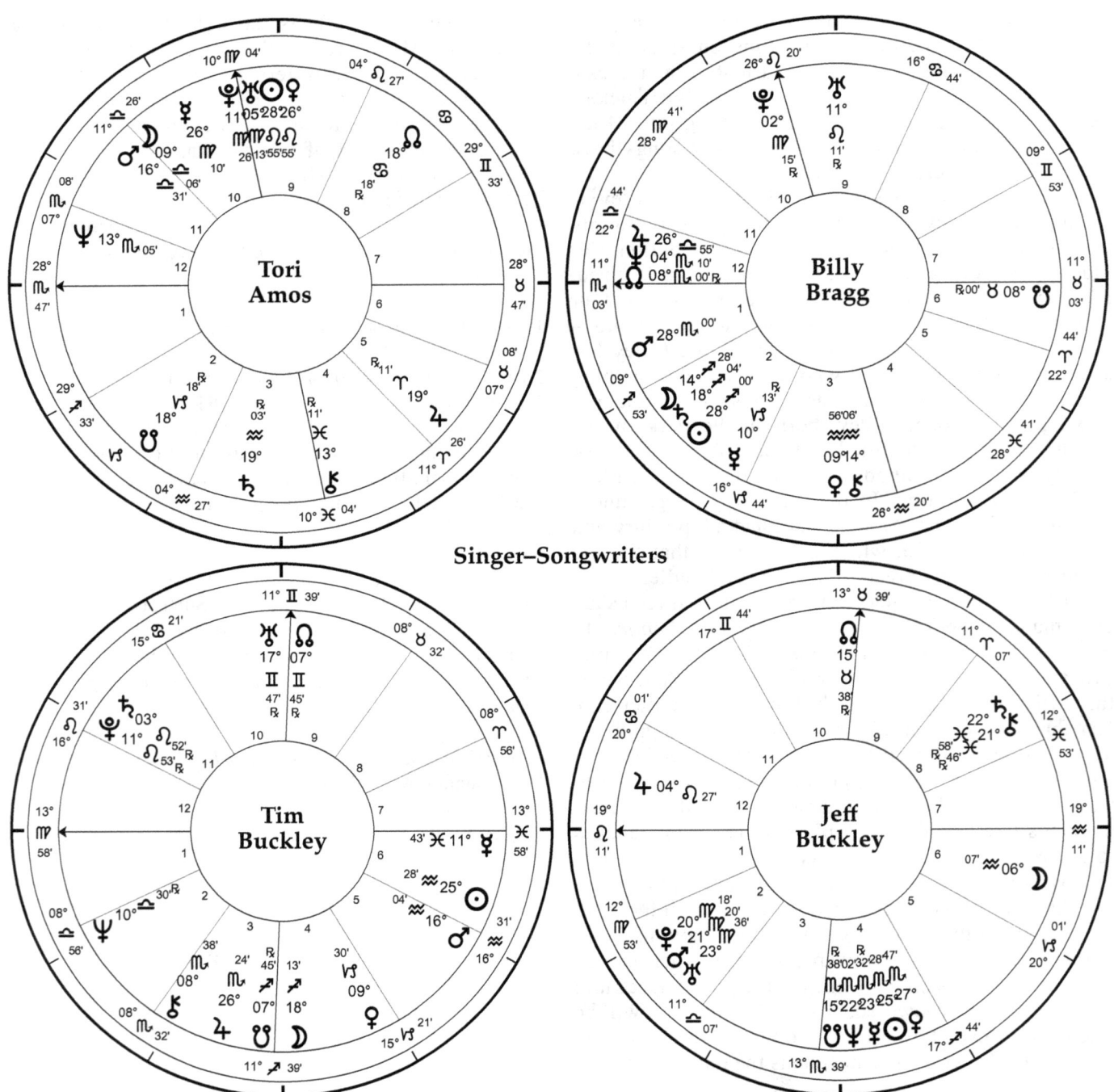

Singer–Songwriters

Whole Lotta Love: Tim and Jeff Buckley

Mark Jones

As I listen to classic Miles Davis (*Kind of Blue*), the great musical influence on the young Tim Buckley, it's with a certain soulful melancholia that I contemplate the lives of two great musicians: one, the father, who took American folk music deep into the jazz-infused world of the 'voice as an instrument', and the second, the son, who inherited a majestic vocal style and brought that to devastating effect in contemporary 'indie' music.

Both father and son have the Moon's Nodal axis across the MC–IC axis (with the North Node on the Midheaven), and both took the yearning of childhood dreams and condensed it into musical forms that were emotional and hugely influential. In the case of father Tim Buckley, the long-term influence of his music far outweighed its commercial impact in his all too brief life. He was a post-war baby, the son of a war hero, born into the bright possibilities of a new world.

The generation of musicians born in the mid-1940s all have Pluto conjunct the North Node of Neptune. Neptune, in itself and as the higher octave of Venus, has often been a planet linked to music. The generation born with the individual and collective intensification of Pluto on Neptune's North Node includes such luminaries as David Bowie, Marc Bolan, Richard Carpenter, Cher, Brian Eno, Jimi Hendrix, Elton John, Freddie Mercury, Liza Minnelli, Van Morrison, Jim Morrison, Jimmy Page, Diana Ross, Cat Stevens, Bobby Womack, Neil Young and many more. It is as if a surge of creative energy streamed into collective humanity after the crisis in western civilization brought by war, the dark revelations of the Holocaust and the atomic bomb.

Tim Buckley also has the North Node of Uranus conjunct his North Node–Midheaven conjunction, as well as Uranus in his 10th House. The urge to escape his home life and individuate – and in so doing to make an impact on the world – was very strong in him. It was there in his youthful inability to cope with the pressures of marriage and fatherhood and in his leaving to pursue his career (Uranus in the 10th House opposite the Moon in Sagittarius). This departure would have an enormous impact on the life of his son. It represents, in evolutionary terms, the unresolved karma of the wide conjunction of the Moon to its own South Node. It also involves his Mercury in Pisces conjunct the Descendant and square the Nodes of the Moon: the promise of love seemingly easier than the reality of commitment and domestic responsibility.

The resulting guilt echoes from his own dutiful childhood conditioning (Venus in Capricorn) as he fell short of his own ideals of fairness and harmony (Venus square Neptune in Libra) which, alongside the striving for new musical forms, led into heroin dependency, in stark emulation of his jazz heroes. Addiction hurried his untimely death just before his first Saturn Return.

Buckley's young son Jeff would be haunted by the elusive, Mercurial talent of his father, whom he only met once, at the age of eight. We can feel the tremendous energy of the young man in his tight Pluto–Mars–Uranus conjunction opposing the retrograde Saturn in Pisces: the hurt of the all-significant, yet completely absent, father. We can sense the anger that pushed him to find his own expression – equal to that of the missing man he heard on CD; it was fuel for his own musical training.

The wide conjunction of the stellium in Scorpio (Neptune–Mercury–Sun–Venus) to the South Node is very significant in evolutionary terms, revealing how the past weighed heavily on this young man: idealism and the sense of betrayal of the ideal that he was born to experience. An exploration of the fate of his father became the overriding expression of his intensity.

In the midst of work on his second album, *Sketches for My Sweetheart the Drunk*, as his band flew into Memphis to start recording, Jeff Buckley swam out into the Mississippi River, singing along as 'Whole Lotta Love' by Led Zeppelin played on his ghetto blaster. A wave from a passing tugboat pulled him under and, although the friend with him organized a search, his body was not found for days. He was thirty years old – just past his Saturn Return, transiting Saturn forming a Yod to Pluto and the South Node of the Moon, and transiting Uranus conjunct his Moon.

Genetics might explain the quality of voice, even the pull of music, but do genetics explain the eerie parallels in the life and death of father and son? What are genetics anyway but the biological codification of meaning, the symbols of inheritance? The birth chart expresses its own twelve-strand DNA through the twelve archetypes of the zodiac. Does even that symbolism explain the parallel trajectory of father and son?

At the news of Jeff Buckley's death, I sat with friends and listened to his album *Grace* as a mark of respect for the talent and humanity of this unique man. The number of references in his lyrics to love experienced as a tide that drowns the individual is truly uncanny. I would suggest a therapeutic dimension to the mutuality of father and son's fates, at least from the point of view of Jeff Buckley, revealing the unconscious loyalty of the child.

When small, the child totally relies on the parents. Lacking language and utterly dependent for all needs, the child cannot conceive any fault in the parents. The imperative is to successfully bond with them. The loyalty and strength of this bond can be phenomenal. When a parent is absent – only present through the mysterious expression of their art – the capacity for a compensatory idealism is added to this loyalty. I have witnessed clients unconsciously sabotage a given area of their experience because, through the bond of unconscious loyalty, they do not want to outshine the parent who failed in that dimension. This is the power of the undifferentiated love of the child that has not had the chance to mature into a more constructive form.

I feel that it was a whole lot of love for his absent father – mixed certainly with anger, hurt and abandonment, but a decisive childlike love of this father image – that sustained Jeff Buckley, and even fathered his talent. Yet a love that, in a final twist, left him with a fatal unconscious allegiance to the parabola of his father's life. The power of the unconscious, the roots of love itself, becomes a form of fate.

Singer–Songwriters

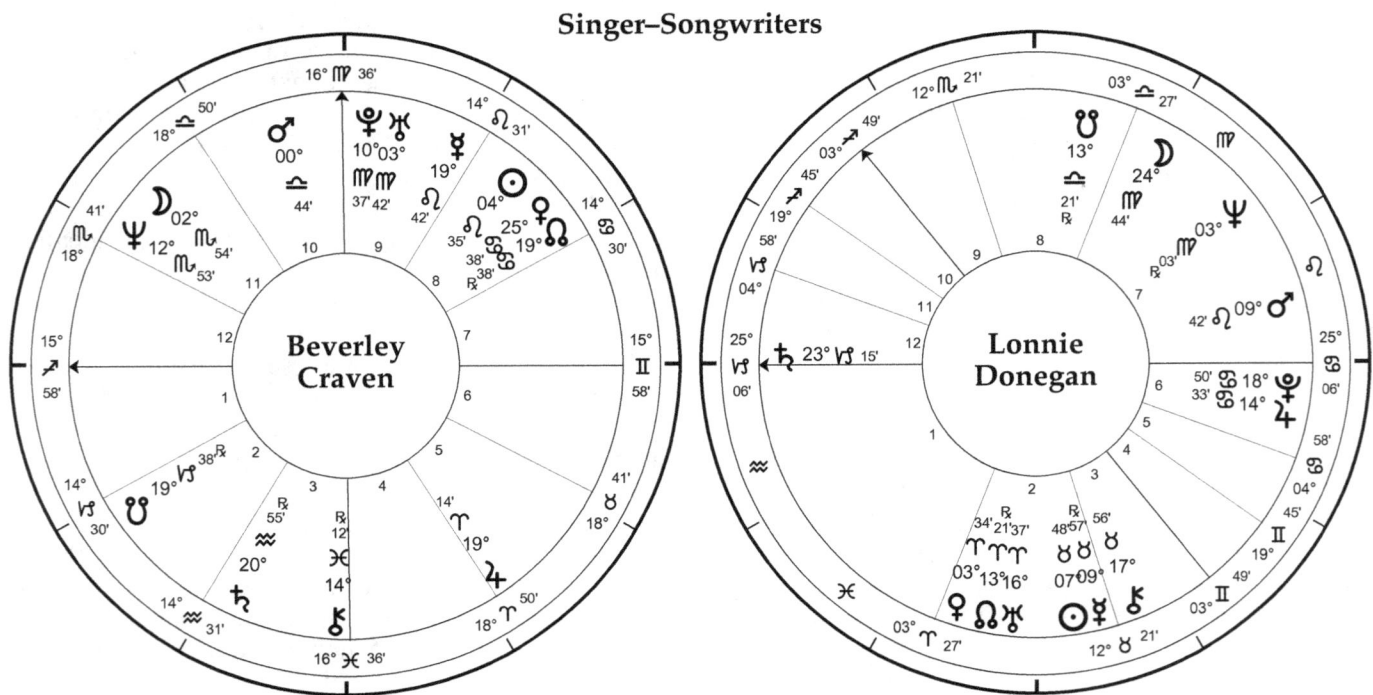

Country & Singer–Songwriters

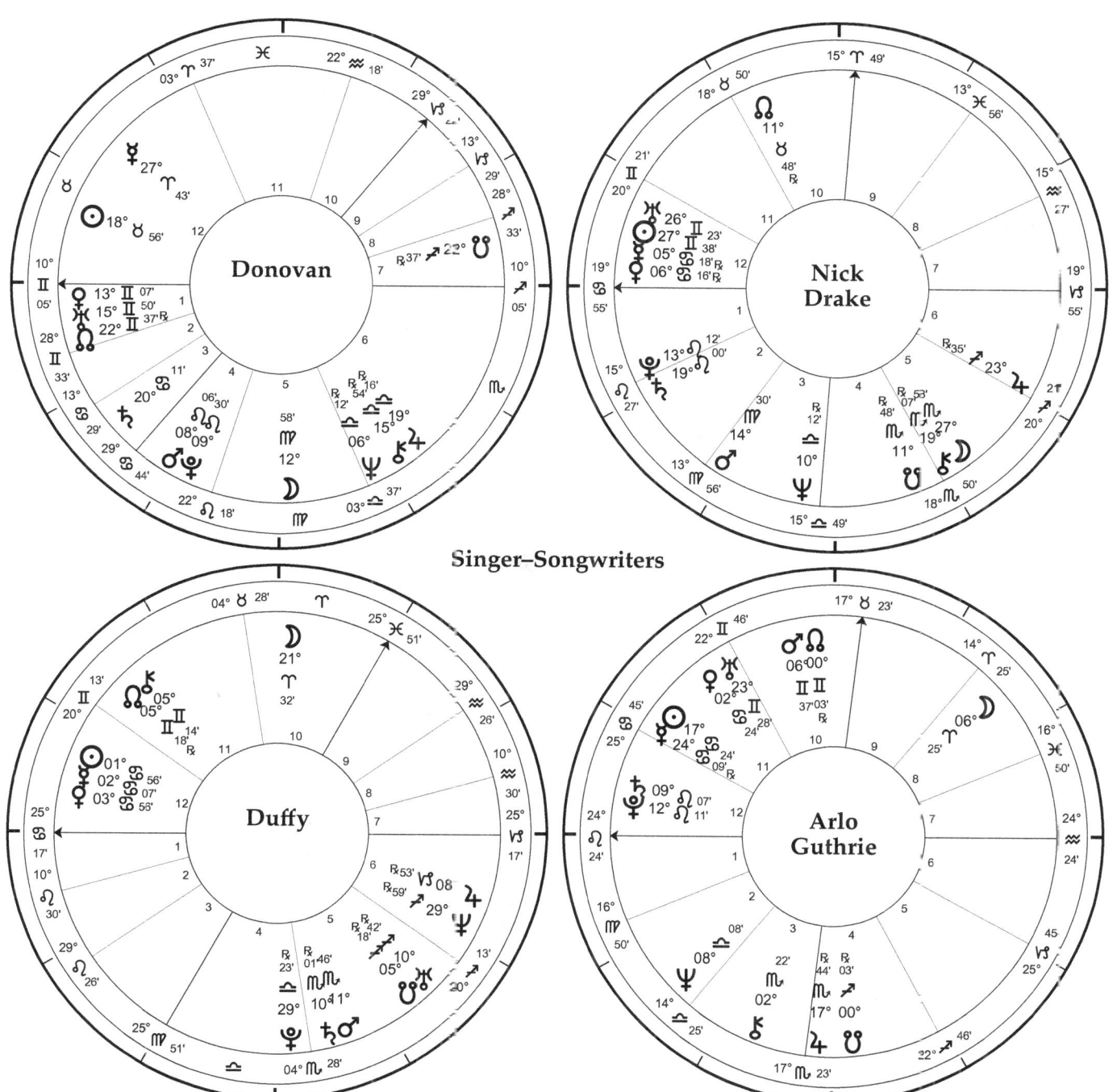

Singer–Songwriters

88 *The Book of Music Horoscopes*

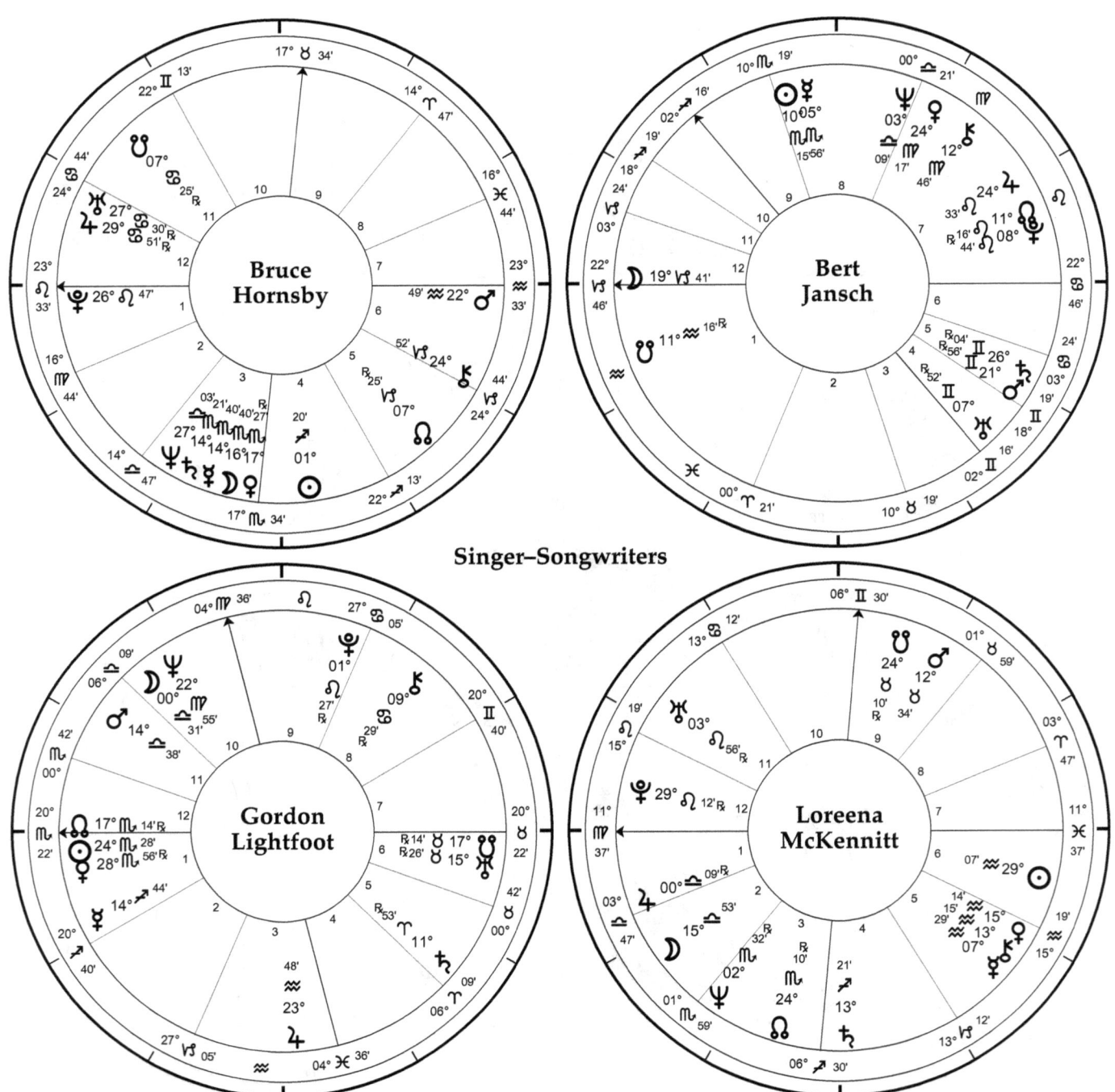

Singer–Songwriters

Country & Singer–Songwriters

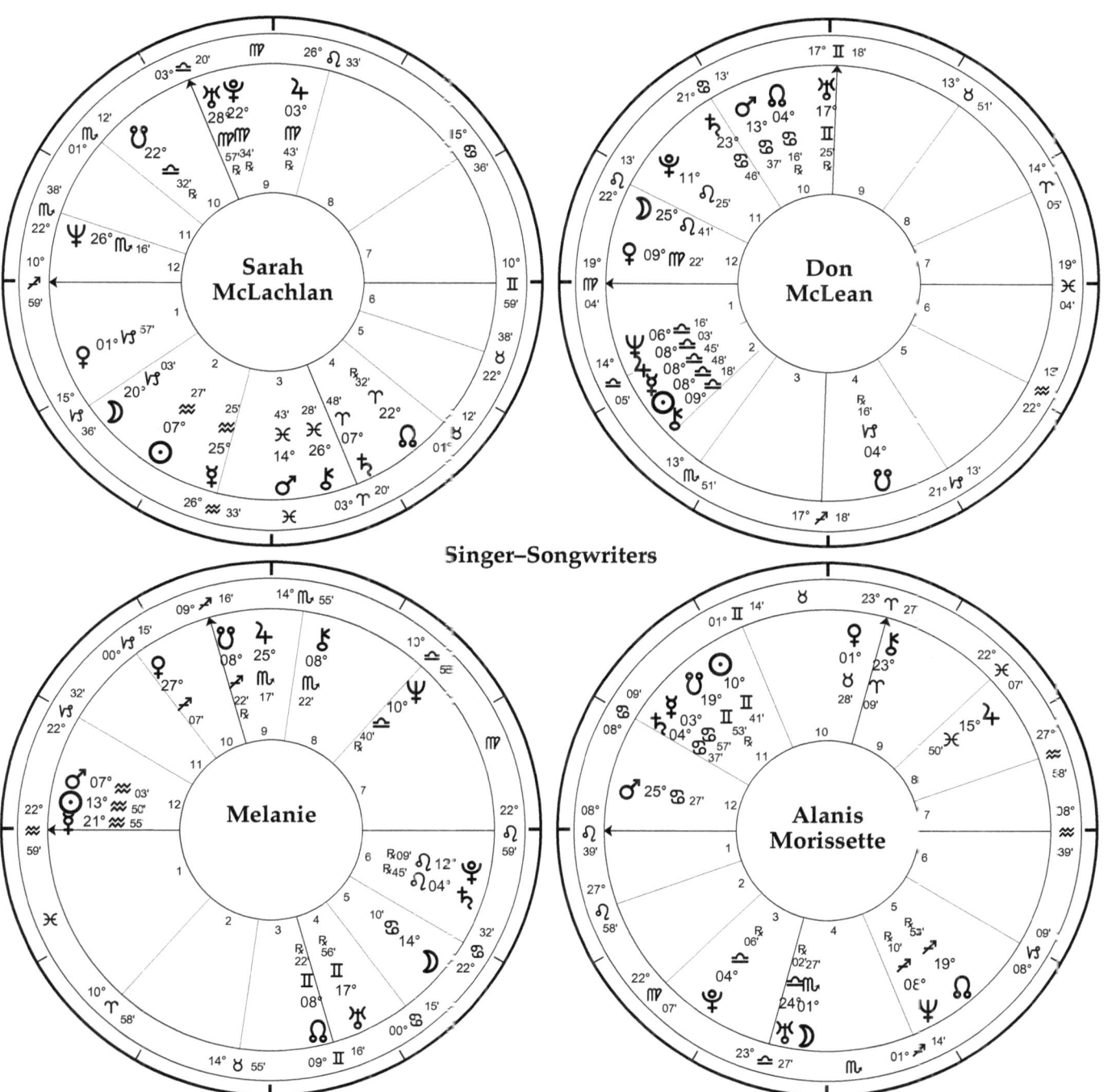

Singer–Songwriters

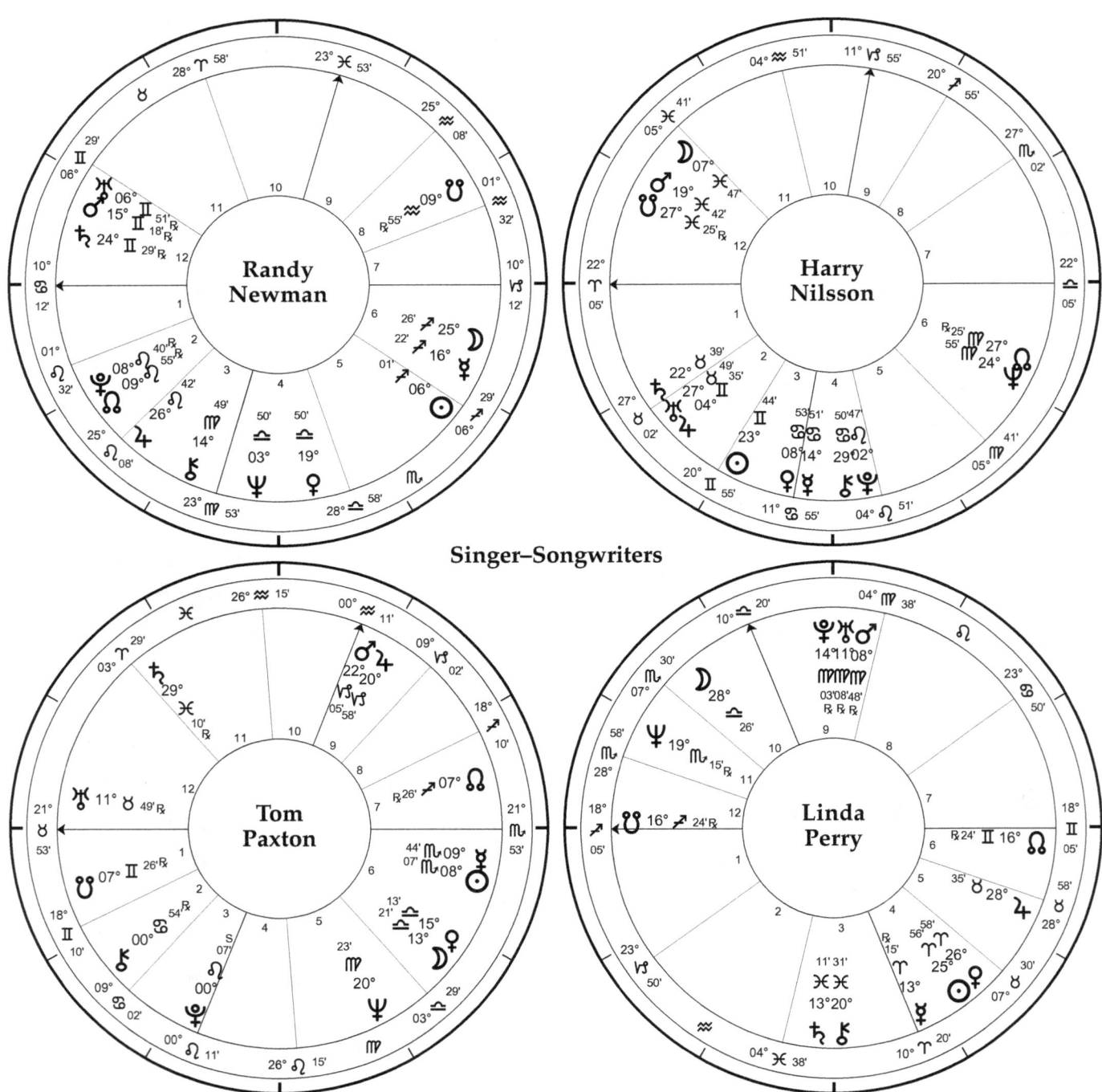

Singer–Songwriters

Country & Singer-Songwriters

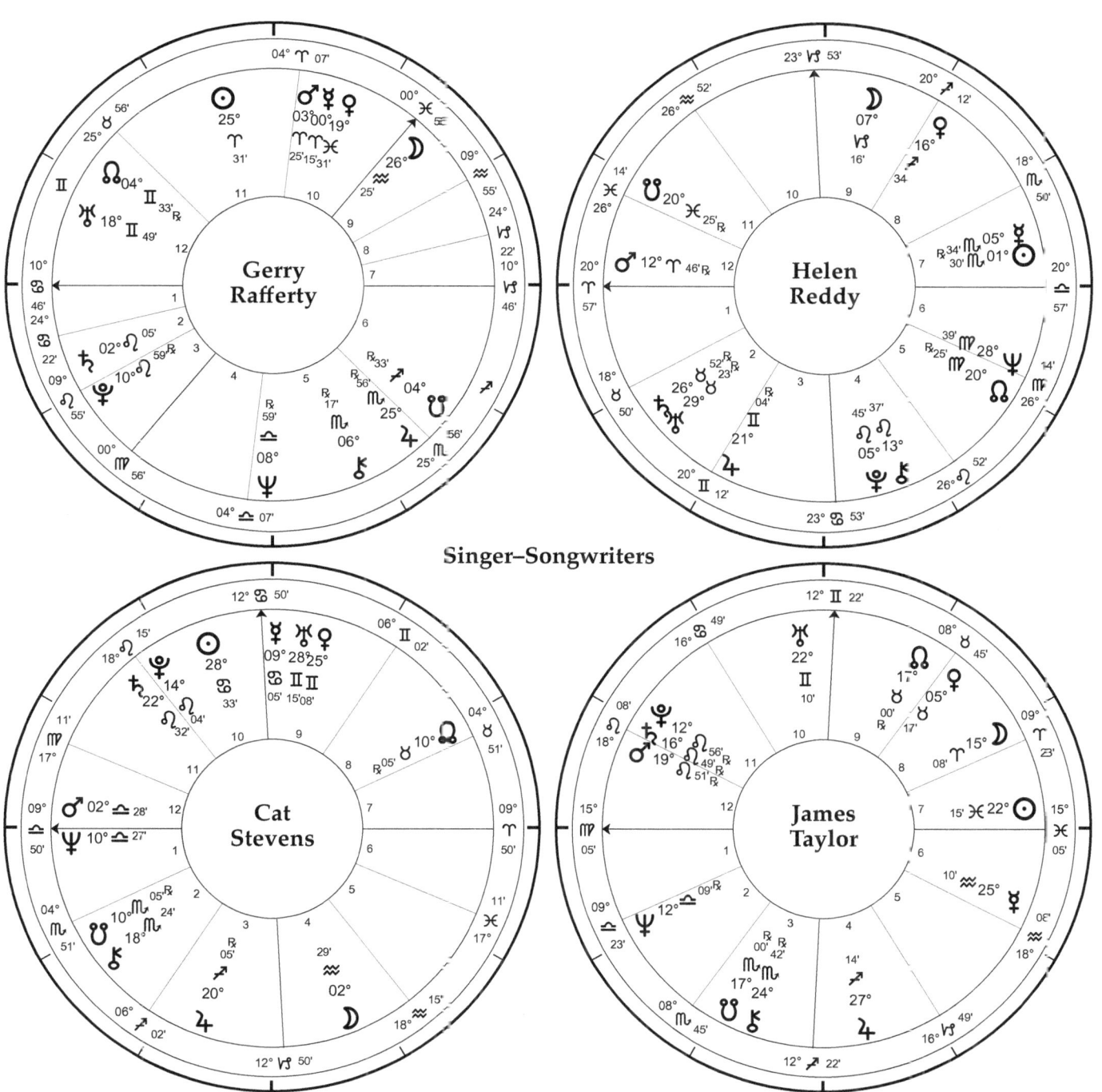

Singer–Songwriters

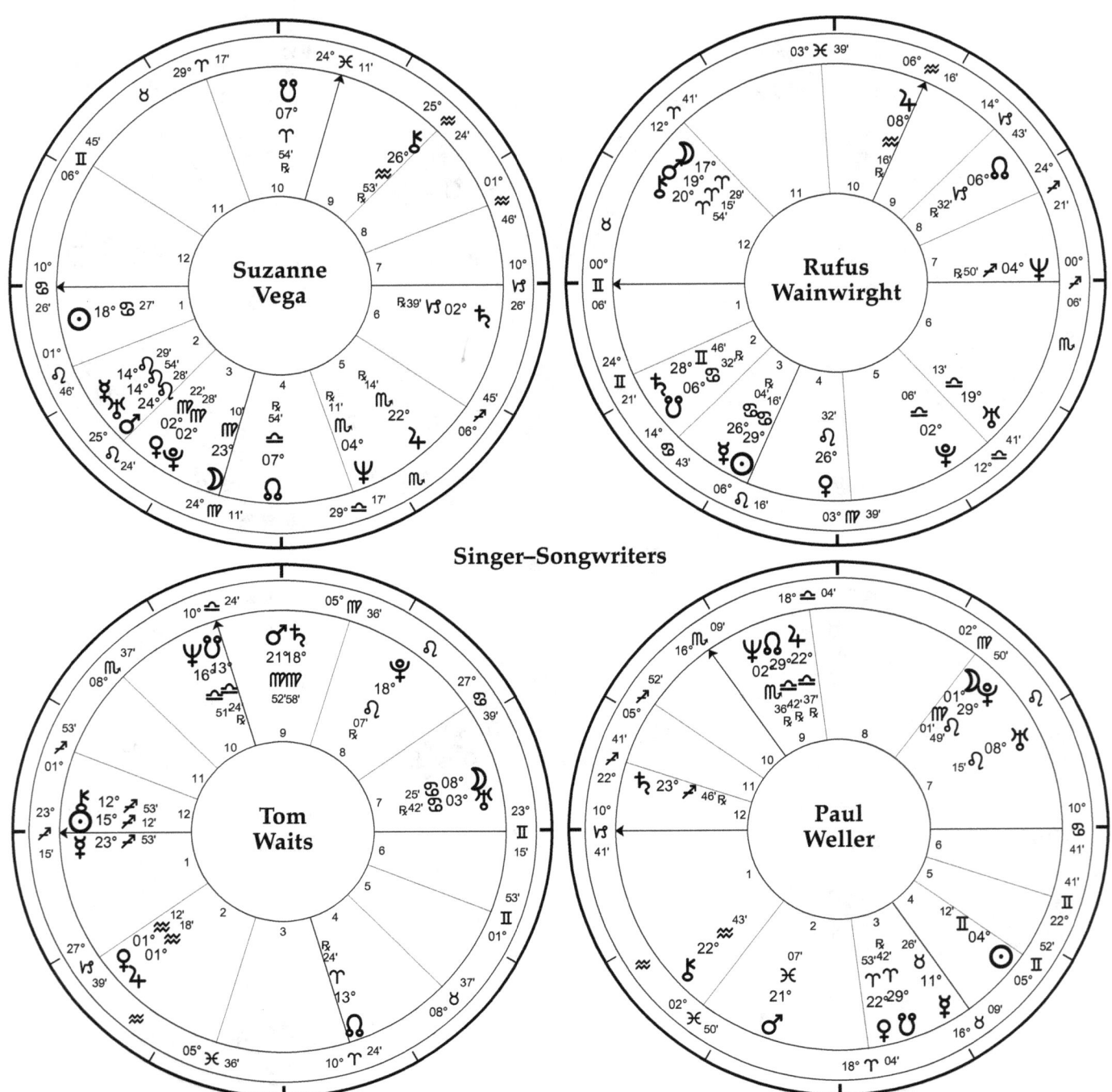

Singer–Songwriters

MUSIC ROYALTY

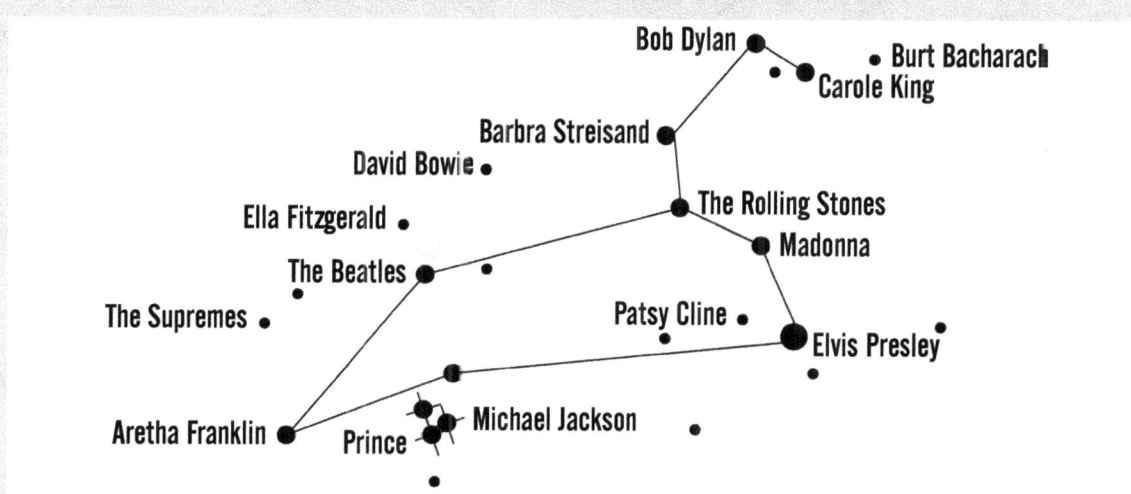

Music Royalty – General

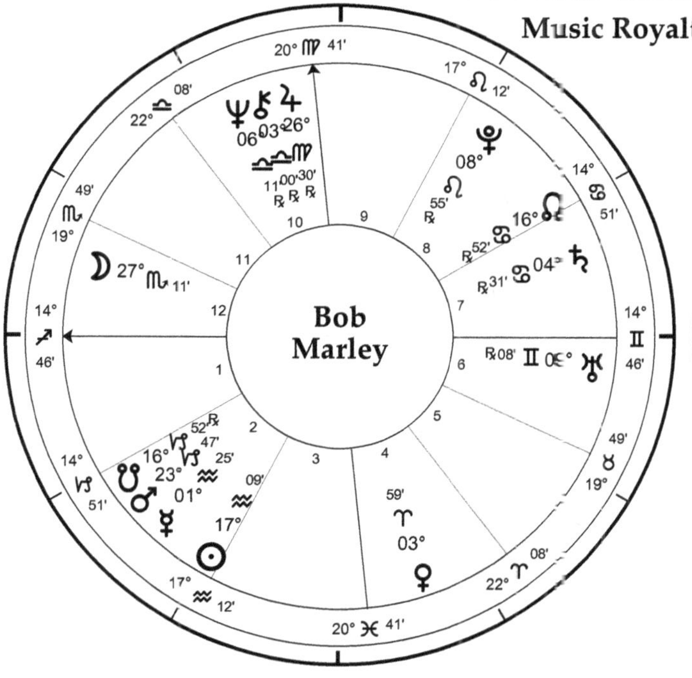

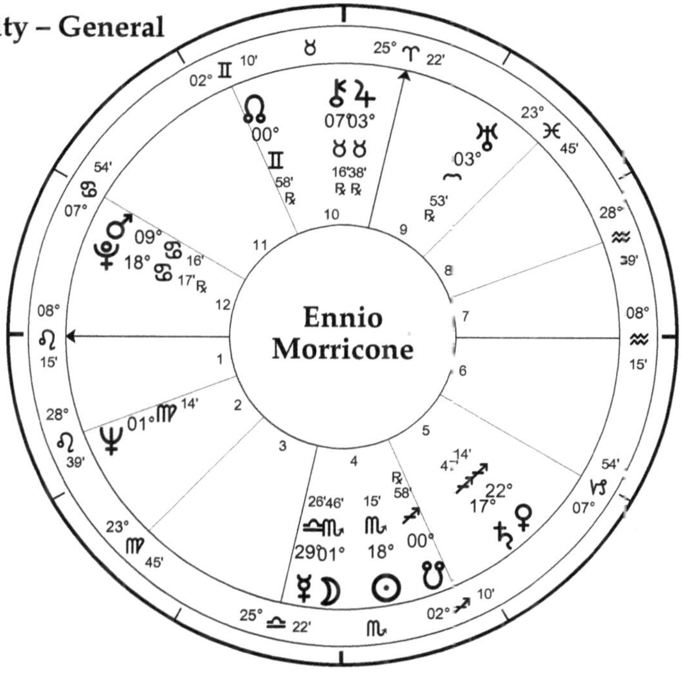

94 The Book of Music Horoscopes

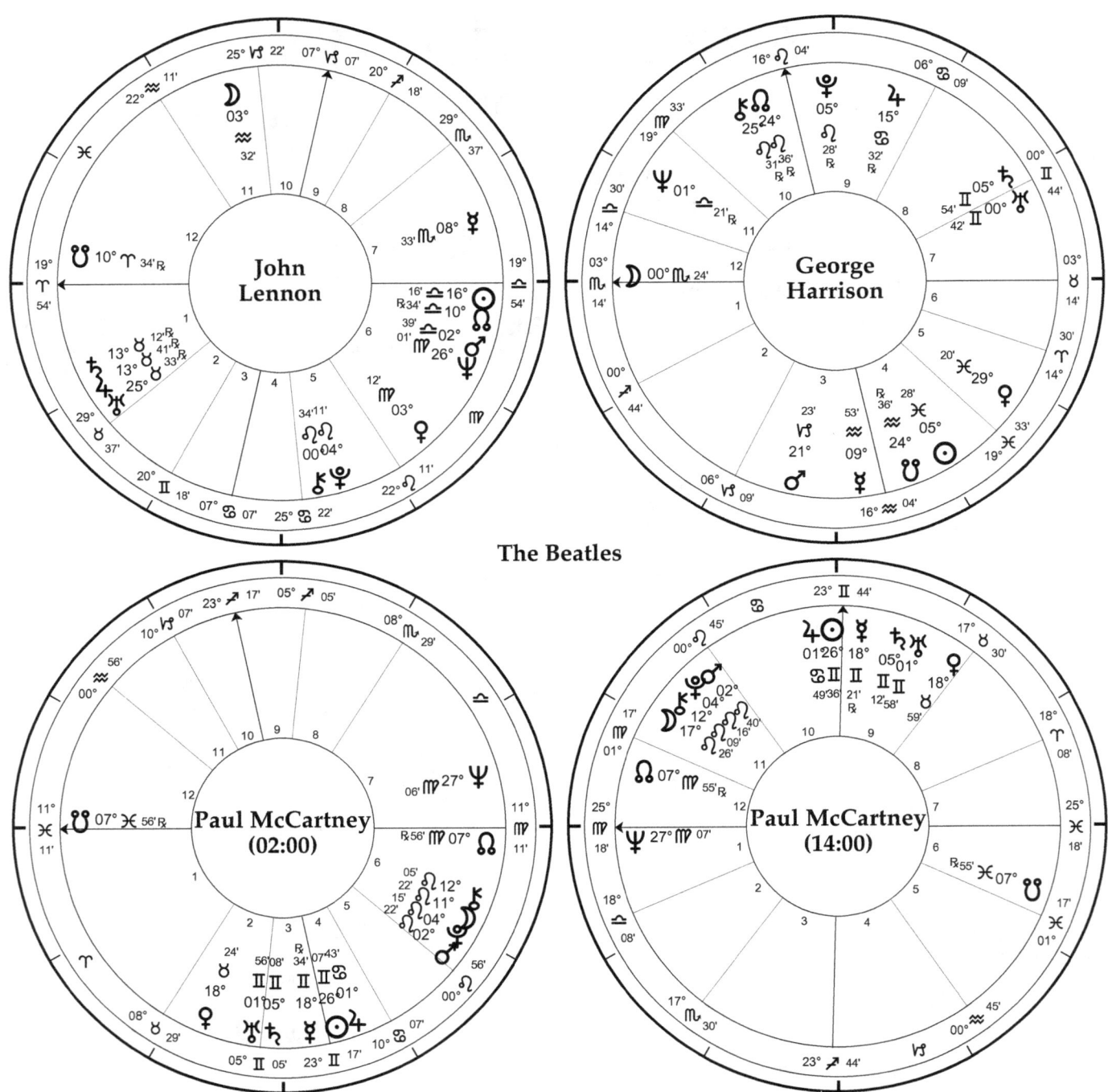

The Beatles

Music Royalty 95

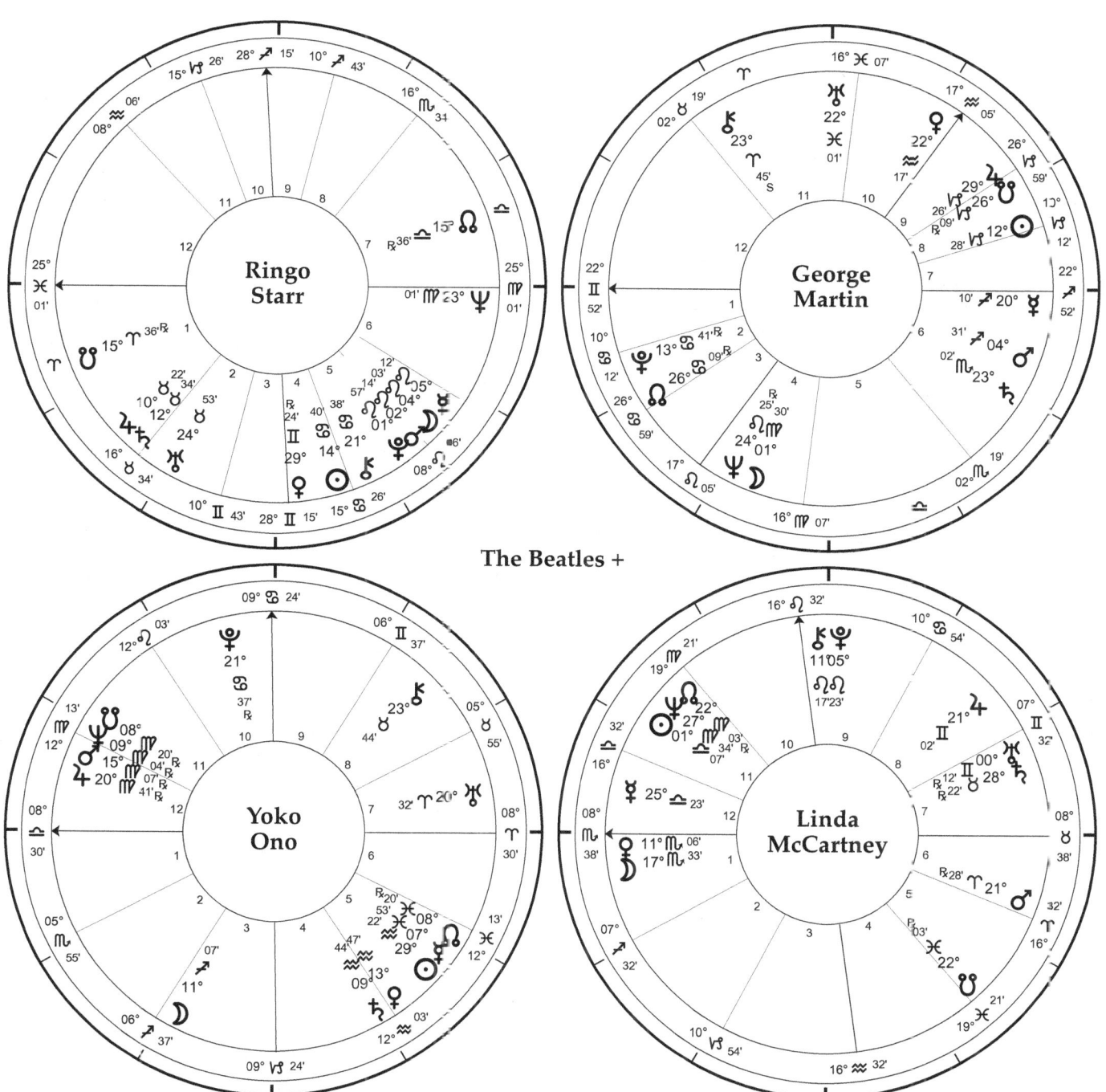

The Beatles +

George Harrison

Pete Watson

John and Paul were Sun-in-Air Beatles; George and Ringo the Sun-in-Water Fabs. Zipping through the airwaves, lodging in so many minds, Lennon and McCartney's songwriting talent charmed the public. Working from their communicative, Sun in Air core, this Libra–Gemini partnership had ideas aplenty and Beatle leadership agendas to push. Equipped with an overview, endlessly witty and clever, they naturally thrived among the excitement of Beatlemania, feasting on opportunities to express themselves. Supplying the words and overt direction, they instinctively left George and Ringo in whatever background could have been available to a Beatle.

But the Beatles' appeal is not merely witty, cerebral, poetic and smart. It's about words and music together – a mixture of ideas and feeling, of conscious and subliminal stimulation, a blend of the brainy/smart Air and intuitive/felt Water. The counterbalance to all that Air was made by George and Ringo who added the sheer musical *feel*.

George's chart is by far the most Watery of the Beatles, with the Moon and Ascendant in Scorpio and the Sun in Pisces. In life, water is everywhere; we are mostly made of it. It shifts between states, seeps and steams, sometimes ugly, often beautiful, changeable and powerful.

In astrology, Water corresponds to the emotions, the everywhere and nowhere of personal, intimate, felt experience. That subtle, illogical, hard-to-communicate arena, rooted in the heart, was where George came from and where he felt most comfortable.

It's not surprising to find that the quiet Beatle lived a 'Watery' life, spiritual interests soon becoming central, with privacy and intimacy more appealing than showbiz. Thrust into too bright a spotlight, he found Beatlemania disturbing and was the first to want to leave the band. Which provokes the question: how and why could he allow himself to arrive at the centre of that unwanted storm in the first place?

A further examination of his chart clears this up. Air is the second strongest element. Chatty Mercury in wacky Aquarius (useful for all those press conferences), structural Saturn and the more 'out there' energies of Uranus and Neptune are all in Air. So while the nucleus of George's chart is soaked in Water, the outer reaches are in Air. It's as if the far-from-Earth planets pulled George into the limelight and away from his centre. A look at the aspects adds to this theory, with the Sun and Moon making aspects to Uranus and Pluto, pointing to something big and powerful impinging on the contentment of a Sun–Moon trine in Water. It's as if being a Beatle was unnatural for George, as though his Air sign talents satisfied *part* of him but not his *essence*.

George's challenge was squaring the circle of where he found himself and how he felt about it. Primarily he wanted answers to Piscean questions of spirit and soul, yet he was also a Beatle and media star. He found spiritual solutions in chanting, meditation and the religious traditions of India. These gave him something to communicate, at last healing his Water–Air split and releasing greater confidence. His new concerns suffused his lifestyle and songwriting and they soon spilt out into the band and beyond. The idea of chanting (using the voice – an Air activity) to seek the Watery goal of spiritual truth appealed to John and Paul, and involvement with the Maharishi and a full Beatle trip to India followed.

George's interest in the question of death was noticeable from an early age and could still be heard in songs such as 'Within You Without You' and 'All Things Must Pass'. While we can pin his interest in the world beyond on a Sun in Pisces, Scorpio Moon and Saturn in the 8th House, there is clearly something extra at work here. It's no surprise to find his Sun in tight, challenging aspect to both Mars (semi-square) and Saturn (square),[1] since the Mars/Saturn midpoint is considered the death axis. Mars–Saturn suggests the restless experience of 'driving with the brakes on' and a strong awareness of endings and limitations. Applied to his Sun, there are impulses to move forwards and shrink away, to live brightly or hide oneself. 'Here Comes the Sun' and 'Blow Away' move towards bright futures from desolate starting points, while others, such as 'My Sweet Lord', carry the driven, questing discipline of these forces working together.

Post-Beatles George lived this way, only jumping into the limelight when he felt comfortable, happier tending his family and huge garden than promoting albums and films. Like John, he had a powerful Moon–Pluto aspect, lived out in a demand for privacy. In practical terms, George found a way of putting this aspect to work outwardly through the massive home renovation project he took on when he bought his country pile, Friar Park.

George's unusual, divergent interests away from the core of religion and music make sense when we look at his elemental balance. A lack of Fire loves frenetic activity and excitement – such as dancing – to lift the spirits and re-establish some *joie de vivre*, particularly if it hits a depressive rut. George found his exciting lift by driving fast cars and developed a passion for Formula 1 racing, as well as effectively gambling by funding film projects. Film was an involvement which also necessitated jumping back into the public eye for brief periods, satisfying his Leo Midheaven and elevated Pluto.

Someone with a lack of Earth can feel rootless and disassociated from their body and from Earth itself; somehow the connection needs to be re-made. George appears to have solved this problem by buying a grand old run-down country house and spending much time fixing the house as well as renovating the garden, sinking his feet in the mud. All this would have also satisfied the need to be alone and work on difficult projects found in those hard Sun–Mars–Saturn aspects.

His musical career can be seen in the Aries Point opposition between Venus and Neptune, tightly semi-square and tri-octile the Leo Midheaven. This found expression in other ways too: his life-altering experiences with LSD, the George–Pattie Boyd–Eric Clapton love triangle and his involvement in the vagaries of funding films.

George participated in the lunacy of the Beatles through his rising Moon in Scorpio – a configuration he shares with Charlie Chaplin. We see the lovable yet distant Beatle, moods flickering across his face – but also a powerful connection with the public. The astrology connects with his affection for comedy, lived out through movies such as *The Life of Brian*. George the comedian even took part in *All You Need Is Cash*, the excellent spoof documentary by Beatles doppelgangers The Rutles.

Ultimately, George Harrison was a complex man driven by myriad urges which were lived out in diverse actions and interests. Post-Beatles, he would walk past pictures of himself 'as if it were someone else entirely'[2] – the self-denial of Sun square Saturn kicking in hard. His influence in the areas of music, cross-culturalism and spirituality continue to percolate through the western world. He remained, to the end, ever hopeful that the dreams of the Sixties would be realized and he went to his death chanting. George contributed more to the world than most of us realize: his charitable foundation continues to give aid and his invention of the big charity rock concert lives on. He lived out so much of his complex chart. Yet a great deal is explained when we remember that he was a Pisces, perhaps even an enigma to himself and always swimming in two directions – at the very least.

1 It's interesting to note that Pattie Boyd, his first wife and fellow Pisces, had a very similar pattern with her Sun being square a Mars–Saturn conjunction in Gemini. She was also very much a spiritual seeker and encouraged George in this direction.
2 Olivia Harrison quoted in *The Independent*, 19 October 2005.

98 *The Book of Music Horoscopes*

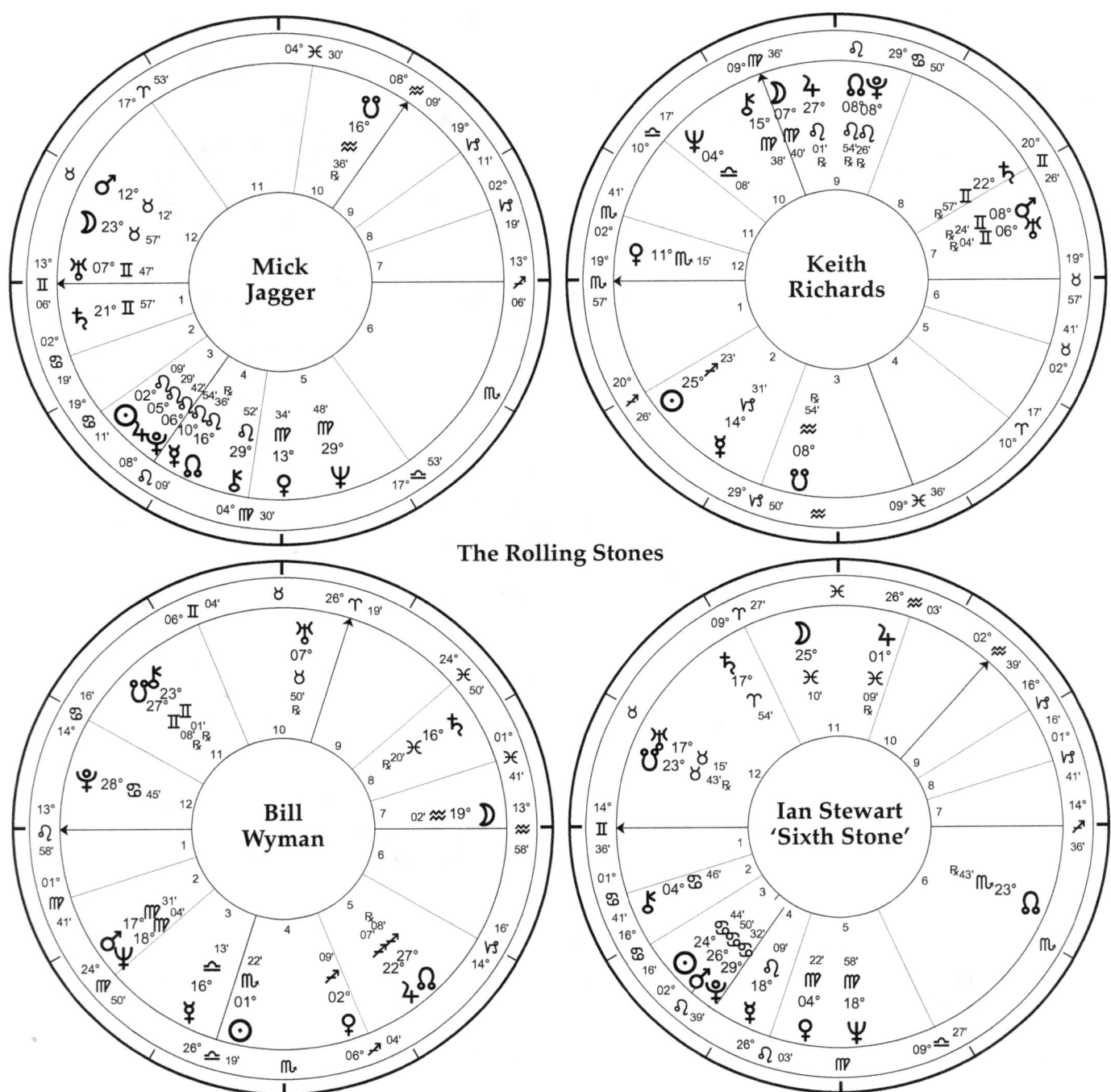

The Rolling Stones

Music Royalty

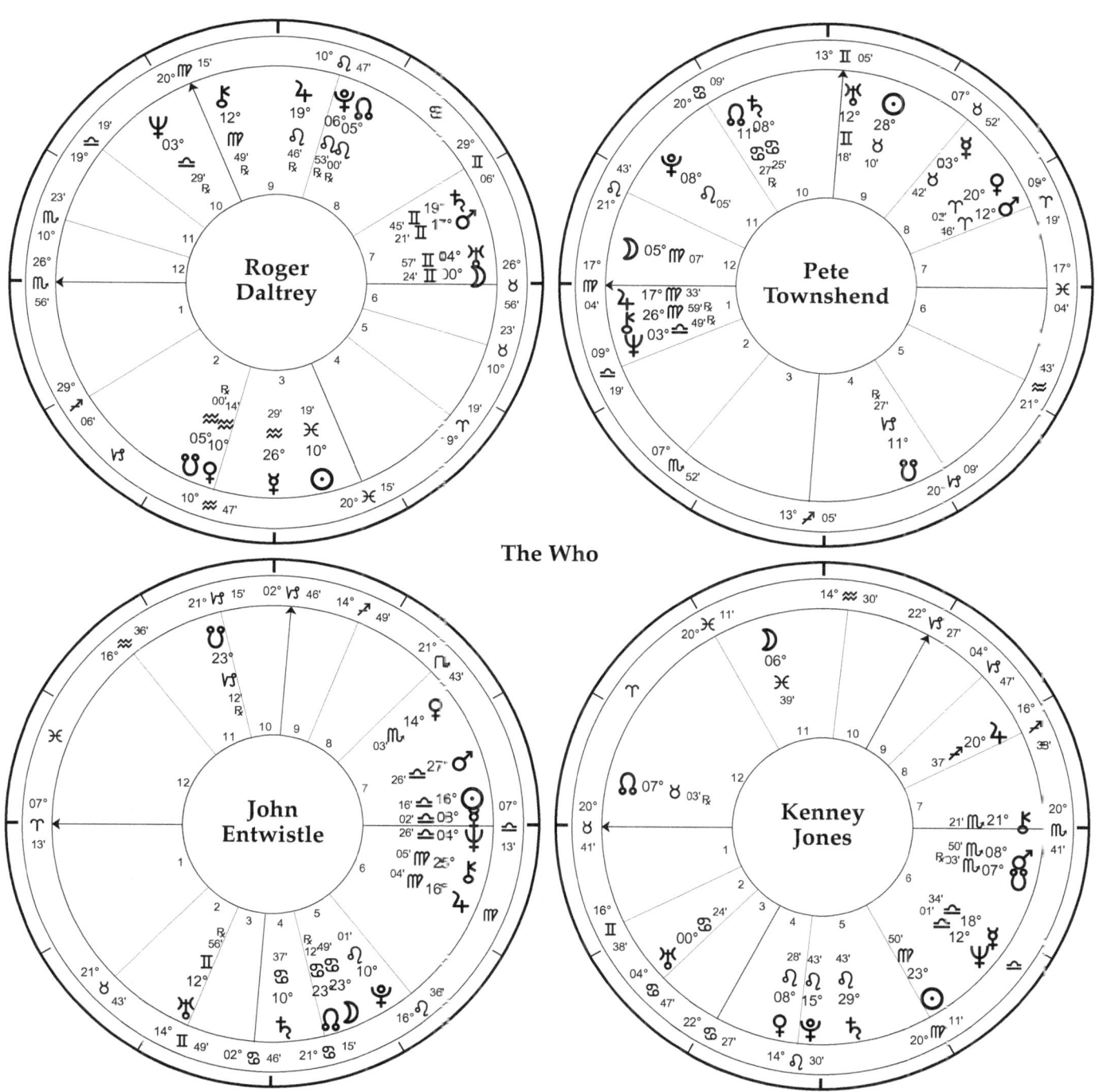

The Who

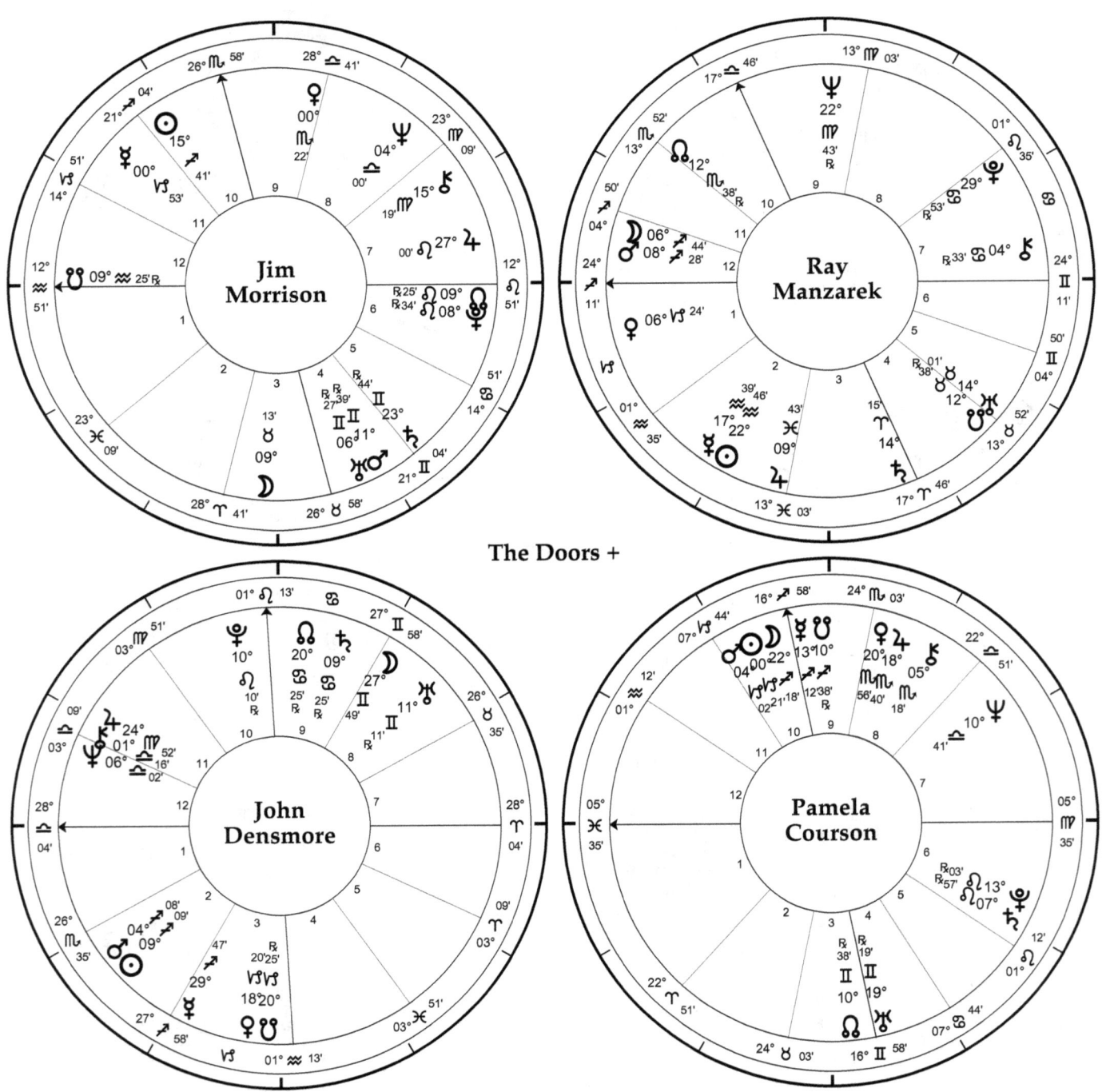

The Doors +

Music Royalty 101

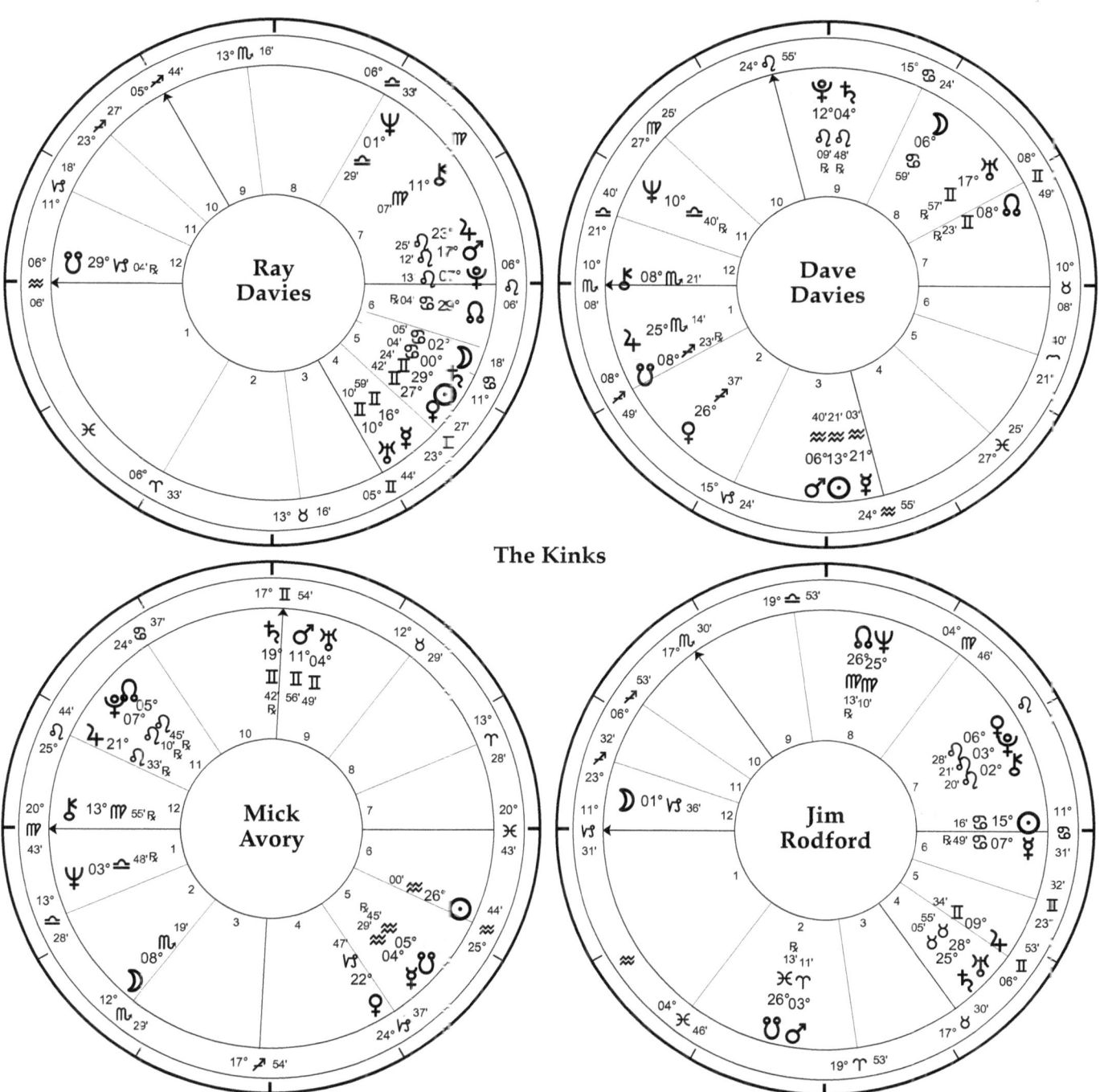

The Kinks

102 The Book of Music Horoscopes

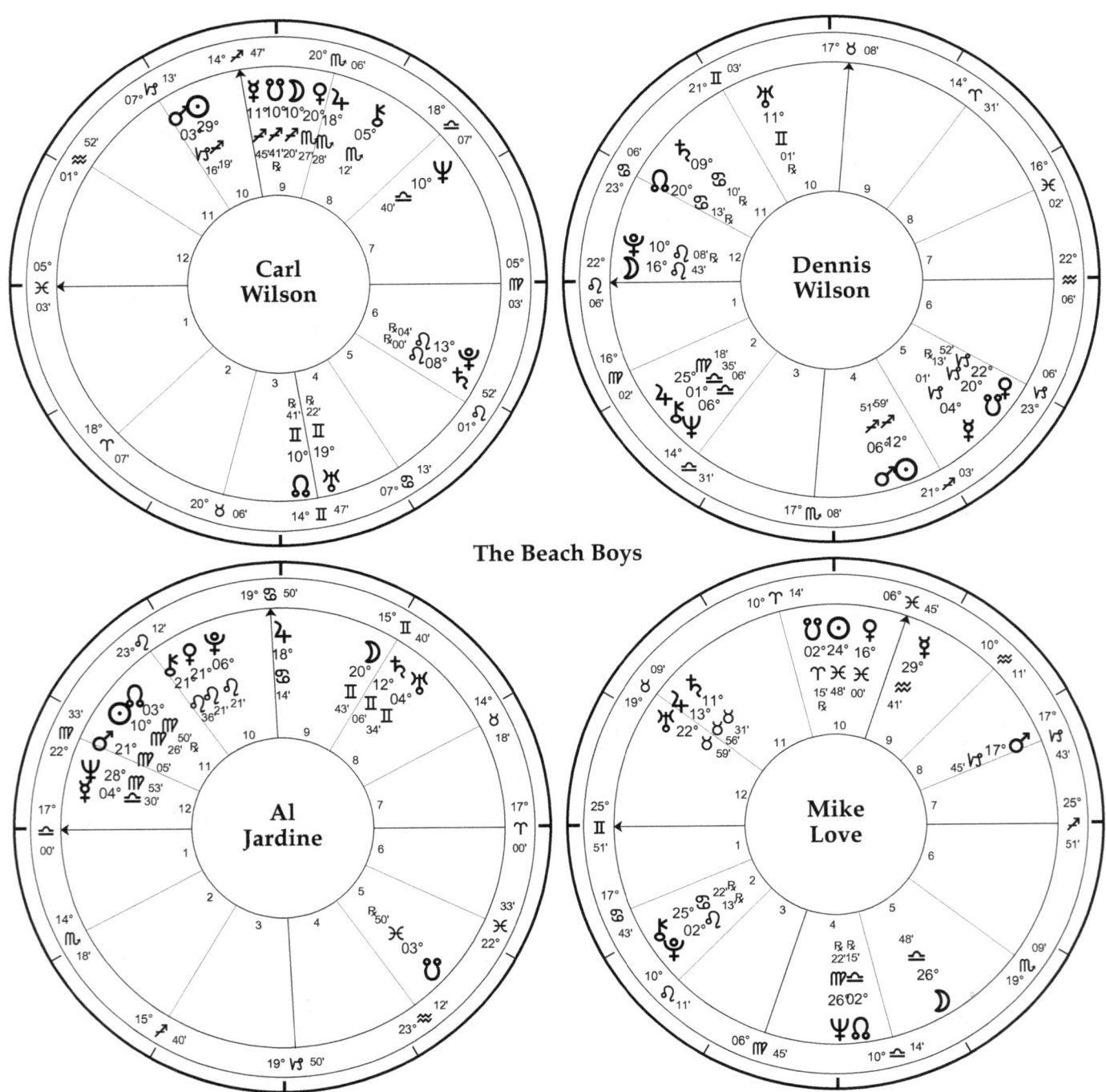

The Beach Boys

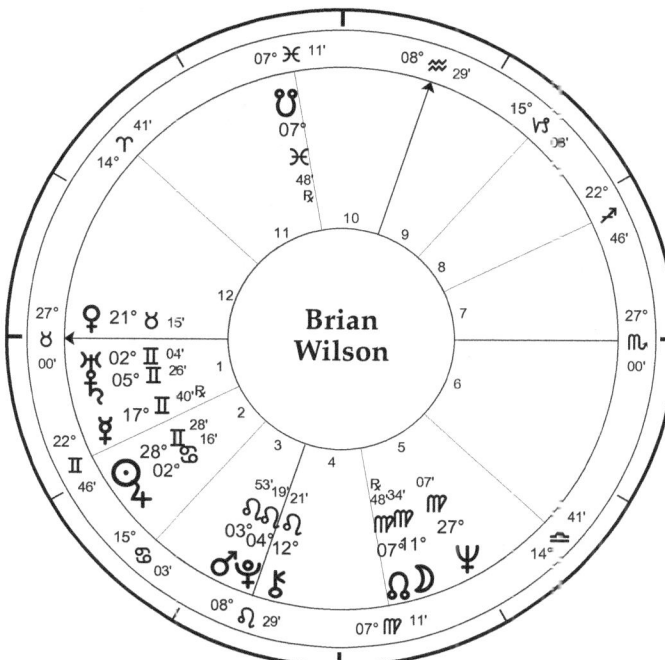

Good Vibrations: The Mutable Chart of Brian Wilson

Paul F Newman

The Beach Boys rode professional triumphs alongside personal tragedies during the ebb and flow of their existence. The three Wilson brothers – Brian, Dennis and Carl – their cousin Mike Love and their friend Al Jardine were all born with the Sun in a mutable zodiac sign. Brian was a Gemini, Dennis and Carl both Sagittarius, Mike a Pisces and Al a Virgo. The line-up was weighted towards Sagittarius, but it was a completely mutable set.

Brian Wilson, with his Sun in Gemini and Moon in Virgo, was the main songwriting and creative force. With the Sun square Neptune, Brian was the seeker of harmony and beauty in an uncertain world who almost drowned in his own talent. Yet he survived to tell the tale. He was born on a day when over half the planets were in mutable signs. Four, including the Sun, were in Gemini and two, including the Moon, in Virgo.

For a Sun Gemini and Moon Virgo, life can be full of nervous moments. But the eternal spirit of optimism during life's anxieties, so beautifully expressed in such songs as 'Wouldn't It Be Nice' and 'Don't Worry Baby' sprang surely from Brian's Sun conjunct Jupiter. Apart from the obvious family connection with his two Sagittarian brothers, Jupiter was his great protector, the energy that pulsed good vibrations into his nervy Sun.

The classic songs of the Beach Boys are Jupiterian. They are joyously uplifting in melody, harmony and message. Perhaps Brian's strong Jupiter is best observed in those songs where the warmth of the Sun breaks through despite whichever uncertain circumstance his Mercury mind is worrying about. The Jupiterian feeling of well-being suddenly floods in, seemingly to the astonishment of the writer. For example, in 'You're So Good To Me' Brian sings as if he can hardly believe anyone could be so nice to him. ('How come you are?')

His chart is focused on the lower left-hand quadrant (the first three houses), a pattern that can illustrate a reluctant leader. Brian Wilson gave up touring with the Beach Boys early in their career although he still sang, wrote and produced most of their recorded work. Inevitably with his mutable chart, the monotony of touring and singing the same songs every night, plus the stresses of trying to do too much creatively, resulted in a series of nervous breakdowns. There was no chance to think, he acknowledged in later interviews – a classic statement from a Gemini with a Taurus Ascendant. But his inventive genius blossomed in the studio, climaxing in such albums as the renowned *Pet Sounds* and the multi-million-selling masterpiece 'Good Vibrations'.

'Good Vibrations' is a musical illustration of Brian Wilson's chart. It is so mutable that the tempo changes several times during its course, making it a delight to hear but a nightmare to dance to. Recorded over a period of six months in four different studios, the need for absolute perfection is, again, Brian's Moon in Virgo. Endlessly juggling and synthesizing at the console, he eventually melded Geminian chunks of disconnected melodies into a seamless whole. In less experienced hands, 'Good Vibrations' could have ended up as a jerky pastiche, an unrelated glob of bits and pieces hacked off and stuck together. Yet his Airy Sun supported by the glow of Jupiter took it all into ethereal realms where church organs, purple dresses (and lots of other Jupiter things) blend like air currents in a flowing entirety.

With little effort Brian fits the image of the eccentric creator/inventor (Uranus rising in the 1st House and Aquarius on the Midheaven). Venus is rising too but in the 12th House, bringing inspiration to his music from a deeper, meditative source. Chart-ruling Venus in its own sign of Taurus is sensitive and compassionate here, with a need to retreat into peace and solitude. Perhaps, through his indulgence in drugs and other eccentricities (including heaping up sand in the studio so he could feel it under his feet while he composed at the piano), Brian regressed too much into an enclosed 12th House prison. Such introspection and lack of mobility led his Jupiter to seek another method of expression. Instead of bursting out in hit-song fragments, the giant planet turned physical and Brian became obese.

Of the three Wilson brothers only one is still alive, and perhaps against all odds it is Brian. (Dennis drowned in 1983, aged 39, and Carl died of cancer in 1998, aged 51.) In his sixties and seventies Brian returned to touring, recreating and singing his classic hits to packed audiences in sell-out tours. Jupiter is the preserver, they say. Jupiter is lucky, they say. But if Jupiter inclines one to overdoing things when the Moon is whispering 'small is beautiful', a lot of mental give and take is required to preserve the balance.

Surfers believe, rightly or wrongly, that there is a hidden rhythm in the waves that break. Amid the laws of random probability, there is a harmony, they believe. Brian Wilson's chart illustrates the endless mutable belief that, however unpredictable life's variety, Jupiter will find and preserve the timeless fragments.

The Carpenters

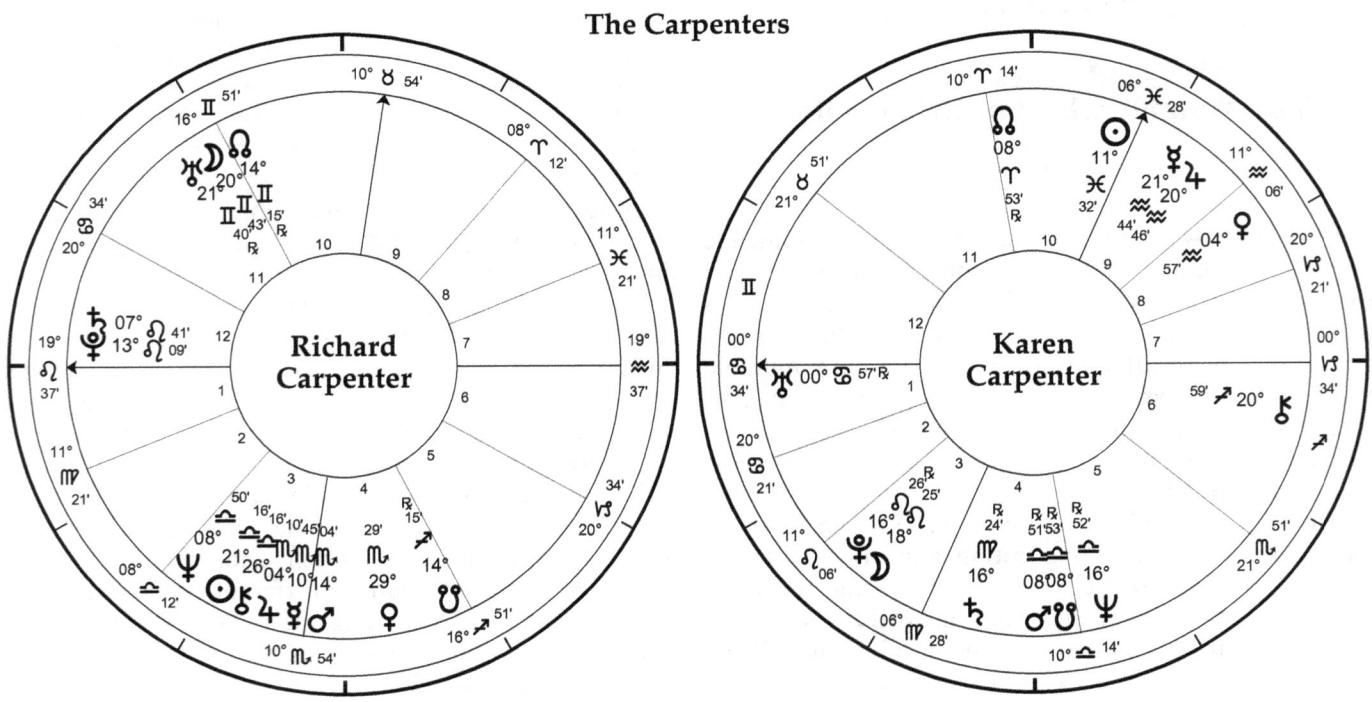

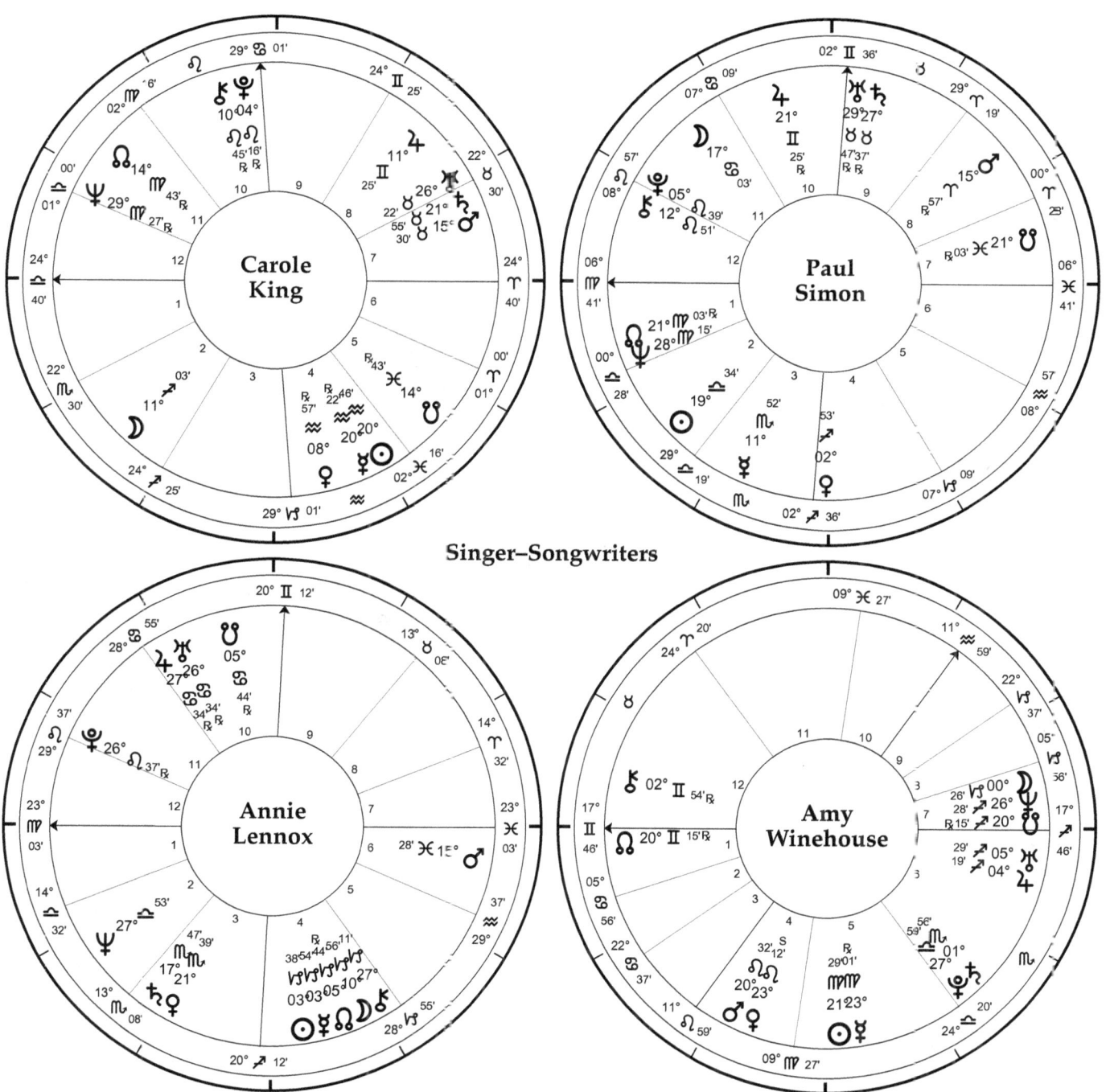

Singer–Songwriters

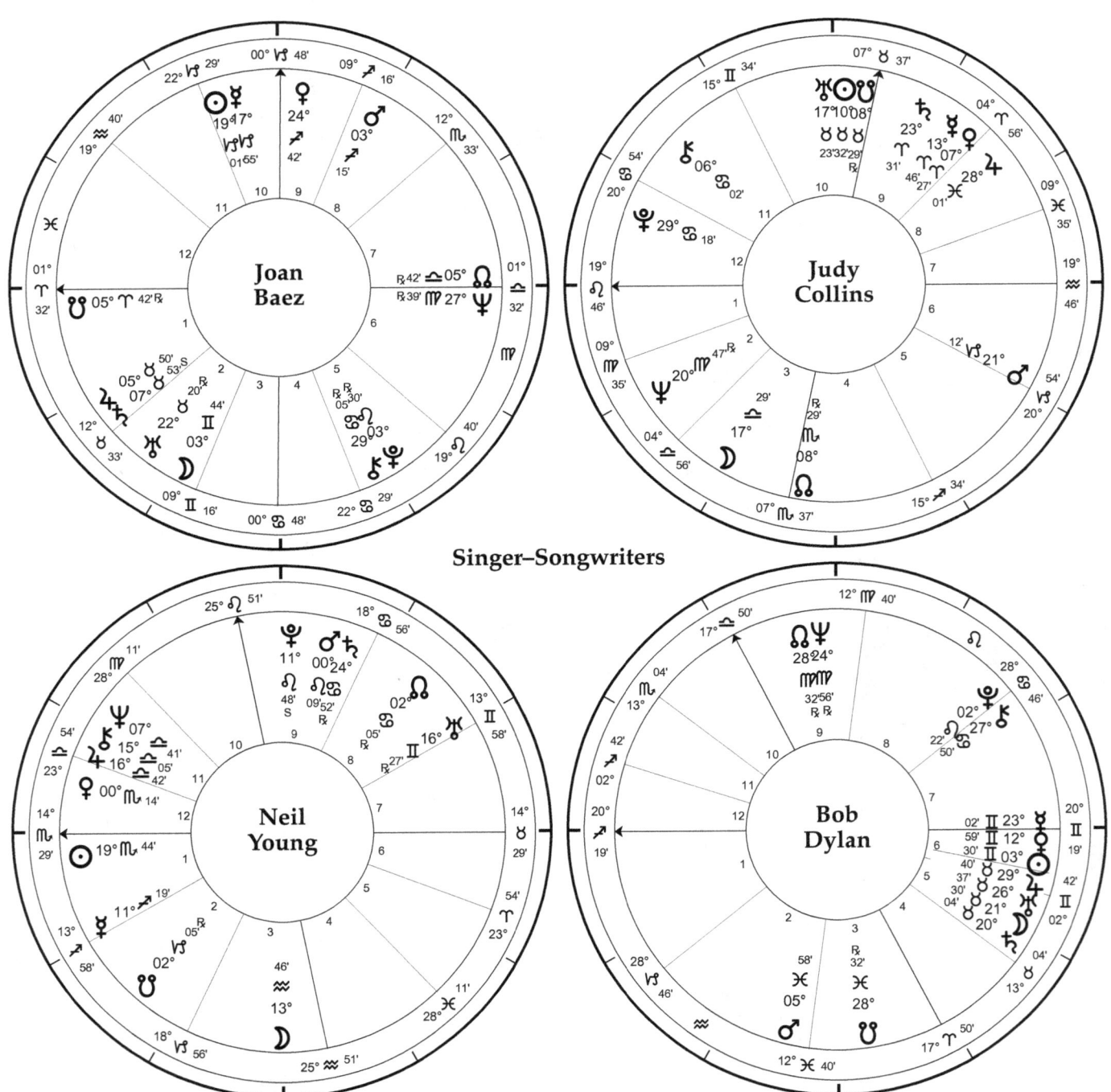

Singer–Songwriters

The Wild Mercury Musical Journey of Bob Dylan

Sue Merlyn Farebrother

The songs are there. They exist all by themselves just waiting for someone to write them down.[1]
  Bob Dylan

Bob Dylan's Mercurial muse has been picking up songs and writing down his own songs for his entire adult life. Exposure to an extraordinary collection of folk songs, Dust Bowl blues and traditional music was a major influence and inspiration for Bob Dylan's early musical experimentation in New York in the 1960s, forming a strong basis for his own creative outpouring of words and music. As he says himself, looking back:

Folk songs were the way I explored the universe, they were pictures and the pictures were worth more than anything I could say. I knew the inner substance of the thing.[2]

His intensity and speed in absorbing prolific amounts of new songs through delving into the past was legendary during this period. In his own words:

I did everything fast. Thought fast, ate fast, talked fast and walked fast. I even sang my songs fast.

Dylan's fifty-year musical journey has been, and continues to be, an ever-changing trip of exploration, of experimentation, of spiritual searching. He constantly re-invents his own past work, and keeps on keeping on into the future.

In his chart all these qualities jump out. He has a stellium in Gemini – Sun, Venus, Mercury, with Mercury on the Descendant – opposite his Sagittarius Ascendant, square Neptune in Virgo conjunct the North Node and trine his Libra MC. Inspiration comes to him in the form of tunes, words, poetry and images. His ability to compose music, to play and sing the words he has written is perhaps shown by his other stellium: Saturn, Moon, Uranus and chart ruler Jupiter all in Taurus. His Sun–Moon midpoint falls exactly between Jupiter conjunct Uranus and further suggests that he has known his own destiny since he was young: to express his inner being and to inspire millions of followers, fans and fellow musicians alike.

His chart ruler Jupiter is at 29° Taurus: the Earthy sign and house of his Jupiter in its strong position in the last degree of Taurus grounds his muse, makes it real and manifest. He has also switched the musicians around him many times, as his approach to his work and his co-workers undergoes yet another change as the years progress. There is a restless seeking after the ideals of precision and excellence and a poetic mastery of imagery – sword-swallowers, jewels and binoculars, howling beasts and Egyptian rings haunt Dylan's lyrics. These reflect his predominantly mutable chart, the stellium across Taurus and Gemini, the multiple trines to Neptune in the 10th House, and the squares to Mars in Pisces in the 3rd.

Dylan takes his creative work very seriously and has an excellent memory (Moon conjunct Saturn, both quincunx Ascendant). It is perhaps this blend of a serious attitude to his own radical variations that makes Dylan's appeal so unique and widespread. The Moon–Saturn conjunction also embodies Dylan's ironic sense of humour, seen in songs like 'Maggie's Farm' and 'Rainy Day Women #12 and #35'.

Although love, romance and sex have featured prominently throughout his private life (according to the gossip press, he has had at least two wives and a countless number of lovers), Dylan's personal inner world and his concerns – what he has experienced, heard, seen, researched and dreamed about – are written into his songs.

'Change' is Dylan's middle name. He rarely, if ever, does the same thing twice. His followers know this about him and often delight at his concerts in trying to figure out which song Dylan is singing now, only recognizing one of his well known songs several lines (or verses) in because its rhythm or instrumental backing has been altered so radically.

The musicians that back him are also subject to short-termism. Dylan seems to be a perfectionist with a low level of tolerance – at times that requires his bands to follow his eccentric shifts. His musical styles have been equally diverse, from his youthful protest songs through his experiments with blues, country, rock, gospel, jazz and ballads – and with all kinds of different instruments in his backing band. With the Moon–Uranus–Jupiter–Sun, he does it his way – a crowd pleaser he ain't.

Dylan has a reputation for reclusiveness, is known to frequently refuse to be interviewed, and to give obscure or evasive answers to questions. He has used, Gemini-style, a number of different names, among them Blind Boy Grunt, Lucky Wilbury and Jack Frost. The inner mystery of this man has made an enigma of him, a subject of fascination to millions over the years – even within the music business – with, as he says himself, 'a gazillion books on me either out or coming out in the near future.' Yet from this inner world, a Gemini world where he says himself 'I fought with my twin, that enemy within, till both of us fell by the way' ('Where Are You Tonight?'), a massive encyclopedia of songs, music and paintings will be Bob Dylan's legacy.

His autobiography, *Chronicles Volume One*, however, published in 2004, reveals much of his personal world and experiences. Perhaps because it is his own choice of what to include, or maybe he is simply older. The book seems strikingly honest. Maybe one day there will be another volume.

His Jewish upbringing instilled a sense of religion in him, being sent by his father to study for his bar mitzvah as a young teenager. Although he did not seriously practise Judaism for a large part of his adulthood, he has always had a desire to know and understand, often to an obsessive degree. During the mid-1970s, with the release of the albums *Desire* and *Street Legal*, it is evident if you listen to some of the lyrics that Dylan was then exploring systems of meaning which included astrology and tarot. He was still suffering after his divorce from his 'Scorpio sphinx in a calico dress'[3] wife Sara. This period evolved into his well known born again Christian period in 1978-9, which lasted on and off into the 1980s.

Perhaps it is no surprise that transiting Pluto crossed Dylan's MC in late 1978, as he became swept up in this compelling new belief system and undertook to dedicate his life and future direction to Jesus. 'Gotta Serve Somebody' is the first track on *Slow Train Coming*, released in 1979, and containing the lines 'it may be the Devil or it may be the Lord, but you're gonna have to serve somebody.' He did experience an inner revolution, which partially took the form of feeling the presence of God. Close on the heels of the first hit of transiting Pluto conjunct his MC, transiting Neptune crossed Dylan's Sagittarius Ascendant. Dylan was baptized by oceanic immersion, which symbolized burying guilt and being reborn into a new life, according to the Church. Added to which he also had transiting Saturn square Venus, transiting Neptune sextile MC, transiting Uranus opposition Saturn, among other indications of important changes – it was a true period of transformation. The songs that emerged during this time mostly did not sit well with Dylan's fans – or with his own children who were upset, having been raised in the Jewish faith.

With Sagittarius rising and the Sun conjunct chart ruler Jupiter, Bob Dylan's journey has always been a spiritual one, though it has taken the form of the adventurer, the researcher, the traveller and pioneering explorer – and also the recluse. All these phases of experience are inbuilt in his music. A fellow musician once said of Bob that 'he moves into mysticism at the drop of an E minor chord'.[4]

Bob Dylan's wild Mercury musical journey continues with several acclaimed albums of new material in the last decade or so, such as *Modern Times* (2006), *Together Through Life* (2009), *Tempest* (2012) and an album reviving Frank Sinatra songs, in his own unique style, *Shadows in the Night* (2015). He did it his way.

1 *Down the Highway*, Howard Sounas, quote from Bob Dylan, p. 326.
2 *Chronicles Volume One*, Bob Dylan, p. 18.
3 Line from 'Sara' on the album *Desire*.
4 *Rolling Thunder Logbook*, Sam Shepard, p. 148.

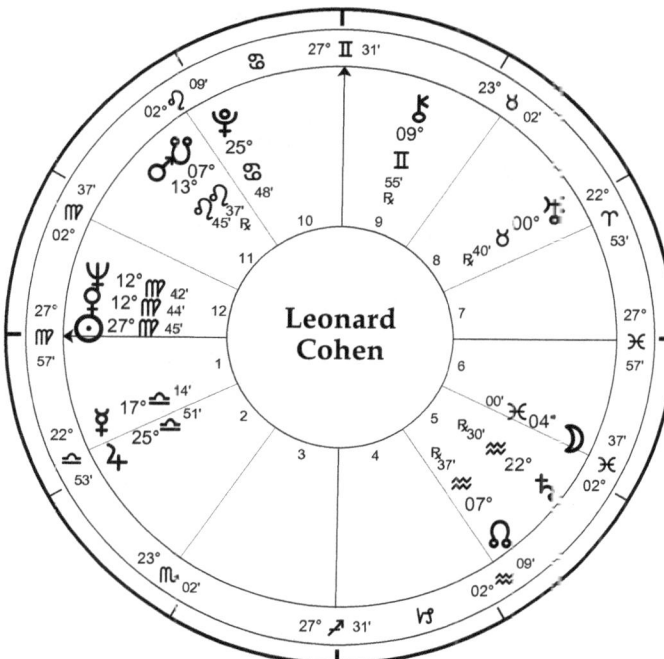

**Dance Me to the End of Love:
Leonard and his Muses**

Brian Clark

Leonard Cohen was 15 when Chance revealed her hand in a used bookstore in his hometown of Montreal. Amidst countless volumes he found a book of poems by Spanish bard Federico García Lorca. Between its pages he was introduced to the *duende*, an earthy spirit who seizes artists, confronts their mortality and inspires them to create passionate 'black sounds',[1] possessing not only the artist, but its audience as well.

The soulfulness and depth of imagination represented by Cohen's Venus–Neptune conjunction in the 12th House resonated with Lorca's poetry. Three times in that year Saturn would traverse this creative 12th House combination, awakening his *anima*, compelling it to find its worldly face. In Leonard's life, Saturn would transit this house twice more and on each of these occasions his connection to the soul of the *duende* would be strengthened.

In Leonard's chart, lyrical poetry, artistic expression, beauty and musical love affairs are the legacy of Venus conjunct Neptune in the 12th House, a bittersweet blend of passion and sorrow, devotion and escape, sacrifice and longing, and Love Itself,[2] all reproduced in his lyrics and his lovers. This conjunction echoes throughout his artistry, his spirituality and his prosperity. The oceanic 12th House tides sweep this conjunction up in fantasy, deceit, romanticism, bleakness and yearning for what is unattainable, and poetry and music would become the instruments to express these formless haunting soul sounds.

Leonard's time of birth is quoted as 'daybreak' (approximately 6.45 a.m.) 'according to the records' and from his mother's memory; however, I have often wondered if the records and the memory have, like Leonard, become romanticized, as this moment happens to be the same as the rising Sun.[4]

Yet, at the same time, muses are rising. The asteroids Erato and Melpomene are named after two of the nine mythological Muses. Each is within 40' of the Ascendant. Erato, the Muse of lyric poetry, expresses the force of love through emotional and romantic poetry. Her sphere of influence is closely linked to Eros, the multi-faceted god who incarnated as a primal force of creation. Synchronistically the asteroid Eros had risen a few minutes earlier and is conjunct Leonard's Anti-Vertex, symbolizing an intoxicating erotic force behind his Virgoan persona. Melpomene is the muse of tragedy who celebrates in dance and song. In fact all the Muses rejoice when they dance with Apollo, the Sun god; so in a way the Ascendant is highly mythologized with the Sun and Muses rising. The Muses are melodic back-up singers to the commanding lead vocals of Neptune and Venus and his mythically inspired Sun–Ascendant arrangement.

Some of Cohen's mortal muses are named in song, some are not. Suzanne is perhaps best known. She was a bohemian dancer who, as in the song, made her gypsy clothes from secondhand fabrics bought at the Salvation Army Store on Rue Notre Dame. Suzanne lived in Old

Montreal near the St Lawrence River. When Leonard visited she would invoke the Spirit of Poetry before the tea and mandarins from Chinatown were served. Suzanne embodied Leonard's inner feminine, ultimately the reflection of his own half-crazy gypsy dancer. Intimate in song, yet never in reality, Suzanne was an early personification of enmeshing love with fantasy.

'Suzanne' was published as a poem in 1966 and recorded by Judy Collins the same year. The opening verse was a poetic account of the time Cohen spent with Suzanne in the summer of 1965, just before the first of three Uranus–Pluto conjunctions in Virgo. Pluto had gone direct, having excavated his Venus–Neptune conjunction over the previous two years; Uranus was also going direct and transiting the conjunction for the last time while Saturn was retrograding in opposition. The muse and the music had been dug up, freed and set to work.

A few years later he would meet the mother of his two children at the Scientology Center in New York. Ironically, her name was Suzanne. When they separated nearly ten years later, Leonard lamented 'where is my gypsy wife tonight?' Fourteen years after his gypsy muse, the first Suzanne, got him on 'her wavelength', Saturn was again in his 12th House, traversing the Venus–Neptune conjunction, just as it had done when he first encountered Lorca and the *duende* of the poet. Personal feelings of love and grief, emptiness and sorrow became entangled with mourning for his inner muse.

It was the 'Summer of Love' in 1967 and Judy Collins was organizing a workshop at the Newport Folk Festival where Leonard would participate and perform. An author, poet, songwriter, he was now coming out as a singer. Another workshop member was Joni Mitchell. Like Leonard, Joni was on the cusp of becoming famous. On 16 July 1967, their paths crossed at the festival and they became lovers. He took her to Montreal and his room at the Chelsea Hotel. Joni also has a Venus–Neptune conjunction. Her Venus at 28°29' Virgo wraps around Leonard's Sun–Ascendant. Both Canadian, they share a Moon in Pisces and the *duende*. But he came from the east and a privileged Jewish urban background, while she was raised a western prairie girl in poor and unsophisticated surroundings. And Joni was her own muse.

For the first time he became the lyrical inspiration for another's music. Joni's Piscean Moon sits exactly on his Vertex, which highlights the poetry of this destined connection. Was Leonard the one who 'stood out like a ruby in a black man's ear' in 'That Song about the Midway', the face she sketched twice 'on the back of a cartoon coaster' in 'A Case of You', or the holy man on the FM radio who she watched sleeping in 'Rainy Night House'? Joni's Chiron at 13°12' Virgo falls right on Leonard's Venus–Neptune conjunction; the pain of an unattainable love may have been stirred for both artists.

Thematic in many of Leonard's lyrics is the split or sometimes the amalgam between the saintly and the sexual feminine, another symptom of Venus–Neptune. But in the song 'Chelsea Hotel', his sexual partner who gives him 'head on the unmade bed' had no angelic aura. When introducing the song in concert he outed Janis Joplin as the woman who shared this one-night stand at the Chelsea Hotel. Being attainable and carnal, she conflicted with the sacred side of his Venus–Neptune. In a 1994 BBC interview, Leonard apologized for the indiscretion of naming Janis; but it was an apology to a ghost. Janis had died on 4 October 1970, as Pluto lay exactly on Leonard's Sun–Ascendant.

In 1994, Chiron transited his Venus–Neptune, soothing some of his own inner relational wounds. Leonard had taken up monastic residence the year before. Dwelling in his 12th House he reflected on his obsession with unrequited love and his inability to reply to what love offered. He self-analysed that it was due to 'some fictional sense of separation'.[5]

He was masterful at weaving the fiction into his lyrics, but not into his personal life. He became caught in a repetitive circuit of desire for the muse he could not have. Or if he could, she ceased to be the muse. For instance, in the late 1960s, while living in New York, he met Nico, lyricist and singer with the Velvet Underground. He longed for this striking, aloof and icy unattainable beauty. Her Mars–Neptune conjunction (at 24° and 22° Virgo) closely touched his Sun–Ascendant. Desiring what he could not have he wrote, 'Something in me yearns to win such a cold and lonesome heroine.'

As the inspiration for the song 'Joan of Arc', Nico was another appearance of Leonard's inner muse. Shaped by Venus–Neptune in Virgo, Leonard's muse was holy when unattainable but unsustainable in the flesh. It was the dilemma he expressed in the same song: 'I long for love and light, but must it come so cruel and oh so bright.' Venus–Neptune may fear being annihilated by the loss of love or drowned in its oceanic feelings. This imagined or fictional loss is repeated in each encounter, making it feel real. In the transition from his love life to his monastic life he began to become aware of what his music had always known.

His five-year relationship with Rebecca De Mornay had faded before entering the monastery. Rebecca has four planets in Virgo straddling Leonard's 12th House. They share Venus in Virgo and her Mars is conjunct his Sun–Ascendant; hence another suitable muse for his soul. Ironically, he remembers meeting her when she was very young at a boarding school in England. Rebecca was about six, but he was in his early thirties performing a concert at the school she attended. Years later when Rebecca asked Leonard how he could remember her twenty-something years ago, he said: 'It was something about your light.'

The light is not light seen with the eyes; the memory is the soul's. A Saturn cycle had passed between the times he wrote 'Suzanne' and saw Rebecca's 'light' and entered the monastery. The monastic life gave Leonard the opportunity to express the Venus–Neptune conjunction in another way. But, while he was becoming spiritually affluent, his financial resources were being siphoned away. When Leonard left the monastery to rejoin the world, it eventually became apparent that his manager Kelley Lynch, a former lover, friend and helpmate, had drained his bank accounts. Love and larceny could also be attributed to his Venus–Neptune conjunction, as the financial affairs of this aspect are difficult to value in a material way. Yes, there is the possibility of deceit and deficit; yet equally there may be magic and salvation.

As a way to regain his financial footing, the theft propelled Leonard back into the public spotlight. On 11 May 2008 at 8.05 p.m., after fourteen years, he took centre stage in Fredericton, Canada to commence his world tour that would last nearly three years. This tour would be drug-free: no escape into alcohol or cigarettes. He would rely on the truth that he now knew: he could not command the music; rather he was its instrument.

When he stepped on stage the applause was thunderous. At that moment Venus was setting; Neptune had reached the lower meridian. And transiting Saturn sat again on the cusp of his 12th House. During the tour it would transit his 12th House for the third time, evoking the first time he encountered the *duende*, the second time when he knew his gypsy wife was his own soul, not a woman, and now. Impoverished, yet enriched, he nervously began to sing his ode to Venus–Neptune, 'Dance me to your beauty with a burning violin …' Uranus was in Pisces (21°49') opposite where it had been during the 'Summer of Love' at the Newport Folk Festival (21°17' Virgo). Reviews of the tour likened his concerts to a love-in, a religious ceremony, a papal visit. The *duende* was moving through Leonard and casting its spell on his audiences. He was its channel, not its casualty.

Leonard not only recouped his losses but he became applauded and appreciated in new places and new ways. The chords of Venus–Neptune had found another octave and the Muses once again danced around the Sun.

1 This is Lorca's own expression – see Federico García Lorca, *In Search of Duende*, New Directions, NY: 2010. See Liel Leibovitz's description in *A Broken Hallelujah*, W.W. Norton & Company, NY: 2014. p.54.
2 This is the title of one of Cohen's musical poems that captures the archetypal essence of this 12th House union. See Leonard Cohen's 'Love Itself', from *Book of Longing*, Penguin, London: 2007, p.54.
3 Sylvie Simmons, *I'm Your Man, The Life of Leonard Cohen*, Harper Collins, New York, NY: 2013, p.4.
4 See John Etherington's article 'Leonard Cohen's "Secret Chart"' from *Apollon* magazine.
5 Sylvie Simmons, *I'm Your Man*, p.413.

112 *The Book of Music Horoscopes*

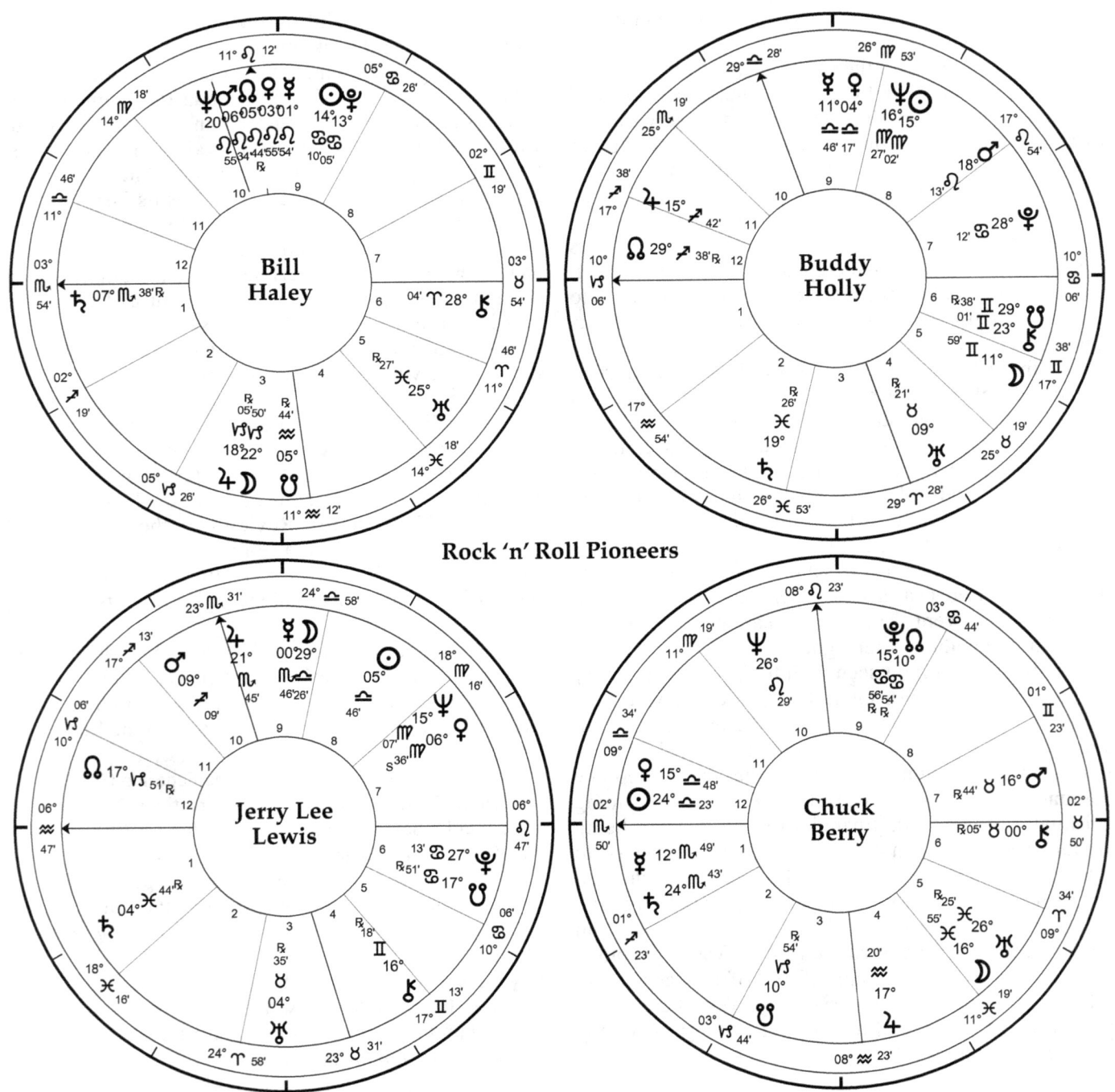

Rock 'n' Roll Pioneers

Music Royalty 113

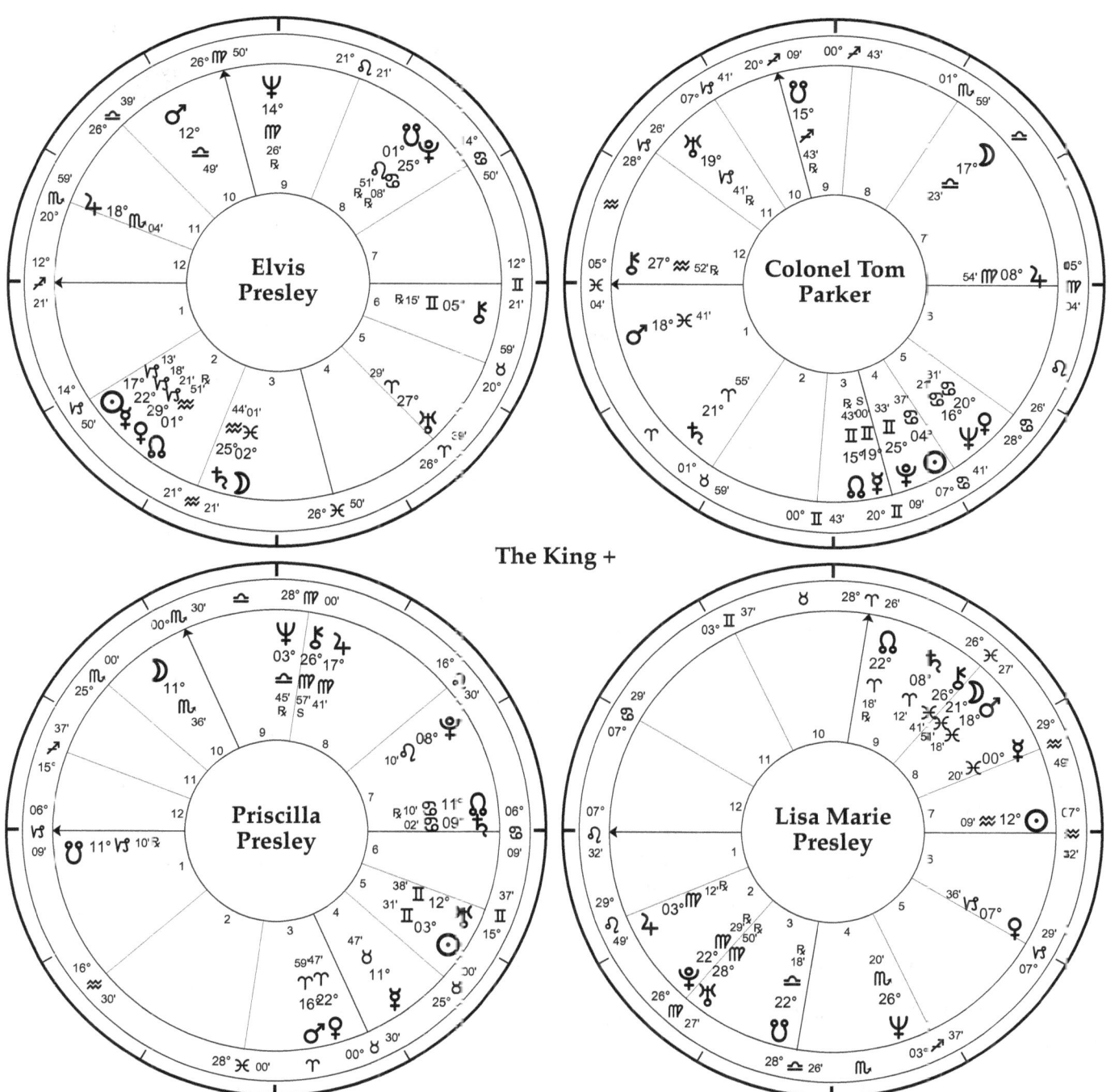

The King +

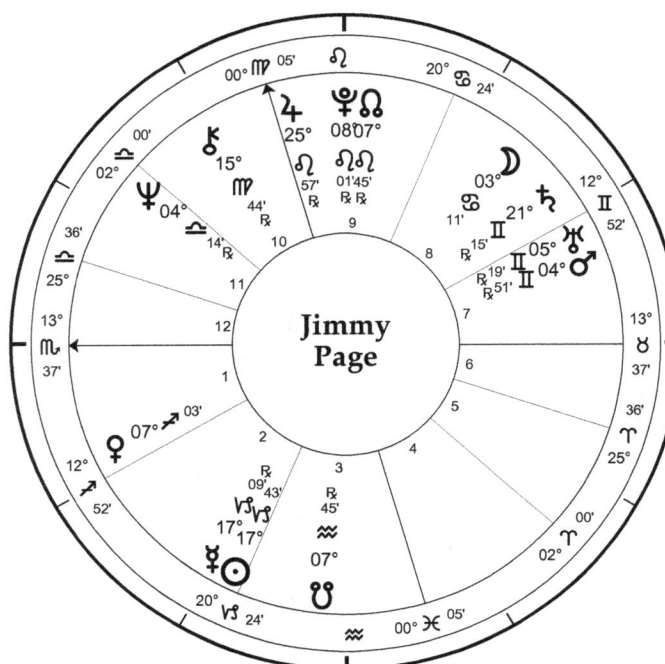

Jimmy Page:
Dwelling with the Devil in the 8th House

Mandi Lockley

Jimmy Page may be one of rock's great guitar heroes, but he's just as well known for the intrigues surrounding his private life: the clandestine love affairs; his fascination with the occult; a need for privacy said to border on the paranoid; his shrewd business sense and reputed meanness with money. Much of this is 8th House stuff, the house associated with psychological death and rebirth, sexual and emotional intimacy, shared feelings and resources, emotional and material security, our values in relation to others, and how we seek to achieve mastery over ourselves and others.

Saturn falls in Jimmy's 8th House. In Gemini, it speaks of the need to apply discipline and patience to his craft. It's easy to imagine a young Jimmy alone in his room for hours, perfecting each chord, tweaking each riff over and over. Jimmy doesn't remember having any playmates until he was five: 'That early isolation probably had a lot to do with the way I turned out. A loner. A lot of people can't be on their own. They get frightened, but isolation doesn't bother me … It gives me a sense of security.' This not only reflects his Saturn but his Moon in Cancer, also in the 8th.

Saturn in Gemini echoes Page's Sun in Capricorn conjunct Mercury, suggesting a deep thinker, which was expressed in his softly spoken seriousness and careful eloquence in interviews. The Sun and Mercury fall in the 2nd House, emphasizing the 2nd–8th axis. According to astrologer Howard Sasportas in *The Twelve Houses* (Flare, 2007), 'The 2nd House sees the face value of something, while the 8th House looks underneath to detect the hidden significance.'

This search for hidden significance seems most evident in Page's involvement in the occult. Why such an obsession? Yes, it was a sign of the times and the environment in which he found himself, but his interest went beyond fashionable dabbling. His 8th House offers some clues.

The 4th-century astrologer Firmicus described the 8th House as the Gate of Hell, and while modern astrology doesn't describe it so lyrically, this part of the nativity shows the need to journey through the metaphorical underworld, to face one's psychological demons, to explore the underlying laws of life. The 8th symbolizes what our own personal underworld feels like. Saturn, that old devil, in the 8th demands that we face our fears; the occult offers a structured pathway.

Legend has it that Led Zeppelin made a pact with the Devil in return for success and Page's obsession with occultist Aleister Crowley did nothing to dispel that rumour. A serious collector of Crowley artefacts, Page purchased Crowley's former home in Loch Ness and financed an occult bookshop, stocking it with Crowley's writings.

Here's Jimmy, speaking from his 8th: 'Magic is very important if people can go through it … We're all still seeking the truth – the search goes on.' Seeking the truth through magic, if you can face it. What could be more Saturn in Gemini in the 8th?

In 1972, Jimmy bought the gothic-style Tower House in London, famed for its astrology hall with a zodiac painted on the ceiling. It's said that Page doesn't trust easily and when he agreed to write the soundtrack for Kenneth Anger's *Lucifer Rising*, he let Anger use Tower House, but the filmmaker complained of being confined to the basement – he was forbidden access to the rest of the house. Page's 8th House planets – Saturn and the protective, security-conscious Moon in Cancer – along with Scorpio rising describe this lack of trust and suggest that Page was protecting not only his privacy but his home's valuable contents, too.

After Page and Anger fell out (Page's compositions were never used), Anger described Tower House as an 'evil fantasy house' and cast doubt on Page's occult credentials, saying he had 'turned into an undisciplined, rich dilettante, at least as far as magic and any serious belief in Aleister Crowley's work was concerned.'

Was his occult interest only an aesthetic, reflected in stage costumes embellished with dragons, astrological glyphs and his personal ZoSo symbol? (The meaning of ZoSo was never revealed, if it ever had a meaning, but is thought to be adapted from the alchemical symbol for Saturn.) His chart suggests he did take magic seriously. But was he a magician? True to the spirit of his 8th House and Scorpio rising, he will probably never tell, but here's what former girlfriend Lori Maddox said: 'You'd hear a lot about Jimmy being a sorcerer or a wizard ... the only evidence I saw of that was just what I felt over myself ... I can't explain it, but I think he's got a lot of power ... I always felt like I was under his spell.'

Page's relationship with Lori reads like a re-enactment of the story of Hades and Persephone, a myth for the 8th House. Lori was fourteen when an obsessed Jimmy had his roadie bring her to him during his June 1972 American tour. Arriving at his hotel suite, she encountered a devilish Saturn in the 8th sitting in the corner of a dimly lit room, tapping a cane and looking 'mysterious and weird'. She was also meeting his Scorpio Ascendant, intimidating yet intriguing.

Being on the groupie scene, Lori must have known it was a rare honour to be invited into Jimmy's private lair and, once inside, she encountered his deep 8th House Cancer Moon. Lori said, 'He's the most romantic person in the world. He's so sweet and gentle, like the perfect man ... And it was really innocent, beautiful, perfect love ... It was like a fantasy or fairy tale.' When Jimmy met Lori, transiting Neptune was making a quincunx to his Moon, intensifying the natal square with Neptune, which describes romantic idealism, emotional naïveté, an insatiable need for emotional nourishment and a longing to merge with another.

But 8th House and Venus–Pluto relationships are also an arena for destruction and control, and at the start of their affair transiting Venus (in a retrograde phase) made three conjunctions to Page's natal Saturn. Lori was under age and like Persephone in the Underworld she was kept locked away at all times over fears he would be deported if their affair was discovered. It was, however, an enduring romance. Once he had her in his realm, perhaps he would not have been willing to let her go easily.

Jimmy's 2nd House Sun and Mercury in Capricorn emphasize the issues around money, values and possessions shown by his 8th House Moon and Saturn, suggesting a respectful approach, a mindset that enough is never enough, a need to hold on to what is earned. However, the ruler of his 2nd, Jupiter in Leo, is on his MC and reflects the substantial amounts of money he made from performing.

Back in the early 1960s, seventeen-year old Page earned £20 a week with his first band the Crusaders, at a time when bus drivers earned £10. Said to be too tight-fisted to get his own place, he stayed with his parents until in 1967, by then a wealthy man, he purchased a boathouse on the Thames – a good choice for his watery Moon. When Led Zeppelin was formed there in 1968, his penniless bandmates were shocked when he asked them to help pay for beer and food during rehearsals.

Notorious for his shrewd business sense, Page ran Led Zeppelin as a commercial enterprise from day one. The band brokered record-breaking fees for their US tours and in October 1968 manager Peter Grant negotiated an unprecedented royalty deal. Jupiter, transiting Page's 10th House, had just squared his

Saturn, a transit bringing opportunity and a realization of ambition, but also commitment and responsibility.

In January 1975, Led Zeppelin began their inevitable tax exile from the UK. Page had Saturn transiting the 8th opposing his Sun and Mercury in Capricorn in the 2nd, symbolizing responsibility and limitation around earned money and assets.

Speaking in 2014, Page explained why the band didn't carry on after drummer John Bonham died in 1980. 'Led Zeppelin was an affair of the heart. Each of the members was important to the sum total of what we were ... And what were we going to do? Create a role for somebody, say, "You have to do this, this way?" That wouldn't be honest.'[1] With Moon in Cancer in the 8th Bonham's death must have felt like the loss of a close family member and the intimate connection between the four bandmates would have seemed impossible to replicate with anyone else.

After Zeppelin disbanded in December 1980, Jimmy became a recluse. That need for a private emotional cleansing period, a shedding of baggage and a sifting through the rubble of the past is not uncommon for 8th House people; it's often deemed necessary for one's 'survival', to enable psychological rebirth. Eventually Jimmy returned to music and has again become part of the rock firmament, but even as a silver-haired grandee he will never shake off his status as the dark man of rock.

What comes across strongly in Page's biography is that his answer to dealing with tough times was to work hard. He may be a romantic idealist, a product of a wild era, but his Saturn/Capricorn discipline and pragmatism saw him through and no doubt saved him from a Moon–Neptune/8th House descent into emotional chaos. Saturn in Gemini was always there to take a firm hold of his hand during his psychological journey through the underworld. The old devil has his uses.

1 http://www.rollingstone.com/music/features/jimmy-page-led-zeppelin-was-an-affair-of-the-heart-20141028#ixzz3QWGCpBUN

Quotes and anecdotes from *Hammer of the Gods The Led Zeppelin Saga* (Sidgwick and Jackson, 1985).

Sphinxes of the Music World: The Leo–Virgo Connection

Victor Olliver

Bowie has it. But not Elton John. Kate Bush, Prince, Grace Jones, Madonna, Mick Jagger, Ozzy Osbourne – yes, they've all got it. But no, not Lady Gaga. The 'it' is mystique, the veil that tantalizes with peekaboo flash and concealment. Not all rock and pop stars have to have it – Sir Elton's done all right – but it is pure gold in building lucrative brand worship. Horoscopically, does mystique (from the Ancient Greek μυστικός [mustikós, 'secret, mystic']) have a birth chart signature common to image-driven songsters whose cool (if not glacial impenetrability) and slippery personae are part of the come-on?

I wondered about this myself as I prepared to write about the flamboyant but puzzling French singer-songwriter Mylène Farmer, who in 30-odd years has sold over 30 million records. Her stunning stage shows anticipate Gaga's baroque extravaganzas by a decade or two yet a mummified pharaoh is an open book compared to mysterious Mylène.

In the Francophone world – and in Russia and Eastern Europe – Farmer commands an awe that her declared all-time heroine, Hollywood's elusive 'Swedish Sphinx' Greta Garbo, would recognize in its passion and dedication. She dedicated a song to Garbo ('Greta') on her debut album *Cendres de Lune* in 1986. Plainly, Farmer identifies with Garbo's statuesque otherliness and need to be let alone.

So to start with, I examined Farmer's and Garbo's birth charts in my astrological probe of mystique.

The Sun in Virgo duo each has four planets in Earth, the element traditionally linked to practicality, to the realization of dreams. Both have Earth Grand Trines linked to the chart's career point, assuring fairly easy success in all kinds of creative work (such as music) and material comfort, though warning of complacency. Both have only one planet in Water: Neptune, symbolic of glamour and illusion, among other things. In astrology,

Music Royalty 117

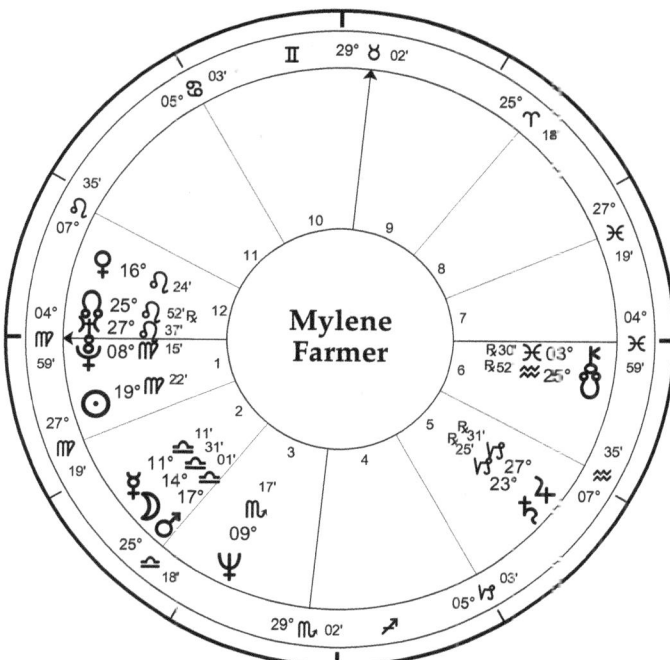

Water represents emotion/feelings, intuition, empathy, receptivity, creativity, imagination.

Capricorn David Bowie, arguably the greatest modern theatrical pop and rock star ever, also has just one planet in Water: Jupiter, which traditionally co-rules Pisces with Neptune.

The virtual absence of Water in these charts (and those below) may make it an especial focus of compensation. In psychology, 'compensation' is described as a mechanism by which an individual attempts to make up for some real or imagined deficiency of personality or behaviour by substituting a different form of behaviour. If a 'weak' Water horoscope describes an individual beset by notable challenges in establishing a rapport with other people – and Bowie, Garbo and Farmer were or are painfully shy, particularly in childhood, seeking escape into private worlds – then creativity, performance and theatrical image projection can be interpreted as counterbalancing expressions of Water. And, in a sense,

this counterbalancing forges a rapport with others, albeit an impersonal or distant one: part of 'mystique'.

The charts of Farmer and Garbo are both ruled by Mercury (Garbo's rising sign is Gemini; Farmer's Virgo), an indicator of 'living in the head', of self-preoccupation but also of huge curiosity and scepticism, logical analysis and cool decision-making. The basic Virgo nature of Farmer and Garbo analyses, dissects and evaluates: activities of essential dispassion. A cool detachment exists in the heart of the Virgin. In general, the behaviour of both stars – controlling, independent, curious and 'perverse' or seemingly capricious and driven by personal, causative thought – fits the Mercurial label.

At this point it's apposite to bring in the late, inscrutable, low-Water King of Pop, Michael Jackson. Both the Jackson and Farmer birth charts (Bowie's also) have well populated Leos (including Venus and Uranus), boosting theatricality and image impact. And both have super-conjunctions or concentrations of planets and points across Leo–Virgo, combining fiery

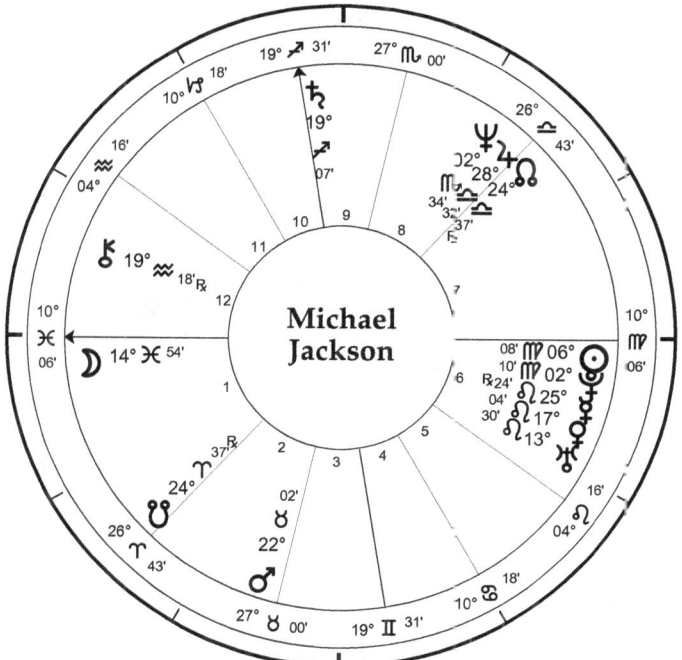

projection with a cool, analytical and controlling inner self: the perfected Sun–Mercury marriage at the heart of the sphinx, as we shall see.

And since we're thinking of a certain type of glacial or highly self-controlled theatrical performer, what about stalwart pop goddess Madonna? Her birth chart, too, has a Leo–Virgo preponderance with six planets (the Moon, Mercury, Pluto, the Sun, Uranus and Venus) in those two signs. Like Garbo and Farmer, she has just one planet in Water – once again, Neptune. Her chart ruler is Mercury (also rising) with Virgo on the Ascendant.

I mentioned earlier that Garbo was known as the Swedish Sphinx. The monolithic provenance of 'sphinx' is of course the Great Sphinx of Giza itself. The word 'sphinx' derives from the Egyptian term *shesep ankh*, meaning 'living image' (according to British Egyptologist and linguist Sir Alan Gardiner). The limestone Giza colossus is thought by many specialists to be a representation of Leo and Virgo in its lion's body (Leo – spirit) and human head (Virgo – human form; possibly Isis).

It seems more than coincidental – but also irrationally puzzling to me – that this Leo–Virgo Frankenstein's monster mystery finds a mirror in the Leo–Virgo horoscopes of modern celebrity sphinxes. The union of Leo–Virgo – organic or mineral – appears to result in conundrums in its most successful expression.

Let's spot a few more examples. Freddie Mercury? Most definitely. All his stage flamboyance as rock band Queen's lead vocalist yielded to a circumspect sensitivity once the limelight had dimmed. He was a Virgo with four planets (Sun, Mercury, Saturn and Pluto) in Leo–Virgo and he had no Water in his chart. Taurus Grace Jones? Certainly. A *Guardian* profile labelled her a creature of the night, a 'pensionable vampire', in a mythical world of her own creation called Graceland. Jones (19 May 1948) has three heavyweight planets (Mars, Saturn and Pluto) in Leo–Virgo – and very little Water. Near-mute Prince? Yes, again. Leo–Virgo bestride the top of his Sun-in-Gemini horoscope with mystifying but forceful Pluto in Leo (personalized) bang on his career point Midheaven, right on the Leo–Virgo cusp between the

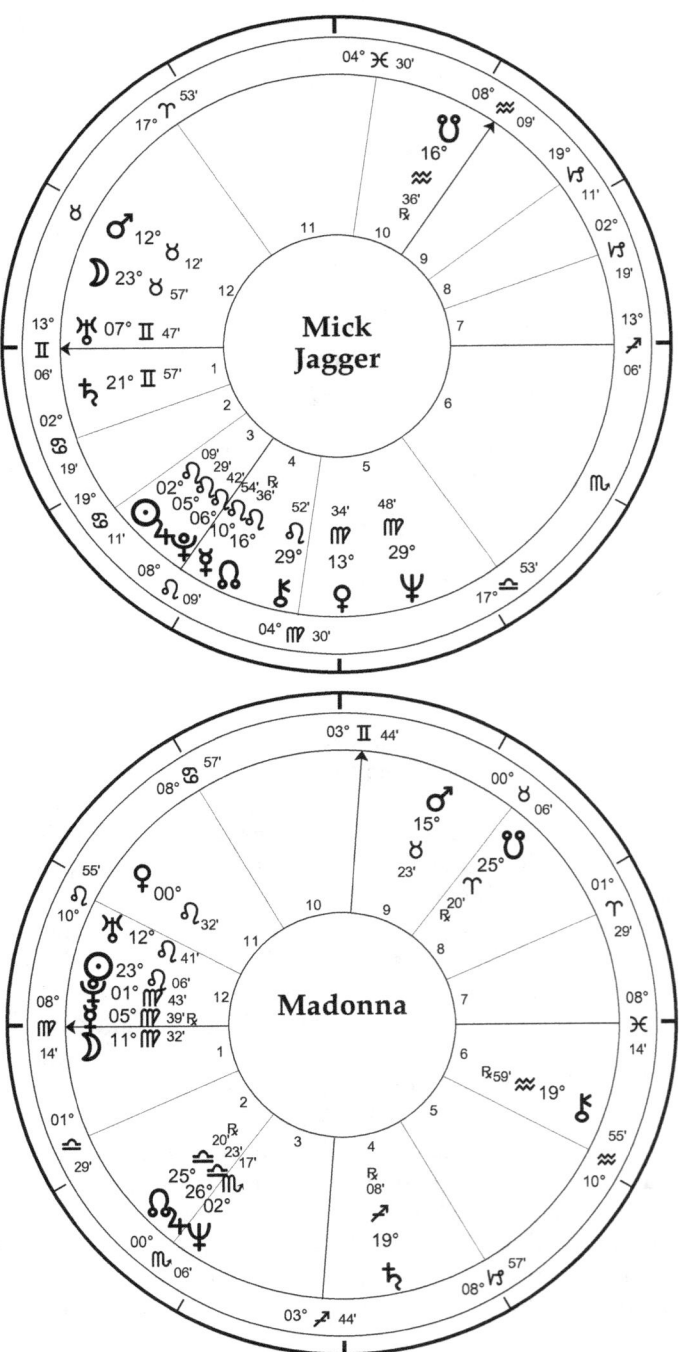

the 10th and 11th Houses, missing Virgo by just two minutes.

The Garbo of British contemporary music is Kate Bush (another self-confessed Farmer pin-up), also a Leo (30 July 1958) with only two planets (Venus and Neptune) in Water. Like Farmer, she's prone to disappearing for years between albums. Bush's Earth–Fire chart demonstrates a link between the two signs and this elusive sphinxlike quality, comprising one two-planet conjunction apiece in Leo (Sun–Uranus) and Virgo (Mercury–Pluto).

Leo Sir Mick Jagger parades himself on and off stage, yet actually says very little for public consumption: he hides behind teasing ironic humour, and has attained a certain kind of impenetrable world glamour. Six planets (Sun, Mercury, Venus, Jupiter, Neptune and Pluto) occupy Leo–Virgo, which also shelter the True North Node, Pars Fortuna and Chiron. He has no Water and his chart is Mercury-ruled with Gemini rising.

And what of shape-shifting Bowie? If anyone's horoscope should hold the Leo–Virgo signature it's his. At first glance, perhaps not. As in Prince's chart, Bowie's Virgo is unoccupied. Oh, but hang on. According to a mid-way estimate of two quoted birth times (9 a.m. and 9.30 a.m.), two of the three planets in Leo that form a bridging stellium over his Descendant are in his 6th House – the traditional zone of Virgo. His chart opens up a different Leo–Virgo variant on the showy–mystery theme. With Aquarius rising, his personalized Uranus is in Gemini – another variant, this time on Mercury's role in a sphinx's chart.

Some may question Madonna's inclusion as a sphinx. Her extrovert performance sexuality alone might appear to blast away mystique. A closer study of her personality reveals much complexity, not least in the way she has evolved through many alter egos since the 1980s, all the while exhibiting a distant relationship with her public. The sheer variety of her work alerts one to her readiness to role-play and to adorn masks for commercial–creative purposes. Her planetary triple (Venus, Uranus and the Sun) in hot-blooded Leo is not wasted even as her Virgo Mercury–Moon graces her work with research and practical calculation. Sting once described her as 'inscrutable' in her transition from 'sex goddess [Leo?] to a yogi [Virgo?]'. She's a one-off not easily read at all.

The above names were first selected blindly. I asked myself: who among the celebrated fit my inscrutable, theatrical, image-creating criteria? Chart analyses of the people I chose followed. The names were not cherry-picked from a mass of celebrity horoscopes to confirm a bias. I was strict about the required elements of sphinxes, and most performers do not measure up. For instance, Aries Sir Elton John is a spectacular stage pop monarch: he has two planets (Saturn and Pluto) in Leo and nothing in Virgo – but then no one would describe him as a sphinx. What don't we know about this blokey soccer-loving living legend? He's walking tantrums and tiaras (or was). Virgo's restraint – or gag – simply does not exist in his planetary make-up.

Mylène Farmer, I discovered, is just one of many Leo–Virgo sphinxes adept at dazzling display with smoke and mirrors. And they're not confined to music: Kevin Spacey (26 July 1959), Tom Cruise (3 July 1962), Anna Wintour (3 November 1949) and so many other cryptic celebs embody the Isis and the Lion in their charts. A thought which perhaps adds to the mystery.

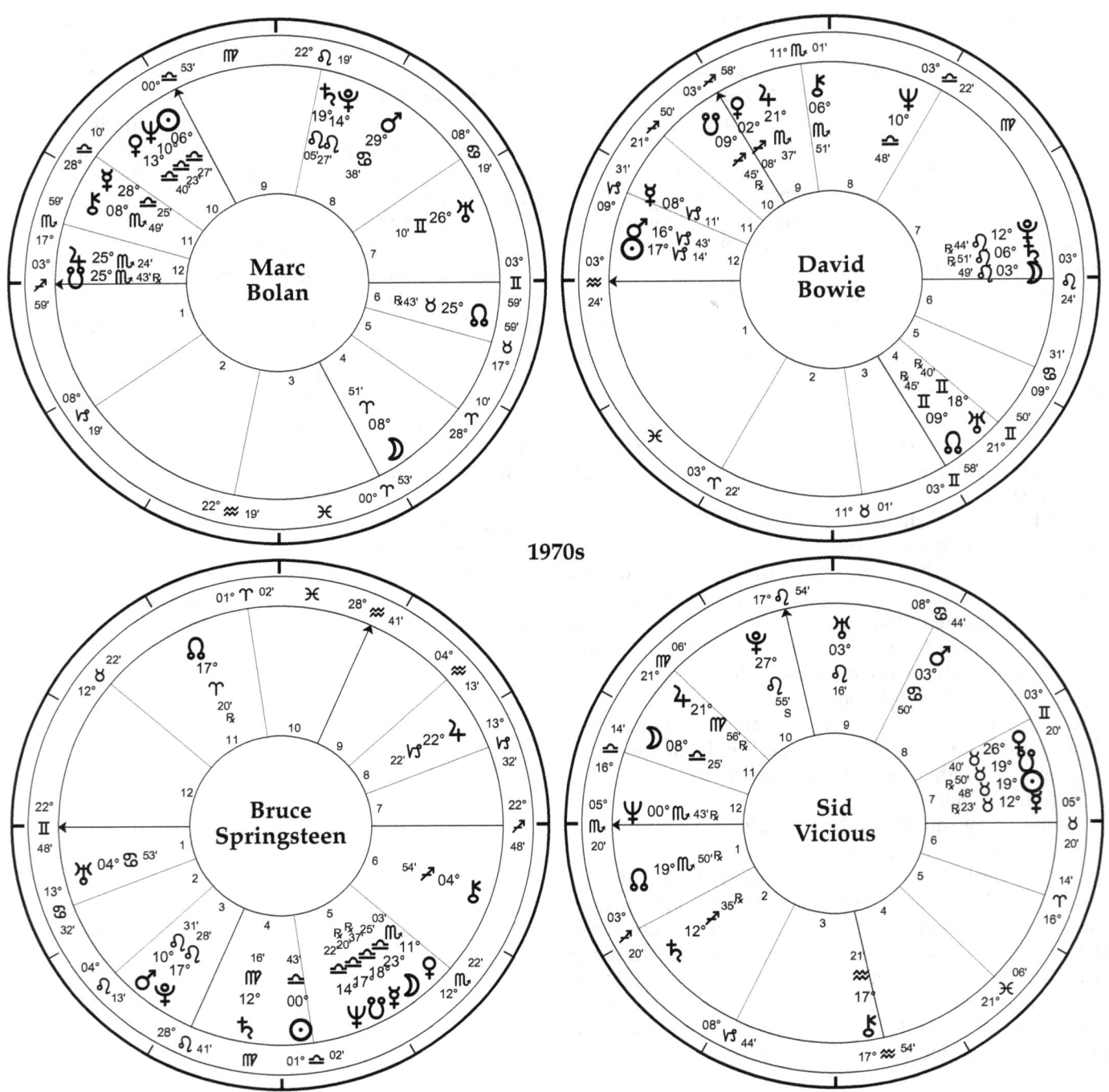

1970s

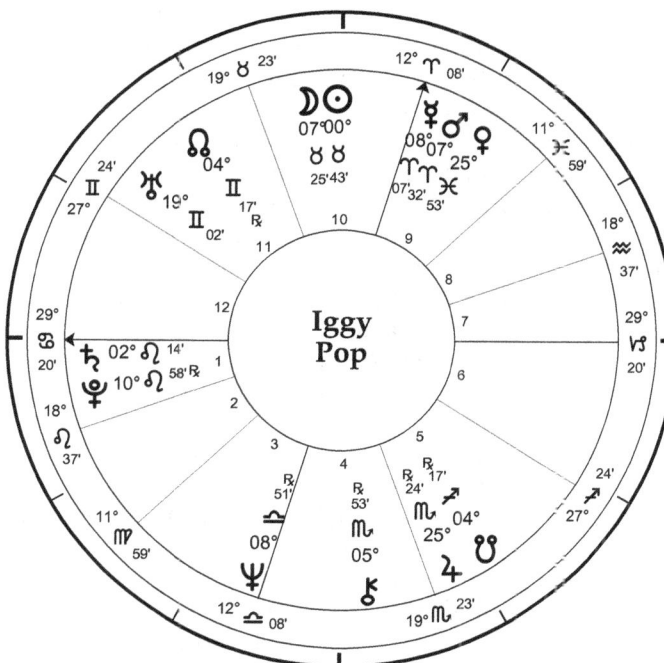

Lust for Life: the Fertile Ground of David Bowie and Iggy Pop's Friendship

Diana McMahon-Collis

David Bowie and Iggy Pop were born in 1947 into different material lifestyles. Bowie grew up in a conventional, middle-class English household (4th House ruler Mercury is in Capricorn conjunct the Sun and Mars), while Pop was raised in a USA trailer park (4th House ruler Venus is in rootless Pisces trine freewheeling Jupiter). Yet they shared common creative – sometimes destructive – impulses in a relationship that produced acclaimed music and a personal friendship that enabled each other to recover from addiction. This essay follows that thread of friendship, collaboration and competition over several decades – one that provided often surprising creative and financial vitality.

Bowie and Pop shared similar intellectual interests in avant-garde and performance art and worked together, in Berlin, on a series of new ventures, driven by Bowie's (self-admitted) desire to use Pop as a 'guinea pig' for electronic music experimentation. Pop has the Sun and Moon in Taurus; Bowie has the Sun, Mercury and Mars in Capricorn. Intertwining elements in their lives and careers include the common ground of hard work and a desire to manifest creativity – both traits found in Earth signs.

Their friendship blossomed, initially, through admiring one another's music and a meeting in New York in 1971, just before Bowie – enjoying a Jupiter transit to his 10th House – released Hunky Dory, the album that would ensure ten years of success with RCA Records.

Musical paths crossed more firmly in 1976, with Bowie inviting Pop – whose career had been flagging due to alcohol and heroin excesses in his band – to gig on his *Station to Station* tour. Bowie took Pop under his semi-parental wing (his Moon–Saturn–Pluto on the Descendant is close to Pop's own 1st House Saturn–Pluto). The protective embrace and generosity of a warm Leo Moon made a nurturing difference to Pop's failing self-image of invincibility. Pop had recently exited rehab in a mental institution, where Bowie was one of his few visitors. The transit of Jupiter in March 1976 to Pop's natal Sun in the 10th House reflected his changing fortunes, and Bowie's grand gesture about the tour helped Pop back on his musical feet.

Bowie's chart has narcotic Neptune square shape-shifting Mercury (conjunct volatile Mars and creative Sun) straddling the blurry 12th House. Cracks in his life were less visible, but he was aware of his own struggles. Barely surviving on a meagre diet consisting mostly of milk (Moon–Saturn sparsity) in LA, which he termed the 'hellhole' (associating it with paranoia and terror due to drug-induced hallucinations), he missed the groundedness of Europe and moved himself to sanitary Switzerland, as his Moon progressed (in April 1976) to health-orientated, Earthy Virgo.

The men's charts share the fixed placements of Jupiter in Scorpio and Saturn in Leo – the most determined Water and Fire signs respectively. This combination plumbs the depths (Scorpio) and finds the gold (Leo) hidden in the sludge – a potent symbol for near-drowning/destruction (Scorpio), followed by a bounce back to success (Jupiter/Leo). Over the years, these planetary gifts kept on giving professionally – from one man to the other. Pop's 'China Girl' (from his Bowie-produced 1977 solo album, *The Idiot*) became a best-seller for Bowie (who co-wrote it) in 1983, while the Bowie-produced tracks 'Nightclubbing' and 'Lust for Life' were resurrected for the 1996 soundtrack to the movie *Trainspotting*, reigniting interest in Pop's back catalogue.

In Berlin, a quick tour for Pop's *The Idiot* (which ended on 16 April 1977) was followed rapidly by recording sessions – with Bowie producing Pop's next album, *Lust for Life*. Pop said it took only eight days to write, record and mix the album. He got by on very little sleep – elevated, ambitious Mercury–Mars in Aries racing to the finishing post – not wanting any Venus in Pisces-type confusion to muddy the waters: 'Bowie's a hell of a fast guy … I realized I had to be quicker than him, otherwise whose album was it gonna be?'[1]

Pop spoke of Bowie's 'executive ability', attributing a main talent for 'repositioning the brand' as his key to success.[2] Bowie's exalted Mars in Capricorn conjunct the Sun describes 'commanding authority', which might have echoed Pop's own father's dominating personality and workaholic drives. Either way, it appears Pop helped Bowie as much as Bowie helped him. Pop's spontaneous method of devising lyrics inspired Bowie to improvise his own words on *Heroes*, Bowie's next personal album project.[3]

Pop also referred to Bowie's 'cultural vampirism' and Bowie described himself (in a 1976 *Playboy* interview and variously) as 'a tasteful thief', 'an artistic plagiarist' and 'musical magpie', rather than an original thinker. Ironically, his chart shows original Uranus in Gemini, a sign often described as having magpie connotations. Even so, Bowie, who sadly died in 2016, continues to be remembered as the great innovator he no doubt was – Aquarius rising and three key, personal planets in cardinal Capricorn. With Mars and the Sun quincunx Uranus, he may have had a blind spot about his own originality.

Notably, overall, both men's charts have Mars in equally strengthened and compromised positions. Pop's Mars (ruler of the MC and conjunct Mercury) is dignified in its own sign of Aries, desiring to be fast and first. But it opposes Neptune in Libra, where the lines of individual genius become hazy. Bowie's 12th House Mars conjuncts Mercury too, but also conjuncts the Sun, which traditionally is 'combust' or burnt up/impotent. The three planets in the 12th square Neptune, so the lines are again blurry – but the emphasis on the 12th House suggests a necessary spiritual translation of creativity where single egos cannot rule. The solid path of success is the result of a team effort – even if a somewhat competitive one, at times.

When Bowie died in January 2016, Iggy Pop told *The New York Times*, '[Bowie] salvaged me from certain professional and maybe personal annihilation … He resurrected me. He was more of a benefactor than a friend in a way most people think of friendship. He went a bit out of his way to bestow some good karma on me.' Pop compared the relationship to *My Fair Lady's* Henry Higgins and Eliza Doolittle: 'He subsumed my personality, lyrically, on that first album.' In *Rolling Stone* (27 January 2016), Iggy said, 'He appreciated oddballs – people who looked different and spoke in a certain way. He had a very strong curiosity and had very absolute aesthetic values.' On Twitter, he said it simply: 'David's friendship was the light of my life.'

1 *The Complete David Bowie*, Nicholas Pegg, 2016.
2 *Starman: David Bowie – the Definitive Biography*, Paul Trynka, 2012.
3 *Iggy Pop: Open Up and Bleed: The Biography*, Paul Trynka, 2008.

Music Royalty

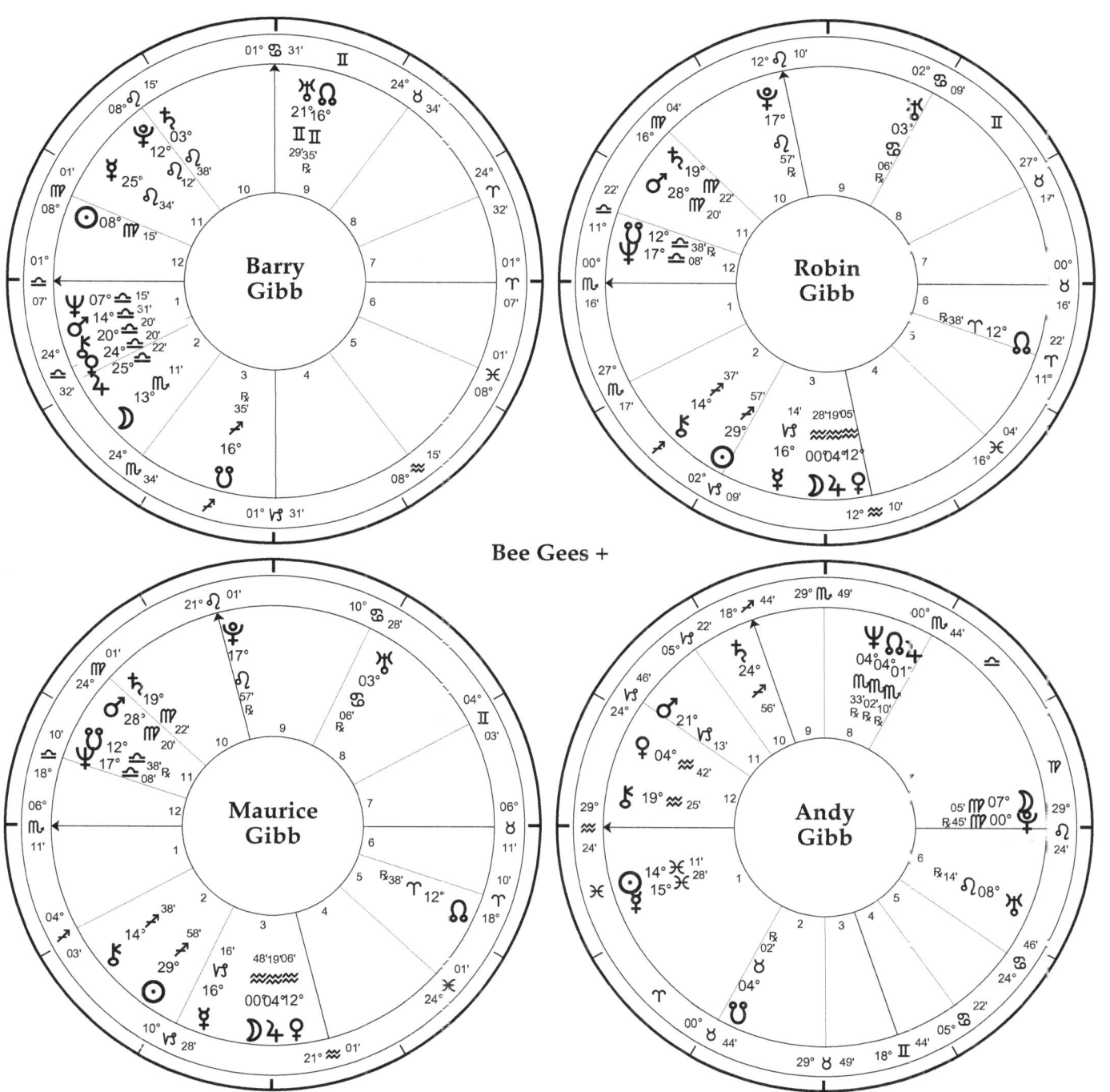

Bee Gees +

124 *The Book of Music Horoscopes*

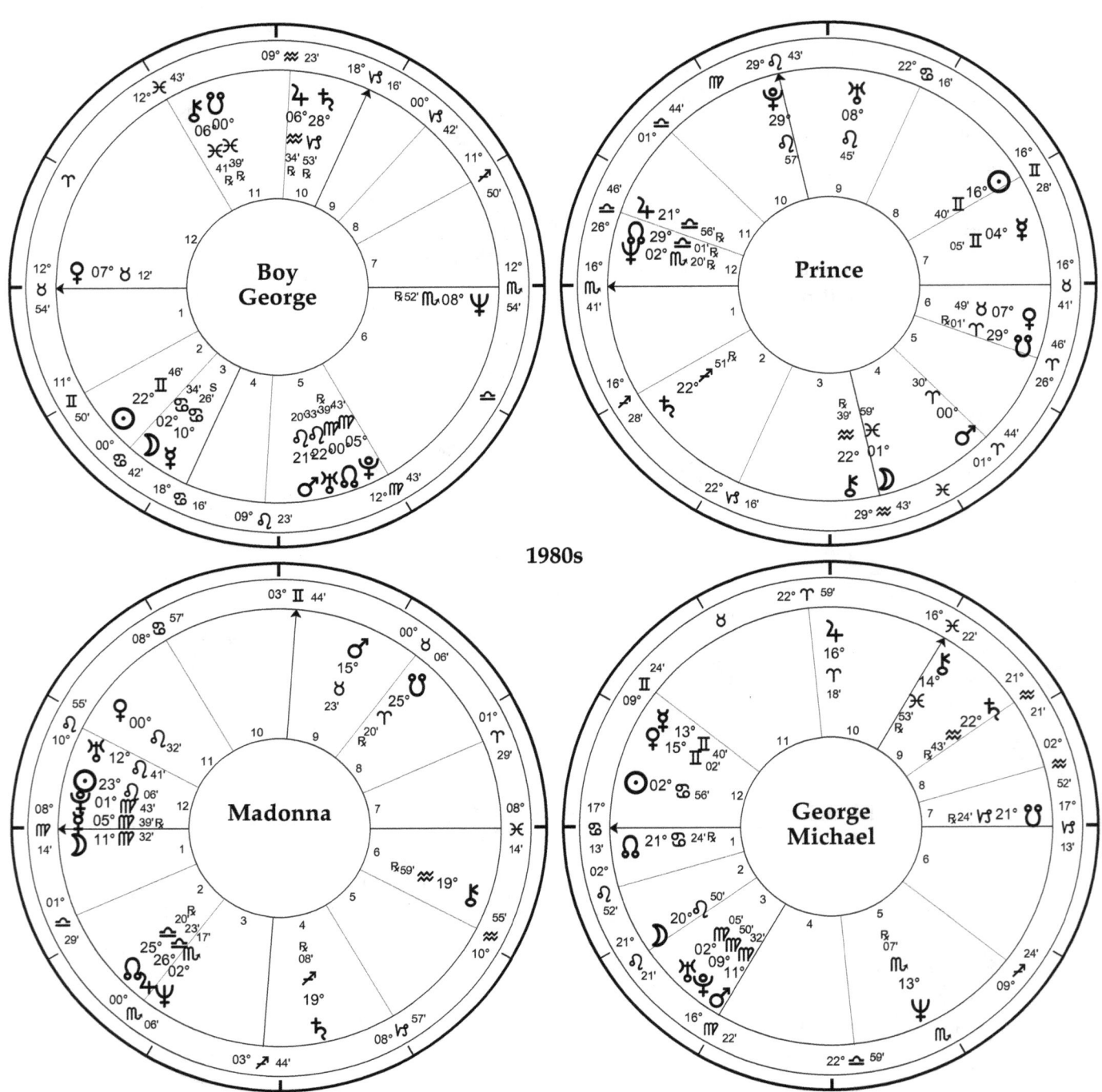

1980s

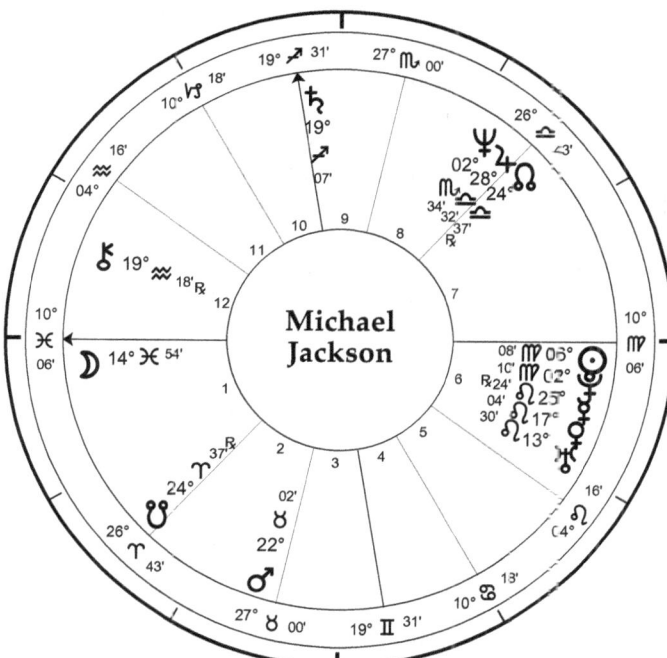

Michael Jackson: Liquid Precision, Fallen Angel

Glenn Perry

As everyone surely knows, Michael Jackson suffered a fatal cardiac arrest on 25 June 2009 at his rented Los Angeles home. Only a few hours earlier, he was excited about rehearsals for his heralded comeback tour. Jackson was in the final stages of preparation for his 'This Is It' concert series – an unprecedented fifty shows slated to start on 13 July at the London O2 Arena. It was to be an exhilarating overview of his entire musical career. Jackson hoped it would not only redeem his public image but also regenerate his sagging finances.

Astrologically, it seems oddly fitting that feverish preparation for this series of redemptive performances might have proved too much for his fragile heart. Performance and the heart are both ruled by the Sun, whereas Pluto is the planet of death and rebirth. In Jackson's horoscope, his Sun is conjunct Pluto, suggesting that creative performance is linked to regenerative power. Unfortunately, time ran out for Michael; there would be no rebirth, no regeneration of image or renewal of wealth, only death.

Jackson was born during a Full Moon in Pisces right on the Ascendant, indicating an otherworldly, translucent femininity immediately apparent in his personality and style. Yet, the Moon's square to Saturn ensured that the delicacy of his emotional nature would be severely stressed by an authority figure with harsh, unrelentingly high standards: his father. The Moon square Saturn symbolizes not only the impingement of adult responsibilities into a truncated childhood but the resulting loneliness and despair that haunted Michael his entire adult life.

Jackson's three planets in Leo (Uranus, Venus and Mercury) correspond, in brief, to a dazzlingly original and brilliant artistic creativity. With Pluto conjunct the Sun in Virgo, they form a five-planet stellium in the 6th House. A stellium is an aspect of intensely focused force, like a troupe of wild-eyed dancers moving forwards with ferocious energy. Jackson's videos for 'Thriller' and 'Beat It' capture exactly this image. Also noteworthy is the Plutonic dimension of underworld hoodlums coming together for gang fights in the videos for both 'Bad' and 'Beat It'. Even more telling is the image of zombies emerging from graves to dance in unison down a nightmarish street in 'Thriller' The exacting precision of his Virgo stellium is evident in the perfectly orchestrated movement of the choreographed dancers; each moving in exact mimicry of Jackson's every gesture and gyration. His performance in these videos – as lead singer-dancer – is a fitting expression of the solar component of the stellium. The King of Pop spent most of his life honing, refining and improving such creative productions.

With Jackson's Sun and Mercury in mutual reception, all the planets involved in the stellium are contained in a feedback loop that is self-stimulating and self-reinforcing. This further underscores how his stellium is a closed system of concentrated creative power. As he put it, 'Being on stage is magic. When it's time to go off, I don't want to. I could stay up there forever.'[1]

After achieving six Top 10 albums with his brothers, Michael went on to a successful solo career. In 1979, when he turned 21, Jackson teamed up with music arranger Quincy Jones to produce an entirely different sound. *Off the Wall* was the first authentically Michael Jackson album. Gone were the infectious melodies and upbeat lyrics of the feel-good, bubblegum soul that propelled the Jackson Five to the heights of teenybopper stardom. *Off the Wall* had raw, primitive rhythms that were more intense and blatantly sexual than anything that preceded it, and more befitting of Michael's Sun conjunct Pluto.

It was also the year that he had his first plastic surgery, as if to put a punctuation mark on his childhood and announce to the world that a new, different Michael Jackson had arrived. Sun–Pluto signifies Jackson's compulsion to reform, remake and reinvent his ego-identity, which is reflected in the fact that he had an estimated 25 facial operations, ultimately coming to look like one of the ghoulish phantoms that populated his 'Thriller' video.

With the release of the album *Thriller* in 1982, Jackson's career went stratospheric. It sold 100 million copies – the biggest-selling album of all time – and earned him seven Grammy Awards. That same year, Michael transformed the entertainment world with a singular performance at Motown's 25th anniversary show. As he sang his hit 'Billie Jean', he electrified the crowd with a levitating dance move that made him appear to be going forwards while he was moving backwards. This surreal dance step – the Moonwalk – caused an immediate sensation and seemed to encapsulate Jackson's emerging status as a performer without limits.

The very name of the dance step – Moonwalk – reflects his Pisces Moon on the Ascendant. The Ascendant sign (and any planets in the 1st) reveals what is associated with the most primitive and instinctive of impulses – assertion and the need to survive. With the Moon on the Ascendant, lunar qualities were pronounced in Jackson's appearance and basic orientation to life. He was consistently described as sweet, gentle and sensitive – qualities we attribute to the Moon, but which are ill-fitted to 1st House requirements. Many wondered whether Jackson was strong enough to survive the harsh realities of life.

The Moon's sign position, Pisces, describes how Michael expressed his need for emotional connection. As the Moon is a Watery planet (ruling Cancer) and Pisces is a Watery sign, we can expect that themes of flow, fluidity and plasticity are likely to be pronounced. Given that Pisces is also Jackson's rising sign, these qualities were especially apparent in the way that he instinctively moved and surrendered to his music, felt its rhythms coursing through his body and moved with an instinctive grace that seemed surreal.

Martin Scorsese, who directed the music video of 'Bad', said that watching Jackson was like seeing quicksilver in motion. 'Every step he took was absolutely precise [Sun in Virgo] and fluid [Moon in Pisces] at the same time.'[2] One reviewer described Jackson: 'Aided by the burn and flash of silvery suits, he seems to change molecular shape at will, all robot angles one second and rippling curves the next. So sure is the body that his eyes are often closed, his face turned upward to some unseen muse.'[3] Film director Steven Spielberg referred to Michael as 'an emotional star child', which is an interesting choice of words in light of the aforementioned configuration – Moon (child) and Pisces (transcendent, cosmic). In fact, Spielberg chose Jackson to narrate the soundtrack to his film, *E.T.*, knowing that Michael would instinctively identify with E.T.'s plight. The problem was that Michael would always cry when he got to the part where E.T. was dying. This reflects the extraordinary emotional sensitivity of the Moon in Pisces on the Ascendant. Tearfulness also overwhelmed him when he sang certain songs, including 'She's Out of My Life', which made recording difficult. 'Every time we did it, I'd look up ... and Michael would be crying,' said Quincy Jones.[4]

When high-functioning, the Moon in Pisces can be a conduit to a higher consciousness. The individual is readily able to enter a flow state and become a vehicle for a transcendent intelligence that comes through the emotional body. Jackson explained that many of his songs came to him in dreams.

I wake up from dreams and go, 'Wow, put this down on paper.' The whole thing is strange. You hear the words, everything is right there in front of your face. And you say to yourself, 'I'm sorry, I just didn't write this. It's there already.' That's why I hate to take credit for the songs I've written. I feel that somewhere, someplace, it's been done and I'm just a courier bringing it into the world. I really believe that.[5]

Also worth mentioning is Saturn in Sagittarius at the Midheaven. As previously described, Saturn's square to his Moon would seem to correspond to the imposition of adult responsibilities into a shrunken childhood. Saturn's sign position constitutes an area of serious focus, often corresponding to an aspect of life that proves frustrating and burdensome. Sagittarius, of course, rules the domain of legality, courts, lawsuits, ethics and morality.

Clearly, Saturn in Sagittarius correlates to Jackson's chronic legal troubles, including two cases of child sexual molestation and numerous other lawsuits involving breach of contract.

The Midheaven signifies one's public image and accomplishments. With Saturn in Sagittarius there, Jackson was renowned for suffering the legal and ethical consequences of sleeping with children. His notoriety as a suspected paedophile who was dragged into court by protective parents left an indelible stain upon his reputation.

1 Hirshey, G. 'Cover Story: Michael Jackson: Life in the Magical Kingdom', Rolling Stone, Issue 389, 17 February 1983, p. 2 http://www.rollingstone.com/news/story/22775354/michael_jackson_life_in_the_magical_kingdom/2
2 'Let's Go to the Videos!', TV Guide, Special Collector's Edition, Summer 2009, p. 16
3 Ibid., p. 5
4 Ibid., p. 4
5 Ibid., p. 11

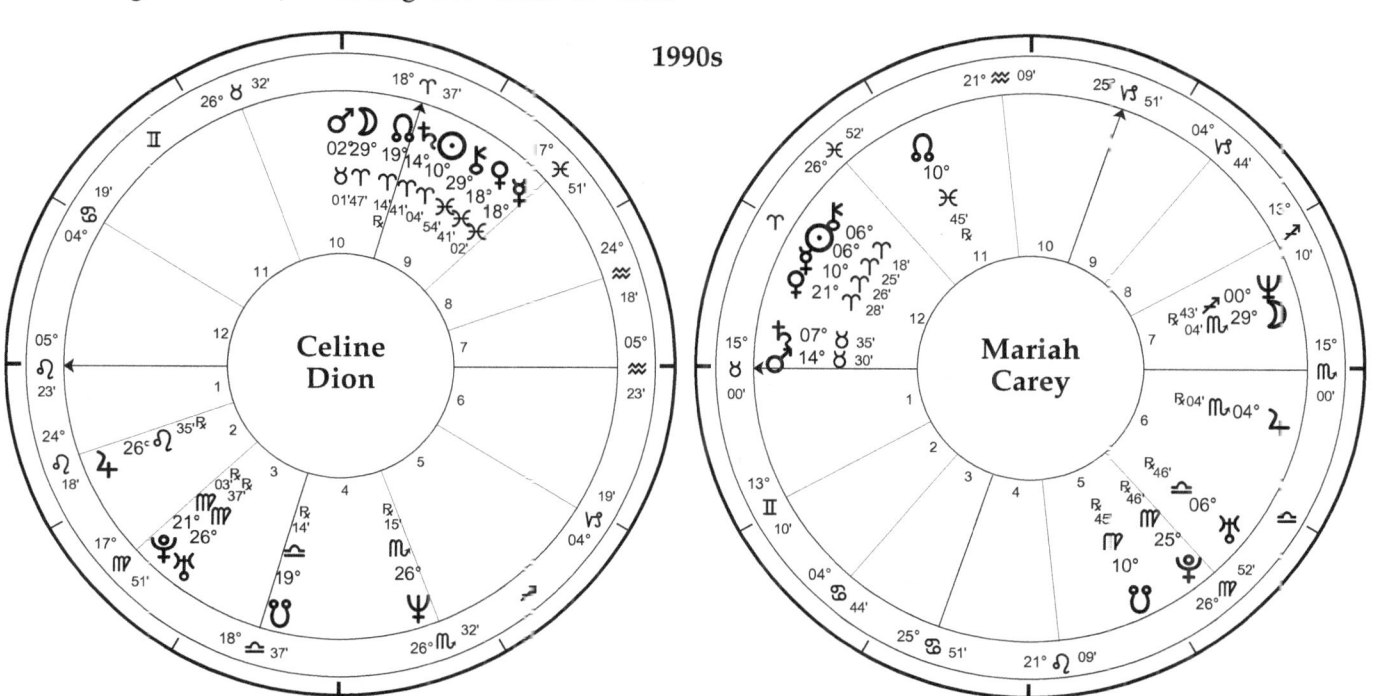

1990s

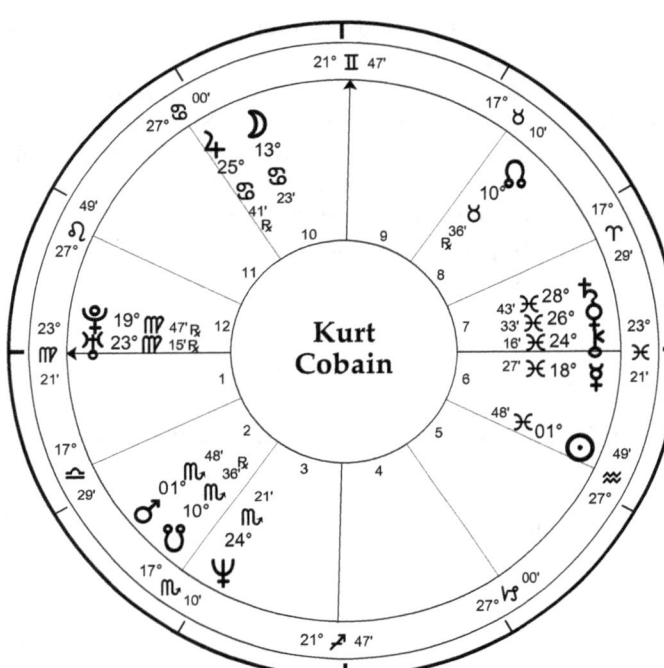

Neptune and the Search for Nirvana

Carole Bone

If you were to seek definitions of the term 'nirvana', you'd find something along these lines: 'A transcendent state in which there is neither suffering, desire, nor sense of self; release from the effects of karma and the cycle of death and rebirth; a state of perfect happiness; an ideal or idyllic place.' (English Oxford Living Dictionaries) This description also relates to astrological Neptune, a planet that rules the Water sign of Pisces.

Astrologically, Neptune is intuitive, idealistic, compassionate and empathic. The lyrics of artists who have its signature etched in their charts are often emotive and reveal the deep waters of their writers' emotions and vulnerability. No matter the music genre, a boundless longing permeates the listener to awaken feelings – stirring the soul and merging singer, song and listener.

In naming his band Nirvana, the astrological symbolism of Neptune was immediately stamped on the innovative 1990s grunge rock band by its charismatic lead singer, Kurt Cobain. His lyrics are diffuse, vague and hotly debated as to their meaning, but many say they illustrate a profound understanding of the drug culture and the identity confusion of a generation that was born of the idealism of the hippy era.

Kurt's birth chart is dominated by Water, with Pisces and its ruler Neptune strong:

- Four planets in Pisces, plus Chiron and a striking eight planets in Water signs
- Nine trines forming a Grand Water Trine of Neptune–Jupiter–Mercury/Chiron/Venus/Saturn
- The angular stellium in Pisces is opposed by Uranus–Pluto, which is pinned tightly to the Virgo Ascendant
- Neptune squares the Sun

Growing up with Neptune

Born and raised near Seattle, Washington, Kurt remembered his early childhood fondly. His time was spent drawing and singing along to the songs of The Beatles. But he was diagnosed as a hyperactive pre-schooler and given the amphetamine-based drug (Neptune) Ritalin as a child. The side effects of the drug were countered with sedatives to help him sleep at nights. His parents' divorce in 1975 was an emotional catastrophe for eight-year old Kurt, who always felt he was somehow to blame. Afterwards his mother had violent, abusive relationships and drank heavily, and Kurt went from being a normal student to a troubled one. Angry and confused, he became sullen and antagonistic towards his bewildered mother, who finally sent him to live with his father.

Kurt continued to rebel by refusing to share in his father's enthusiasm for sports. Joining the Junior High wrestling team, he allowed his opponent to win while his disappointed father watched. Kurt dropped out of high school before graduation (refusing his two state Art scholarships), skipped college and worked part-time as a janitor at his high school. He took drugs, drank, vandalized cars and lived life on the streets.

Here we can see Neptune's negative signature developing. For Neptunian people, situations can leave them feeling overwhelmed and 'all at sea' in their personal lives. Feelings of confusion, blame and self-sacrifice are common, and often drink or drugs are used to soften life's 'hard edges'.

Neptune, Music and Fame
Kurt found enjoyment and expression in music. His main influences were The Beatles, AC/DC, Queen, Aerosmith, The Pixies, Velvet Underground, The Sex Pistols and The Clash. In 1987, Cobain and bassist school friend Krist Novoselic formed Nirvana and were signed to Geffen Records in 1991. Their most famous album, *Nevermind*, would go on to sell over ten million copies worldwide. Kurt was singled out by music critics and shot to superstar status, but his personal life continued to fall apart. Uncomfortable with fame, he continued his Neptunian drug habit of heroin and alcohol.

Continuing in the Neptune vein, Kurt met Courtney Love and the couple bonded over music and their mutual drug habit. They married on 24 February 1992 but their addiction to drugs fuelled fights between them and proved difficult to conquer. In March 1994, Kurt was rushed to hospital in a coma after an unsuccessful suicide bid in which he washed down about fifty prescription painkillers with champagne. It was officially deemed an accident.

On 8 April 1994, Kurt's body was found in the couple's Seattle home. Police believe he had died of a self-inflicted shotgun wound to the head three days earlier. His death shocked the nation and several distraught teenagers in America and Australia also committed suicide. Controversy surrounded his death; not everyone believed it was suicide. He left a one-page note written in red ballpoint pen describing his personal demons, unhappiness, addictions, discomfort with celebrity status and his domestic disputes.

Neptunian Reflections
Kurt's heavy Water chart with a Pisces–Neptune emphasis suggests enormous wells of sensitivity and creativity; a longing to belong and merge with something greater than oneself. There is a yearning to connect to someone or something higher, combined with the receptive, perhaps oversensitive, Cancer Moon and the passion and bite of Mars in Scorpio. Here is some Water–Pisces–Neptune symbolism:

- Nirvana's most famous album, *Nevermind*, shows a child swimming underwater (Pisces/Neptune)
- There is a 'hidden' track on the album called 'Endless, Nameless' (Neptune)
- A later album was titled *In Utero*, Latin for 'in the uterus' (Cancer)
- Cobain's suicide note read: '... but I still can't get over the frustration, the guilt and empathy I have for everyone. There's good in all of us and I think I simply love people too much, so much that it makes me feel too fucking sad. The sad little, sensitive, unappreciative, Pisces, Jesus man.'

For the Water signs, feelings run deep – sometimes to the point of being all-consuming. With the element of Air virtually missing from his chart, Kurt would have had a hard time dealing with others in a light or superficial manner.

His chart's Grand Trine in Water reveals powerful possibilities and latent talents. It suggests an idealistic and romantic personality capable of loving and feeling – not only at a personal level but for mankind, too. There is much creativity, love, empathy and good in this configuration. But Grand Trines can often indicate talents that go unrecognized or wasted if there is insufficient drive to put them to practical use.

In the horoscope, the Ascendant (rising sign) represents among other things our physical appearance and approach to the world. Kurt has Virgo on the Ascendant. Virgo, the opposite sign to Pisces, is its own harshest critic; there is often a humbleness and lack of self-confidence.

Uranus–Pluto tightly conjunct the Virgo Ascendant suggests an unusual and contradictory need to project himself as unique and deep, yet in a modest, unglamorous way (grunge – Virgo). The tight conjunction is split by house: Uranus is below the horizon while Pluto is above. Uranus in the 1st is readily visible as the wild man in such music videos as 'Smells Like Teen Spirit'. His desires to be contrary and bring about change by going against expectations would have been strong. Perhaps the need to be at one with humanity yet to rebel against society (as shown by Uranus opposite the Pisces stellium) was the source of much inner conflict and restlessness.

Any planet in the Neptune/Pisces-associated 12th House can be a point of much preoccupation, and can also suggest a powerful drive to master the areas that bring much trouble and pain. In the 12th House, a planet is under the surface and on the verge of expression. Pluto here – ruling death and rebirth – gives a strong need to regenerate, and a striving for meaning and purpose. It is dramatic and needs to get to the bottom of things, to bring light to inner darkness. If not used constructively, this placement can coincide with overwhelming feelings of futility. There is a dark, brooding quality that can border on the obsessive, with a desire for power and a tendency to self-analysis that can be self-destructive.

Kurt's lyrics and later his journals all expressed a deeply withdrawn, extremely sensitive personality – with all the anger, pain and cynicism of someone who felt very alone and disconnected. Those very feelings managed to speak to a massive audience, but in many ways this was one-way and on a collective, not a personal, level. Since the 12th House rules, among other things, isolation, we can see how a strong Water–Pisces–Neptune emphasis would be fitting for Kurt's feelings of desolation and hopelessness.

Neptune's gifts often demand some kind of sacrifice or loss. With great artistic talent often comes great sensitivity, and Kurt's suicide illustrates that tragically. The singer-songwriter Don McLean, who has Neptune as part of a stellium in Libra, perhaps put it best when he wrote in one of his most famous songs about artist Vincent Van Gogh (also strongly Neptunian): 'This world was never meant for one as beautiful as you.'

Soulful Stars

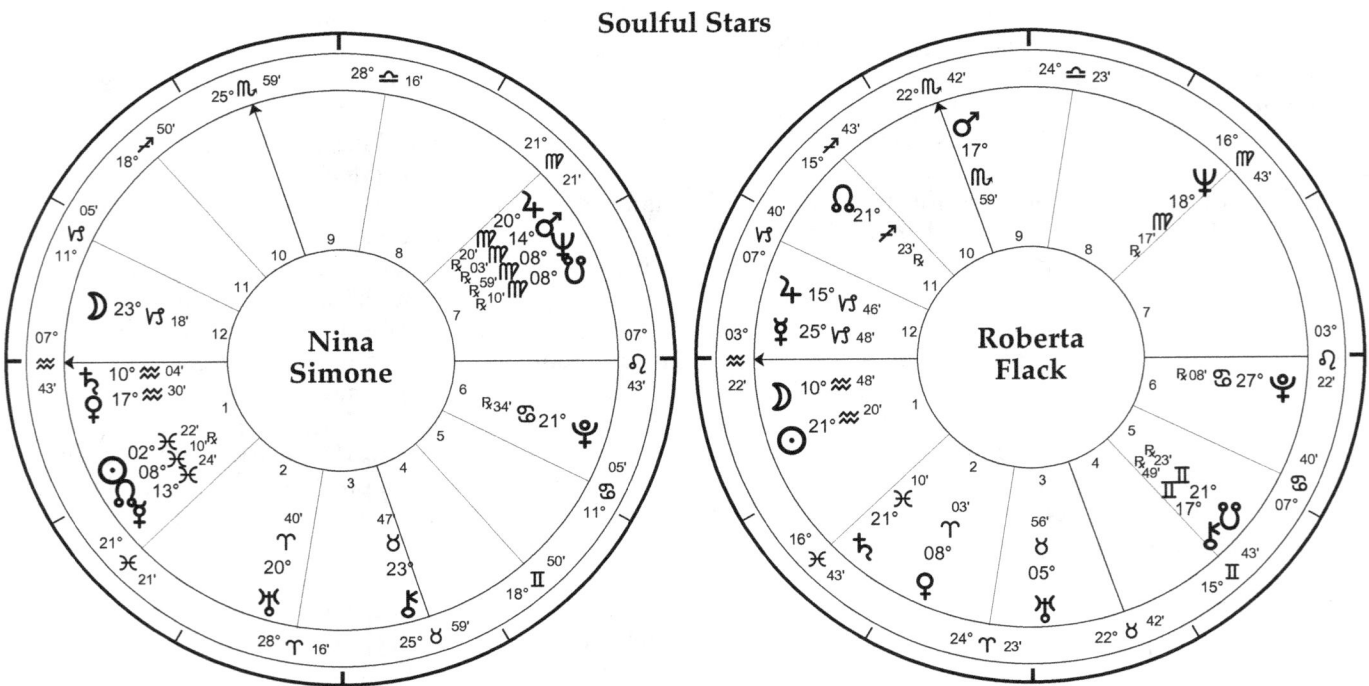

Music Royalty 131

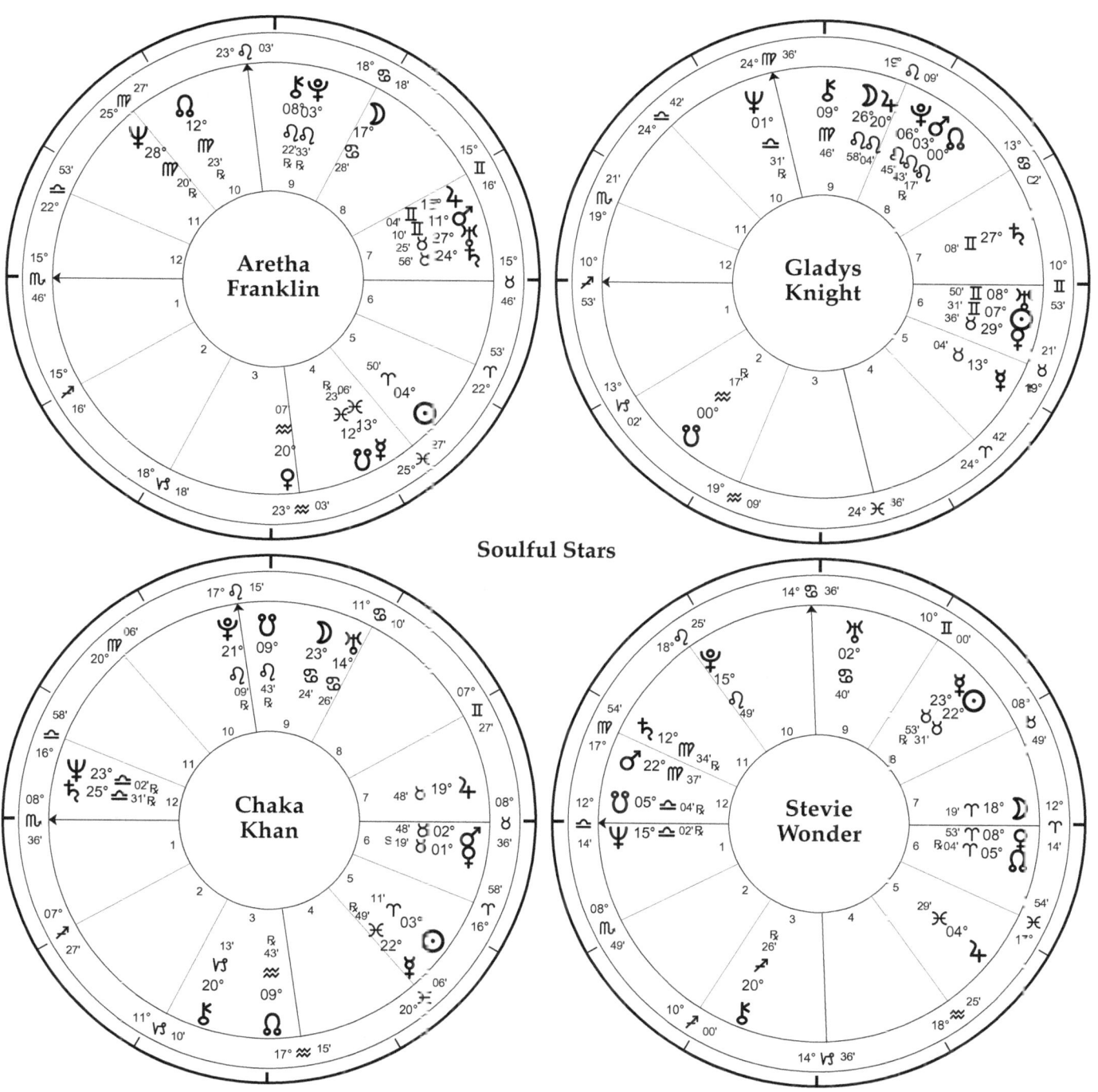

Soulful Stars

132 The Book of Music Horoscopes

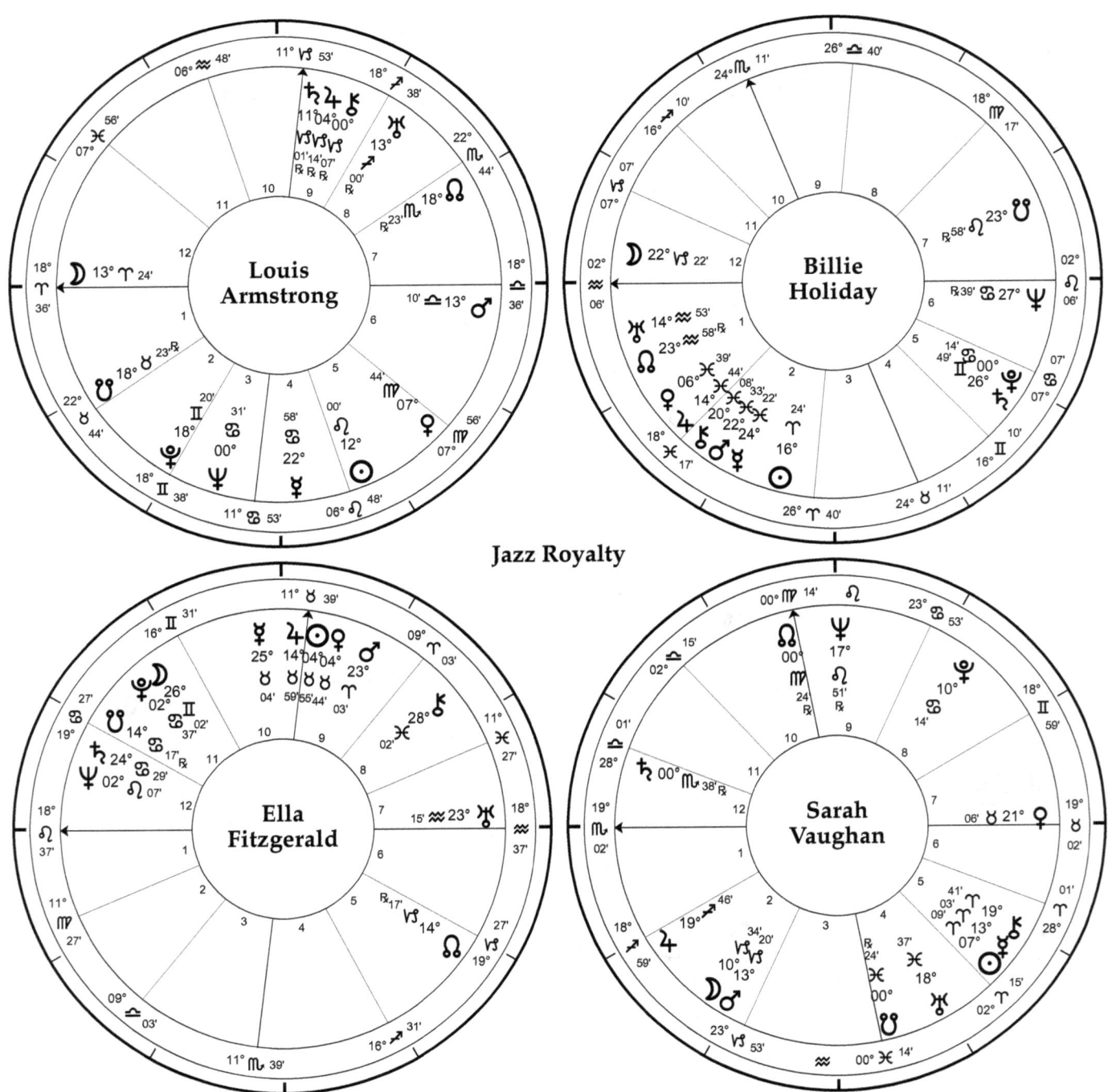

Jazz Royalty

'I know that deep blue sea Will soon be calling me'

Fernanda Paiva

It was some time ago that I started sensing the powerful Neptunian signature in Billie Holiday's horoscope. I had always loved her music and my natal Venus square Neptune could easily resonate with it; listening to her tunes while having a bath allowed me to express the Neptunian aspect of my own psyche.

I also remember the live versions of her songs being my least favourite in my early twenties because I could never sing along. Contrary to most of the singers I enjoyed listening to, Billie Holiday would always interpret her songs differently live than when in the studio. From one concert to another it seemed like she was giving birth to a new tune. I could never keep up with the rhythm, and that used to bother me. I don't think I had the emotional awareness at that time to feel her performances deeply.

Singing entered Billie Holiday's life in a very authentic way. Never rehearsing and without almost any influence from other singers (being unable to afford the luxury of having a record player in her youth), Billie Holiday based her technique on feelings. There were songs she couldn't personally relate to and would refuse to sing a single note of them, and there were songs that seemed made for her.

In her autobiography, *Lady Sings the Blues*, Billie talks about her approach as a song stylist: 'If you find a tune and it's got something to do with you, you don't have to evolve anything. You just feel it, and when you sing it other people can feel something too. With me, it's got nothing to do with working or arranging or rehearsing. Give me a song I can feel, and it's never work.'

Each planet in the horoscope represents a different drive coexisting in our psyche. Billie had many of those driving forces either in Pisces, aspecting Neptune or falling in the 12th House – giving rise to a very powerful Neptunian signature. The singer's stellium in Pisces is in the house that governs resources and talents (the 2nd), and some of the planets (Mars and Mercury) make an almost exact trine to her MC (reputation) in Scorpio. There wasn't much separation between her professional and private lives: Billie's suffering was the raw material that she converted into music and she was famous for all the dramas in her personal life, problems with the law, drugs and abusive relationships.

In her book *The Astrology of Fate*, Liz Greene writes that a dominant theme in the horoscope is the 'spinal column of the chart' and reflective of a person's key life stories. The energies represented by the symbols aren't only 'potential seeds' but an intrinsic pattern that will be manifested somehow in life by the individual.

When we are faced with such a strong motif in the chart, as with Billie Holiday, that archetypal dimension will feature so powerfully that perhaps the person's individual choice is somehow reduced from within. The outside factors also have an influence upon how prepared the individual can be to work with the energies given and reflected by the heavens. Billie Holiday was born to a thirteen-year old mother in a poor financial situation and in a society stricken by racial prejudice; she experienced much turmoil from an early age.

Neptune represents the dissolution of boundaries and, to a certain extent, so does Pisces. Pisces is about channelling creative energy and transcending the limits of mundane life in some way. Liz Greene refers to it as 'creative madness'. Other Piscean traits include the inherent capacity for empathy, great sensitivity, the melting down of barriers, and the potential to go beyond one's ego and separateness into a state of union with the whole.

We can imagine Billie's stellium as a kind of driving force that could have taken her closer to actualizing the purpose of her Sun in Aries – a pioneer of some kind. But perhaps Billie Holiday's fate was to carry the Neptunian archetype and Piscean myth – not only in her personal life, but also for the collective. That is possibly the main reason why her talent was so promptly and vastly recognized. The realness and intensity with which she performed could melt the space between her and the audience, and her voice powerfully expressed this archetypal energy through her music.

134 *The Book of Music Horoscopes*

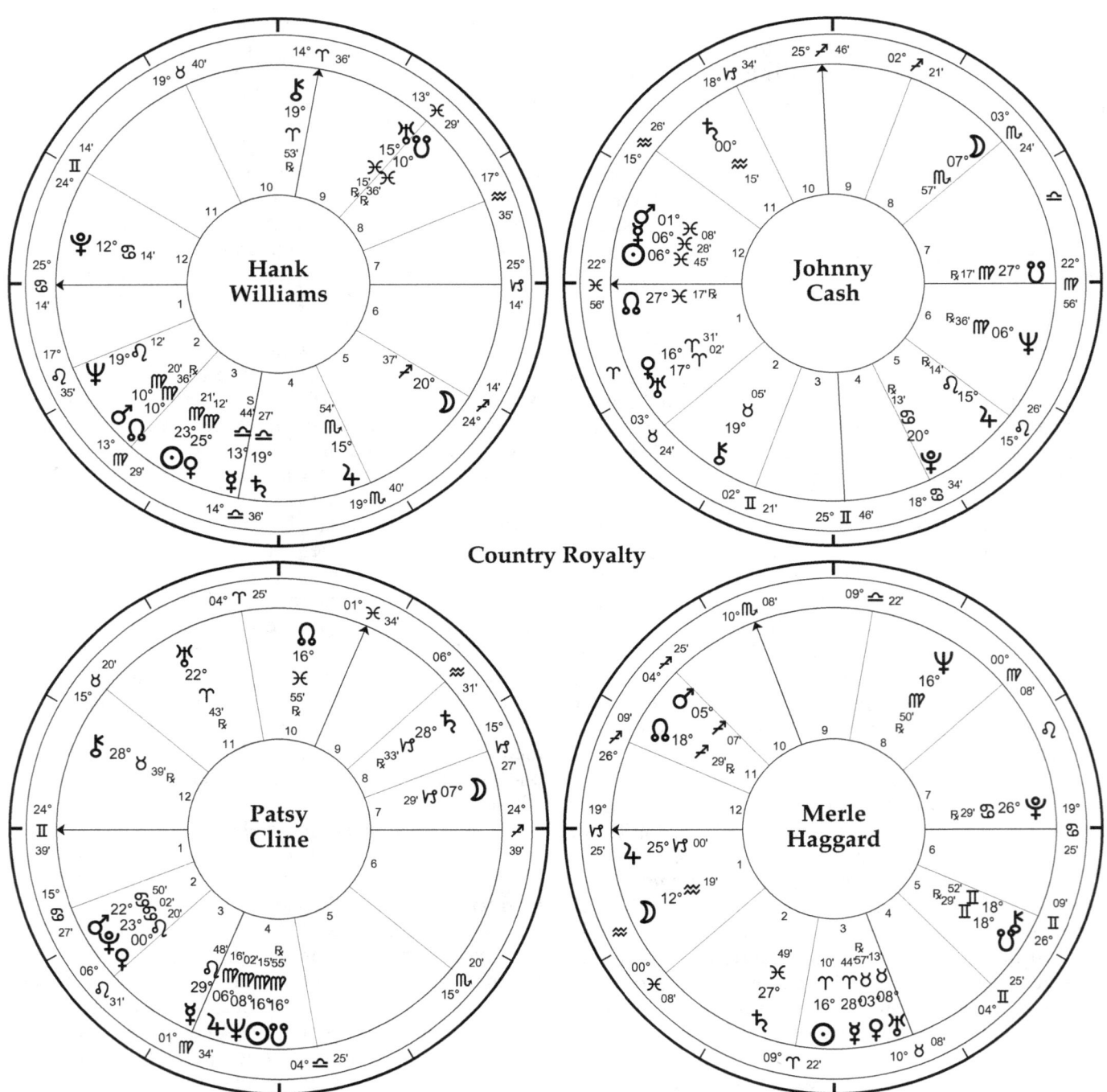

Country Royalty

Music Royalty 135

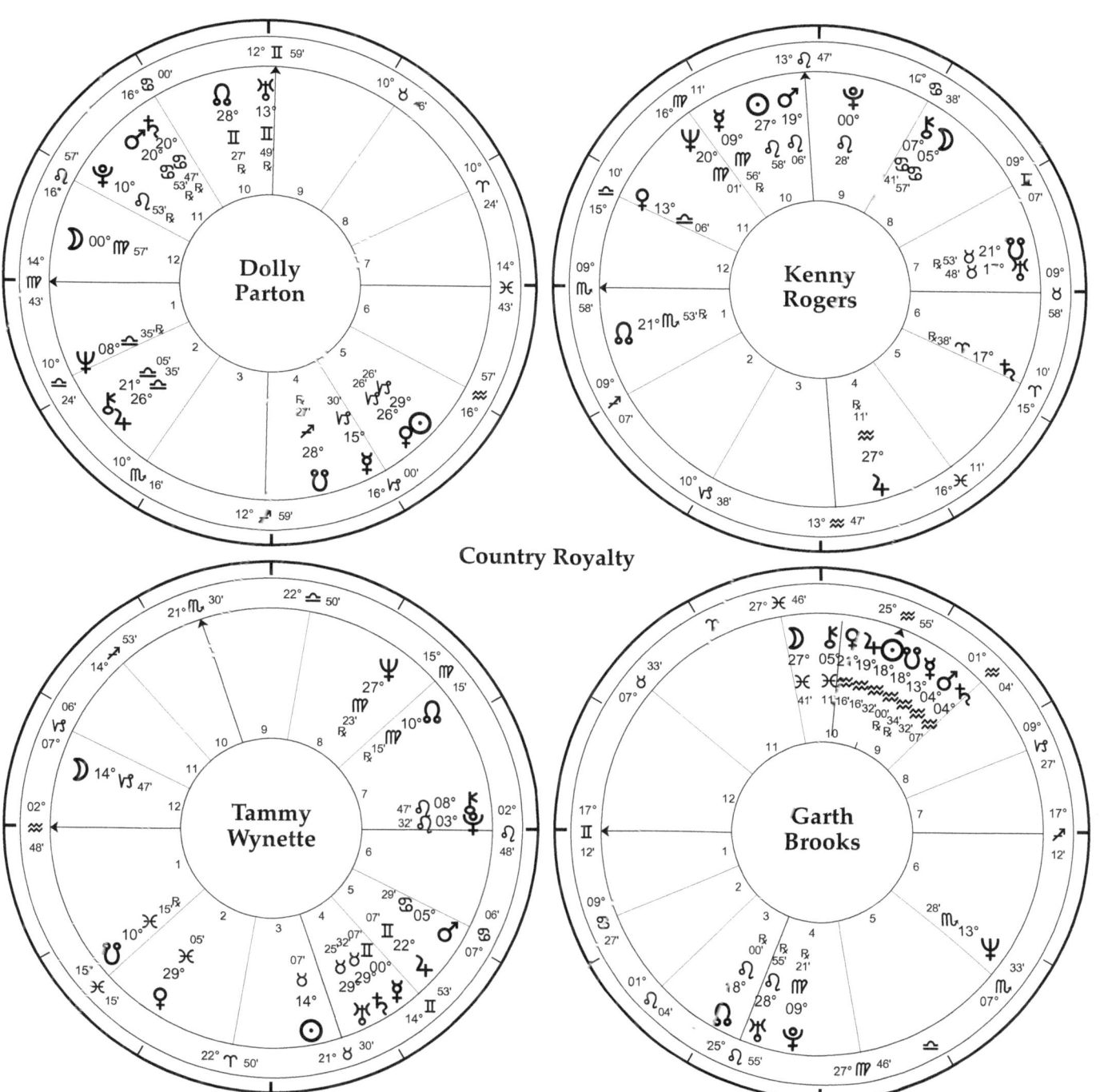

Country Royalty

136 *The Book of Music Horoscopes*

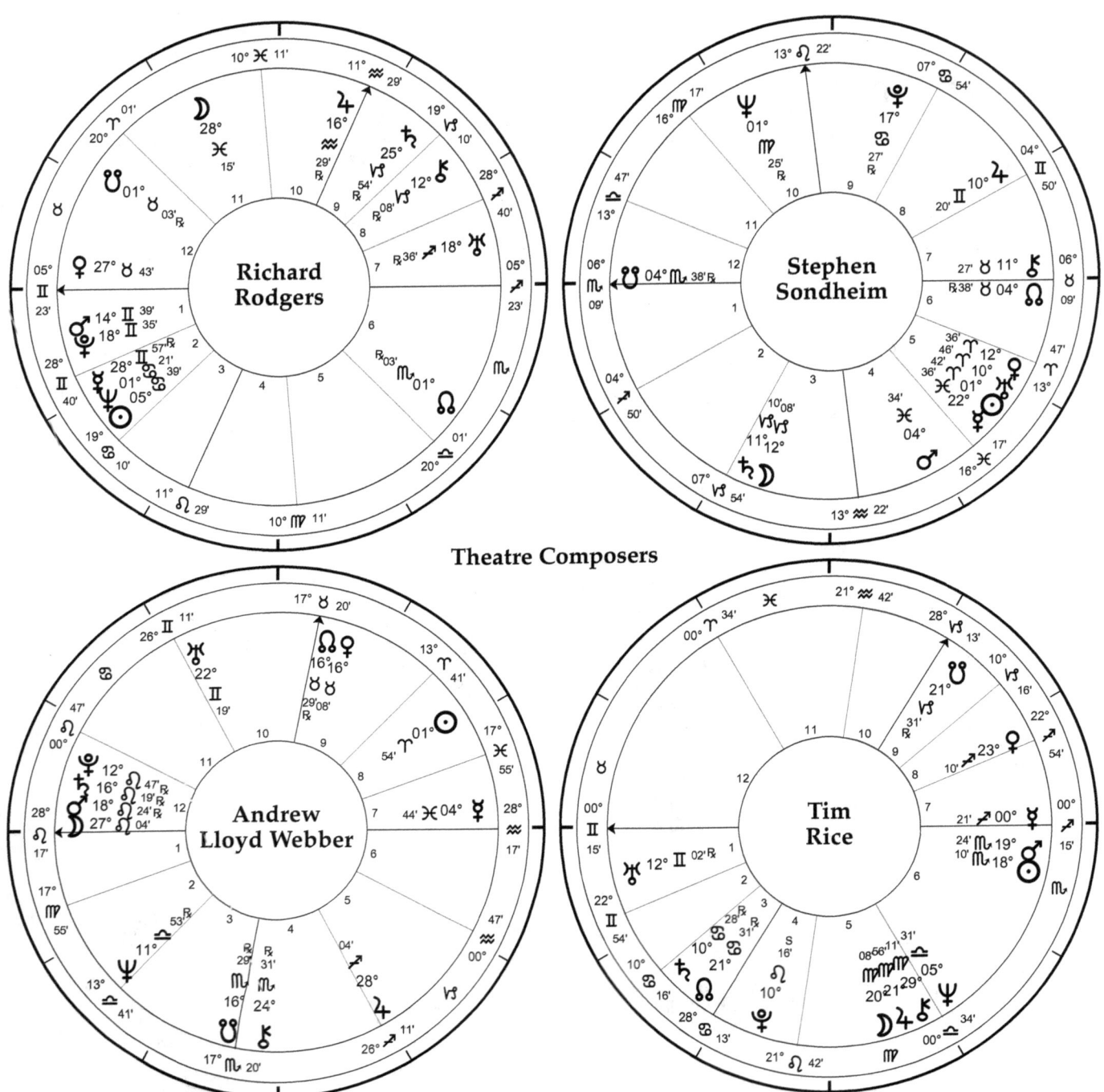

Theatre Composers

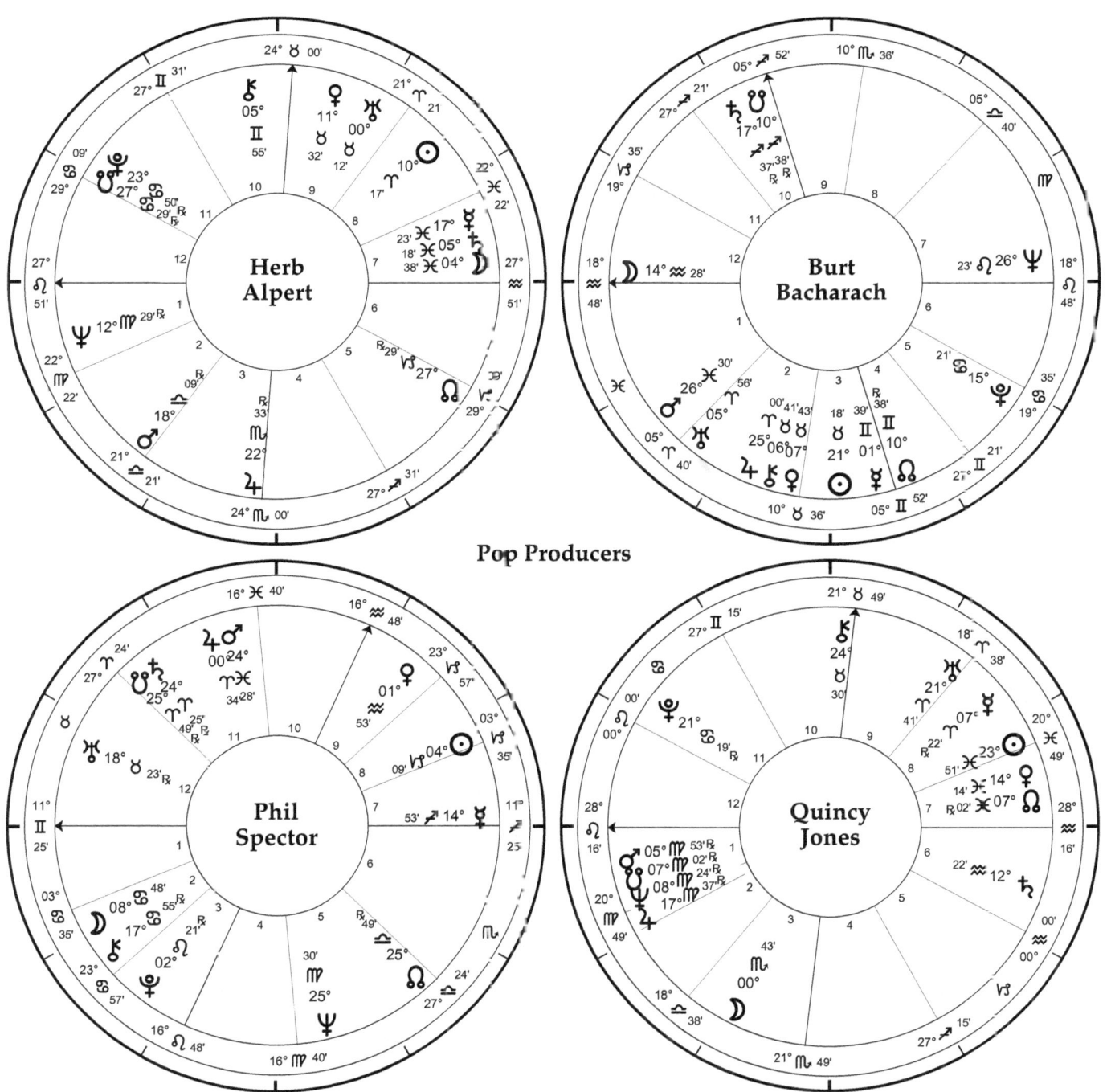

Pop Producers

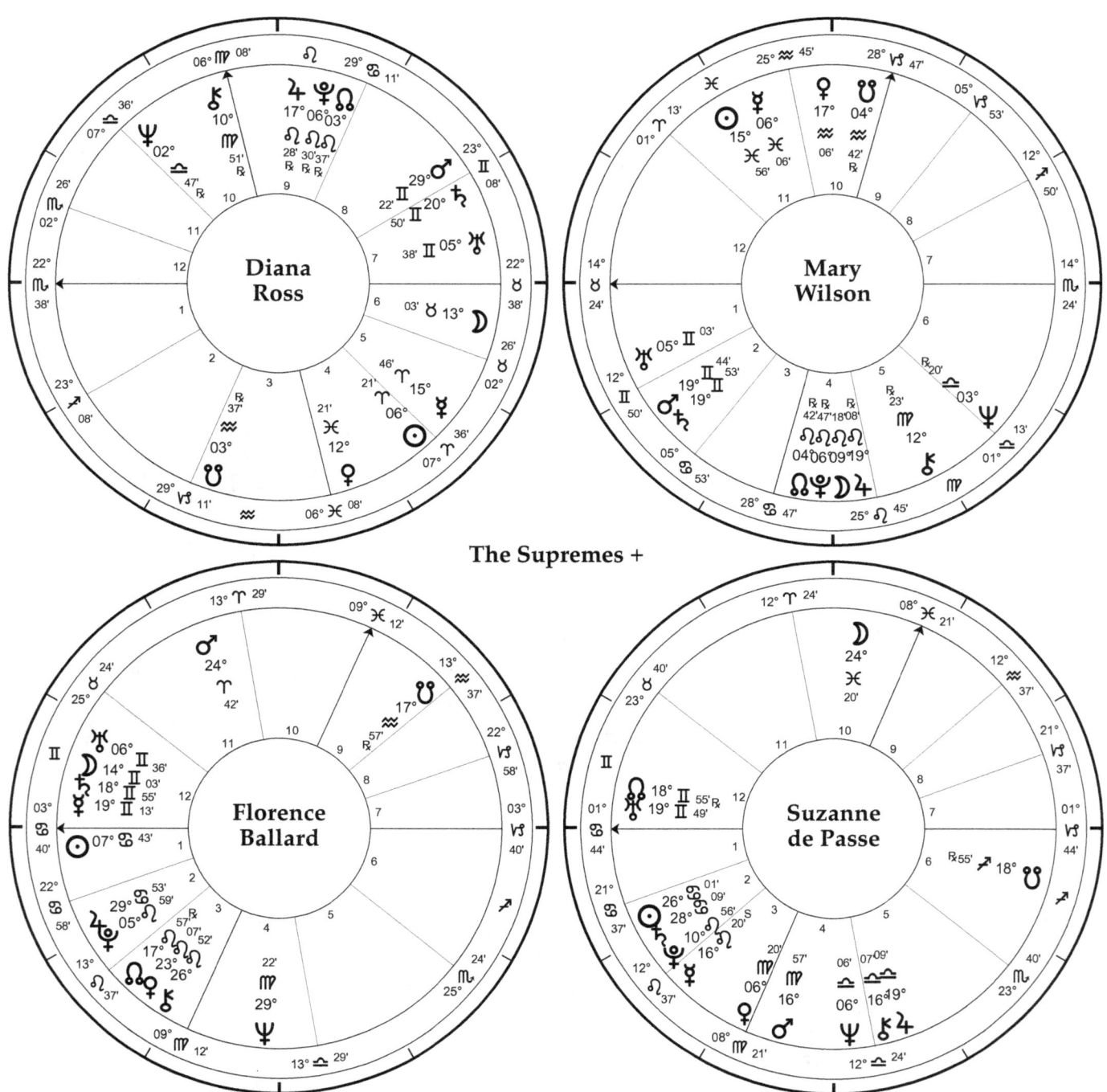

The Supremes +

It's All About the Performance!

Michele Finey

Jupiter is by far the largest planet in our solar system. Astrologically, it represents the capacity to expand, to grow and to explore. In classical mythology, Jupiter/Zeus was the king of the gods. He was all-powerful. No one dared to question his supremacy or authority.

Symbolically and psychologically, astrologers associate Jupiter with confidence and self-belief. Other character traits linked to Jupiter include generosity, optimism, hubris, excess and a tendency to show off. The typical Jupiter type is extroverted and proud. Somehow they seem larger than life. They have their fair share of good luck and staying power. People engaged in public performance need an abundance of Jovian qualities in their personal make-up, so we would therefore expect to see Jupiter emphasized in some way.

Michel Gauquelin found that Jupiter was often rising or culminating in the charts of actors and politicians. His groundbreaking research provides compelling evidence that if Jupiter is in one of the 'Gauquelin plus zones' it means that the individual concerned is likely to be imbued with the necessary confidence required for a high-profile profession and public life. His research into musicians, specifically military bandmasters, also showed that Jupiter was prominent.

The Sun–Jupiter conjunction is another combination we might expect to find in the charts of dynamic performers. We see this aspect in the charts of Mick Jagger, Josephine Baker, Maria Callas, Bob Dylan, Paul McCartney, Donna Summer and Ritchie Valens.

Stationary Planets

Throughout the history of astrology, astrologers have not been able to agree on how to interpret slow-moving planets that are about to change their apparent direction. It's worth noting that Ptolemy viewed stationary planets as being similar to rising planets in terms of their potency. In her book, *Retrograde Planets*, Erin Sullivan says of the stationary retrograde (SR) planet:

> One often finds it difficult if not impossible to express oneself to one's satisfaction. This can result in obsessive or compulsive types of behaviour or dedication to rigorous detailed work which through its thoroughness satisfies one's sense of completion and success.

Stationary retrograde planets can challenge us. We have to dig deep to find the inner fortitude required to harness their energy. SR planets foster endurance, staying power, focus and dedication. Of the stationary direct planet (SD), Sullivan writes:

> [It] has already constelled a great amount of power and is virtually trembling for an avenue for expression. Unless there are other aspects to the planet that promote a channel for the energy, then it is likely to have little grounding in the early years of one's life.

In resuming forward momentum the stationary direct planet urges us to get moving, but at the same time this planet is not easy to harness, especially early in life. It's raw and fresh. Over time we have an opportunity to develop and utilize this planet and express it outwardly as it gains momentum and speed, but at first it can be a real monkey on our back.

My initial research into stationary planets yielded some very interesting results that support the idea that stationary planets are indeed very powerful. Those born when a planet is slow or stationary tend to embody the nature of this planet, for better or worse, to a large degaree, but its lack of motion means that this can take a great deal of stamina and time. Some people will find motionless planets to be an insurmountable hurdle, while others will rise to the challenge: a fact that may account for the different ways that astrologers interpret them.

Jupiter Stationary

In terms of both their profession and their personality, people born when Jupiter was slow or stationary can strongly embody the Jupiter archetype. It's possible that Jupiter is actually stronger when slow than when fast. By extension, we may have to rethink the way we interpret all stationary and slow-moving planets.

Jupiter has a synodic cycle of 399 days, from one solar conjunction to the next. Its average daily speed is 4'59". When moving at its slowest pace, Jupiter will travel 8'50" in retrograde motion per day, compared to its fastest daily motion which is 15'40". Using this as a benchmark, I searched for birth charts that had Jupiter moving at between 2' of arc retrograde and 3' of arc direct per day. I created a database of 739 performers that include musicians, singers, actors and dancers. Of these 739 performers, 109 were found to have Jupiter within these parameters. This is 14.75 per cent. To make a comparison I built a database of 739 random charts using the same years and locations of birth as the performers. In this control group I found that 84 (11.37 per cent) had Jupiter moving at between minus 2' and plus 3' of arc per day: far less than the performers.

Of the 109 who had Jupiter slow or stationary, there was a distinct tendency for Jupiter *not* to be in a cadent house: Angular (39), Succedent (46), Cadent (24).

Sun–Jupiter Aspects
It should be noted that Jupiter's stations occur when it makes a trine to the Sun. So is it the Sun–Jupiter trine, rather than Jupiter's stations, that is the significant factor here? It appears not. In searching through the 109 performers' charts where Jupiter was stationary or slow, only 36.7 per cent (or 40 charts) had a Sun–Jupiter trine within a 5° orb. In 69 charts there was no Sun–Jupiter trine within this orb range. There were also fewer Sun–Jupiter trines in the control group (26) compared to that of the performers (40). More than half the performers (395 individuals) had no major aspect between Jupiter and the Sun, compared to 428 in the control group. But as we might expect, Sun–Jupiter conjunctions were almost twice as common in performers' charts as in the control group – by 27 to 15. The number of Sun–Jupiter semi-squares was also noticeably higher in the performers' than in the control's group. It seems that being born with Jupiter slow or stationary (or a Sun–Jupiter conjunction or semi-square) is a real asset for those in the performing arts.

'All You Need is Your Own Imagination, So Use It – That's What it's For' – Madonna

Deborah Perera

This is a line from Madonna's single 'Vogue' and it seems she has used her Leo–Virgo 12th House planetary line-up to do just that. This grouping includes her Sun in Leo – a rather hidden and self-sacrificing placement for a creative, self-expressive and attention-seeking Leo Sun. So could it be possible that a fear of going unnoticed has driven her to achieve such global stardom? The lack of boundaries present in the 12th House could also mean that her ego-driven Sun in Leo achievements would need to be limitless for her to feel good about herself. Given the extremes of 12th House energy, her Uranus in Leo is perhaps saying there isn't anything she wouldn't do to shock or create controversy. She has said that she's not interested in being the best singer or dancer around – what she likes is to 'push people's buttons'.

We also see extremes of Virgoan energy, with a ruthless and wilful Pluto conjunct a sharp, fault-finding Mercury in the 12th House. This suggests someone with an outspoken, critical tongue who will not hesitate to voice her opinions or complain if something is not up to her high standards. These planets close to her Virgo Ascendant imply that she likes to have total control over her immediate environment and suggest an enormous drive for perfection, particularly in her work. They also provide her with the discipline (for example, her diet and punishing daily exercise routine) to achieve this. But we must remember the depth of imagination and the need to transcend the mundane that are the gifts from the 12th House. Madonna's music and dancing are perfect vehicles for this.

Madonna's Moon is in Virgo in the 1st House conjunct her Ascendant and Mercury, suggesting someone who needs to express their emotions and, although they can be maternal, will often put their own needs first. Virgo Moons can worry about being at fault, so Madonna will work hard at being totally prepared for anything.

Given her very public Moon, she is able to express her emotions through her performance and perhaps she sees it as a form of Virgoan service. Interestingly, she has often referred to her work as a 'job'.

Madonna was only six when her mother died and she has said this tragedy initiated her drive to achieve global success. We see this reflected in her chart with her Virgo Moon square to Saturn in Sagittarius in the 4th, suggesting pain and a lack of female nurturing early in life. Being the eldest girl of six children, maternal responsibilities would have manifested when she was young. We can observe this square in operation later in life because she has expressed guilt at having to divide her time between her career, travelling and her family life. With Sagittarius on the IC Madonna often ends up with a travelling 'family', which includes her entourage. However, the Moon is strong in this chart so she needs to be a good mother as well as a top performer.

Madonna's Moon and Ascendant receive a further boost from an Earthy trine from a 9th House Mars in Taurus. This combination of the musical talent of Taurus and the physical energy of Mars results in her gift for singing and dancing. This trine is perhaps the physical manifestation, the sheer hard work behind Madonna's fiery, creative ideas demonstrated in her spectacular live shows. She began her career by studying dance at university, beautifully reflected by Taurus on the cusp of the 9th House and Mars placed here. From the beginning, Madonna's work has often had a strong sexual content (another manifestation of Mars in Taurus). Mars is square to Uranus in Leo in the 12th, so her use of sexual imagery is frequently shocking and extreme. Because the 9th and 12th Houses are involved, she has also used religion in this manner. (The contents of her 1989 video 'Like A Prayer' caused huge controversy and ended up being condemned by the Vatican.) Mars in Taurus is stubborn and likes to get what it wants, so it is unlikely that Madonna would have been willing to compromise on her art. It is important to note that Mars–Uranus indicates that she may be unpredictable and could have a volatile reaction if things do not go her way.

Madonna's spiritual beliefs are important to her and they emerge in her work and private life. Her heavily occupied 12th House is key to this, with a fiery Sun and Uranus forming trines to Saturn in Sagittarius. The Sun and 4th House Saturn may be her connection to her disciplinarian father and Catholic upbringing. Although her relationship with her father was not always easy, her love and respect for him are well documented and she has clearly benefitted from his strict discipline and work ethic. Perhaps she needed to impress him and gain his attention amid the sibling rivalry, so she became in her father's words a 'high achiever', although self-discipline, confidence and the will to succeed can come easily to a Sun–Saturn trine.

To quote the song 'Keep It Together': 'I want to be different, I want to be on my own but Daddy said listen, you always have a home.' Here, she is possibly describing her trine between Saturn and Uranus. This may reflect her need to move away from her Catholic roots – her traditional upbringing – and to break away in an effort to become independent. This trine not only reflects her inventiveness and originality but could also suggest a need to explore another spiritual path – one that is rooted in mysticism and the metaphysical. In recent years she has become a devoted Kabbalist – this would work well with her Mercury conjunct Pluto as she would be attracted to learning about hidden knowledge and uncovering the mysteries of the universe, particularly as this conjunction is sextile to Neptune in Scorpio in the 3rd. It is worth mentioning that Madonna's 1989 album *Like A Prayer* was written and recorded during her Saturn Return and contains songs such as 'Oh Father' and 'Keep It Together', a song about early family life. It is a mature, sensitive piece of work and deeply reflective of a Sagittarius Saturn returning to her IC and 4th House. The album received huge acclaim and marked a point in her career where her music began to taken seriously by the critics. All this you might expect from a strong natal Saturn and its subsequent Return.

I'd like to give the final word on Madonna to her younger brother, Christopher, who provided emotional and professional support from the beginning. In summing up her life and work he once said, 'She is her own masterpiece.'

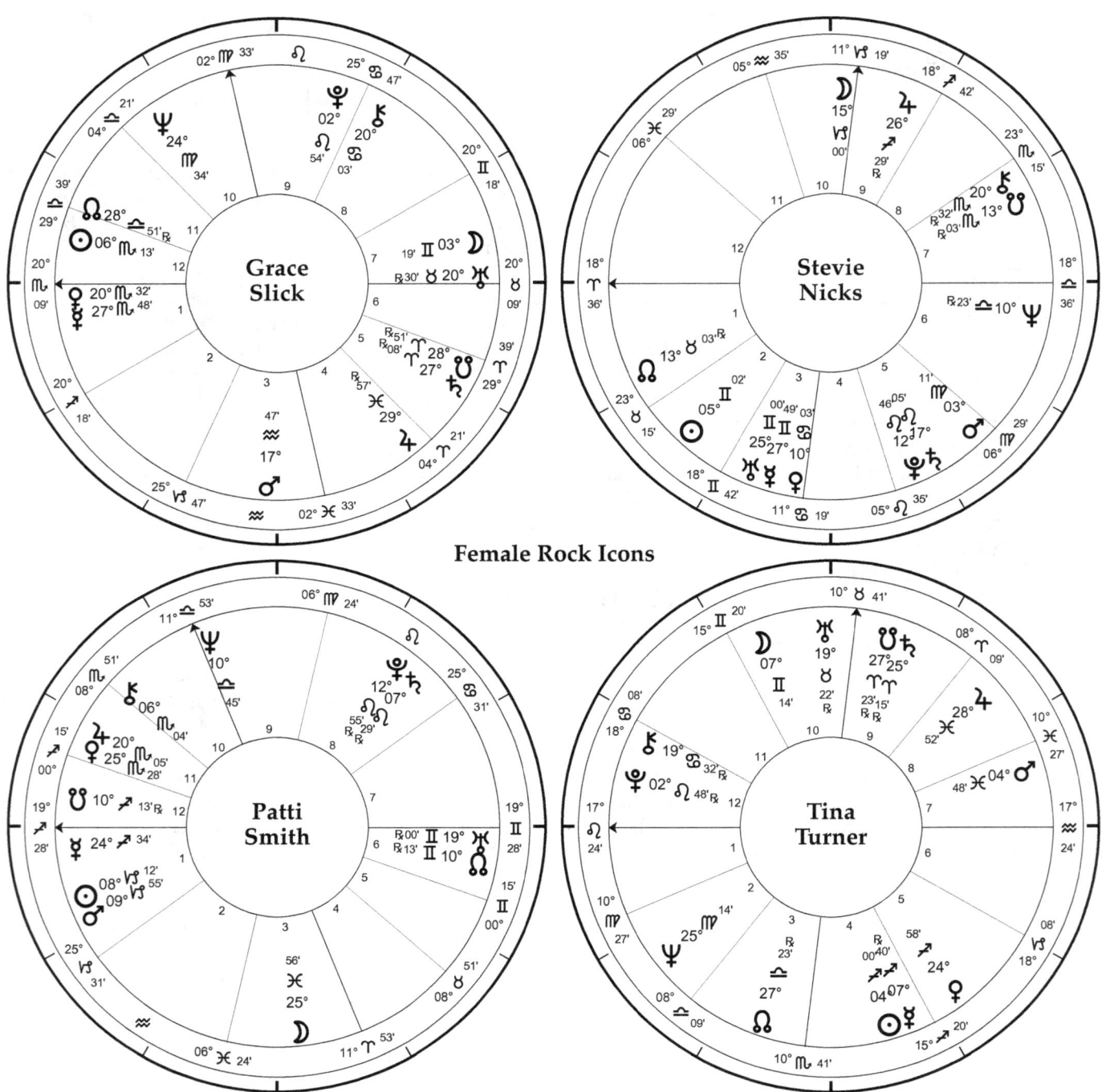

Female Rock Icons

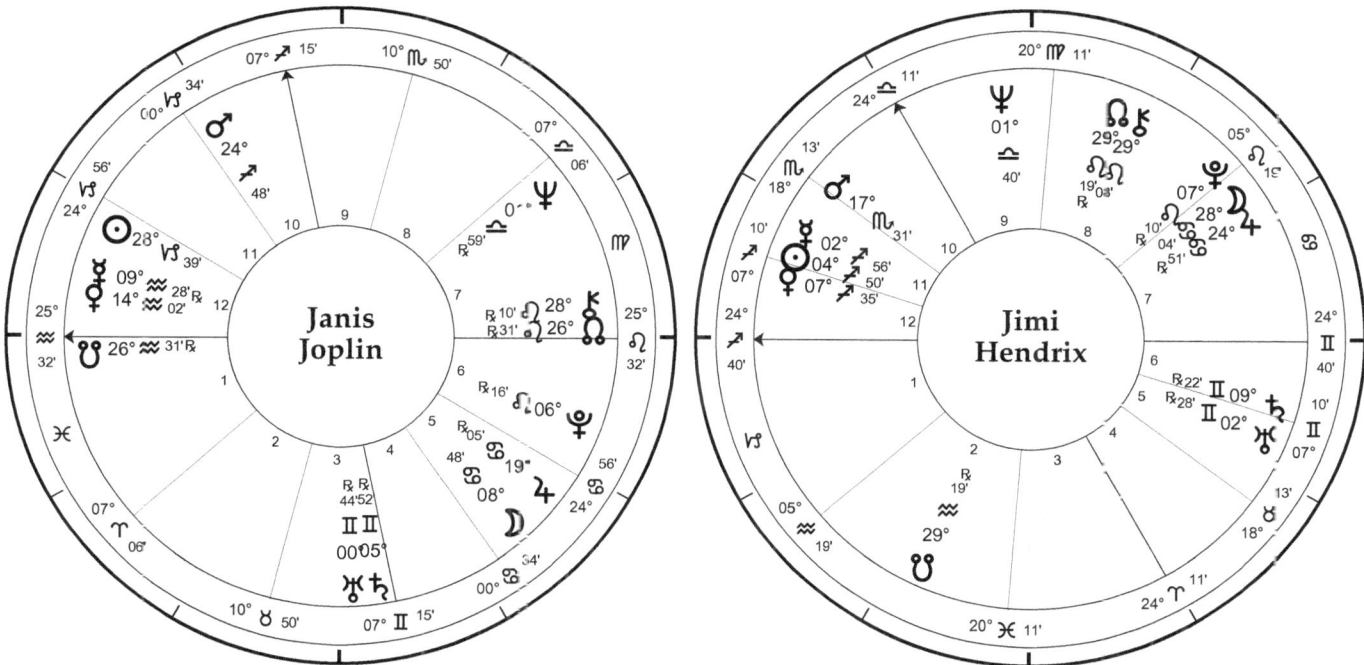

Rock Rebels:
Janis Joplin and Jimi Hendrix

Kim Farley

The only people for me are the mad ones, the ones who are mad to live, mad to talk, mad to be saved, desirous of everything at the same time, the ones who never yawn or say a commonplace thing, but burn, burn, burn like fabulous yellow roman candles exploding like spiders across the stars and in the middle, you see the blue center-light pop, and everybody goes ahh …
> Jack Kerouac, *On the Road*

Ahh, indeed. Janis and Jimi flared and burst across the skies of the late 1960s and seared the world for a handful of years. A white singer from a southern town who ripped the screaming raucous blues out of the depths of her soul like nobody before or since and a black guitarist from a northern city who played howling extraterrestrial psychedelic science fiction rock. Both of them groundbreaking, mould-smashing, ear-scorching children of a Saturn–Uranus conjunction in Gemini.

Only a few years back, in a record shop on Liverpool's Bold Street, I saw a Hendrix bootleg called *He's Not Gone, He's Just Dead*. That's a line from one of his own songs and yet it sums up how Jimi is still with us. Janis, too – there's a fashion line called Made for Pearl so that we can all dress like 'God's idea of a rock star'. Seventy-odd years since they were born, forty-eight since they died at the now-legendary age of twenty-seven and neither of them has ever really gone away.

That Saturn–Uranus conjunction had actually hit its exact point at 29°20' Taurus on 3 May 1942 (Richard Idemon had a thing for the final degree of a sign, suggesting it holds Neptunian vibes) and, any way you look at it, the themes are highly significant in Jimi's and Janis's charts. Jimi was born on 27 November that year and Janis came along a couple of months later on 19 January 1943. War babies, in other words. Big times worldwide. And they both have the retrograde conjunction in the early degrees of Gemini, with Saturn slightly ahead of Uranus. The cycle repeats itself over a 45-year period (meaning that the following conjunction was in late Sagittarius in 1988 and gives us a glimpse into the radicalization of some of those in their late-twenties/early-thirties now: think Occupy, student riots, grass roots movements).

Janis is a Capricorn Sun (she's been called the female Elvis, another Capricorn, because of the impact she made) and her Mercury–Venus conjunction is in Aquarius with all three planets in the 12th House. Chuck in Aquarius rising and that makes Saturn and Uranus the (co)rulers of all of this, additionally creating a mutual reception with Mercury. Then the icing on the cake: the conjunction falls on her IC which is 7° Gemini – so the power of the combination is like a huge neon sign in the darkness. (There's also an off-kilter Grand Trine created with her Sun and Neptune.) Now you're thinking, yes, that sounds like it, right? Capricorn Suns aim high, work hard, flog themselves. And they like to set their own rules. But when you bump Saturn up next to Uranus, the odds shoot up that the person will also identify as wild at heart and weird on top. Aquarius rising can be many things, but ordinary is not usually one of them.

Similarly, Jimi has a packed (Equal) 12th House, with the Sun, Mercury and Venus all in cosmic Sagittarius bang opposite Saturn and Uranus in the 6th. Sagittarius is also rising. More is more – right? Mercury not only rules his Descendant (and of course disposits the Saturn–Uranus conjunction itself) but falls within half a degree of an exact opposition to Uranus. There's some glorious crosstown traffic here with the Nodes, whose axis ('Bold as Love' …) falls across his (Equal) 9th–3rd Houses in Leo–Aquarius respectively. Talk about surfing on a higher plane. Mutable signs and cadent houses reflect restlessness, seeking and gathering knowledge and (cue drum roll) experience.

So at heart (Sun) both were different, they thought (Mercury) differently and they dressed (Venus) differently. Uranus rattled Saturn's cage, taking Saturn's framework and bending it into crazy shapes. Unexpected connections and progressive ideas/ideals were normal to them. As Sue Tompkins puts it in *Aspects in Astrology*: 'In personal terms, people with these contacts often have a gift of looking at an old subject in an entirely new way.'

A conjunction fuses two (or more) principles. And I go with the view that outer planets carry rather more heft. So with Saturn and Uranus we have the electrifyingly original (Uranus) mixed with the established structure (Saturn) in a way that shakes up (Uranus) all the rules (Saturn). We have the classic battle between stasis (Saturn) and change (Uranus), but I would definitely see the 'struggle' factor to be much lower than in a square or an opposition. For me, the conjunction combines the best of both worlds. We get revolutionary (Uranus) manifestation (Saturn) and innovative (Uranus) organization (Saturn). What is unusual (Uranus) can be respected (Saturn) and what is alternative or maverick (Uranus) can be grounded and given form (Saturn). And so the progressive spirit (Uranus) meets the established norm (Saturn), wakes it up (Uranus) and achieves longevity (Saturn). Certainly, the groundbreaking (now, there's a Saturn–Uranus word) talents and output of both Janis and Jimi have continued (Saturn) to illuminate (Uranus) every generation of musicians and artists since, despite their sudden (Uranus) end (Saturn). I'd say it's the Uranus component that keeps things fresh and relevant, no matter how much time (Saturn) passes.

With Janis's chart there's a really strong sense of her chafing against her roots (IC). She was born into a middle-class family in Port Arthur, a Texan town founded on oil refineries. Segregation was the norm. Janis had no sympathy for the uptight white attitudes and everyday racism prevalent, the small minds and big injustices. As she herself said, 'Texas is OK if you want to settle down and do your own thing quietly, but it's not for outrageous people, and I was always outrageous.' Even before she had fully flowered into her own unique style she was already standing out as being freer than those around her. At university in Austin, the campus newspaper *The Daily Texan* ran a profile of her in the issue dated 27 July 1962, headlined 'She Dares to Be Different'. It began, 'She goes barefooted when she feels like it, wears Levi's to class because they're more comfortable, and carries her Autoharp with her everywhere she goes so that in case she gets the urge to break into song it will be handy. Her name is Janis Joplin.'

The bands she would ultimately front have various Saturn–Uranus overtones: Kozmic Blues Band, Big Brother and the Holding Company, and Full Tilt Boogie. These days it seems everyone and his mother are inked, but she was way ahead in having decorative tattoos (scandalous! permanent!) and in wearing gorgeously individual (Uranus) vintage (Saturn) clothes. Jimi was also known for his extraordinary threads and flamboyant style – psychedelic prints and feather boas, satins, silks and velvets looked as good on him as they did on Janis. It's hard to overstate the impact they had on white-bread, post-war America.

On *The Dick Cavett Show*, screened on 9 September 1969, Jimi was famously asked about his wild and controversial playing of the American national anthem and the ensuing outcry, and he responded straight-faced and mildly that he didn't think it was unorthodox at all.

In another literal example of things being turned on their head, he usually played right-handed guitars which were turned upside down and restrung for his left-handed playing. When still dirt-poor and unknown, he regularly had to borrow guitars while his own was in hock and would simply flip them (sans restring) and instantly play them better than their owners. How's that for classic Gemini (hands) 6th (skill/technique) in action? His 6th House conjunction is no doubt the foundation for his stunning ability to craft and develop experimental sounds – he had such creative and technical genius and no limits to what he could dream up. He took elements from jazz, rock and roll and R&B, and synthesized his own unique sound, experimenting with distortion and feedback in entirely new ways.

Even in his brief days as a paratrooper (honourably discharged for 'unsuitability' – yet another Saturn–Uranus kerchiiiing) he would find ways to make his guitar echo the sounds around him: clanging aircraft doors or screaming engines. So Jimi took the framework of his musical heritage (legendary blues musicians such as Muddy Waters and BB King, and early pioneer rock and rollers such as Chuck Berry and Little Richard) and broke away from it – literally distorting and pushing his sound to extremes. Janis found her own brand of freedom by defying her segregated roots and looking to older African-American artists such as Odetta and Bessie Smith for inspiration and a new direction. Each in their own way, true to the spirit of Saturn–Uranus.

Vocally, Janis was also completely out there. There's famous concert footage from Monterey of an astonished Mama Cass gazing up in disbelief as Janis performs 'Ball and Chain' with an indescribable intensity. Unmistakable truth simply poured out of her when she was on stage: the full power of the Saturn–Uranus conjunction scorched through her vocal cords like an amazing voltage for which she was the uninhibited channel. At the height of her powers, she had all the raw vulnerability and excitement of an electrical storm on the edge of an active volcano, and to watch her was to be baptized by the white light of pure emotion.

Listen to Janis's and Jimi's stuff. It sounds like freedom and breakthrough and worlds colliding and changing, chaos and order spinning each other round the floor. Listen. Even after decades it still sounds new.

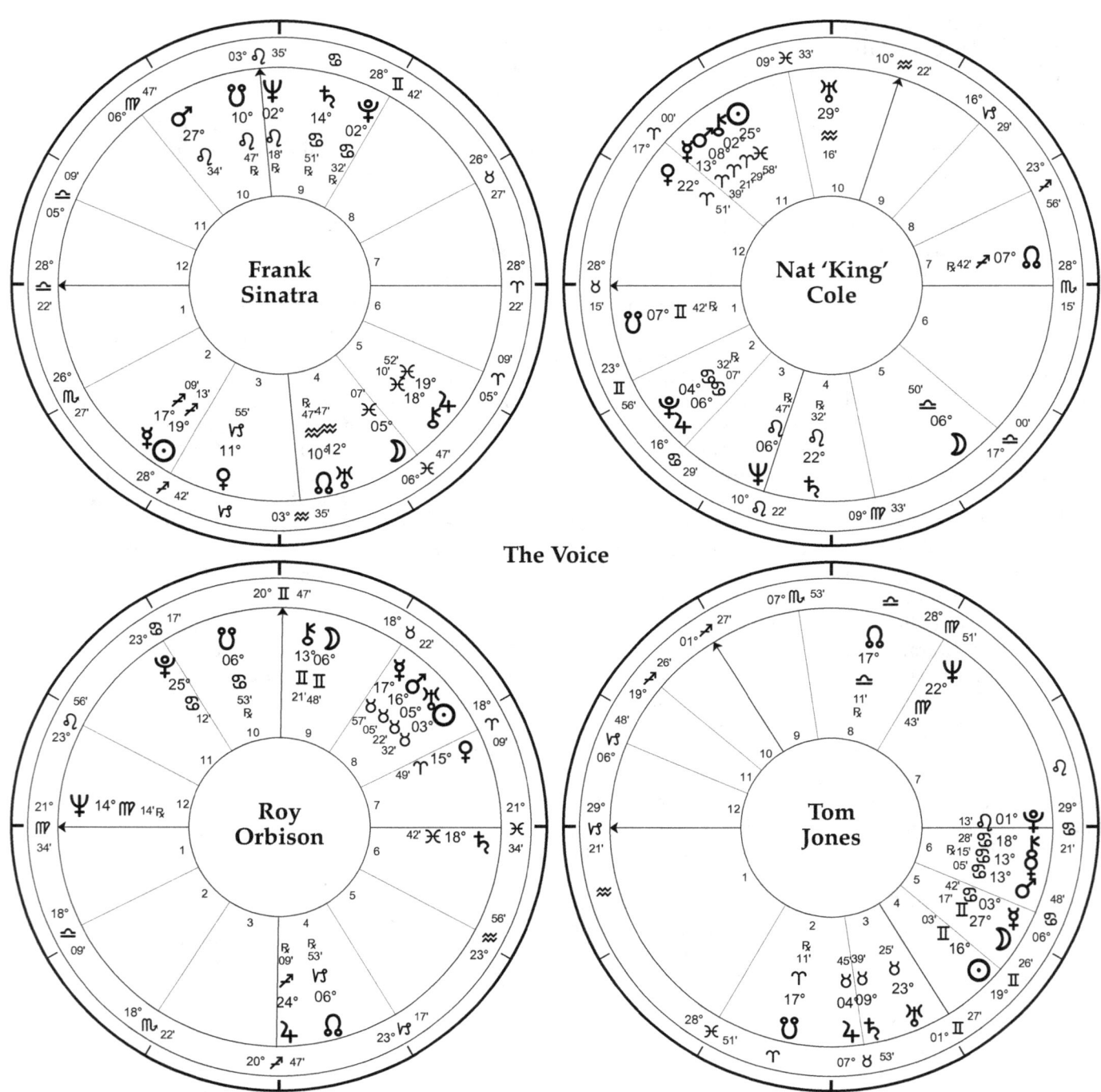

The Voice

Music Royalty 147

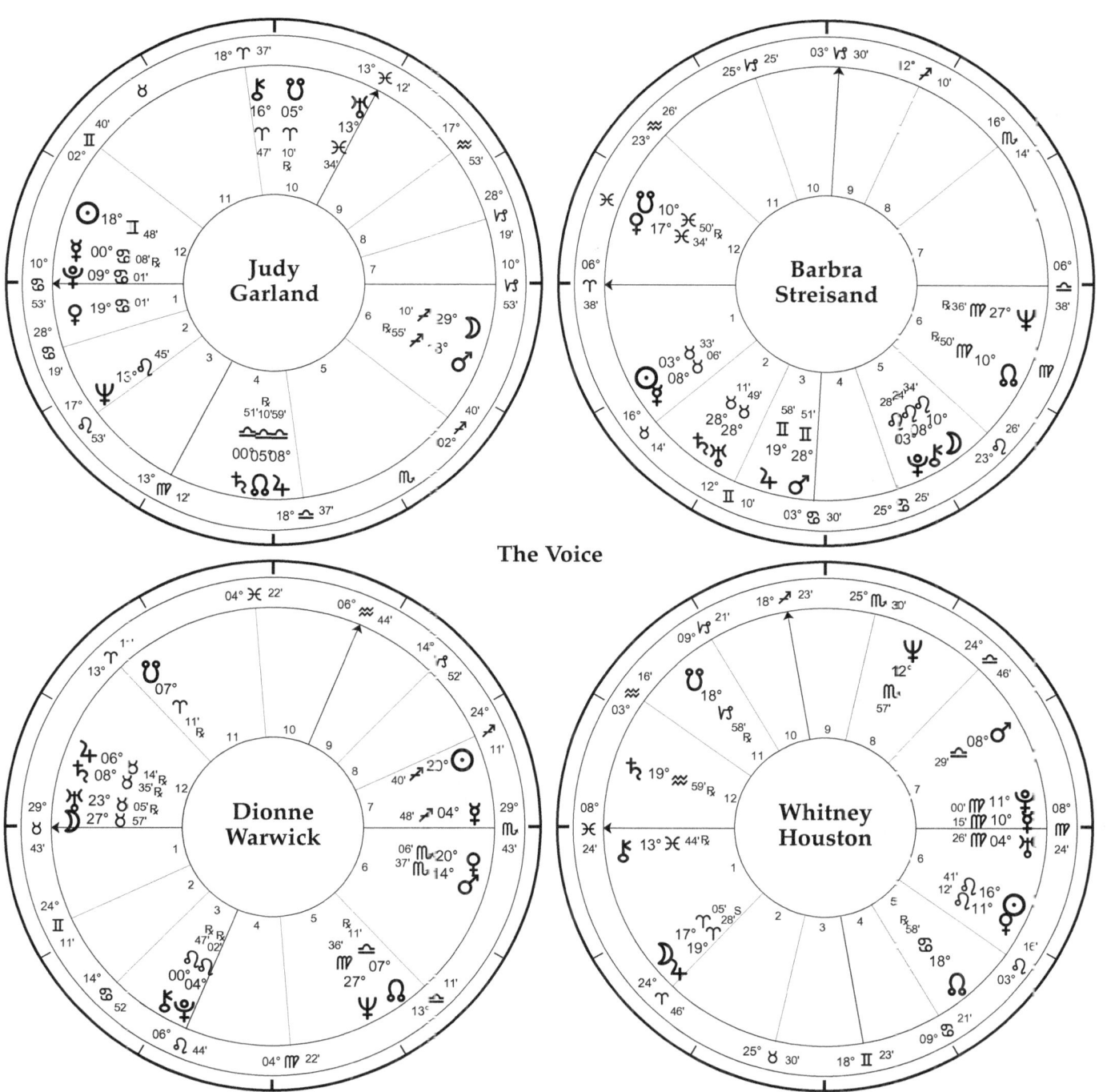

The Voice

Music and the Saturn–Neptune Cycle

Bruce Scofield

Trends in music throughout history follow the Saturn–Neptune cycle, and it appears that peaks in musical activity of all kinds occur around the conjunction and opposition. Saturn conjoins Neptune approximately every 36 years, with the opposition occurring about 18 years after the conjunction. Each conjunction of these planets takes place about 80 degrees (roughly three signs) ahead of their previous conjunction. For example, the conjunction of 1953 was at 21° Libra, that of 1989 was at 11° Capricorn, and in 2026 Saturn and Neptune will conjoin at 0° Aries. In this short article I've noted some obvious correlations between this astronomical cycle and the history of music in the West since the 18th century.

In 1738 Saturn conjoined Neptune near 0° Cancer. It was in this year that J.S. Bach composed his *Mass in B Minor*, one of his greatest masterpieces. Not long after, in 1741, Handel composed *The Messiah*. Perhaps we could say that around this date the Baroque movement in music was at its peak. In 1756 Saturn and Neptune were in opposition and during that year Mozart was born. Three years later, Haydn composed his first symphony. The next conjunction occurred in 1773, a year during which the waltz became fashionable in Vienna, the centre of musical activity in Europe. Between this conjunction and the next opposition, Mozart produced all his major works. He died shortly before this opposition, which occurred in 1792. Mozart's creative life, from conjunction to opposition of these two planets, established the highest standards of the classical form. Also in 1791, the waltz became fashionable in London. Time and fashions moved more slowly for most back then.

Throughout the 19th century, major works and the births and deaths of famous musicians seem to have taken place close to the conjunctions and oppositions of Saturn and Neptune. The 1828 opposition was near in time to the birth of Stephen Foster, the great American songwriter, and also the death of Beethoven. The 1846 conjunction of Saturn–Neptune occurred in Aquarius when the Paris Opera was lit up for the first time by electric lights, and Adolphe Sax patented the saxophone.

The Saturn–Neptune opposition of 1900 correlates with several important events in the history of music that took place in the US. Ragtime was developing around this time, and both Aaron Copland and Louis Armstrong were born. During the next few years the first major musical recordings were made. But it was the conjunction of 1917 in Leo that began one of the major musical movements of the 20th century. Jazz was sweeping the country.

It can be argued that the origins of jazz are located well before this 1917 conjunction, but it was only by this date that the several strands of gospel, blues and marching band combined and took a definite form. In 1917 Storyville, the red-light and gambling district of New Orleans, was closed down by municipal order. This was a major blow to the musicians who were employed there and they migrated to other parts of the country (notably Chicago), taking their music with them. In a very real sense, jazz was born when it was forced to expand out of New Orleans. The first jazz recordings were also made around this time and Chicago became the world jazz centre.

Jazz changed around the time of the 1936 opposition of Saturn and Neptune – it became 'swing', a wildly successful popular form of jazz. This was the time when Fats Waller, Teddy Wilson, Duke Ellington, Count Basie, Lionel Hampton and Louis Armstrong made their best recordings. It appears that jazz as an art form ran its course between two Saturn–Neptune conjunctions and peaked at the opposition in the middle.

Shortly after the 1953 conjunction, the first Newport Jazz Festival was held. But was jazz now simply a form of American classical music which needed special festivals to keep it alive? One thing can be said for sure, far fewer jazz artists were making the charts in the 1950s and the 1960s than they were in the 1930s and 1940s. The conjunction of Saturn and Neptune in 1953 occurred in square to the planet Uranus and foreshadowed the development of a musical form more disruptive than any the world had ever seen.

During the early 1950s, a number of black rhythm and blues artists hit the charts with best-selling records. These were the seeds of what became rock 'n' roll when, in 1954, white artists, many with country music backgrounds, began to cover the same material. The dominance and power of the electric guitar also began to be felt during the mid 1950s. By 1954, just one year after the Saturn–Neptune conjunction, the groundwork for an entirely new form of music had already been laid and Elvis Presley, a white country and gospel singer who sang songs written by black artists, took centre stage.

Over the next few years, early rock 'n' roll peaked with both black and white artists, including Elvis, Chuck Berry, Little Richard, Jerry Lee Lewis and Buddy Holly. The material became more aggressive and the lyrics more threatening to the white, middle-class Establishment. Some tried to ban this new music, a confirmation of the Uranus square to the conjunction. But by 1962, when Saturn was forming a square to Neptune, many of the early rockers began to lose their influence as corporate control of the music industry asserted itself. Other musical currents, including folk music and watered down jazz, began to fill the void. Rock music had hit the rocks as Saturn hit Neptune with a hard square in fixed signs. But just as the square began to separate in 1964, new lifeblood, in the form of The Beatles and other English groups, crossed the Atlantic hitting the charts and the performance halls. In essence, rock music was rescued by English interpretations of the original black American musical form. Along with The Rolling Stones, The Kinks, The Animals and The Yardbirds, The Beatles transformed a young musical tradition and brought it towards maturity in the late 1960s just before Saturn and Neptune opposed each other.

Everything fell apart around 1971, the year the opposition occurred – deaths and suicides of major stars made it the year 'the music died'. In many respects, rock music never surpassed its 1960s' peak. The music recorded then still remains viable and fresh-sounding. Even though recording techniques have improved considerably since this time, and there have been steady improvements in the quality of the vocals and the playing of instruments, the fact that many radio stations today play nothing but 'classic rock' is evidence of this statement.

In 1979 Saturn again squared Neptune, and again rock music was in the doldrums. Disco, primarily a dance movement, had been dominant for several years, and the rebellious and aggressive tradition in rock music had been sanitized by the corporations. But then rock showed its staying power and we saw the emergence of punk and new-wave rock music. This trend sought the primitive roots of rock music and celebrated the right to be an individual. Much of the material expressed frustration and even violence. Also around this time hip hop (rap) and new age music began to develop as genres.

In 1989, there was another Saturn–Neptune conjunction, this one in Capricorn. But the planet Uranus was again in the picture, this time as part of the conjunction. The conjunction of these three planets is quite infrequent, the last having occurred during the early 14th century with the Ars Nova movement, a major development in the history of music. In 1989, we saw the rise of what was called alternative rock music, mostly from musicians who bypassed the corporations and signed with independent record labels. Today a lot of this music is referred to as indie rock. This time also marked the golden age of hip hop (rap) music, which celebrates individual expression, and techno which is certainly Uranian.

In 2006, Saturn opposite Neptune appears to have marked the watershed for digital music downloads (which have basically killed the music album). The music industry was turned upside down in just a few years as bands began to distribute their music for free. This was the rise of music sharing, YouTube music videos and the corporate creation of music stars in TV shows like *Idol*. The next Saturn–Neptune conjunction occurs in 2026 at 0° Aries. A fresh start? We shall see.

This is a reduction and update of a much larger article published in a 1988 issue of The Mountain Astrologer.

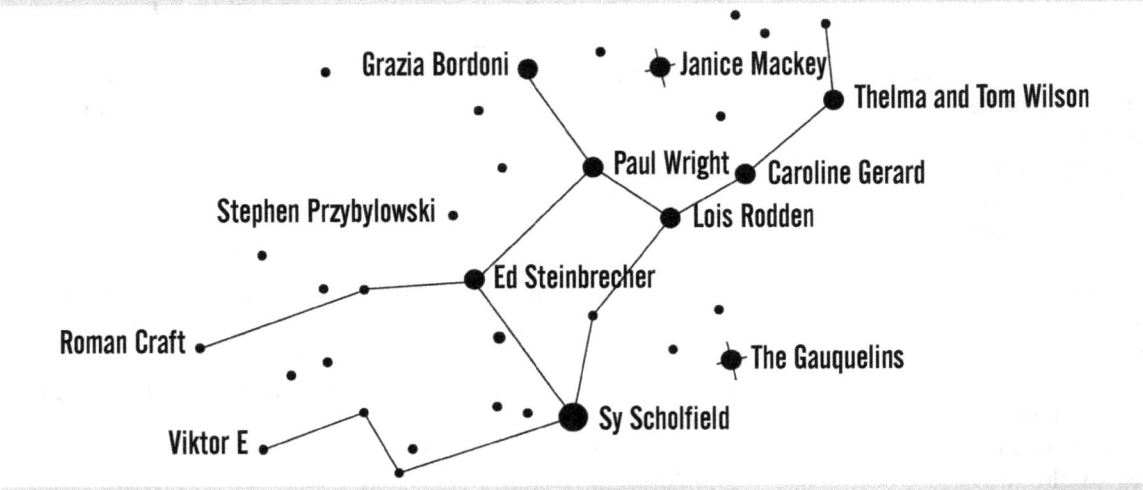

Birth Data

In this section you'll find the birth data and sources for all the performers presented within these pages – along with a page reference for where their horoscope appears. For space reasons, I've not given coordinates for the birth places (only including information on the specific borough/province when there is more than one place with the same name) and where relevant I've referred to the source being 'a biography' rather than listing the name and publication details. For further details of biographies and other sources quoted, please visit www.astrodatabank.com. Much of the data entered onto this website have been edited by Sy Scholfield (www.syscholfield.com), who has also checked the data included in this book.

The data presented in this book are based on information that is as accurate as we currently have available. Only in a handful of cases have I presented charts where there is a major, known difference of opinion (e.g. Mariah Carey, Diahann Carroll, Nat 'King' Cole and Quincy Jones). In one instance (Paul McCartney), I have printed two charts side by side because both sources of these conflicting birth times appear equally valid.

Sadly, I've not been able to include many well known performers (from Elton John to Lady Gaga) because their birth times are not known or haven't been verified. Please feel welcome to send in any updates (directly to me at info@flareuk.com) for future editions or to contribute additional birth data (ideally with documented sources) of people we've not been able to include. My deepest thanks to all the collectors who have helped me directly and indirectly over the 20+ years that I've been researching and accumulating sourced data.

Chart Data & Sources

Name, page	Day, month, year, time (24hr clock), time zone, place, country. (Source and collector)
Paula Abdul, 174	19 Jun 1962, 14:32 PDT, Los Angeles, CA, USA. (BC* from Frank Clifford)
Christina Aguilera, 58	18 Dec 1980, 10:46 EST, Staten Island, NY, USA. (Mother to Kevin Bold)
Jewel Akens, 33	12 Sep 1933, 19:40 CST, Houston, TX, USA. (BC* from Sy Scholfield)
Alaska, 178	13 Jun 1963, 13:00 CST, Mexico City, Mexico. (Bio quoted by Eduardo Castellanos)
Alizée, 178	21 Aug 1984, 08:55 MEDT, Ajaccio, France. (BC from Paddy de Jabrun)
Debbie Allen, 57	16 Jan 1950, 21:45 CST, Houston, TX, USA. (BC* from Frank Clifford)
Marc Almond, 172	9 Jul 1957, 05:00 GDT, Southport, England. (His letter to Garry Heaton; autobio states Leo rising)
Herb Alpert, 137	31 Mar 1935, 14:46 PST, Los Angeles, CA, USA. (BC from Janice Mackey)
Tori Amos, 84	22 Aug 1963, 13:10 EST, Newton, NC, USA. (BC from Jennifer Albert)
Trey Anastasio, 222	30 Sep 1964, 06:32 CST, Fort Worth, TX, USA. (Father as quoted in the Phish Google forum)
Ian Anderson, 198	10 Aug 1947, 07:30 GDT, Dunfermline, Scotland. (BC* from Ed Steinbrecher)
Lynn Anderson, 68	26 Sep 1947, 18:36 CST, Grand Forks, ND, USA. (BC from Janice Mackey)
Julie Andrews, 235	1 Oct 1935, 06:00 GDT, Walton-on-Thames, England. (Bio quoted by Lois Rodden)
Adam Ant, 54	3 Nov 1954, 06:20 GMT, London, England. (Autobio* quoted by Sy Scholfield)
Billie Joe Armstrong, 198	17 Feb 1972, 04:02 PST, Oakland, CA, USA. (BC from Viktor E)
Louis Armstrong, 15, 132	4 Aug 1901, 22:00 CST, New Orleans, LA, USA. (BC for date, PBC documentary for time)
Ashanti, 33	13 Oct 1980, 13:32 EDT, Glen Cove, NY, USA. (Birth announcement from Roman Craft)
Fred Astaire, 238	10 May 1899, 21:16 CST, Omaha, NE, USA. (BC from Ed Helin)
Gene Autry, 68	29 Sep 1907, 04:30 CST, Tioga, TX, USA. (BC from Sy Scholfield)
Mick Avory, 101	15 Feb 1944, 20:30 GDT, Hampton Court, England. (Mother and him to Debbi Kempton-Smith)
Charles Aznavour, 167	22 May 1924, 00:15 GDT, Paris, France. (BC from The Gauquelins)
Mel B, 219	29 May 1975, 17:59 GDT, Leeds, England. (Autobio* quoted by Frank Clifford; same from mother on Twitter)
Burt Bacharach, 137	12 May 1928, 01:15 CST, Kansas City, MO, USA. (BC* from Ed Steinbrecher)
Erykah Badu, 34	26 Feb 1971, 01:10 CST, Dallas, TX, USA. (Her to a mutual friend of Frank Clifford)
Joan Baez, 106	9 Jan 1941, 10:45 EST, Staten Island, NY, USA. (BC* from Ed Steinbrecher)
Pearl Bailey, 229	29 Mar 1918, 07:00 EST, Newport News, VA, USA. (Her to a mutual friend of Joan McEvers)
Gavin Bain, 43	25 May 1981, 08:30 EET, Vanderbijlpark, South Africa. (Him to Stefanie James)
Chet Baker, 22	23 Dec 1929, 03:45 CST, Yale, OK, USA. (BC in biopic quoted by Michael Tierney)
Josephine Baker, 234	3 Jun 1906, 11:00 CST, St Louis, MO, USA. (Autobio* and sister's bio; Baker also gave 11:30)
Florence Ballard, 138	30 Jun 1943, 05:45 EWT, Detroit, MI, USA. (BC* from Frank Clifford)
Tony Banks, 217	27 Mar 1950, 07:30 GMT, East Hoathly, England. (Him to Marjorie Orr)
Gary Barlow, 58	20 Jan 1971, 12:20 MET, Frodsham, England. (Autobio* quoted by Frank Clifford and Sy Scholfield)
Jimmy Barnes, 198	28 Apr 1956, 16:30 GDT, Glasgow, Scotland. (BC from Caroline Gerard)
John Barrowman, 169	11 Mar 1967, 17:25 GMT, Glasgow, Scotland. (BC from Caroline Gerard)
Kathleen Battle, 228	13 Aug 1948, 00:50 EST, Portsmouth, OH, USA. (BC* from Frank Clifford)
Beck, 198	8 Jul 1970, 23:59 PDT, Los Angeles, CA, USA. (Bio* quoted by Sy Scholfield)
Lou Bega, 179	13 Apr 1975, 18:00 MET, Munich, Germany. (Him to Manfred Gregor)
Harry Belafonte, 166	1 Mar 1927, 10:30 EST, New York, NY, USA. (BC quoted by him to B. Redding)
Andy Bell, 173	25 Apr 1964, 03:30 GDT, Peterborough, England. (Official website quoted by Sy Scholfield)
Maggie Bell, 192	12 Jan 1945, 00:45 GDT, Glasgow, Scotland. (BC from Caroline Gerard)
Robert Bell, 34	8 Oct 1950, 20:25 EST, Youngstown, OH, USA. (BC* from Frank Clifford)
Ronald Bell, 34	1 Nov 1951, 04:13 EST, Youngstown, OH, USA. (BC* from Frank Clifford)
Chuck Berry, 112	18 Oct 1926, 06:59 CST, St Louis, MO, USA. (Autobio quoted by Lois Rodden)
Justin Bieber, 58	1 Mar 1994, 00:56 EST, London, Ontario, Canada. (Bio* and documentary quoted by Frank Clifford)

Björk, 177	21 Nov 1965, 07:50 WAT, Reykjavik, Iceland. (Approx time from info in her interview with Jon Savage)	
Clint Black, 69	4 Feb 1962, 19:30 EST, Long Branch, NJ, USA. (BC from Stephen Przybylowski)	
Andrea Bocelli, 226	22 Sep 1958, 05:15 MET, Lajatico, Pisa, Italy. (BC* from Grazia Bordoni)	
Marc Bolan, 120	30 Sep 1947, 12:30 GDT, Hackney, London, England. (Him to Adam Fronteras)	
Michael Bolton, 58	26 Feb 1953, 01:32 EST, New Haven, CT, USA. (BC from Stephen Przybylowski)	
Jon Bon Jovi, 218	2 Mar 1962, 20:45 EST, Perth Amboy, NJ, USA. (BC* from Stephen Przybylowski)	
Bono, 199	10 May 1960, 02:00 GDT, Dublin, Ireland. (Him, quoted by Ed Steinbrecher; 'Two on the dot', a.m./p.m. not specified)	
Sonny Bono, 214	16 Feb 1935, 21:21 EST, Detroit, MI, USA. (BC from Janice Mackey)	
Debby Boone, 166	22 Sep 1956, 14:37 EDT, Hackensack, NJ, USA. (BR* from Ed Steinbrecher)	
Pat Boone, 166	1 Jun 1934, 18:40 EST, Jacksonville, FL, USA. (BC from Janice Mackey)	
Miguel Bosé, 179	3 Apr 1956, 14:30 EST, Panamá, Panamá. (Bio* quoted by Su Scholfield)	
David Bowie, 120	8 Jan 1947, 09:00 GMT, Brixton, London, England. (Parents in bio quoted by Lois Rodden; Bowie gave Gary Lorig 09:30)	
Billy Boyd, 43	31 May 1980, 17:10 GDT, Londonderry, Northern Ireland. (Him to Stefanie James)	
Boy George, 124	14 Jun 1961, 02:50 GDT, Bexley, England. (Baby book* info given on Twitter quoted by Sy Scholfield)	
Susan Boyle, 63	1 Apr 1961, 09:50 GDT, Blackburn, West Lothian, Scotland. (BC from Caroline Gerard)	
Billy Bragg, 84	20 Dec 1957, 04:00 GMT, Barking, England. (Him to Neil Spencer)	
Jacques Brel, 178	8 Apr 1929, 03:00 GMT, Schaerbeek, Belgium. (BR from Luc de Marre)	
Dee Dee Bridgewater, 22	27 May 1950, 04:00 CST, Memphis, TN, USA. (Her to Paddy de Jabrun)	
Sarah Brightman, 231	14 Aug 1960, 05:45 GDT, London, England. (Her and mother to Pamela Crane)	
Elkie Brooks, 192	25 Feb 1945, 20:00 GDT, Salford, England. (Her to J. Argyle)	
Garth Brooks, 135	7 Feb 1962, 13:07 CST, Tulsa, OK, USA. (Him to Basil Fearrington)	
Bobby Brown, 40	5 Feb 1969, 05:21 EST, Boston, MA, USA. (BC* from Frank Clifford)	
Chris Brown, 40	5 May 1989, 12:30 EDT, Tappahannock, VA, USA. (Mother on Twitter)	
Clifford Brown, 23	30 Oct 1930, 10:32 EST, Wilmington, DE, USA. (Wife to David Hayward)	
Ruth Brown, 34	12 Jan 1928, 15:30 EST, Portsmouth, VA, USA. (Her to Lynn Palmer)	
Jack Bruce, 199	14 May 1943, 02:10 GDWT, Glasgow, Scotland. (BC from Paul Wright)	
Lindsey Buckingham, 215	3 Oct 1949, 01:53 PST, Palo Alto, CA, USA. (BC* from Frank Clifford)	
Betty Buckley, 229	3 Jul 1947, 11:44 CST, Big Spring, TX, USA. (BC* from Frank Clifford)	
Jeff Buckley, 84	17 Nov 1966, 22:49 PST, Anaheim, CA, USA. (BC* from Frank Clifford)	
Tim Buckley, 84	14 Feb 1947, 19:12 EST, Washington, DC, USA. (BC from Janice Mackey)	
Jimmy Buffett, 69	25 Dec 1946, 01:08 CST, Pascagoula, MS, USA. (Autobio quoted by Marion March)	
Eric Burdon, 199	11 May 1941, 00:00 GDWT, Newcastle upon Tyne, England. (Him to Jenni Harte)	
Donald Byrd, 23	9 Dec 1932, 06:00 EST, Detroit, MI, USA. (BC from Janice Mackey)	
David Byrne, 199	14 May 1952, 14:00 GDT, Dumbarton, Scotland. (BC* from Aaron Fischer)	
Monserrat Caballé, 227	12 Apr 1933, 21:00 GMT, Barcelona, Spain. (Bio quoted by Frank Clifford)	
Glen Campbell, 69	22 Apr 1936, 20:14 CST, Delight, AR, USA. ('TV Guide' quoted by Lois Rodden)	
Nick Cannon, 40	8 Oct 1980, 20:49 PDT, San Diego, CA, USA. (BC from Viktor E)	
Captain Beefheart, 200	15 Jan 1941, 16:25 PST, Los Angeles, CA, USA. (BC* from Sy Scholfield)	
Captain Sensible, 200	24 Apr 1954, 05:00 GDT, Balham, London, England. (Him to Marjorie Orr)	
Irene Cara, 57	18 Mar 1959, 10:41 EST, Bronx, NY, USA. (BC quoted by her to Lynn Rodden)	
Mariah Carey, 127	27 Mar 1970, 07:27 EST, Huntington, NY, USA. (Date and time from her 'Rolling Stone' interview; 1970 from her twins' BCs and from mother; place from online; some evidence for 1969)	
Belinda Carlisle, 54	17 Aug 1958, 19:17 PDT, Los Angeles, CA, USA. (BC* from Frank Clifford)	
Roberto Carlos, 179	19 Apr 1941, 10:00 BZT, Cachoeiro de Itapemirim, Brazil. (BC from Marcello Borges)	
Kim Carnes, 192	20 Jul 1945, 10:14 PWT, Los Angeles, CA, USA. (BC* from Frank Clifford)	

Karen Carpenter, 104	2 Mar 1950, 11:45 EST, New Haven, CT, USA. (BR* from Ed Steinbrecher)
Mary Chapin Carpenter, 69	21 Feb 1958, 05:46 EST, Princeton, NJ, USA. (BC* from Frank Clifford)
Richard Carpenter, 104	15 Oct 1946, 00:53 EST, New Haven, CT, USA. (BR* from Ed Steinbrecher)
Vikki Carr, 180	19 Jul 1940, 15:00 MST, El Paso, TX, USA. (BR* from Ed Steinbrecher)
Rafaella Carra, 180	18 Jun 1943, 16:00 MEDT, Bologna, Italy. (BC from Grazia Bordoni)
José Carreras, 225	5 Dec 1946, 04:00 MET, Barcelona, Spain. (BC* from Frank Clifford)
Diahann Carroll, 229	17 Jul 1935, 21:55 EDT, New York, NY, USA. (BC* from Thelma and Tom Wilson; BC unclear: 21:35?)
Johnny Cash, 134	26 Feb 1932, 07:30 CST, Kingsland, AR, USA. (Mother to Coleen Gauthier)
Rosanne Cash, 70	24 May 1955, 20:00 CST, Memphis, TN, USA. (Autobio quoted by Sy Scholfeld; BC has no time)
David Cassidy, 51	12 Apr 1950, 09:55 EST, New York, NY, USA. (Him to a mutual friend of Robert Jansky)
Shaun Cassidy, 51	27 Sep 1958, 15:34 PDT, Santa Monica, CA, USA. (BC* from Thelma and Tom Wilson)
Gustavo Cerati, 180	11 Aug 1959, 06:30 ADT, Buenos Aires, Argentina. (Mother to Eduardo Castellanos)
Carol Channing, 229	31 Jan 1921, 21:00 PST, Seattle, WA, USA. (BC* from The Gauquelins; autobio states 20:30)
Cher, 214	20 May 1946, 07:25 PST, El Centro, CA, USA. (BC from Janice Mackey)
Maurice Chevalier, 167	12 Sep 1888, 02:00 LMT, Paris, France. (BC* from Sy Scholfield)
George Chisholm, 23	29 Mar 1915, 07:05 GMT, Glasgow, Scotland. (BC from Paul Wright)
Charlotte Church, 228	21 Feb 1986, 22:28 GMT, Cardiff, Wales. (Autobio in 'The Sunday Times' quoted by Bill Sheeran)
Patsy Cline, 134	8 Sep 1932, 23:15 EST, Winchester, VA, USA. (Hospital record* from FC; BC states 23:05)
George Clinton, 35	22 Jul 1941, 11:55 EST, Kannapolis, NC, USA. (BR from Ed Steinbrecher)
Rosemary Clooney, 164	23 May 1928, 02:30 EST, Maysville, KY, USA. (BC from The Gauquelins)
Kurt Cobain, 128	20 Feb 1967, 19:38 PST, Aberdeen, WA, USA. (Hospital record* from Roman Craft)
Joe Cocker, 200	20 May 1944, 05:00 GDWT, Sheffield, England. (Him to Ruth Nobel)
Leonard Cohen, 109	21 Sep 1934, 06:45 EDT, Montreal, Canada. (Records stated in bio quoted by Sy Scholfield)
Nat 'King' Cole, 146	17 Mar 1919, 09:00 CST, Montgomery, AL, USA (BC* from Thelma and Tom Wilson; BC unclear: 03:00?)
Natalie Cole, 35	6 Feb 1950, 18:07 PST, Los Angeles, CA, USA. (BC from Janice Mackey)
Ornette Coleman, 23	9 Mar 1930, 05:00 CST, Fort Worth, TX, USA. (Him* in print quoted by Sy Scholfield)
Edwyn Collins, 200	23 Aug 1959, 15:20 GDT, Glasgow, Scotland. (BC from Paul Wright)
Judy Collins, 106	1 May 1939, 11:55 PST, Seattle, WA, USA. (BC from Janice Mackey)
Phil Collins, 217	30 Jan 1951, 00:05 GMT, Putney, London, England. (Mother via record company to Garry Heaton)
John Coltrane, 24	23 Sep 1926, 17:00 EST, Hamlet, NC, USA. (BR from Ed Steinbrecher)
Earl Thomas Conley, 70	17 Oct 1941, 02:00 EST, Washington, OH, USA. (BC* from Frank Clifford)
Sam Cooke, 35	22 Jan 1931, 14:10 CST, Clarksdale, MS, USA. (BC* from bio quoted by Frank Clifford)
Rita Coolidge, 70	1 May 1945, 00:17 CWT, Nashville, TN, USA. (BC quoted by her to Marc Singer)
Alice Cooper, 201	4 Feb 1948, 22:33 EST, Detroit, MI, USA. (BC from Janice Mackey)
Chick Corea, 24	12 Jun 1941, 12:40 EDT, Chelsea, MA, USA. (BC from Pat Taglilatelo)
Pamela Courson, 100	22 Dec 1946, 11:10 PST, Weed, CA, USA. (BC from Pamela Young)
Beverley Craven, 86	28 Jul 1963, 15:00 IST, Colombo, Sri Lanka. (Her* to Frank Clifford)
Darren Criss, 59	5 Feb 1987, 12:37 PST, San Francisco, CA, USA. (BC from Viktor E)
Christopher Cross, 168	3 May 1951, 01:01 CST, Fort Sam Houston, TX, USA. (BC* from Frank Clifford)
Sheryl Crow, 70	11 Feb 1962, 09:58 CST, Kennett, MO, USA. (Bio* quoted by Sy Scholfield)
Jamie Cullum, 24	20 Aug 1979, 07:30 GDT, Rochford, Essex, England. (Him to a mutual friend of Frank Clifford)
Billy Ray Cyrus, 71	25 Aug 1961, 17:52 EST, Bellefonte, KY, USA. (BC from Stephen Przybylowski)
Miley Cyrus, 59	23 Nov 1992, 16:19 CST, Nashville, TN, USA. (BR* from Frank Clifford)
Roger Daltrey, 99	1 Mar 1944, 01:50 GDT, London, England. (Autobio 'just before 2 a.m.'; Mother gave 2 a.m.)
Dana International, 63	2 Feb 1969, 22:30 EET, Tel Aviv, Israel. (Her via her mother)
Darius Danesh, 63	19 Aug 1980, 14:34 GDT, Glasgow, Scotland. (BC from Caroline Gerard)
Pino Daniele, 180	19 Mar 1955, 23:00 MET, Naples, Italy. (Him in interview quoted by Grazia Bordoni)

Charlie Daniels, 71	28 Oct 1936, 04:00 EST, Wilmington, NC, USA. (BR from Ed Steinbrecher)
Bobby Darin, 50	14 May 1936, 05:28 EDT, Manhattan, NY, USA. (BC* from Ed Steinbrecher)
Dave Davies, 101	3 Feb 1947, 01:00 GMT, London, England. (Mother to Debbi Kempton-Smith)
Ray Davies, 101	21 Jun 1944, 00:20 GDWT, Fortis Green, London, England. (BC* for date and place; time from mother to Debbi Kempton-Smith)
Miles Davis, 24	26 May 1926, 05:00 CST, Alton, IL, USA. (BC from Pat Taglilatelo; same in BR* from Bob Garner)
Doris Day, 163	3 Apr 1922, 16:30 CST, Cincinnati, OH, USA. (BC* from Frank Clifford)
Suzanne de Passe, 138	19 Jul 1946, 03:50 EDT, New York, NY, USA. (Her to Sharon Timmer)
John Densmore, 100	1 Dec 1944, 04:27 PWT, Santa Monica, CA, USA. (BC from Bob Garner)
John Denver, 71	31 Dec 1943, 15:55 MWT, Roswell, NM, USA. (BC from Janice Mackey)
Giuseppe Di Stefano, 225	24 Jul 1921, 12:00 MET, Motta Sant'Anastasia, Italy. (BC from Arno Müller)
Neil Diamond, 168	24 Jan 1941, 23:04 EST, Brooklyn, Kings, NY, USA. (BC* from Lois Rodden)
Celine Dion, 127	30 Mar 1968, 12:30 EST, Charlemagne, Canada. (Her on radio; also said 'noon')
DMC, 40	31 Mar 1964, 15:31 EST, Manhattan, NY, USA. (BC* shown in documentary)
Plácido Domingo, 225	21 Jan 1941, 22:00 GDT, Madrid, Spain. (BC from Lois Rodden)
Lonnie Donegan, 86	29 Apr 1931, 03:00 GDT, Glasgow, Scotland. (BC from Paul Wright)
Donovan, 87	10 May 1946, 06:15 GDT, Glasgow, Scotland. (BC* from Aaron Fischer)
Jason Donovan, 54	1 Jun 1968, 18:00 AEST, Melbourne, Australia. (Bio* quoted by Frank Clifford)
Daryl Dragon, 215	27 Aug 1942, 01:43 PWT, Los Angeles, CA, USA. (BC from Janice Mackey)
Drake, 41	24 Oct 1986, 02:31 EDT, Toronto, Canada. (BR* from Roman Craft)
Nick Drake, 87	19 Jun 1948, 07:15 LT, Rangoon, Burma (now Yangon, Myanmar). (Mother to John Etherington)
Dr. Dre, 41	18 Feb 1965, 10:56 PST, Los Angeles, CA, USA. (BC from Pat Taglilatelo)
Duffy, 87	23 Jun 1984, 06:55 GDT, Bangor, Wales. (BC* from Frank Clifford)
Dulce, 181	29 Jul 1955, 08:50 CST, Matamoros, Mexico. (BR* from Sy Scholfield)
Johnny Duncan, 71	5 Oct 1938, 22:30 CST, Dublin, TX, USA. (BC from Stephen Przybylowski)
Deanna Durbin, 238	4 Dec 1921, 14:00 CST, Winnipeg, Canada. (Her in an interview; birth year from online)
Bob Dylan, 106	24 May 1941, 21:05 CST, Duluth, MN, USA. (BC* from Bob Garner)
Steve Earle, 72	17 Jan 1955, 12:00 EST, Fort Monroe, VA, USA. (Bio* quoted by Sy Scholfield)
Sheena Easton, 55	27 Apr 1959, 15:40 GDT, Bellshill, Scotland. (BC* from Aaron Fischer)
Brian Eno, 201	15 May 1948, 03:50 GDT, Melton, Woodbridge, England. (Mother to Tony Matthews)
John Entwistle, 99	9 Oct 1944, 18:00 GDT, London, England. (Mother to Debbi Kempton-Smith)
David Essex, 52	23 Jul 1947, 06:05 GDWT, West Ham, London, England. (Autobio* quoted by Sy Scholfield, 'just before dawn')
Gloria Estefan, 181	1 Sep 1957, 13:00 EST, Havana, Cuba. (Her on Twitter)
Melissa Etheridge, 192	29 May 1961, 13:15 CST, Leavenworth, KS, USA. (Bio* quoted by Sy Scholfield)
Don Everly, 213	1 Feb 1937, 14:00 CST, Brownies Creek, KY, USA. (BC from Janice Mackey)
Phil Everly, 213	19 Jan 1939, 19:30 CST, Chicago, IL, USA. (BC printed in bio quoted by Aaron Fischer)
Donna Fargo, 72	10 Nov 1940, 04:30 EST, Mount Airy, NC, USA. (BR from Ed Steinbrecher)
Mylene Farmer, 117	12 Sep 1961, 05:17 EDT, Montreal, Canada. (Her to Dana Haynes)
Fergie, 219	27 Mar 1975, 13:24 PDT, Whittier, CA, USA. (BC from Pat Taglilatelo)
Tiziano Ferro, 181	21 Feb 1980, 15:00 MET, Latina, Italy. (Him to Paolo Crimaldi)
Bryan Ferry, 201	26 Sep 1945, 11:30 GDT, Washington, England. (Him to Ian Richards)
Eddie Fisher, 165	10 Aug 1928, 07:42 EDT, Philadelphia, PA, USA. (BC from Janice Mackey)
Ella Fitzgerald, 132	25 Apr 1917, 12:30 EST, Newport News, VA, USA. (BC from Penelope Sitter)
Roberta Flack, 130	10 Feb 1937, 06:30 EST, Black Mountain, NC, USA. (BR* from Ed Steinbrecher)
Renée Fleming, 228	14 Feb 1959, 12:22 EST, Indiana, PA, USA. (BC from Romy Ransom)
John Fogerty, 201	28 May 1945, 19:28 PWT, Berkeley, CA, USA. (BC from Aaron Fischer)

Chart Data & Sources

Peter Frampton, 202	22 Apr 1950, 06:30 GDT, Beckenham, Kent, England. (Bio* gives time; BC* from Frank Clifford gives date and place)
Connie Francis, 164	12 Dec 1937, 07:28 EST, Newark, NJ, USA. (BC* from Eugene Moore)
Aretha Franklin, 131	25 Mar 1942, 22:30 CWT, Memphis, TN, USA. (BC* from Ed Steinbrecher)
Janie Fricke, 72	19 Dec 1947, 06:03 CST, South Whitley, IN, USA. (Her* to Frank Clifford)
Lefty Frizzell, 72	31 Mar 1928, 00:35 CST, Corsicana, TX, USA. (BC* from Sy Scholfield)
Peter Gabriel, 210, 217	13 Feb 1950, 16:30 GMT, Woking, England. (Him to T.J. Andrews)
Dave Gahan, 202	9 May 1962, 05:00 GDT, Chigwell, England. (Him to Marjorie Orr)
Serge Gainsbourg, 181	2 Apr 1928, 04:55 GMT, Paris, France. (BC from The Gauquelins and Didier Geslain)
Liam Gallagher, 202	21 Sep 1972, 12:58 GDT, Burnage, England. (Him to a mutual friend of Frank Clifford)
Jerry Garcia, 202	1 Aug 1942, 12:05 PWT, San Francisco, CA, USA. (BC from Aaron Fischer)
Judy Garland, 147	10 Jun 1922, 06:00 CST, Grand Rapids, MN, USA. (BC from Janice Mackey; same on BR*)
Leif Garrett, 52	8 Nov 1961, 03:41 PST, Hollywood, CA, USA. (Bio quoted by Lois Rodden)
Larry Gatlin, 73	2 May 1948, 14:30 CST, Seminole, TX, USA. (BC* from Frank Clifford)
Marvin Gaye, 35	2 Apr 1939, 12:00 EST, Washington, DC, USA. (Him to John Etherington)
Crystal Gayle, 73	9 Jan 1951, 01:25 EST, Paintsville, KY, USA. (BC* from Stephen Przybylowski)
Bob Geldof, 203	5 Oct 1951, 14:20 GDT, Dublin, Ireland. (Him and his press agent to Jo Logan)
Andy Gibb, 123	5 Mar 1958, 06:30 GMT, Manchester, England. (BR from mother to Tashi Grady)
Barry Gibb, 123	1 Sep 1946, 08:45 GDT, Douglas, Isle of Man. (Bio; mother gave 9 a.m. to Tashi Grady)
Maurice Gibb, 123	22 Dec 1949, 03:50 GMT, Douglas, Isle of Man. (BC* from Ed Steinbrecher)
Robin Gibb, 123	22 Dec 1949, 03:15 GMT, Douglas, Isle of Man. (BC* from Ed Steinbrecher)
Debbie Gibson, 55	31 Aug 1970, 02:57 EDT, Brooklyn, Kings, NY, USA. (Baptismal record; same from her on Twitter* quoted by Sy Scholfield)
Erica Gimpel, 57	25 Jun 1964, 16:00 EDT, New York, NY, USA. (BC quoted by her* to Frank Clifford)
Mike Gordon, 222	3 Jun 1965, 11:32 EDT, Sudbury, MA, USA. (BC from Pat Taglilatelo)
Luke Goss, 55	29 Sep 1968, 18:11 MET, Lewisham, London, England. (BC* from Frank Clifford)
Matt Goss, 55	29 Sep 1968, 18:21 MET, Lewisham, London, England. (BC* from Frank Clifford)
Ariana Grande, 59	26 Jun 1993, 21:16 EDT, Boca Raton, FL, USA. (Father on Twitter* quoted by Sy Scholfield)
Irene Grandi, 182	6 Dec 1969, 20:30 MET, Florence, Italy. (BC from Grazia Bordoni)
Amy Grant, 73	25 Nov 1960, 03:24 EST, Augusta, GA, USA. (BC from Stephen Przybylowski)
Gogi Grant, 164	20 Sep 1924, 15:45 EDT, Philadelphia, PA, USA. (Mother via Grant's husband to Lynne Palmer)
Peter Green, 215	29 Oct 1946, 21:59 GMT, Bethnal Green, London, England. (Him to Bettina Lee, confirmed by mother)
Josh Groban, 169	27 Feb 1981, 16:13 PST, Los Angeles, CA, USA. (BC from Pat Taglilatelo)
Dave Grohl, 31	14 Jan 1969, 07:33 EST, Warren, OH, USA. (BC* from Frank Clifford)
Arlo Guthrie, 87	10 Jul 1947, 08:45 EDT, Brooklyn, Kings, NY, USA. (Him in an interview quoted by Ruth Dewey)
Merle Haggard, 134	6 Apr 1937, 01:30 PST, Bakersfield, CA, USA. (BC from Janice Mackey)
Bill Haley, 112	6 Jul 1925, 14:30 EST, Highland Park, MI, USA. (Bio and website quoted by Sy Scholfield)
Geri Halliwell, 219	6 Aug 1972, 14:30 GDT, Watford, England. (Her to Barry Street of The Astrology Shop in London)
Johnny Hallyday, 182	15 Jun 1943, 13:00 GDWT, Paris, France. (BC from Patrice Petitallot)
Herbie Hancock, 29	12 Apr 1940, 03:30 CST, Chicago, IL, USA. (BC from Lois Rodden)
Calvin Harris, 177	17 Jan 1984, 17:22 GMT, Dumfries, Scotland. (BC from Caroline Gerard)
Emmylou Harris, 73	2 Apr 1947, 12:10 CST, Birmingham, AL, USA. (BC quoted by her to Ruth Elliot)
George Harrison, 94	25 Feb 1943, 00:10 GDT, Liverpool, England. (BR quoted by sister)
Bobby Hatfield, 214	10 Aug 1940, 02:15 CST, Beaver Dam, WI, USA. (BC from Stephen Przybylowski)
Isaac Hayes, 36	20 Aug 1942, 04:00 EWT, Covington, KY, USA. (BC from Janice Mackey)
Jimi Hendrix, 143	27 Nov 1942, 10:15 PWT, Seattle, WA, USA. (BC* from Janice Mackey)
Woody Herman, 25	16 May 1913, 12:30 CST, Milwaukee, WI, USA. (BC from The Gauquelins)

Patrick Hernandez, 171	6 Apr 1949, 12:45 MET, Le Blanc Mesnil, Paris, France. (BC from Paddy de Jabrun)
Howard Hewett, 174	1 Oct 1955, 14:40 EST, Akron, OH, USA. (BC* from Frank Clifford)
Billie Holiday, 132	7 Apr 1915, 02:30 EST, Philadelphia, PA, USA. (BC in bio* quoted by Frank Clifford)
Buddy Holly, 112	7 Sep 1936, 15:30 CST, Lubbock, TX, USA. (Mother in an interview; 18:10 has been given)
Lena Horne, 235	30 Jun 1917, 23:45 EST, Brooklyn, Kings, NY, USA. (BR recorded by mother, quoted by Horne to Bertucelli)
Marilyn Horne, 227	16 Jan 1934, 15:20 EST, Bradford, PA, USA. (Hospital record quoted by Marc Penfield)
Bruce Hornsby, 88	23 Nov 1954, 23:00 EST, Richmond, VA, USA. (Him to Eileen Grimes)
Whitney Houston, 147	9 Aug 1963, 20:55 EDT, Newark, NJ, USA. (BC* from Kathryn Farmer)
Mick Hucknall, 203	8 Jun 1960, 06:30 GDT, Manchester, England. (Him to Garry Heaton)
Engelbert Humperdinck, 166	2 May 1936, 23:48 IST, Madras, India. (Secretary to his fan club president, quoted by Joan McEvers)
Michael Hutchence, 203	22 Jan 1960, 05:00 AEST, Sydney, Australia. (Him in an interview quoted by Frank Clifford)
Chrissie Hynde, 193	7 Sep 1951, 10:20 EDT, Akron, OH, USA. (BC* from Frank Clifford)
Billy Idol, 203	30 Nov 1955, 16:00 GMT, Stanmore, England. (Him on Twitter)
Julio Iglesias, 167	23 Sep 1943, 11:30 GDWT, Madrid, Spain. (BC* from Frank Clifford)
Pedro Infante, 182	18 Nov 1917, 02:30 LMT, Mazatlán, Mexico. (BC* from Eduardo Castellanos)
James Ingram, 36	16 Feb 1952, 12:49 EST, Akron, OH, USA. (BC* from Frank Clifford)
Chris Isaak, 204	26 Jun 1956, 22:49 PDT, Stockton, CA, USA. (BC from Viktor E)
Ronald Isley, 36	21 May 1941, 07:25 EST, Cincinnati, OH, USA. (BC* from Frank Clifford)
Rudolph Isley, 36	1 Apr 1939, 18:39 EST, Cincinnati, OH, USA. (BC* from Frank Clifford)
Jessie J, 59	27 Mar 1988, 09:27 GDT, Seven Kings, Ilford, England. (Autobio* quoted by Frank Clifford)
Michael Jackson, 117, 125	29 Aug 1958, 19:33 CDT, Gary, IN, USA. (BC quoted by nephew Taj, as given by MJ's mother)
Mick Jagger, 98, 118	26 Jul 1943, 02:30 GDWT, Dartford, England. (Doctor who delivered him, 'between 2 and 3 a.m.'; Jagger gave 06:30)
Etta James, 37	25 Jan 1938, 21:50 PDT, Los Angeles, CA, USA. (BC from Viktor E)
Tommy James, 204	29 Apr 1947, 03:38 EST, Dayton, OH, USA. (BR from Ed Steinbrecher)
Bert Jansch, 88	3 Nov 1943, 14:30 GDT, Glasgow, Scotland. (BC from Paul Wright)
Al Jardine, 102	3 Sep 1942, 10:14 EWT, Lima, Allen, OH, USA. (BC from Ed Steinbrecher)
Jean-Michel Jarre, 177	24 Aug 1948, 04:00 MET, Lyon, France. (BR from Ed Steinbrecher; Jarre gave 04:15)
Maurice Jarre, 224	13 Sep 1924, 13:00 GDT, Lyon, France. (BC from The Gauquelins)
Al Jarreau, 29	12 Mar 1940, 01:20 CST, Wauwatosa, WI, USA. (BC from Stephen Przybylowski)
Waylon Jennings, 74	15 Jun 1937, 10:30 CST, Littlefield, TX, USA. (BC from Stephen Przybylowski; same on BR*)
Joan Jett, 193	22 Sep 1958, 16:00 EDT, Wynnewood, PA, USA. (Her in an interview quoted by Roman Craft)
Jose Alfredo Jimenez, 182	19 Jan 1926, 00:30 MST, Guanajuato, Mexico. (BC from Eduardo Castellanos)
Holly Johnson, 173	9 Feb 1960, 16:15 GMT, Wavertree, Liverpool, England. (Him to Frank Clifford and Sy Scholfield)
Kenney Jones, 99	16 Sep 1948, 20:55 GDT, London, England. (Mother to Debbi Kempton-Smith)
Quincy Jones, 137	14 Mar 1933, 15:40 CST, Chicago, IL, USA. (BC* from Thelma and Tom Wilson; could be read as 8.40 p.m.; Jones states 'Leo rising')
Rickie Lee Jones, 193	8 Nov 1954, 05:50 CST, Chicago, IL, USA. (Her to Tashi Grady)
Tom Jones, 146	7 Jun 1940, 00:10 GDT, Pontypridd, Wales. (Interview with parents; 'just after midnight')
Janis Joplin, 143	19 Jan 1943, 09:45 CWT, Port Arthur, TX, USA. (BC* from Frank Clifford; hospital record states 09:30)
Naomi Judd, 74	11 Jan 1946, 18:45 EST, Ashland, KY, USA. (BC* from Kathryn Farmer)
Wynonna Judd, 74	30 May 1964, 08:52 EST, Ashland, KY, USA. (BC* from Kathryn Farmer)
Rocio Jurado, 183	18 Sep 1943, 12:00 GDWT, Chipiona, Spain. (BC quoted in 'Cyklos' newsletter)
Gene Kelly, 238	23 Aug 1912, 07:00 EST, Pittsburgh, PA, USA. (BC from Janice Mackey)
Jim Kerr, 204	9 Jul 1959, 09:45 GDT, Glasgow, Scotland. (BC from Paul Wright)
Ke$ha, 60	1 Mar 1987, 00:34 PST, Van Nuys, CA, USA. (BC from Viktor E)

Chaka Khan, 131	23 Mar 1953, 21:05 CST, Great Lakes, IL, USA. (BC quoted by her* to Frank Clifford)	
Anthony Kiedis, 204	1 Nov 1962, 05:00 EST, Grand Rapids, MI, USA. (Autobio quoted by Sy Scholfield)	
Carole King, 105	9 Feb 1942, 23:42 EWT, Brooklyn, Kings, NY, USA. (BC quoted by her to Ruth Elliot)	
Freddie King, 37	3 Sep 1934, 12:00 CST, Gilmer, Upshur, TX, USA. (BC* from Sy Scholfield)	
Eartha Kitt, 234	17 Jan 1927, 04:00 EST, North, SC, USA. (Time from registry via The Gauquelins; date and place from her to Frank Clifford)	
Gladys Knight, 131	28 May 1944, 19:52 CWT, Atlanta, GA, USA. (BC from Janice Mackey)	
Jordan Knight, 60	17 May 1970, 04:50 EDT, Worcester, MA, USA. (BC from Frances McEvoy)	
David Knopfler, 218	27 Dec 1952, 22:15 GMT, Glasgow, Scotland. (BC from Caroline Gerard)	
Mark Knopfler, 218	12 Aug 1949, 21:50 GDT, Glasgow, Scotland. (BC from Caroline Gerard)	
Alison Krauss, 74	23 Jul 1971, 19:48 CDT, Decatur, IL, USA. (BC from Stephen Przybylowski)	
Kris Kristofferson, 75	22 Jun 1936, 15:30 CST, Brownsville, TX, USA. (BC from The Gauquelins; BR from Ed Steinbrecher)	
Drew Lachey, 60	8 Aug 1976, 12:57 EDT, Cincinnati, OH, USA. (BC from Viktor E)	
Nick Lachey, 60	9 Nov 1973, 12:29 EST, Harlan, KY, USA. (BC from Viktor E)	
Kendrick Lamar, 41	17 Jun 1987, 15:04 PDT, Compton, CA, USA. (BC from Viktor E)	
Adam Lambert, 63	29 Jan 1982, 22:40 EST, Indianapolis, IN, USA. (Father on Twitter quoted by Sy Scholfield)	
k.d. lang, 75	2 Nov 1961, 02:03 MST, Edmonton, Canada. (BR from her to students of Marion March)	
Angela Lansbury, 230	16 Oct 1925, 00:45 GMT, Regent's Park, London, England. (Her to Karen Christino; place from her)	
Mario Lanza, 167	31 Jan 1921, 09:45 EST, Philadelphia, PA, USA. (BC from Janice Mackey and Eugene Moore)	
Agustin Lara, 183	30 Oct 1897, 04:30 LMT, Mexico City, Mexico. (BC from Eduardo Castellanos)	
Amanda Lear, 171	18 Jun 1939, 16:05 SST, Saigon, Vietnam. (BC printed in Italian newspaper)	
Simon Le Bon, 55	27 Oct 1958, 09:00 GMT, Watford, England. (Him in an interview quoted by Grazia Bordoni)	
Brenda Lee, 75	11 Dec 1944, 15:24 CWT, Atlanta, GA, USA. (BC from Janice Mackey)	
Peggy Lee, 25	26 May 1920, 12:45 CST, Jamestown, ND, USA. (BC from Janice Mackey)	
John Legend, 37	28 Dec 1978, 08:25 EST, Springfield, OH, USA. (BC from Viktor E)	
John Lennon, 94	9 Oct 1940, 18:30 GDT, Liverpool, England. (Step-mother, astrologer Pauline Stone; same from hospital to author David Ryan)	
Annie Lennox, 105	25 Dec 1954, 23:10 GMT, Aberdeen, Scotland. (BC* from Aaron Fischer)	
Adam Levine, 205	18 Mar 1979, 15:24 PST, Los Angeles, CA, USA. (BC from Viktor E)	
Jerry Lee Lewis, 112	29 Sep 1935, 15:00 CST, Ferriday, LA, USA. (BC from Aaron Fischer)	
Gordon Lightfoot, 88	17 Nov 1938, 07:00 EST, Orillia, Canada. (Him to a colleague of Shelagh Kendal)	
LL Cool J, 42	14 Jan 1968, 20:43 EST, Bay Shore, NY, USA. (Autobio quoted by Frank Clifford)	
Andrew Lloyd Webber, 136	22 Mar 1948, 16:00 GDT, Westminster, London, England. (Mother to Pamela Crane)	
Hank Locklin, 75	15 Feb 1918, 01:30 CST, McLellan, FL, USA. (Him in a book interview quoted by Sy Scholfield)	
Julie London, 25	26 Sep 1926, 18:00 PST, Santa Rosa, CA, USA. (BC* from Robert Paige)	
Alan Longmuir, 216	20 Jun 1948, 23:35 GDT, Edinburgh, Scotland. (BC from Caroline Gerard)	
Derek Longmuir, 216	19 Mar 1951, 02:25 GMT, Edinburgh, Scotland. (BC from Caroline Gerard)	
Mike Love, 102	15 Mar 1941, 10:55 PST, Los Angeles, CA, USA. (BC quoted by him to Lois Rodden)	
Madonna, 118, 124	16 Aug 1958, 07:05 EST, Bay City, MI, USA. (Hospital record from father via Tashi Grady)	
Taj Mahal, 37	17 May 1942, 00:45 EWT, Harlem, New York, NY, USA. (Him to Simone Butler)	
Henry Mancini, 224	16 Apr 1924, 11:10 EST, Cleveland, OH, USA. (BC* from Frank Clifford)	
Barbara Mandrell, 76	25 Dec 1948, 15:42 CST, Houston, TX, USA. (BC from Stephen Przybylowski)	
Barry Manilow, 168	17 Jun 1943, 09:00 EWT, Brooklyn, Kings, NY, USA. (Him to Linda Clark; same from mother to Eugene Moore)	
Marilyn Manson, 205	5 Jan 1969, 20:05 EST, Canton, OH, USA. (BC from Lois Rodden and Sy Scholfield)	
Shirley Manson, 193	26 Aug 1966, 17:35 GDT, Edinburgh, Scotland. (BC from Caroline Gerard)	
Ray Manzarek, 100	12 Feb 1939, 03:30 CST, Chicago, IL, USA. (Him to Bob Garner; same in autobio from Sy Scholfield)	

Bob Marley, 93	6 Feb 1945, 02:30 EST, St. Ann's Bay, Jamaica. (Him to Neil Spencer)
Dean Martin, 165	7 Jun 1917, 23:55 CST, Steubenville, OH, USA. (BC* from Frank Clifford)
George Martin, 95	3 Jan 1926, 14:29 GMT, London, England. (Interview with his astrologer son, George Martin)
Mary Martin, 230	1 Dec 1913, 12:00 CST, Weatherford, TX, USA. (Her to Velma Chatham; same in autobio; BC confirms date and place)
Ricky Martin, 183	24 Dec 1971, 17:00 AST, Hato Rey, Puerto Rico. (BC quoted in bio* quoted by Frank Clifford)
Johnny Mathis, 168	30 Sep 1935, 12:00 CST, Gilmer, Upshur, TX, USA. (BC* from Sy Scholfield)
Dan McCafferty, 205	14 Oct 1946, 05:05 GMT, Dunfermline, Scotland. (BC from Caroline Gerard)
Linda McCartney, 95	24 Sep 1941, 10:00 EDT, New York, NY, USA. (Her to Nalini Kanta Das/Tom Hopke)
Paul McCartney, 94	18 Jun 1942, 14:00 GDWT, Liverpool, England. (Wife Linda McCartney to Nalini Kanta Das/Tom Hopke; 'shortly after 2 a.m.' in bio)
Scotty McCreery, 64	9 Oct 1993, 04:14 EDT, Raleigh, NC, USA. (BC from Sue Kay and Sy Scholfield)
Bobby McFerrin, 25	11 Mar 1950, 23:19 EST, Manhattan, NY, USA. (Him to William Stickevers)
Maureen McGovern, 231	27 Jul 1949, 09:10 EDT, Youngstown, OH, USA. (BC from Stephen Przybylowski)
MC Hammer, 42	30 Mar 1962, 11:59 PST, Oakland, CA, USA. (BC* from Frank Clifford)
Loreena McKennitt, 88	17 Feb 1957, 19:00 CST, Morden, Canada. (Mother to Renn Butler)
Les McKeown, 216	12 Nov 1955, 10:10 GMT, Edinburgh, Scotland. (BC from Paul Wright)
Sarah McLachlan, 89	28 Jan 1968, 04:00 AST, Halifax, Canada. (Her to John McKay-Clements via her agent)
Don McLean, 89	2 Oct 1945, 04:17 EST, New Rochelle, NY, USA. (BR from Ed Steinbrecher)
Katharine McPhee, 64	25 Mar 1984, 00:05 PST, Los Angeles, CA, USA. (BC from Pat Taglilatelo)
Meat Loaf, 205	27 Sep 1947, 16:23 CST, Dallas, TX, USA. (BC* from Frank Clifford)
Bill Medley, 214	19 Sep 1940, 08:18 PST, Los Angeles, CA, USA. (BC* from Frank Clifford)
Melanie, 89	3 Feb 1947, 07:35 EST, New York, NY, USA. (Her statement on her album cover 'Born to Be' quoted by Jim Eshelman)
George Michael, 124	25 Jun 1963, 06:00 GDT, Finchley, London, England. (His office to Janey Stubbs; BC* from Frank Clifford confirms date and place)
Bette Midler, 235	1 Dec 1945, 14:19 HST, Honolulu, HI, USA. (BC from Janice Mackey and The Gauquelins)
Mika, 177	18 Aug 1983, 00:01 EET, Beirut, Lebanon. (Him on Twitter quoted by Sy Scholfield)
Steve Miller, 206	5 Oct 1943, 10:31 CWT, Milwaukee, WI, USA. (BC from Stephen Przybylowski)
Mina, 183	25 Mar 1940, 15:00 MET, Busto Arsizio, Italy. (BC from Grazia Bordoni)
Charles Mingus, 26	22 Apr 1922, 21:30 MST, Nogales, AZ, USA. (BC* from Stephen Przybylowski and Sy Scholfield)
Liza Minnelli, 235	12 Mar 1946, 07:58 PST, Los Angeles, CA, USA. (BC* from The Gauquelins and Janice Mackey)
Kylie Minogue, 54	28 May 1968, 11:00 AEST, Melbourne, Australia. (Magazine article quoted by Frank Clifford)
Joni Mitchell, 81	7 Nov 1943, 22:00 MWT, Fort Macleod, Canada. (Her to John McKay-Clements via her agent)
Thelonious Monk, 26	10 Oct 1917, 21:15 EST, Rocky Mount, NC, USA. (BC from Bob Garner)
Giorgio Moroder, 170	26 Apr 1940, 02:45 MET, Ortisei, Italy. (BR* from Grazia Bordoni)
Ennio Morricone, 93	10 Nov 1928, 22:25 MET, Rome, Italy. (BC from Grazia Bordoni)
Sarah Jane Morris, 26	21 Mar 1959, 15:30 GMT, Bassett, Southampton, England. (Her* to Frank Clifford; date and place confirmed by BC*)
Jim Morrison, 100	8 Dec 1943, 11:55 EWT, Melbourne, FL, USA. (Birth registration card* from Bob Garner)
Alanis Morissette, 89	1 Jun 1974, 09:51 EDT, Ottawa, Canada. (Her to Elizabeth Deschenes)
Alison Moyet, 172	18 Jun 1961, 09:30 GDT, Billericay, England. (Her manager to Frank Clifford via Fiona Graham)
MTV, 174	1 Aug 1981, 00:01 EDT, New York, NY, USA. (News on date; NYC was the original home of MTV)
Anne Murray, 76	20 Jun 1945, 10:40 AWT, Springhill, Nova Scotia, Canada. (Bio)
Olly Murs, 64	14 May 1984, 05:10 GDT, Chelmsford, England. (BC* from Frank Clifford; a twin)
Ricky Nelson, 50	8 May 1940, 13:25 EDT, Teaneck, NJ, USA. (BC* from Bob Garner; same from The Gauquelins and Janice Mackey)

Willie Nelson, 76	29 Apr 1933, 23:50 CST, Abbott, TX, USA. (Wife said just before midnight but doctor recorded after midnight; BC* from Sy Scholfield gives 30 Apr at 00:30)
Randy Newman, 90	28 Nov 1943, 20:02 PWT, Los Angeles, CA, USA. (BC from Thelma and Tom Wilson)
New Orleans, 31	28 Nov 1817, New Orleans, LA, USA. (Time not known; midday used for chart)
Wayne Newton, 165	3 Apr 1942, 08:22 EWT, Norfolk, VA, USA. (Wife to William Rogers)
Olivia Newton-John, 53	26 Sep 1948, 06:00 GDT, Cambridge, England. (Her to Debbi Kempton-Smith)
Stevie Nicks, 142	26 May 1948, 03:02 MST, Phoenix, AZ, USA. (BC quoted by her to Tashi Grady)
Harry Nilsson, 90	15 Jun 1941, 02:15 EDT, Brooklyn, Kings, NY, USA. (BR from bio quoted by Sy Scholfield)
Peter Noone, 206	5 Nov 1947, 21:00 GMT, Manchester, England. (Him to Dana Haynes)
Jessye Norman, 228	19 Sep 1945, 01:45 EWT, Augusta, GA, USA. (BC from Janice Mackey)
Gary Numan, 172	8 Mar 1958, 22:30 GMT, London, England. (Autobio quoted by Sy Scholfield)
Pascal Obispo, 184	8 Jan 1965, 23:25 MET, Bergerac, France. (BC from Paddy de Jabrun, Didier Geslain and Patrice Petitallot)
Daniel O'Donnell, 169	12 Dec 1961, 19:30 GMT, Dungloe, Ireland. (Him to Hans Taeger, quoting mother)
Yoko Ono, 95	18 Feb 1933, 20:30 JST, Tokyo, Japan. (Her to Roger Elliott)
Roy Orbison, 146	23 Apr 1936, 15:50 CST, Vernon, TX, USA. (BR* from Ed Steinbrecher; family website gives 15:30)
Donny Osmond, 52	9 Dec 1957, 00:55 MST, Ogden, UT, USA. (Bio quoted by Janice Mackey)
Jimmy Osmond, 52	16 Apr 1963, 06:23 PST, Canoga Park, CA, USA. (BC from Janice Mackey)
Jimmy Page, 114	9 Jan 1944, 04:00 GDT, Heston, London, England. (Him to Jenni Harte)
Patti Page, 164	8 Nov 1927, 08:13 CST, Claremore, OK, USA. (BC from Janice Mackey)
Colonel Tom Parker, 113	26 Jun 1909, 23:00 LST, Breda, Netherlands. (Civil records quoted in bio quoted by Sy Scholfield)
Dolly Parton, 135	19 Jan 1946, 20:25 CST, Sevierville, TN, USA. (BR* from Frank Clifford; Parton gives 03:00)
Laura Pausini, 184	16 May 1974, 17:00 MET, Faenza, Italy. (BC* from Grazia Bordoni)
Luciano Pavarotti, 225	12 Oct 1935, 01:40 MET, Modena, Italy. (BC from Grazia Bordoni)
Tom Paxton, 90	31 Oct 1937, 17:21 CST, Evergeen Park, IL, USA. (BC from Thelma and Tom Wilson)
Nia Peeples, 57	10 Dec 1961, 18:59 PST, Los Angeles, CA, USA. (BC* from Frank Clifford)
Marti Pellow, 56	23 Mar 1965, 00:15 GDT, Clydebank, Scotland. (BC from Caroline Gerard)
Katy Perry, 61	25 Oct 1984, 07:58 PDT, Santa Barbara, CA, USA. (BC from Roman Craft)
Linda Perry, 90	15 Apr 1965, 22:52 EST, Springfield, MA, USA. (BC from Roman Craft)
Steve Perry, 206	22 Jan 1949, 18:05 PST, Hanford, CA, USA. (BC quoted by webmaster to Roman Craft)
Bernadette Peters, 230	28 Feb 1948, 22:45 EST, Jamaica, Queens, NY, USA. (BC* from Thelma and Tom Wilson)
Esther Phillips, 38	23 Dec 1935, 00:10 CST, Galveston, TX, USA. (BC* from Sy Scholfield)
Edith Piaf, 234	19 Dec 1915, 05:00 GMT, Paris, France. (BC* from The Gauquelins and Sy Scholfield)
Iggy Pop, 121	21 Apr 1947, 11:34 EST, Muskegon, MI, USA. (Him to Finnish fan)
'Pop Idol', 67	6 Oct 2001, 19:30 GDT, London, England. (TV listings on date)
Paul Potts, 64	13 Oct 1970, 05:30 MET, Kingswood, South Gloucestershire, England. (Him on Twitter quoted by Sy Scholfield)
Patti Pravo, 184	9 Apr 1948, 18:00 MEDT, Venice, Italy. (BC from Grazia Bordoni)
Elvis Presley, 17, 113	8 Jan 1935, 04:35 CST, Tupelo, MS, USA. (BC* from Bob Garner; same from doctor's record quoted by Sy Scholfield)
Lisa Marie Presley, 113	1 Feb 1968, 17:01 CST, Memphis, TN, USA. (Hospital record quoted by Sy Scholfield)
Priscilla Presley, 113	24 May 1945, 22:40 EWT, Brooklyn, Kings, NY, USA. (Bio quoted by Frank Clifford; BC* from Lois Rodden contains no birth time)
Leontyne Price, 226	10 Feb 1927, 06:15 CST, Laurel, MS, USA. (BC from Janice Mackey)
Charley Pride, 76	18 Mar 1934, 08:10 CST, Nashville, TN, USA. (BC from Buell Huggins)
Prince, 124	7 Jun 1958, 18:17 CDT, Minneapolis, MN, USA. (BC* from Frank Clifford)
Suzi Quatro, 194	3 Jun 1950, 13:40 EST, Detroit, MI, USA. (Her to Andrea Miles via her webmaster)

Queen Latifah, 41		18 Mar 1970, 08:02 EST, Newark, NJ, USA. (BC quoted by her to Basil Fearrington)
Gerry Rafferty, 91		16 Apr 1947, 10:55 GDWT, Paisley, Scotland. (BC from Paul Wright)
Bonnie Raitt, 77		8 Nov 1949, 16:08 PST, Burbank, Los Angeles, CA, USA. (BC* from Thelma and Tom Wilson)
Eros Ramazzotti, 184		28 Oct 1963, 11:30 MET, Rome, Italy. (Him to Peter van Wood)
Helen Reddy, 91		25 Oct 1941, 17:50 AEST, Melbourne, Australia. (Her to Lois Rodden via a private source)
Della Reese, 38		6 Jul 1931, 10:00 EST, Detroit, MI, USA. (Her to Angela Gallo)
Jim Reeves, 77		20 Aug 1923, 22:00 CST, Galloway, Panola, TX, USA. (BC pictured on website quoted by Jim Birke)
Tim Rice, 136		10 Nov 1944, 17:45 GDT, Amersham, England. (Autobio quotes his father)
Keith Richards, 98		18 Dec 1943, 06:00 GDT, Dartford, England. (Him to Ruth Nobel)
LeAnn Rimes, 77		28 Aug 1982, 17:45 CDT, Jackson, MS, USA. (Mother in TV interview; same on Twitter)
Robbie Robertson, 206		5 Jul 1943, 22:25 EWT, Toronto, Canada. (Autobio quoted by Sy Scholfield)
Jim Rodford, 101		7 Jul 1941, 22:00 GDWT, St Albans, England. (Mother to Debbi Kempton-Smith)
Richard Rodgers, 136		28 Jun 1902, 02:30 EST, New York, NY, USA. (Bio quoted by Lois Rodden)
Ginger Rogers, 238		16 Jul 1911, 02:18 CST, Independence, MO, USA. (BC from Ed Helin)
Kenny Rogers, 135		21 Aug 1938, 11:29 CST, Houston, TX, USA. (Bio quoted by Lois Rodden)
Sonny Rollins, 26		7 Sep 1930, 11:40 EDT, Brooklyn, Kings, NY, USA. (Sister and aunt to David Hayward)
Linda Ronstadt, 77		15 Jul 1946, 17:39 MST, Tucson, AZ, USA. (BC quoted by her to Ruth Elliot)
Diana Ross, 138		26 Mar 1944, 23:46 EWT, Detroit, MI, USA. (BC from Janice Mackey)
RuPaul, 171		17 Nov 1960, 18:52 PST, San Diego, CA, USA. (BC* from John McKay-Clements; RuPaul's website states 19:58)
Mike Rutherford, 217		2 Oct 1950, 19:30 GDT, Guildford, England. (Him to Marjorie Orr)
Paul Rutherford, 173		8 Dec 1959, 22:15 GMT, Liverpool, England. (Him to Bettina Lee)
Lea Salonga, 230		22 Feb 1971, 08:55 AWST, Manila, Philippines. (BC from Sy Scholfield)
Richie Sambora, 218		11 Jul 1959, 07:33 EDT, Perth Amboy, NJ, USA. (BC* from Lois Rodden)
Sandro, 185		19 Aug 1945, 03:20 ADT, Buenos Aires, Argentina. (BC quoted in bio)
Carlos Santana, 185		20 Jul 1947, 02:00 CST, Autlán de Navarro, Mexico. (BR* from Ed Steinbrecher)
George Schappell, 189		18 Sep 1961, 11:04 EDT, Reading, PA, USA. (Newspaper birth announcement quoted by Sy Scholfield)
Bon Scott, 207		9 Jul 1946, 23:20 GDT, Forfar, Scotland. (BC from Caroline Gerard)
Ian Shaw, 27		2 Jun 1962, 06:46 GDT, St Asaph, Wales. (Baby book quoted by him to Frank Clifford)
Dinah Shore, 163		29 Feb 1916, 11:45 CST, Winchester, TN, USA. (BC from Janice Mackey)
Beverly Sills, 227		25 May 1929, 01:00 EDT, Brooklyn, Kings, NY, USA. (Mother to John Daniel)
Gene Simmons, 207		25 Aug 1949, 10:15 EEDT, Haifa, Israel. (BC shown in documentary quoted by Isaac Starkman)
Paul Simon, 105		13 Oct 1941, 02:33 EST, Newark, NJ, USA. (BC* from Ed Steinbrecher)
Nina Simone, 130		21 Feb 1933, 06:00 EST, Tryon, Polk, NC, USA. (BC from The Gauquelins; same in autobio)
Jessica Simpson, 61		10 Jul 1980, 16:00 CDT, Abilene, TX, USA. (Mother to Karen Marie Shelton)
Frank Sinatra, 146		12 Dec 1915, 03:00 EST, Hoboken, NJ, USA. (Father to Lynne Palmer)
Siouxsie Sioux, 194		27 May 1957, 21:12 GDT, London, England. (Friend Budgie in an interview quoted by Sy Scholfield)
Ricky Skaggs, 78		18 Jul 1954, 08:10 EST, Louisa, KY, USA. (BC* from Stephen Przybylowski)
Grace Slick, 142		30 Oct 1939, 07:37 CST, Evanston, IL, USA. (BC* from Thelma and Tom Wilson)
Patti Smith, 142		30 Dec 1946, 06:01 CST, Chicago, IL, USA. (Her to Debbi Kempton-Smith)
Robert Smith, 207		21 Apr 1959, 01:00 GDT, Blackpool, England. (Him in an interview quoted by Wojtek Suchomski)
Snoop Dogg, 42		20 Oct 1971, 18:20 PDT, Long Beach, CA, USA. (BC from Pat Taglilatelo)
Hank Snow, 78		9 May 1914, 08:12 AST, Brooklyn, Nova Scotia, Canada. (Him to Brian Clark)
Jimmy Somerville, 173		22 Jun 1961, 15:20 GDT, Glasgow, Scotland. (BC* from Frank Clifford)
Stephen Sondheim, 136		22 Mar 1930, 21:00 EST, New York, NY, USA. (Him to Edith Hathaway; interview with him states previous time of 03:30 is incorrect)

David Soul, 53   28 Aug 1943, 02:55 CWT, Chicago, IL, USA. (BC from Thelma and Tom Wilson)
Britney Spears, 61   2 Dec 1981, 01:30 CST, McComb, MS, USA. (Her and her mother to Barry Street of The Astrology Shop, London)
Phil Spector, 137   26 Dec 1939, 14:55 EST, Bronx, NY, USA. (BC* from Sy Scholfield)
Rick Springfield, 53   23 Aug 1949, 19:00 AEST, Guildford, Sydney, Australia. (Him in a magazine interview; same in autobio quoted by Sy Scholfield)
Bruce Springsteen, 120   23 Sep 1949, 22:50 EDT, Freehold, NJ, USA. (BC* from Sy Scholfield)
Ringo Starr, 95   7 Jul 1940, 00:05 GDT, Liverpool, England. (Him to Lynne Palmer; same in bio)
Tommy Steele, 51   17 Dec 1936, 19:30 GMT, Bermondsey, London, England. (Him to Margaret Dunford)
Gwen Stefani, 194   3 Oct 1969, 14:09 PDT, Fullerton, CA, USA. (BC from Viktor E)
Cat Stevens, 91   21 Jul 1948, 12:00 GDT, London, England. (Him to Richard West)
Risë Stevens, 226   11 Jun 1913, 07:45 EST, Bronx, NY, USA. (Autobio; year from online sources)
Ian Stewart, 98   18 Jul 1938, 01:50 GDT, Pittenweem, Scotland. (BC from Caroline Gerard)
Sting, 207   2 Oct 1951, 01:30 GDT, Wallsend, England. (Him to Arthyr Chadbourne)
George Strait, 78   18 May 1952, 02:00 CST, Poteet, TX, USA. (Father to David Dozier)
Billy Strayhorn, 27   29 Nov 1915, 04:15 CST, Dayton, OH, USA. (BC* from Frank Clifford)
Barbra Streisand, 147   24 Apr 1942, 05:04 EWT, Brooklyn, Kings, NY, USA. (Birth announcement in bio* quoted by Frank Clifford; she gave 05:08 from BC to Ed Steinbrecher via mutual friend)
Yma Sumac, 234   13 Sep 1922, 13:00 EST, Ichocan, Cajamarca, Peru. (BC* from Eduardo Castellanos; exact place is specified online)
Donna Summer, 170   31 Dec 1948, 21:00 EST, Boston, MA, USA. (BC* from Frank Clifford)
Joan Sutherland, 226   7 Nov 1926, 17:30 AEST, Sydney, Australia. (Sutherland quoted by Dennis Sutton)
Sylvester, 171   6 Sep 1947, 01:35 PST, Los Angeles, CA, USA. (BC* from Frank Clifford)
James Taylor, 91   12 Mar 1948, 17:06 EST, Boston, MA, USA. (BC* from The Gauquelins and Frances McEvoy)
Kiri Te Kanawa, 227   6 Mar 1944, 14:00 NZT, Gisborne, New Zealand. (Her to Carol Squires)
Toni Tennille, 215   8 May 1940, 18:15 CDT, Montgomery, AL, USA. (BC from Janice Mackey)
'That's All Right', 17   7 Jul 1954, 21:35 CST, Memphis, TN, USA. ('Rock Almanac' and Wikipedia; Presley bio gives 8 July)
Robin Thicke, 61   10 Mar 1977, 20:54 PST, Canoga Park, CA, USA. (BC from Viktor E)
BJ Thomas, 78   7 Aug 1942, 11:00 CWT, Hugo, OK, USA. (BC from Ellis Steward)
Tiffany, 56   2 Oct 1971, 07:16 PDT, Norwalk, CA, USA. (BC* from Frank Clifford)
Justin Timberlake, 62   31 Jan 1981, 18:30 CST, Memphis, TN, USA. (BC* from Frank Clifford)
Louis Tomlinson, 62   24 Dec 1991, 13:47 GMT, Doncaster, England. (Interview with mother quoted by Roman Craft)
Pete Townshend, 99   19 May 1945, 15:00 GDWT, London, England. (Mother to Debbi Kempton-Smith)
Umberto Tozzi, 185   4 Mar 1952, 16:10 MET, Torino (Turin), Italy. (BC from Grazia Bordoni)
Meghan Trainor, 62   22 Dec 1993, 10:16 EST, Nantucket, MA, USA. (BC from Roman Craft)
Randy Travis, 13   4 May 1959, 06:14 EST, Monroe, NC, USA. (BR* from Ed Steinbrecher)
John Travolta, 53   18 Feb 1954, 14:53 EST, Englewood, NJ, USA. (BC from Eugene Moore)
Tanya Tucker, 79   10 Oct 1958, 02:38 CST, Seminole, TX, USA. (BC from Stephen Przybylowski)
Tina Turner, 142   26 Nov 1939, 22:10 CST, Nutbush, TN, USA. (BR* from Frank Clifford)
Midge Ure, 172   10 Oct 1953, 08:30 GMT, Glasgow, Scotland. (BC from Paul Wright)
Usher, 42   14 Oct 1978, 04:00 CDT, Dallas, TX, USA. (Bio quoted by Dave Campbell)
Ritchie Valens, 208   13 May 1941, 00:56 PST, Los Angeles, CA, USA. (BC from Church of Light)
Chavela Vargas, 185   17 Apr 1919, 23:00 LST, Heredia, Costa Rica. (BC from Eduardo Castellanos)
Sarah Vaughan, 132   27 Mar 1924, 21:45 EST, Newark, NJ, USA. (BC from Janice Mackey and The Gauquelins)
Bobby Vee, 51   30 Apr 1943, 12:15 CWT, Fargo, ND, USA. (BC from Stephen Przybylowski)
Suzanne Vega, 92   11 Jul 1959, 05:18 PDT, Santa Monica, CA, USA. (BC* from Frank Clifford)
Sid Vicious, 120   10 May 1957, 19:09 GDT, London, England. (Mother to Lorraine Exley)

Rufus Wainwright, 92	22 Jul 1973, 01:31 EDT, Rhinebeck, NY, USA. (Him to Nick Dagan Best)	
Tom Waits, 92	7 Dec 1949, 07:25 PST, Pomona, CA, USA. (BC* from Frank Clifford)	
Scott Walker, 208	9 Jan 1943, 17:25 EWT, Hamilton, Butler, OH, USA. (BC* from Frank Clifford)	
Shayne Ward, 65	16 Oct 1984, 21:34 GDT, Ashton-Under-Lyne, England. (BC* from Frank Clifford; a twin)	
Dionne Warwick, 147	12 Dec 1940, 15:08 EST, Orange, NJ, USA. (BC from Gabrielle Hardman; same from Janice Mackey and The Gauquelins)	
Ethel Waters, 38	31 Oct 1896, 09:15 EST, Chester, PA, USA. (Autobio in 1972, correcting year in first 1950 autobio)	
Paul Weller, 92	25 May 1958, 23:45 GDT, Woking, England. (Him to Neil Spencer)	
Dottie West, 79	11 Oct 1932, 04:30 CST, Smithville, TN, USA. (BC* from Frank Clifford)	
Caron Wheeler, 174	19 Jan 1963, 13:00 GMT, Acton, London, England. (Her to Laura Boomer-Trent)	
Barry White, 38	12 Sep 1944, 16:42 CWT, Galveston, TX, USA. (BC* from Frank Clifford)	
Kim Wilde, 56	18 Nov 1960, 20:00 GMT, Chiswick, London, England. (Her to Ananda Bagley)	
Toyah Willcox, 194	18 May 1958, 11:57 GDT, Birmingham, England. (Her to Liz Medler)	
will.i.am, 219	15 Mar 1975, 01:16 PDT, Los Angeles, CA, USA. (BC from Pat Taglilatelo)	
Andy Williams, 165	3 Dec 1927, 06:00 CST, Wall Lake, IA, USA. (BC from Stephen Przybylowski)	
Deniece Williams, 39	3 Jun 1950, 06:45 CDT, Gary, IN, USA. (Her to Marjorie Orr)	
Hank Williams, 134	17 Sep 1923, 01:00 CST, Georgiana, AL, USA. (BC* from Buell Huggins and Sy Scholfield)	
Ann Wilson, 197	19 Jun 1950, 17:20 PDT, San Diego, CA. (BC from Aaron Fischer)	
Brian Wilson, 103	20 Jun 1942, 03:45 PWT, Inglewood, Los Angeles, CA, USA. (BC from Janice Mackey)	
Carl Wilson, 102	21 Dec 1946, 10:48 PST, Los Angeles, CA, USA. (BC from Janice Mackey)	
Cassandra Wilson, 27	4 Dec 1955, 08:30 CST, Jackson, MS, USA. (Time from her in an interview quoted by Sy Scholfield; date and year from bio)	
Dennis Wilson, 102	4 Dec 1944, 22:56 PWT, Los Angeles, CA, USA. (BC from Janice Mackey)	
Mary Wilson, 138	6 Mar 1944, 10:11 CWT, Greenville, MS, USA. (BC quoted by her to Lois Rodden)	
Nancy Wilson, 39	20 Feb 1937, 08:57 EST, Chillicothe, OH, USA. (BC from Janice Mackey and The Gauquelins)	
Amy Winehouse, 105	14 Sep 1983, 22:25 GDT, Enfield, England. (Mother to mutual friend of Margaret Zelinski; same in mother's bio)	
Steve Winwood, 208	12 May 1948, 05:00 GDT, Birmingham, England. (Time from him to Jenni Harte; date and place from autobio* quoted by Frank Clifford)	
Peter Wolf, 208	7 Mar 1946, 10:45 EST, Manhattan, NY, USA. (Him to Ed Steinbrecher)	
Bobby Womack, 39	4 Mar 1944, 08:10 CWT, Cleveland, OH, USA. (BC* from Frank Clifford)	
Cecil Womack, 39	25 Sep 1947, 00:30 EST, Cleveland, OH, USA. (BC* from Frank Clifford)	
Stevie Wonder, 131	13 May 1950, 16:15 EST, Saginaw, MI, USA. (Him to Lynne Palmer)	
Stuart Wood, 216	25 Feb 1957, 17:05 GMT, Edinburgh, Scotland. (BC from Paul Wright)	
Woodstock Festival, 19	15 Aug 1969, 17:07 EDT, Bethel, Sullivan, NY. (Wikipedia)	
Conchita Wurst, 65	6 Nov 1988, 17:52 MET, Gmunden, Austria. (BC from private source to Sy Scholfield)	
Bill Wyman, 98	24 Oct 1936, 23:25 GMT, Lewisham, London, England. (Autobio quoted by Yoe Stein)	
Tammy Wynette, 135	5 May 1942, 01:20 CWT, farm north of Tremont, MS, USA. (BC* from Stephen Przybylowski states Red Bay, AL)	
Trisha Yearwood, 79	19 Sep 1964, 21:23 EST, Monticello, GA, USA. (BC from Stephen Przybylowski)	
Dwight Yoakam, 79	23 Oct 1956, 02:41 EST, Pikeville, KY, USA. (BC from Stephen Przybylowski)	
Neil Young, 106	12 Nov 1945, 06:45 EST, Toronto, Canada. (Bio quoted by Sy Scholfield)	
Will Young, 65	20 Jan 1979, 21:55 GMT, Reading, England. (BC* from Frank Clifford; a twin)	
Lena Zavaroni, 65	4 Nov 1963, 00:45 GMT, Greenock, Scotland. (BC from Paul Wright)	
Renato Zero, 186	30 Sep 1950, 18:15 MET, Rome, Italy. (BC from Grazia Bordoni)	
Zucchero, 186	25 Sep 1955, 18:15 MET, Reggio nell'Emilia, Italy. (BC from Grazia Bordoni)	

EASY LISTENING VOCALISTS

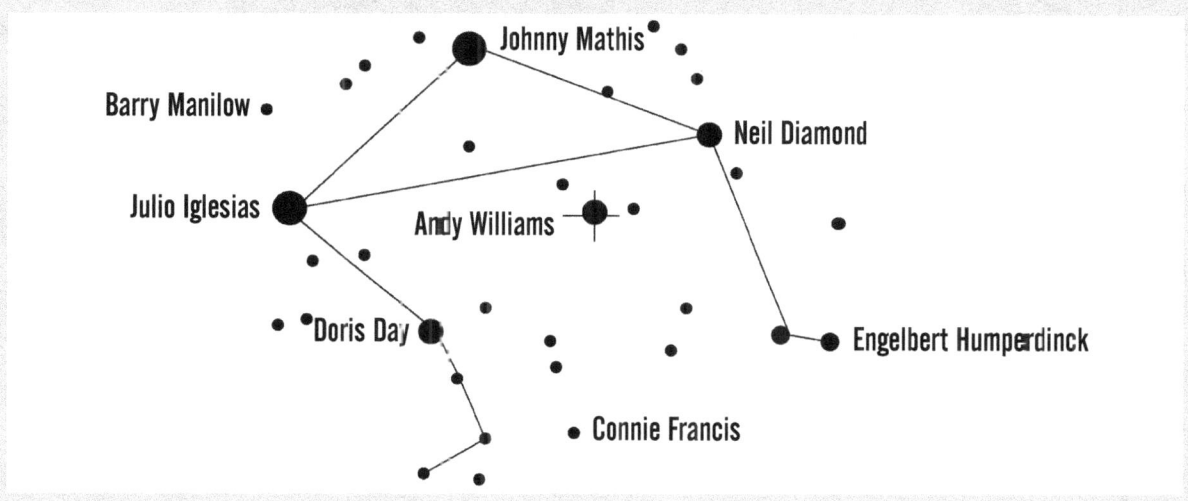

Easy Listening

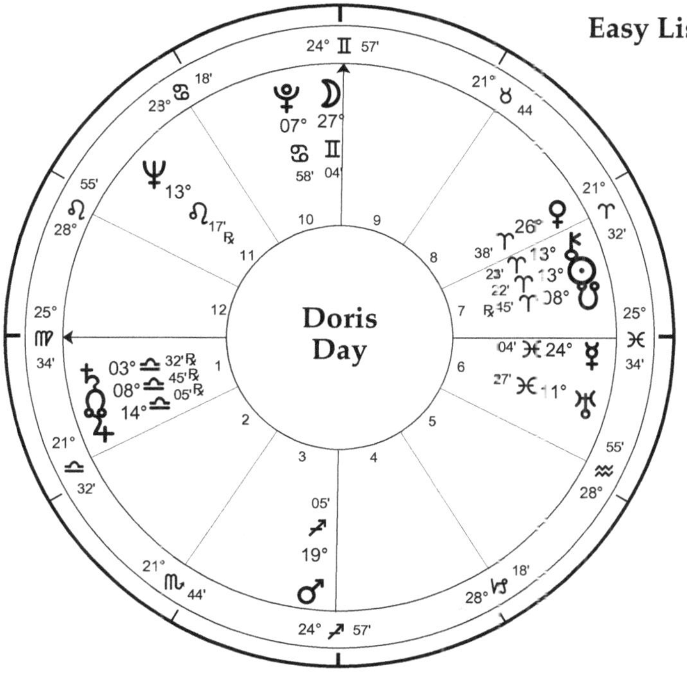

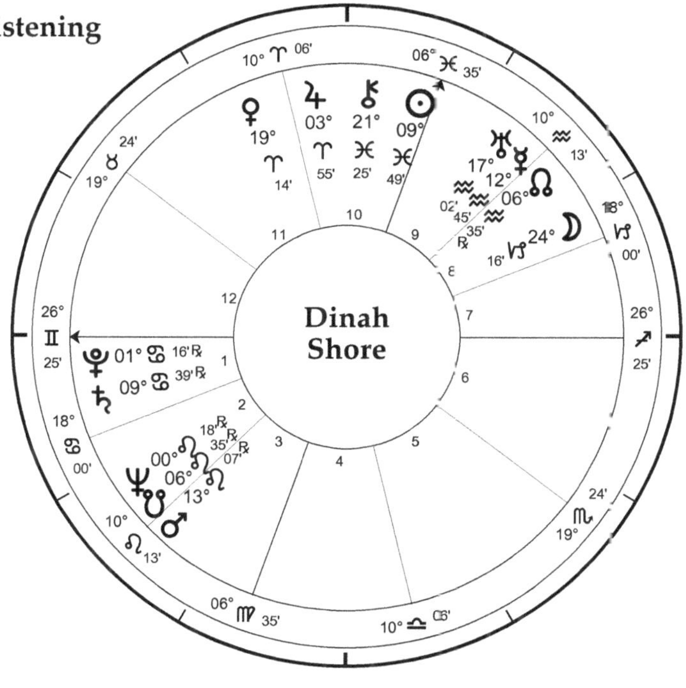

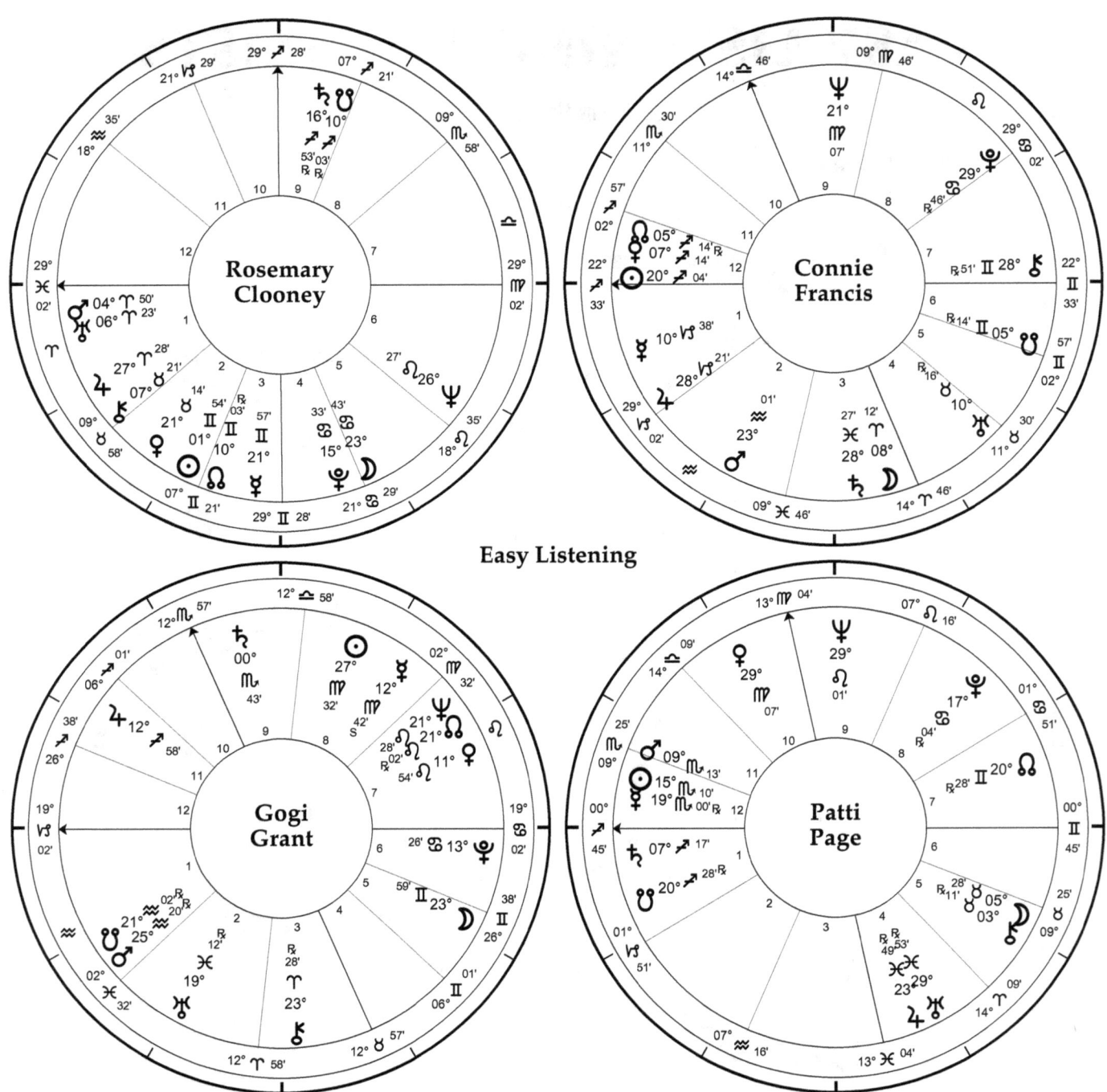

Easy Listening

Easy Listening Vocalists

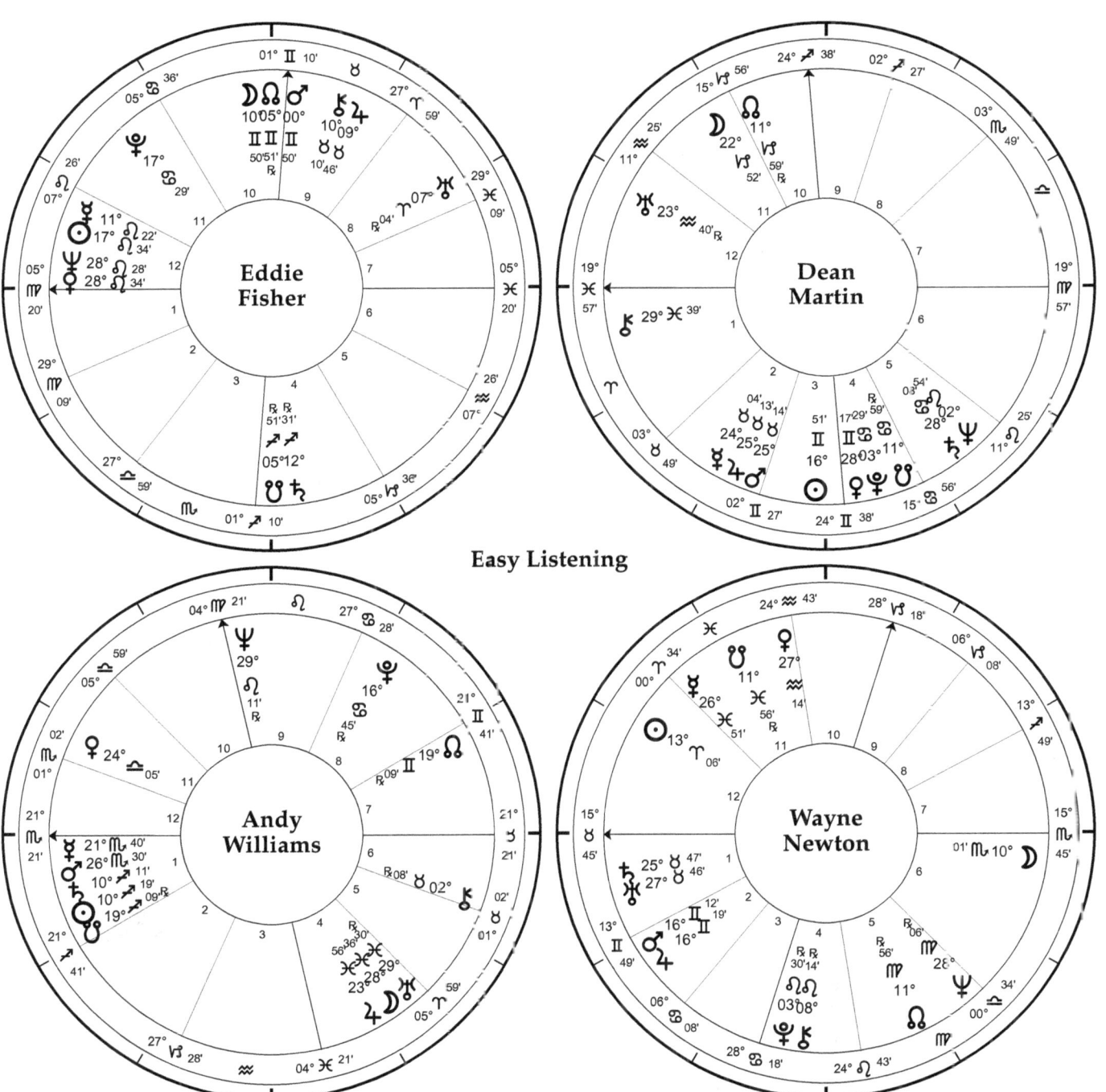

Easy Listening

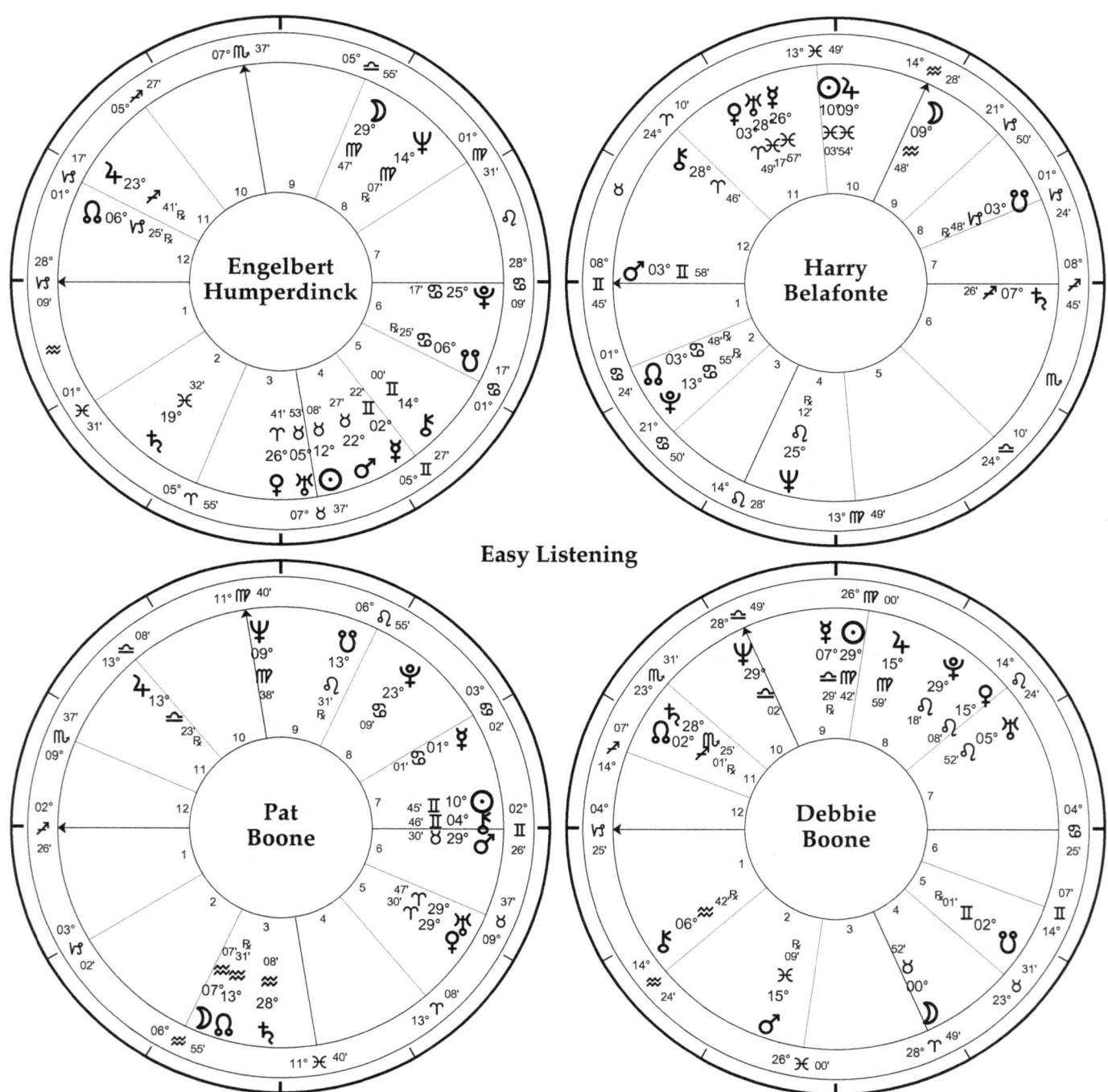

Easy Listening

Easy Listening Vocalists

Easy Listening

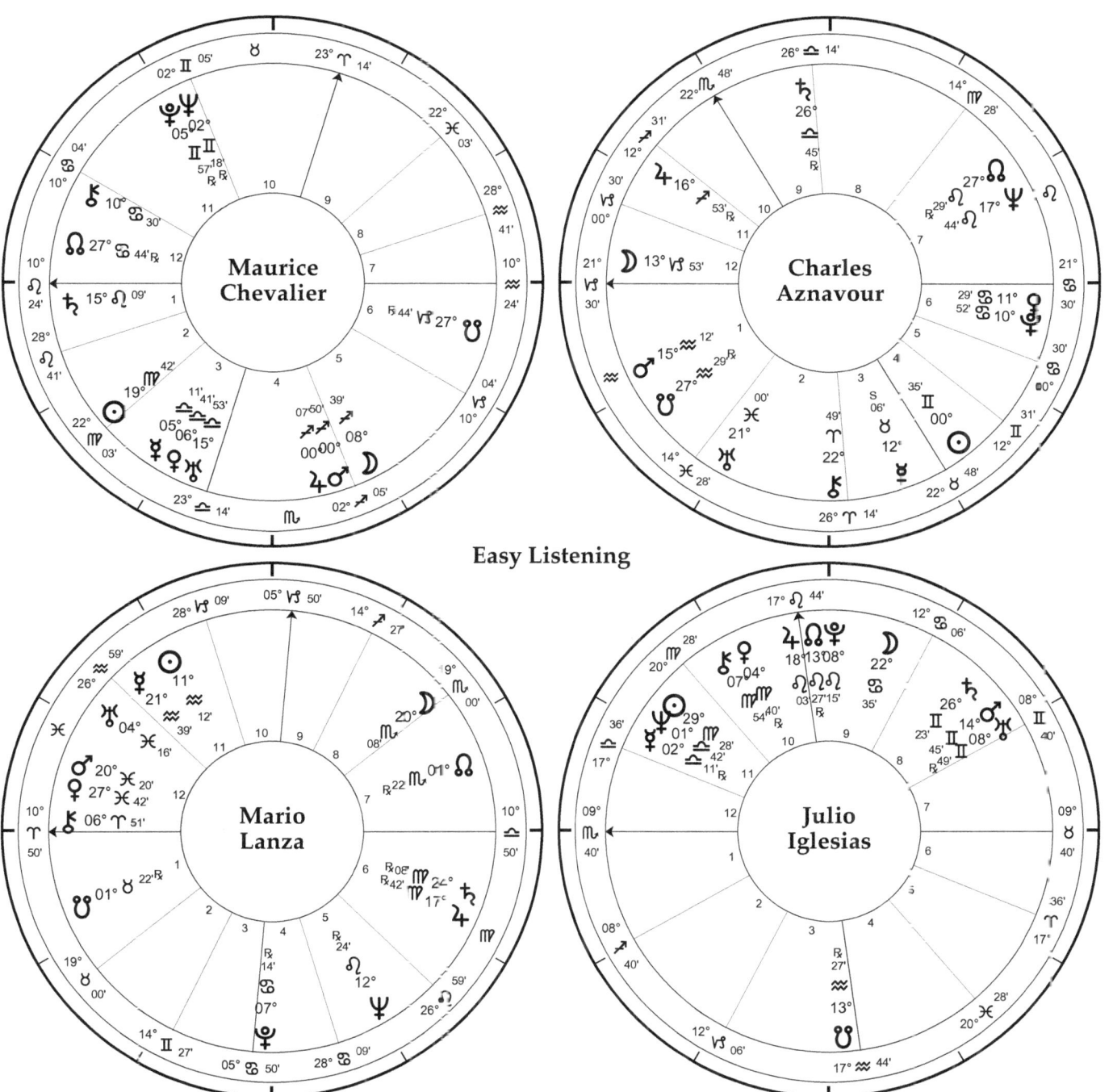

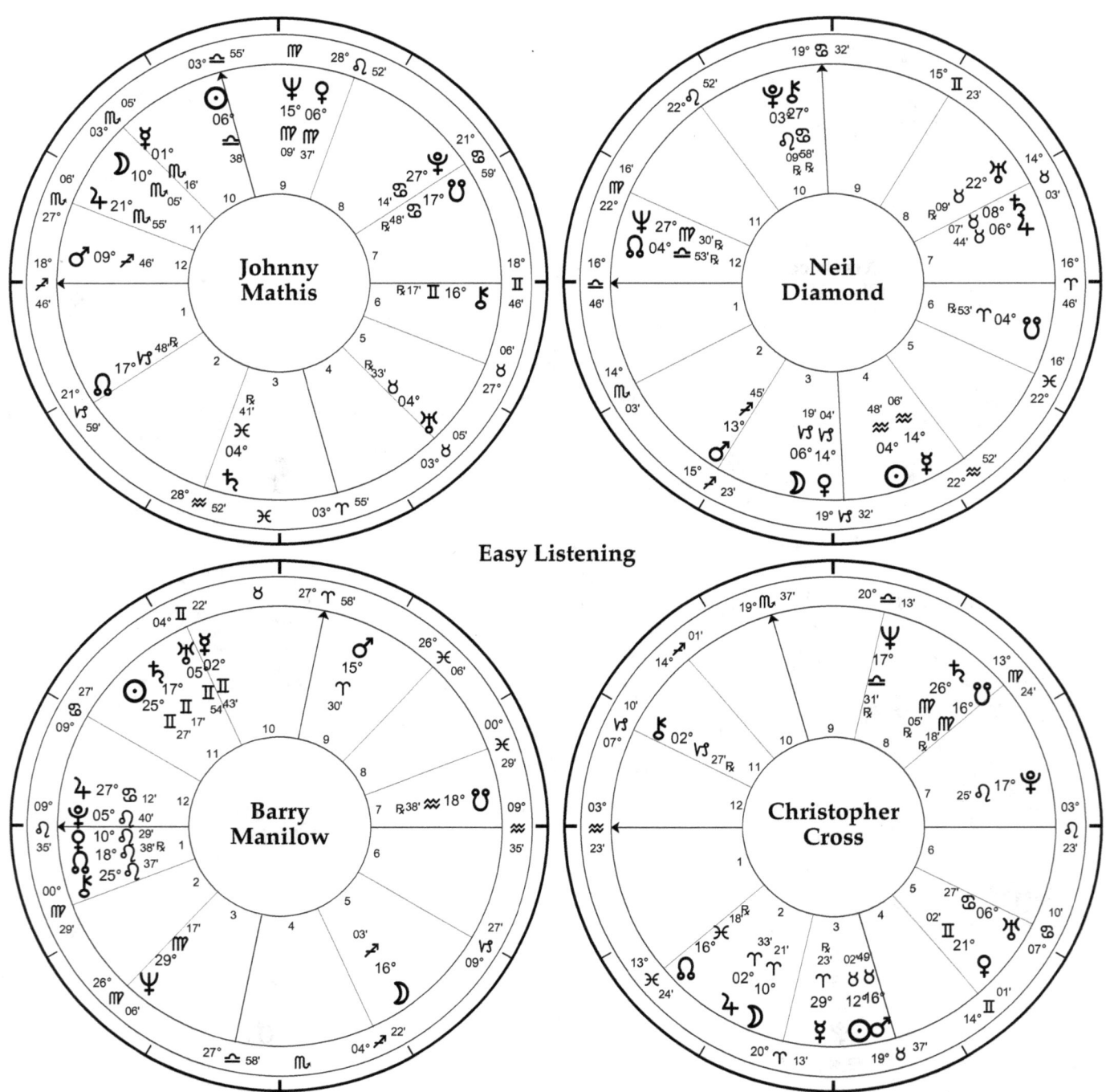

Easy Listening

Easy Listening Vocalists

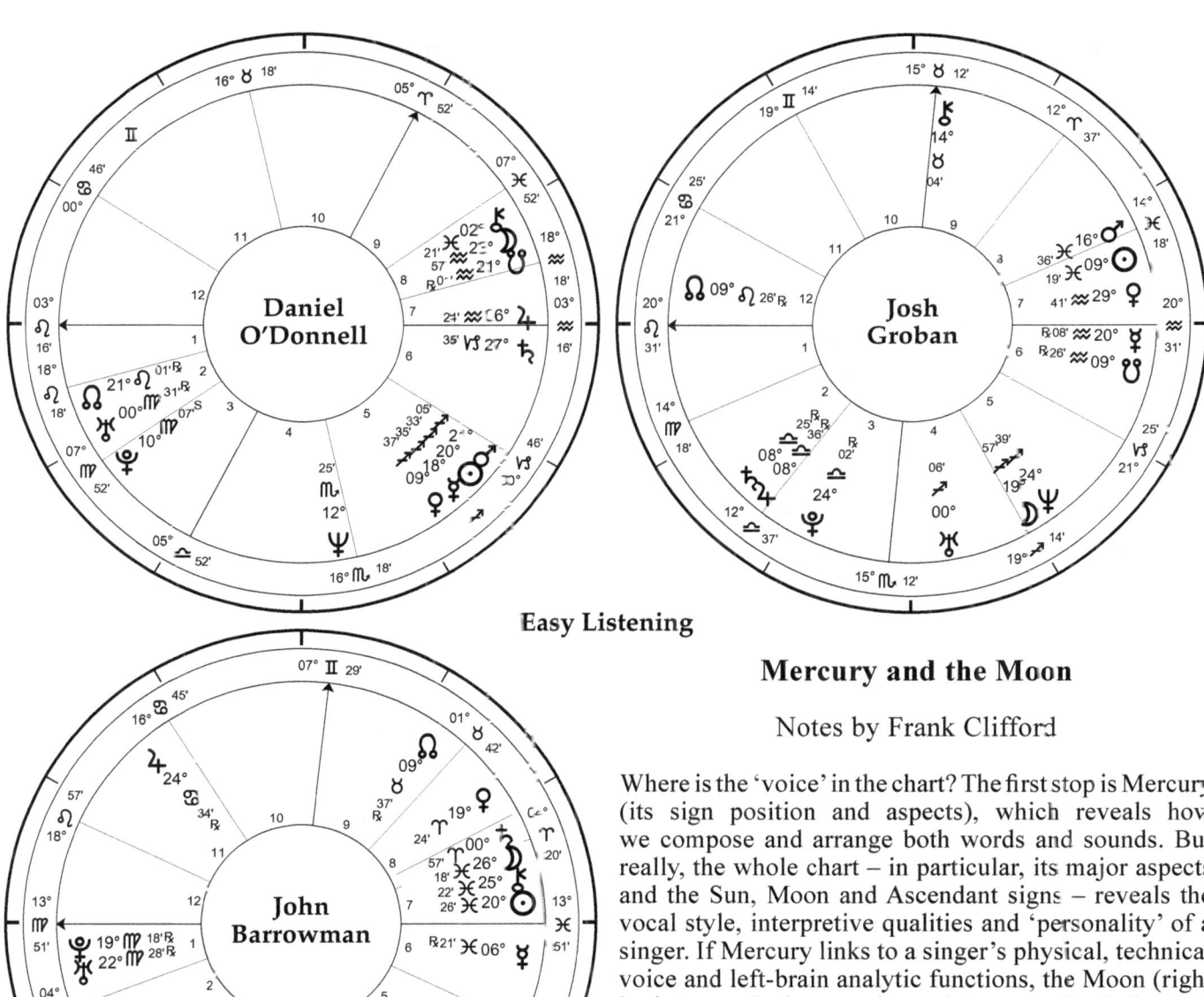

Easy Listening

Mercury and the Moon

Notes by Frank Clifford

Where is the 'voice' in the chart? The first stop is Mercury (its sign position and aspects), which reveals how we compose and arrange both words and sounds. But really, the whole chart – in particular, its major aspects and the Sun, Moon and Ascendant signs – reveals the vocal style, interpretive qualities and 'personality' of a singer. If Mercury links to a singer's physical, technical voice and left-brain analytic functions, the Moon (right brain) reveals how a singer interprets the lyrics and phrases a song. Both planets have specific 'connect and communicate' roles, but the Moon conveys a mood to the audience. Venus has links to harmony, melody, popularity and the type of love song a vocalist sings, rather than being descriptive of the type of voice a singer possesses. Venus is not often a key player – by position or aspect – in the charts of well-known vocalists.

DISCO, DANCE & ELECTRONIC

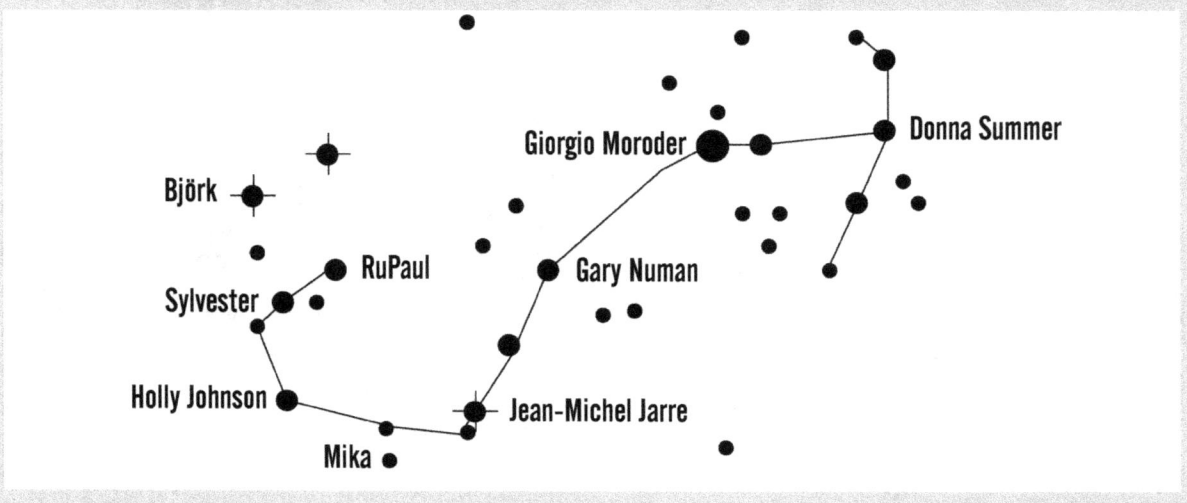

Disco

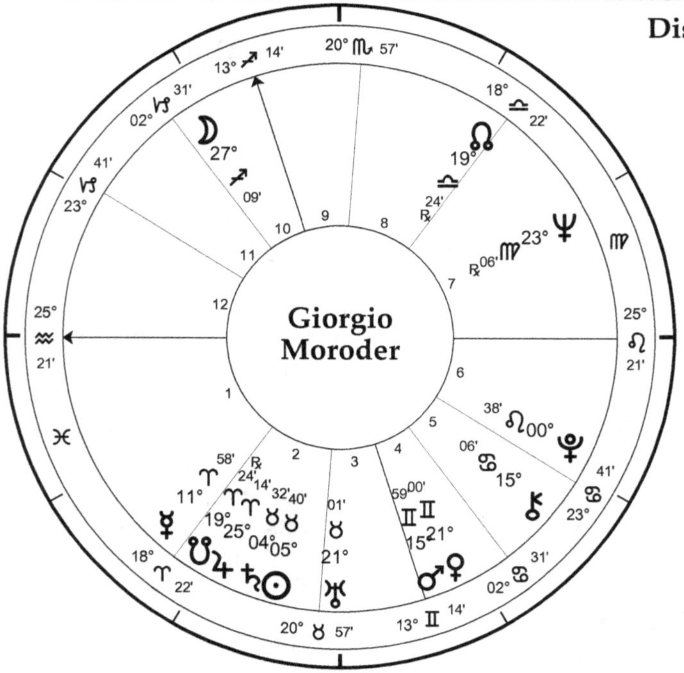

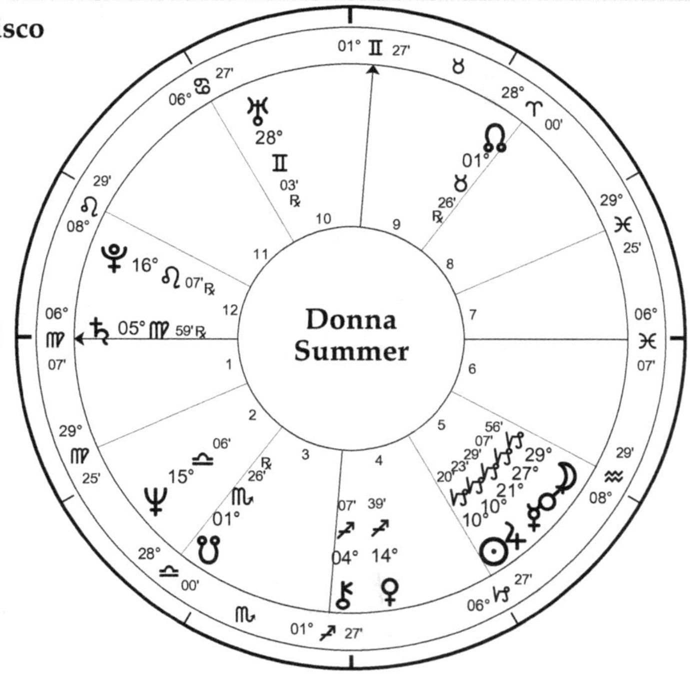

Disco, Dance & Electronic

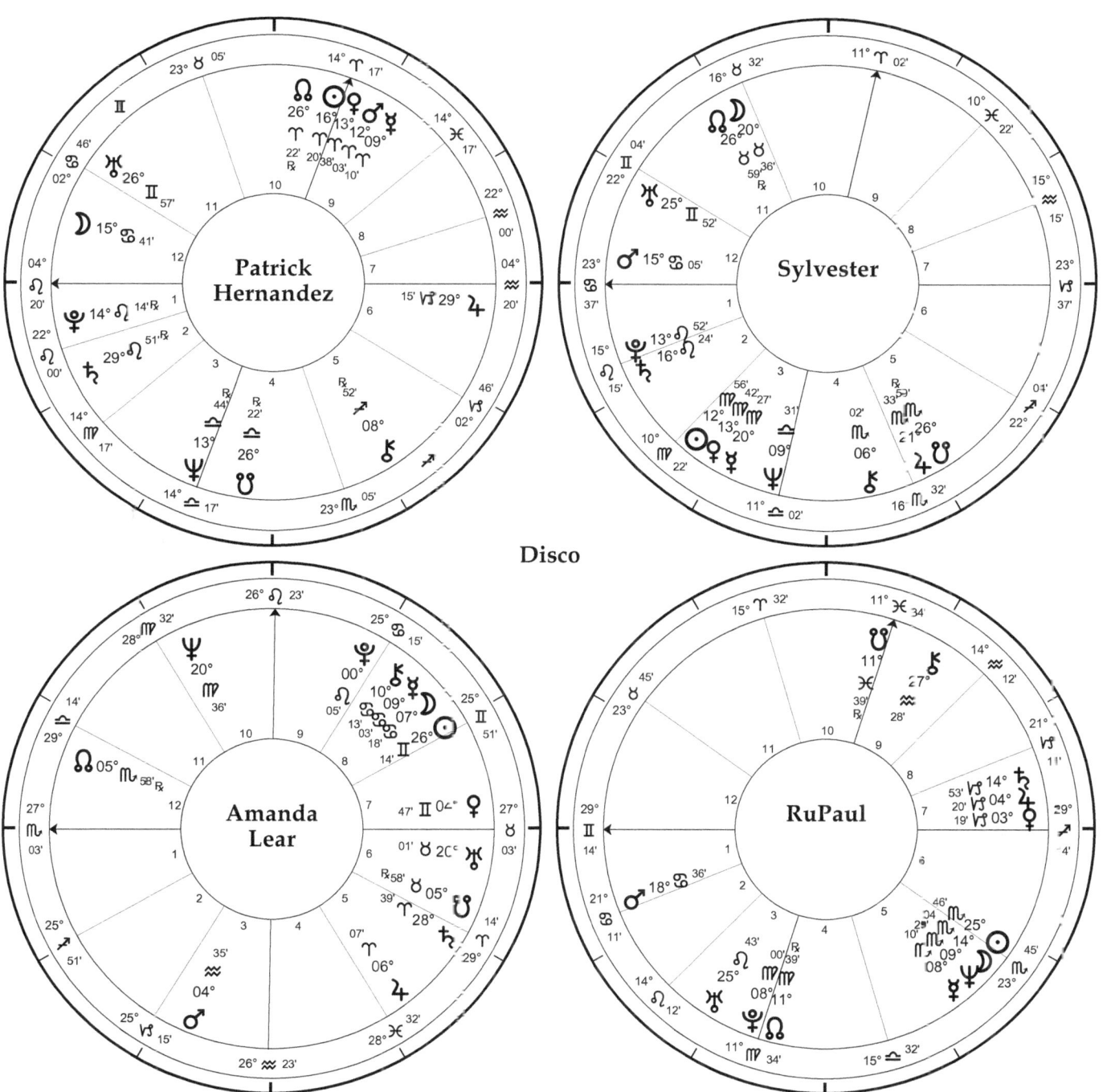

Disco

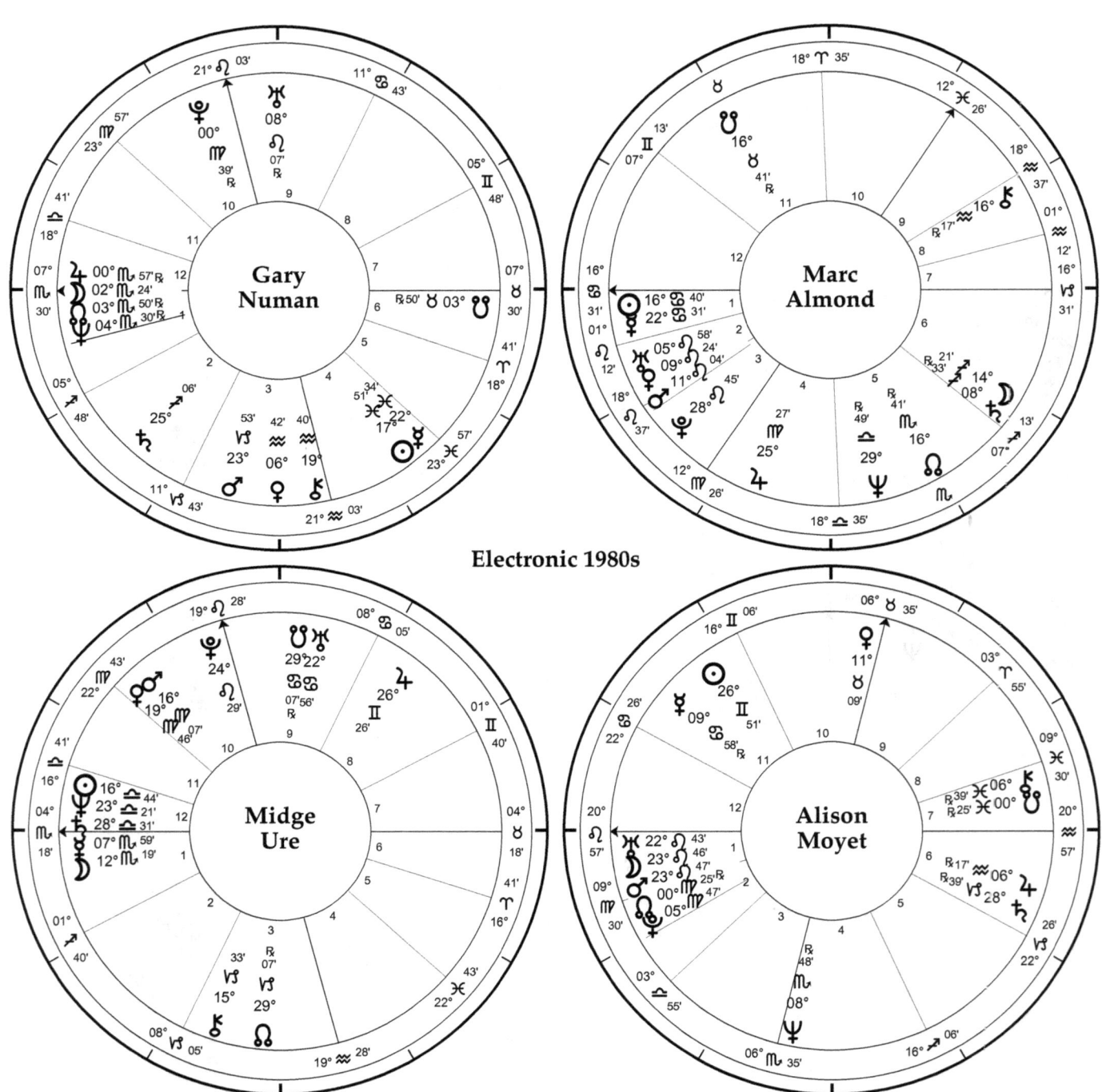

Electronic 1980s

Disco, Dance & Electronic 173

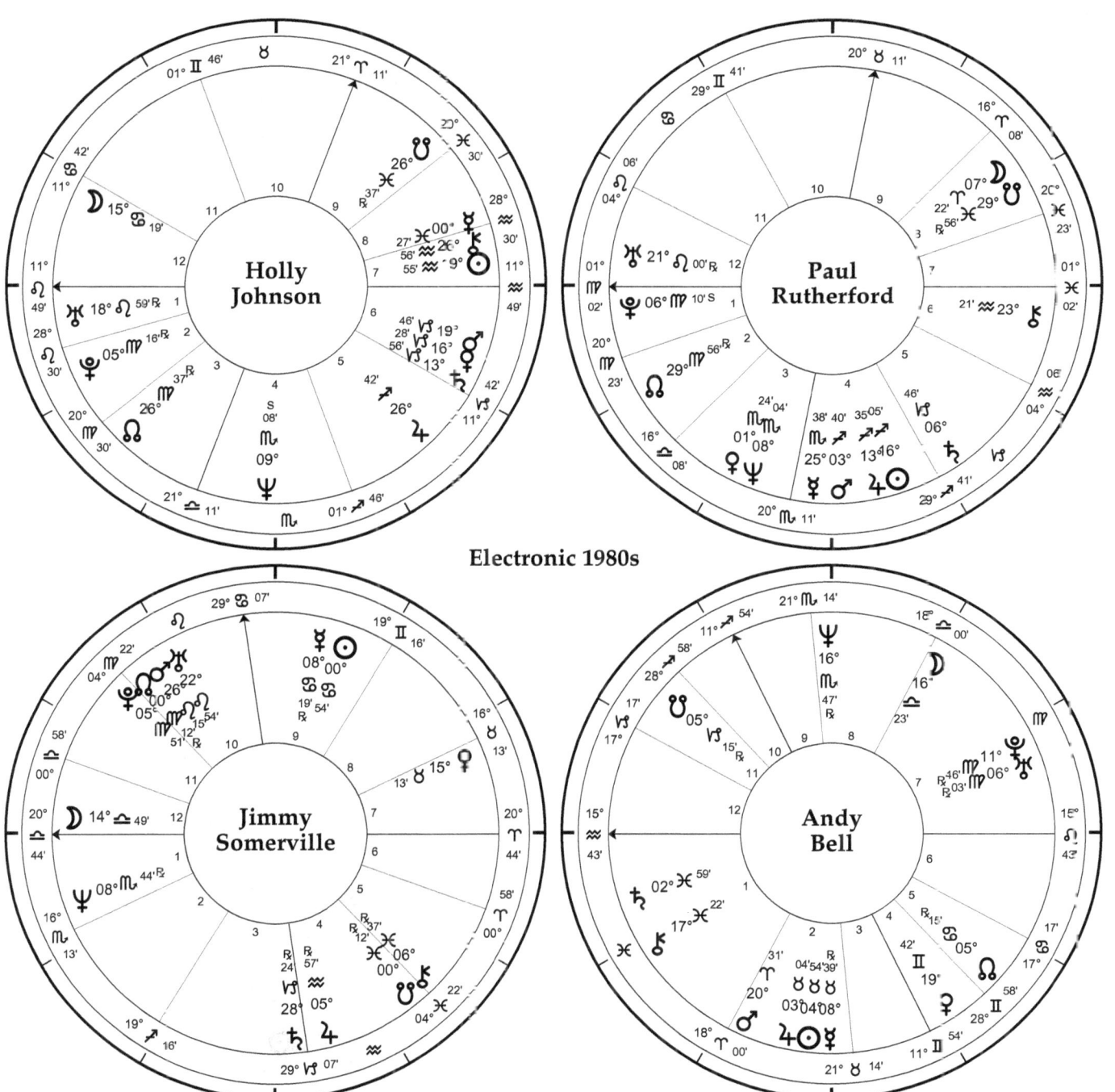

Electronic 1980s

174 The Book of Music Horoscopes

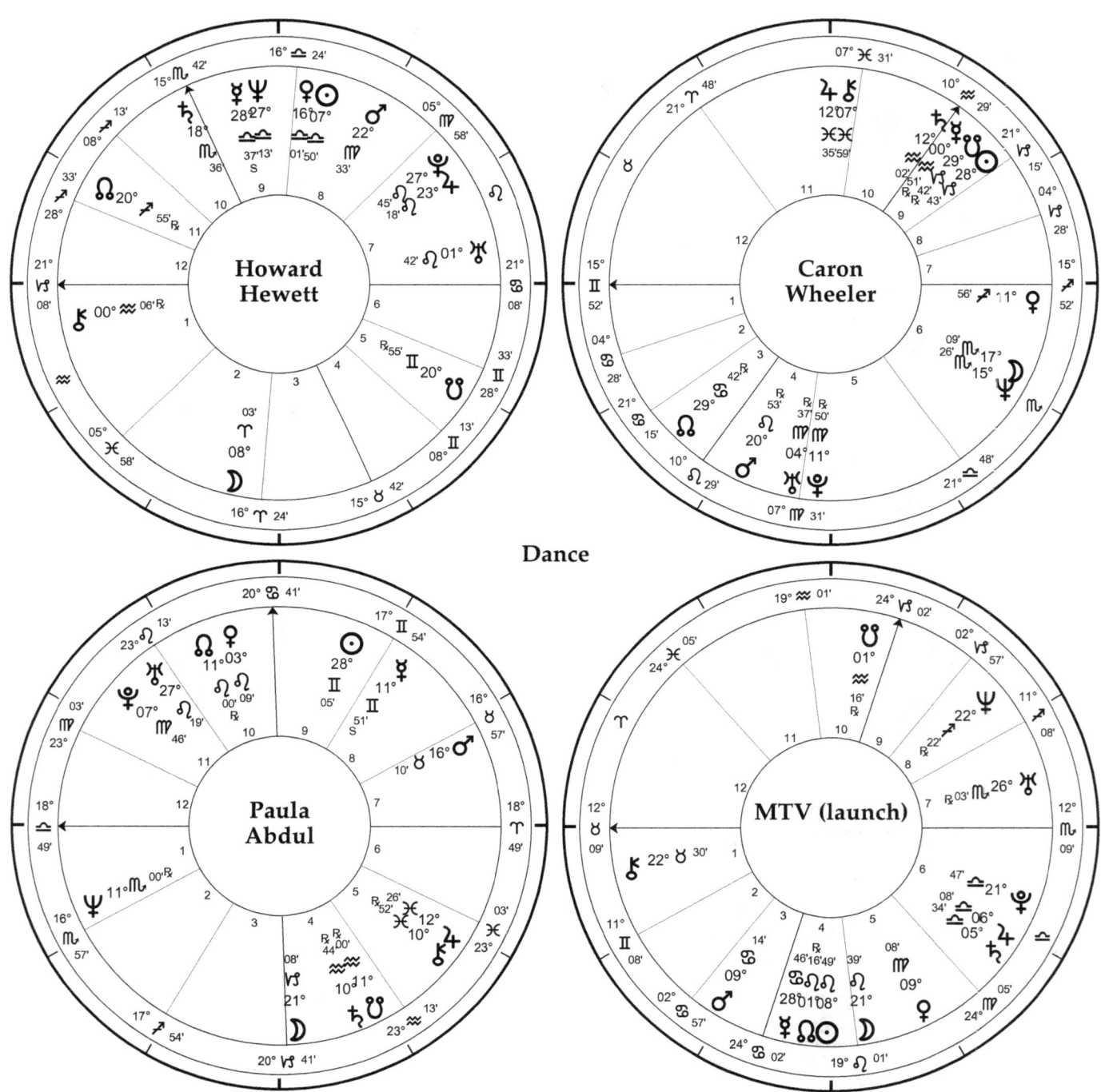

Dance

Astrology and the Evolution of MTV

Emily Chow-Kambitsch

MTV opened with the iconic imagery of the astronaut or 'Moon Man' planting a flag illustrated with the MTV logo on the Moon. Since its inception MTV has been a fixed institution, with 12° Taurus rising, characterized by showcasing art (Venus as chart ruler) and the celebrity image behind it (Sun and Moon in Leo) through music videos. Significantly, the network has also served as a social barometer for American youth culture and its musical and non-musical interests. However, MTV has been accused of harmfully influencing young people through its glamorization of extravagance, sexual experimentation and blatant irresponsibility, discernible in reality shows such as *Jersey Shore* and *Jackass*. This potential for social controversy is signified by the tight square between the Capricorn MC and Pluto, while the MC's ruler Saturn is closely conjunct Jupiter in the 5th House (indicating accusations of corruption of the youth through the encouragement of foolhardy behaviour).

Nevertheless, young people have sought refuge in MTV for its dedication to showcasing their stories, whether in the social experiment of young adults living together in a house in *The Real World*, or in the sometimes painfully raw environments of drug abuse, mental illness and poverty in the documentary series *True Life*. MTV also provided a safe space for young people to gain advice from a medical doctor about relationships, drug addiction and sexuality in *Loveline*. With Chiron in the 1st House trine the Capricorn MC, MTV has a capacity to alert its viewers to the wounds that the young have to bear in modern American society, and to offer inspiration, and even concrete sources, for healing.

Venus and the VMAs

The MTV Video Music Awards (VMAs) have come to be associated with shocking events involving celebrities, particularly concerning the exhibition or repression of the female body and artistic voice. The dynamics of Venus at play in these scenarios indicate the significant role that the VMAs have played in the definition of aesthetics and their cultural value associated with MTV in popular culture. The VMAs debuted on 14 September 1984, when transiting Uranus in Sagittarius was just separating from an exact square to MTV's natal Venus at 9° Virgo. This powerful charge of Uranus to Venus was reflected in Madonna's provocative and electrifying performance of 'Like a Virgin' that, in the words of the MTV archivists, 'gave the MTV Video Music Awards a still-standing reputation as home to the most shocking moments ever seen on an awards show … [and] planted MTV's flag firmly in the pop culture landscape'.

There was another astrological factor in play that prevented the shocking exhibition of art and powerful female sexuality from being relegated only to the debut show. In the quotation above there is a clear impression that, since 1984, the VMAs have occupied a fixed place in the music industry, and in American popular culture more broadly. Furthermore, there is a pattern of VMA performances capturing a critical point in the evolution of an individual artist's image and career direction. It will be difficult to forget Miley Cyrus's infamous, scantily-clad twerking with Robin Thicke in 2013, an opportunity that Cyrus employed to radically redefine her professional image and separate her new persona of bold, complex femininity from her previous identity of the wholesome Disney star. Cyrus, with her natal Venus–Uranus conjunction in Capricorn, propelled significant, ongoing social media discussions on the role of the female entertainer within the corporate entertainment industry.

On 14 September 1984, not only was transiting Uranus squaring MTV's natal Venus but, by Solar Arc (SA), Uranus had just entered 29° Scorpio. At the crisis degree of Scorpio, everything in the realm of the dark, the dangerous and the taboo rises above the surface in a momentary matter of life and death (for the artistic persona, in this case). The VMAs are a platform for public displays of risk-taking; the question is always whether the futuristic vision of art and the feminine (Venus–Uranus) may be too much for an audience to handle (Scorpio).

Gamechangers: 16 and Pregnant and Teen Mom

In 2009, MTV launched the reality documentary *16 and Pregnant*, which endeavoured to communicate, through the experiences of four girls, the various aspects of life that are altered by teen pregnancy. In time, the show *Teen Mom* emerged to continue the stories of the girls from *16 and Pregnant* following the birth of their children. If we observe the astrological events that correspond with the launching of these shows, we can understand the transformative purpose that *16 and Pregnant/Teen Mom* have served and will continue to serve at what clearly is a pivotal point in MTV history. On 11 June 2009, when *16 and Pregnant* debuted, MTV's SA MC was within one degree of exact opposition to the natal Leo Moon in the Equal 4th House (naturally, this would bring the SA IC into conjunction with the Moon). Viewers of *16 and Pregnant/Teen Mom* have a privileged glimpse into the domestic life (4th House) of the young mother (Leo Moon). At the same time SA Venus was at 5°55' Libra, conjoined with the tight natal Jupiter–Saturn conjunction in the Equal 5th House. These young mothers' negotiation of boundaries between independence and restriction in their personal relationships creates a channel for the expression of the Jupiter–Saturn tension in Libra that MTV compulsively explores.

Early 2014 saw another development in relation to *16 and Pregnant/Teen Mom* that would alter American perceptions of the social impact of the shows. Economists Melissa S. Kearney of the University of Maryland and Philip B. Levine of Wellesley College conducted a study that generated a remarkable finding, reported in the *Washington Post*: '*16 and Pregnant* led to a 5.7% reduction in teen births – a percentage that accounts for one-third of the total decline in teen births.' During 13 and 14 January 2014, following the release of the study, headlines in *The New York Times*, Huffington Post and other major media outlets reflected tension between past criticisms of the network and the present recognition of MTV as a healthy influence for young people. Over these two days, SA Mercury travelled from Leo into Virgo. After thirty years of the network primarily serving as a communicator for entertainment purposes (SA Mercury in Leo), the discovery of the social utility of *16 and Pregnant* has ushered in what will no doubt be a new era in the public perception of MTV. The ingress of SA Mercury into Virgo indicates the growth of MTV as a source for promoting health and well being for youth over the next thirty years.

MTV's Future in Youth Culture

The date of 5 November 2016 brought another significant astrological contact for MTV that reflected a major shift in the network's identity as a voice for youth collective consciousness: the ingress of SA Uranus into Capricorn. Occurring three days prior to the US Presidential Election, this ingress reflected MTV's encouragement of youth participation in political debates and social activism. When Donald Trump won the presidency, MTV's election coverage, called (appropriately for natal Sun–Moon in Leo) 'The People's Playhouse', reframed this event – which many young viewers read as a grievous defeat of tolerance and social progress – as an endurable hindrance within a broader historical context of advancement in Civil Rights. Correspondent Marcus Ellsworth encouraged his audience with words reminiscent of the time-honoured social awakener, Uranus in Capricorn: 'We can survive this ... we can push harder, because we are standing on generations of strategy, of community-building, of organizing. We know what the road to freedom looks like, and we know that it goes far beyond who we vote for.'

In late June–early July 2020, transiting Jupiter and Pluto will form a conjunction with MTV's natal MC in Capricorn. This indicates an evolutionary milestone for the network. The combined influence of Jupiter and Pluto implies a simultaneous uprooting and expansion of foundations, particularly in the area of its corporate structure. Subsequently, in May 2021, transiting Uranus will cross MTV's Ascendant, suggesting a major overhaul in how the network will advertise itself. With Uranus in Taurus, there may be a significant change to the logo of the Moon Man, or other iconography that previously stood as symbolic of the fixed position of MTV within the music industry and popular culture. What will MTV become? How will young audiences relate to the transformation? How far will MTV move away from the original identity of 'Music Television'?

Disco, Dance & Electronic 177

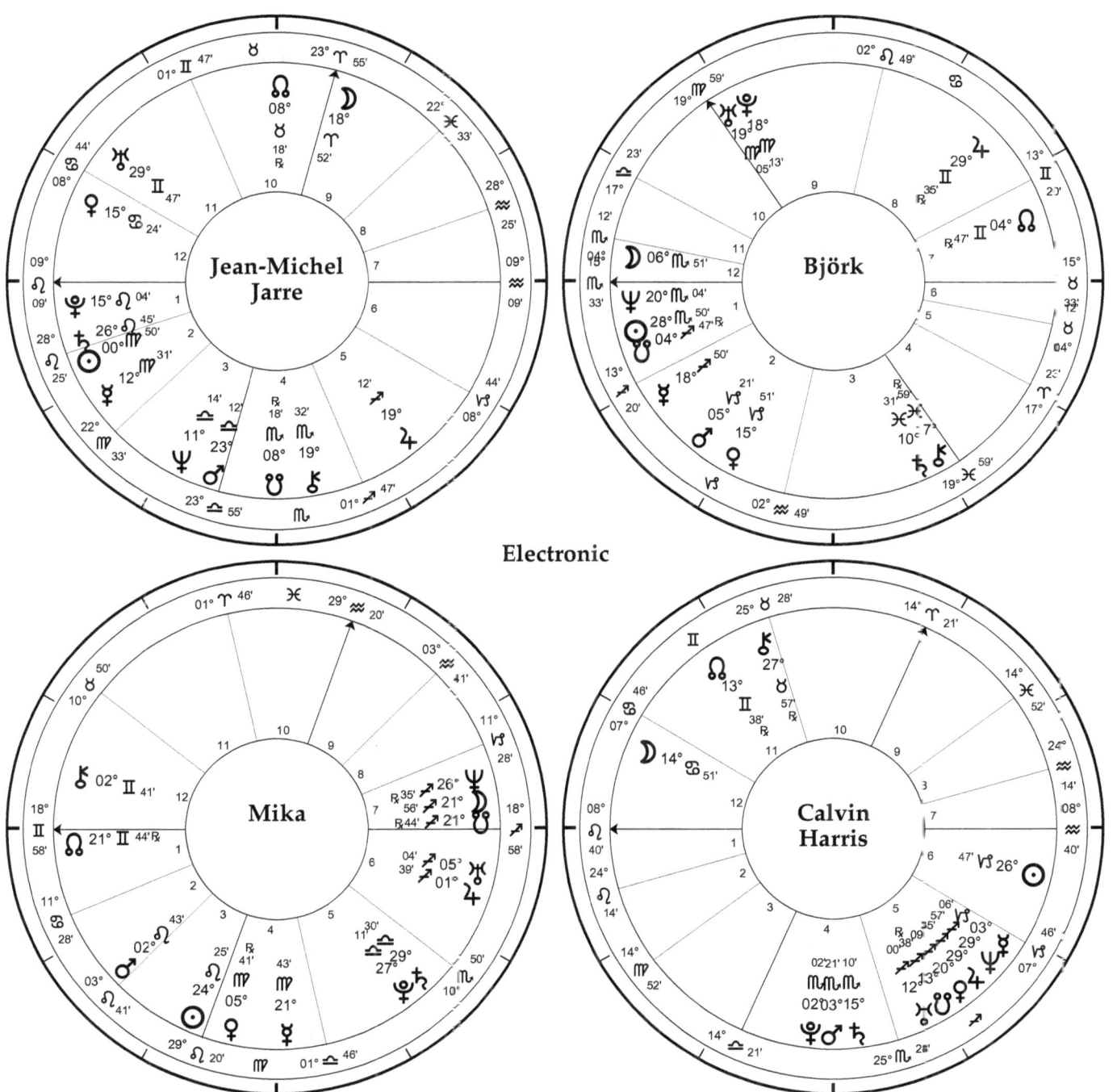

Electronic

LATIN STARS & EURO POP

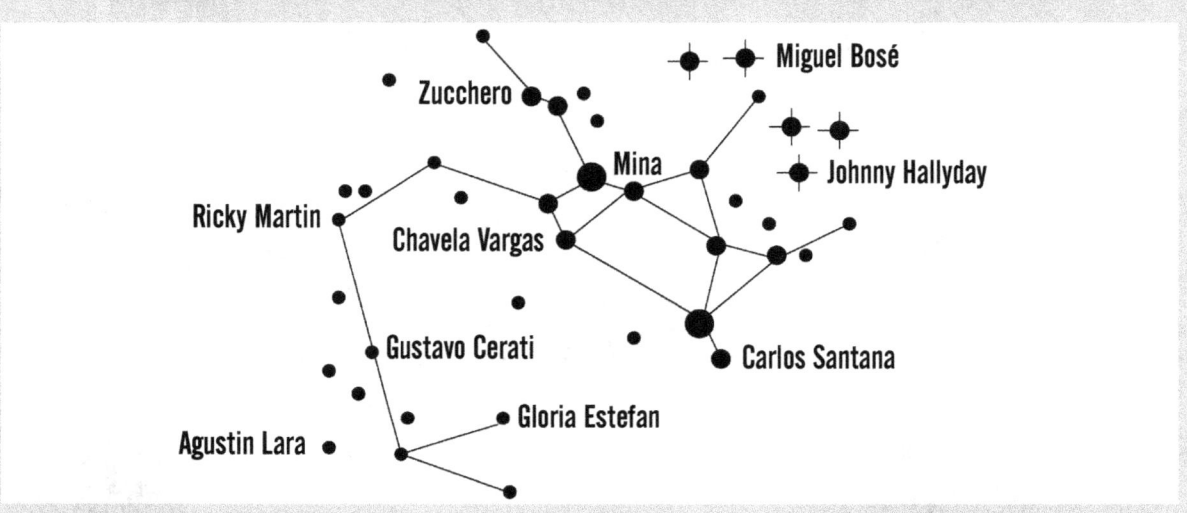

Latin & Euro

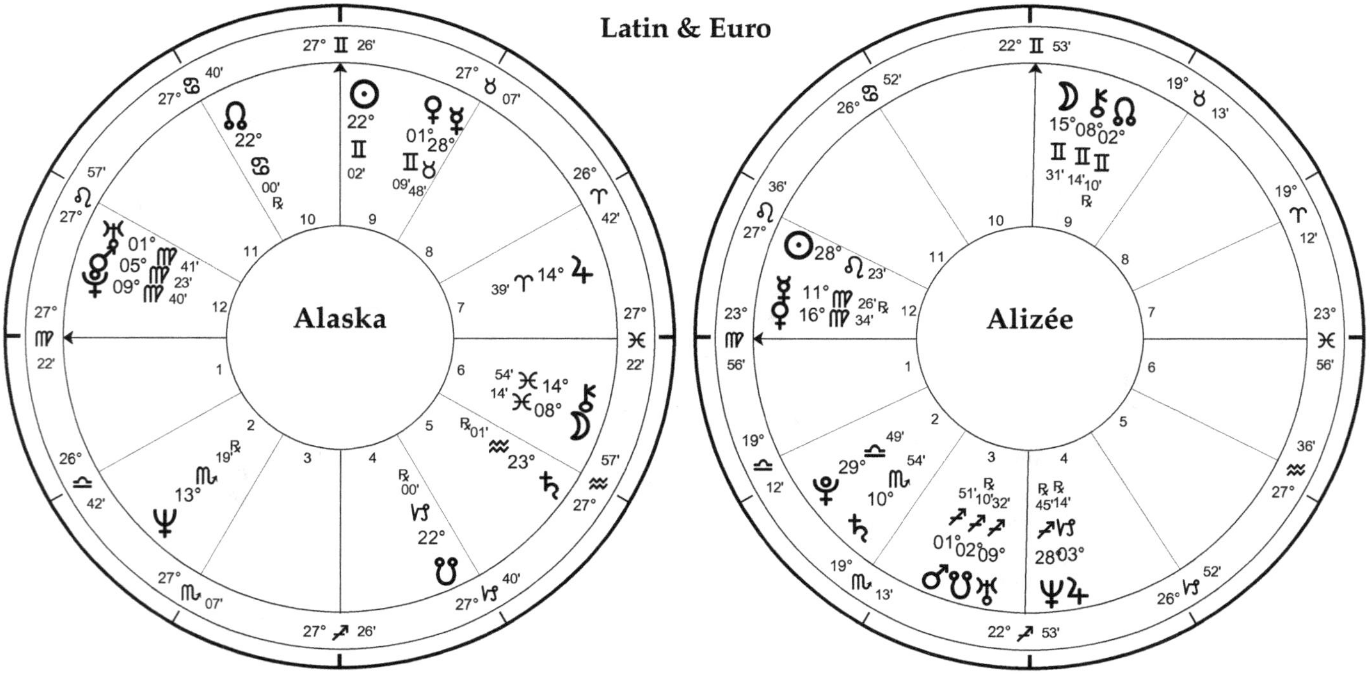

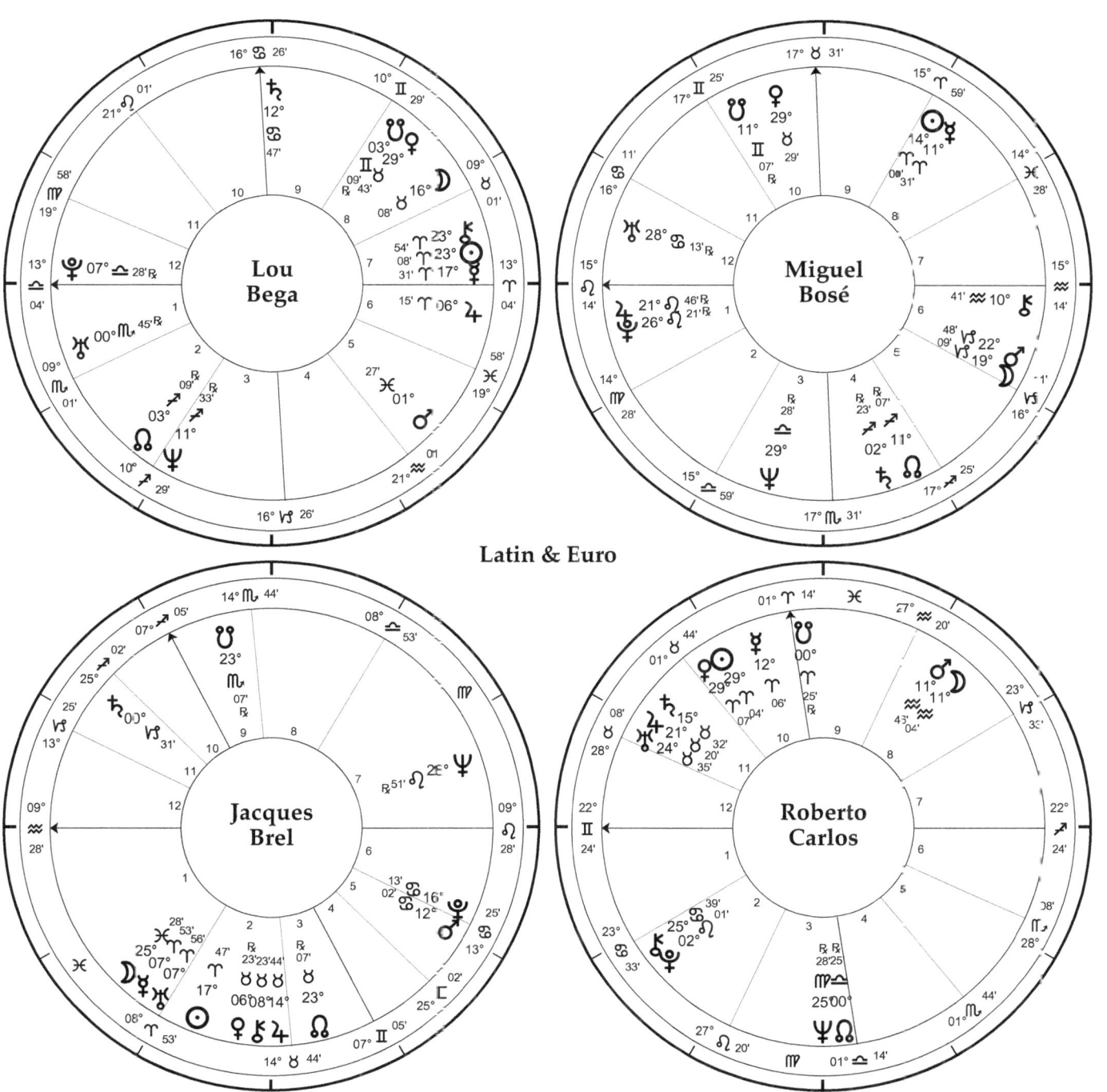

Latin & Euro

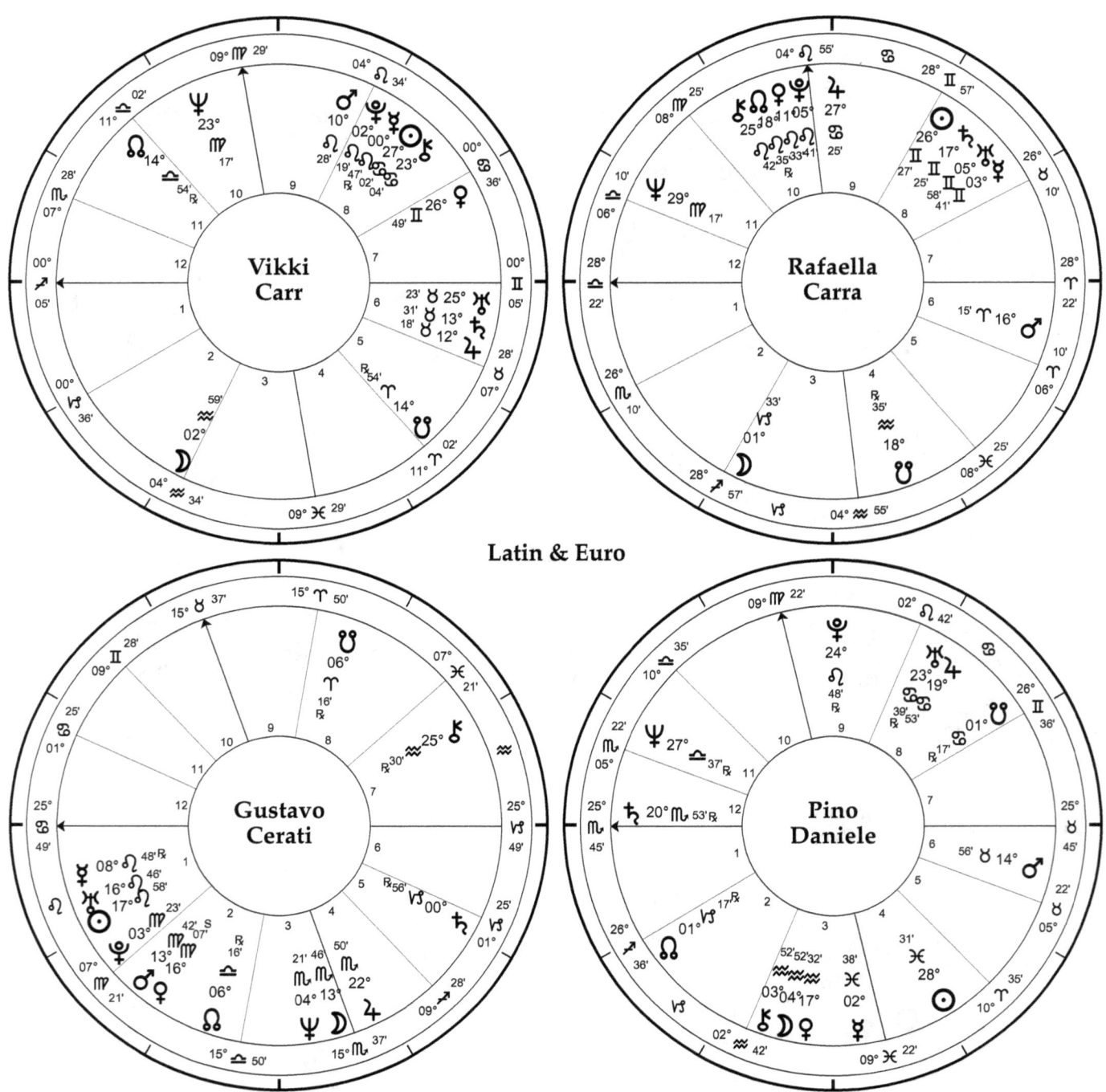

Latin & Euro

Latin Stars & Euro Pop

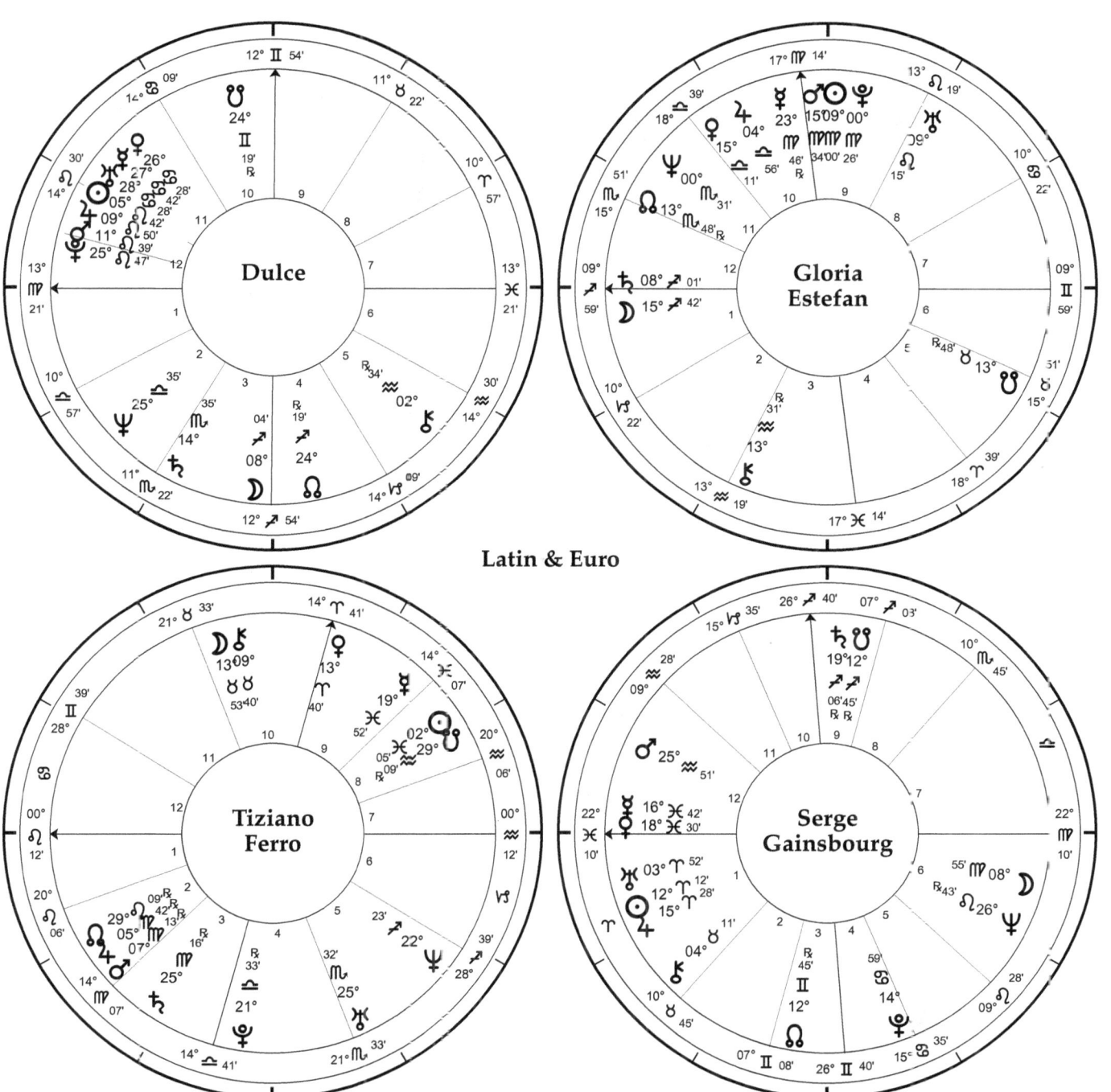

Latin & Euro

182 *The Book of Music Horoscopes*

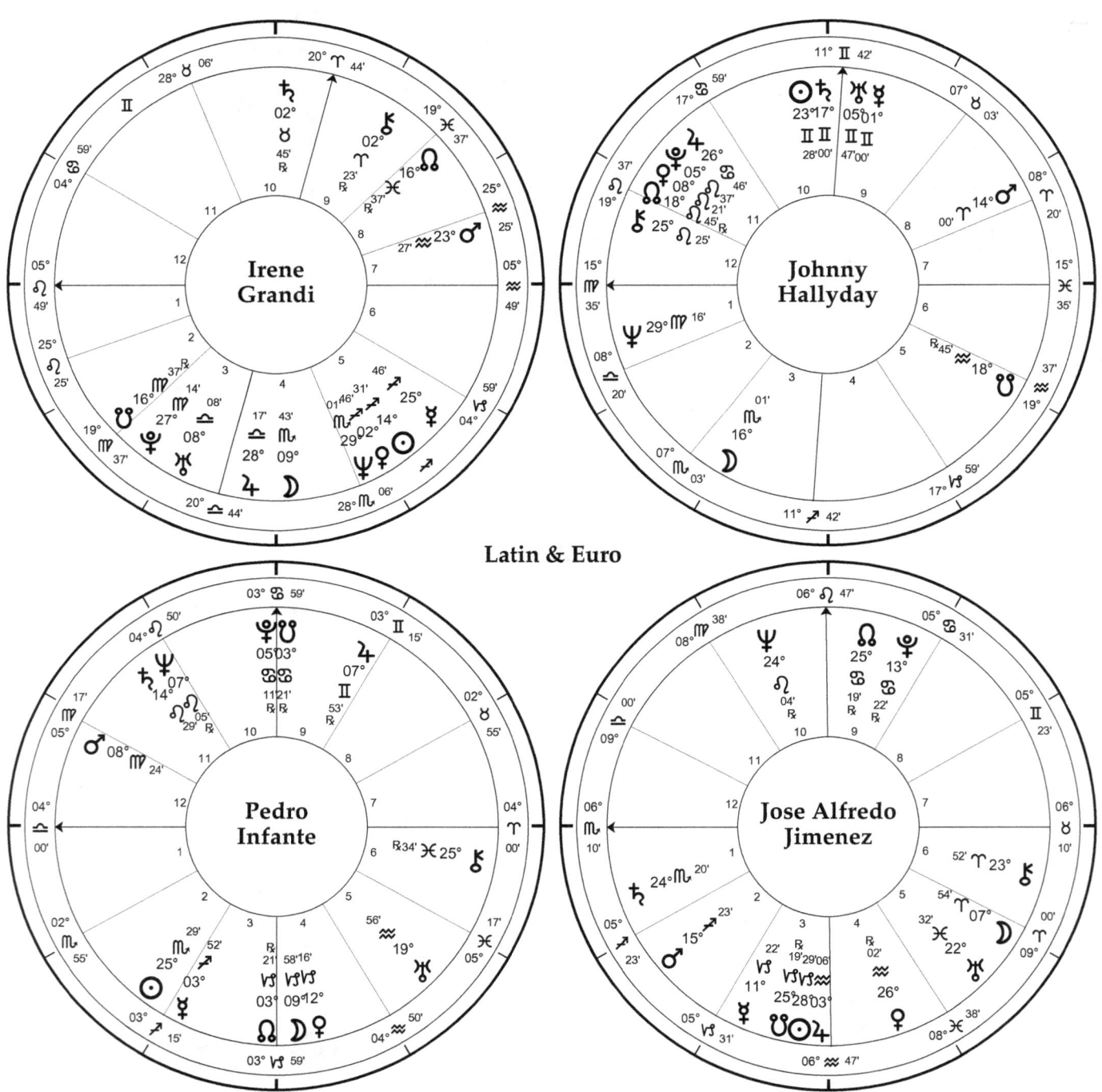

Latin & Euro

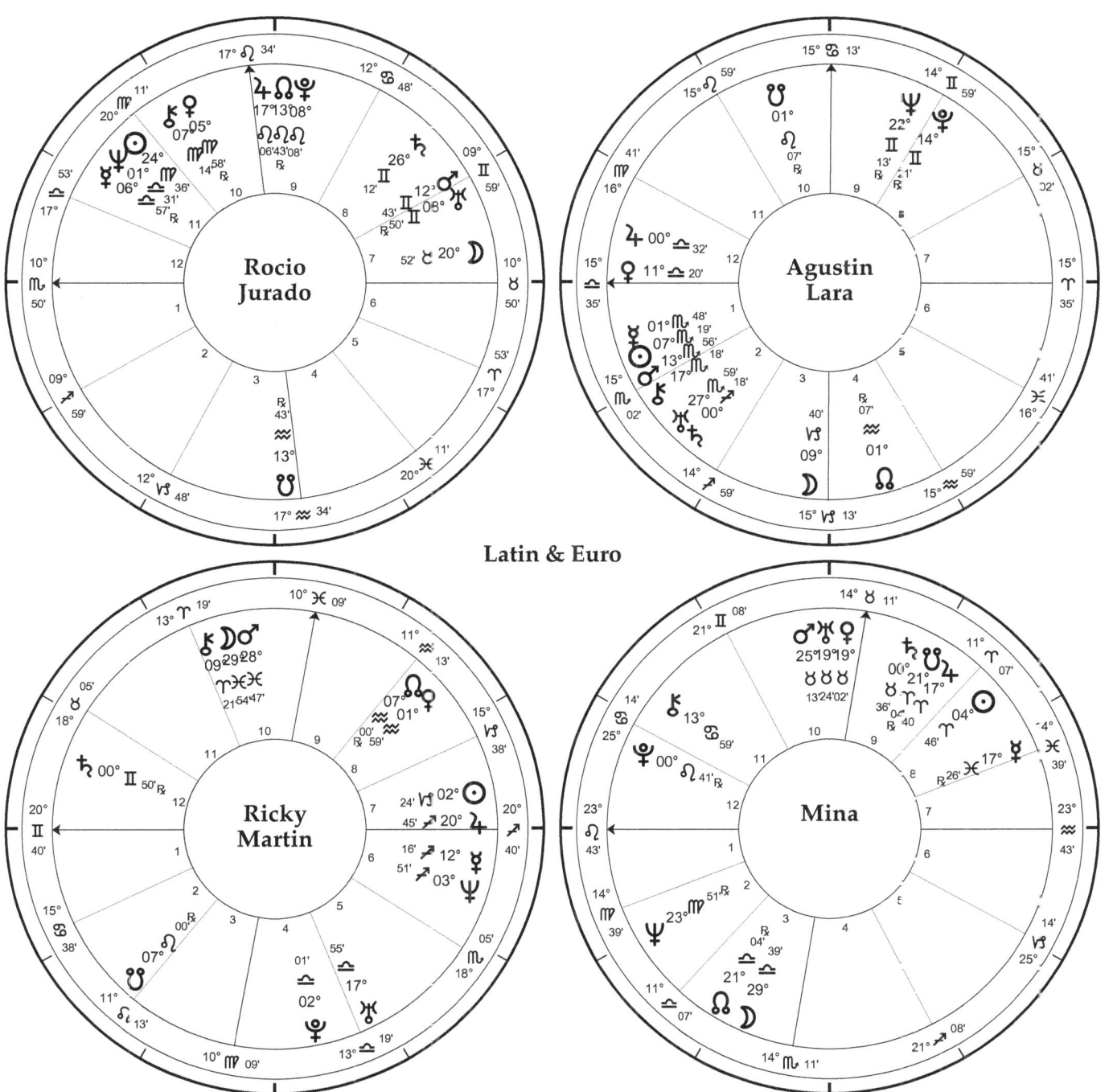

Latin & Euro

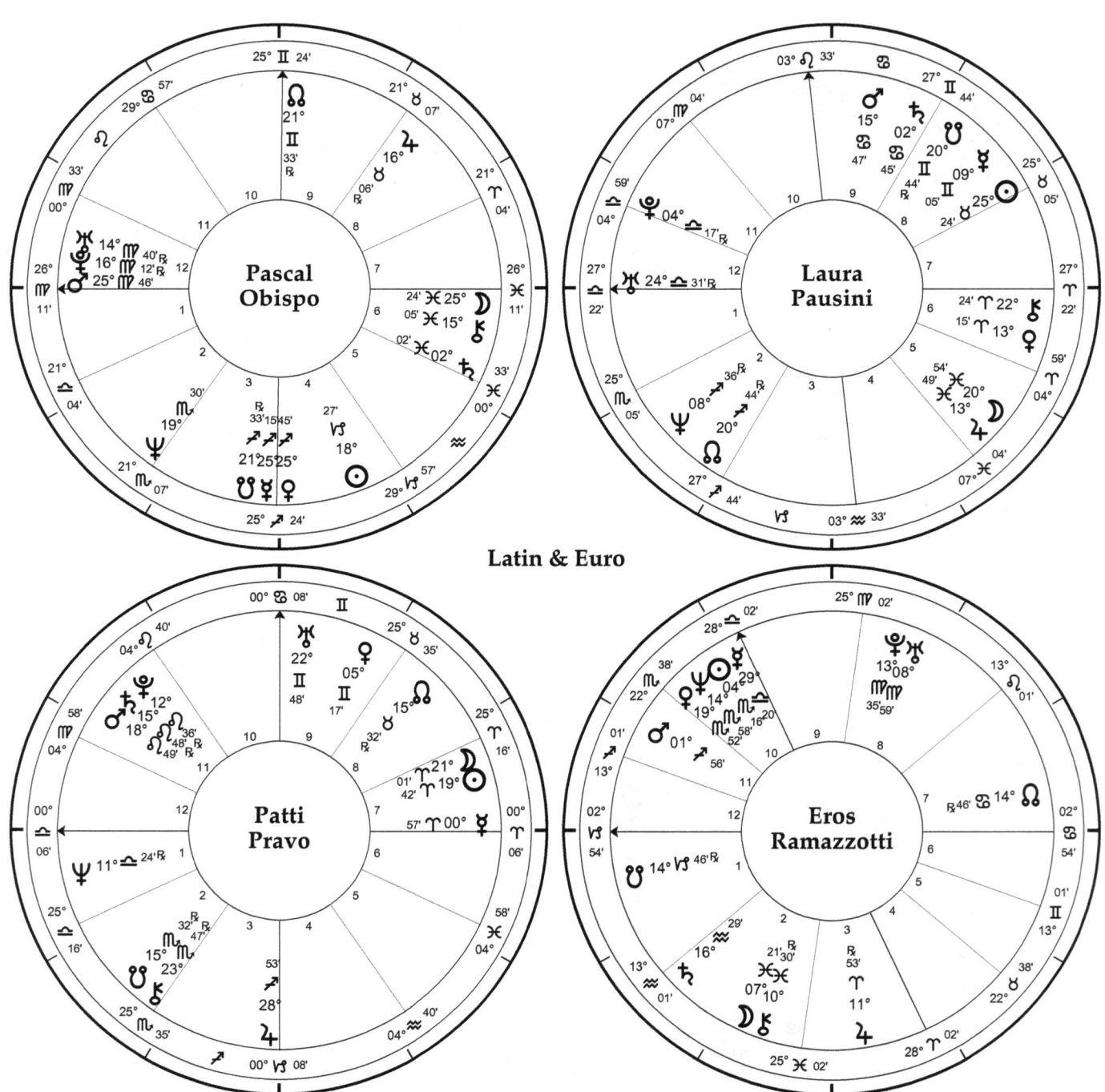

Latin & Euro

Latin Stars & Euro Pop

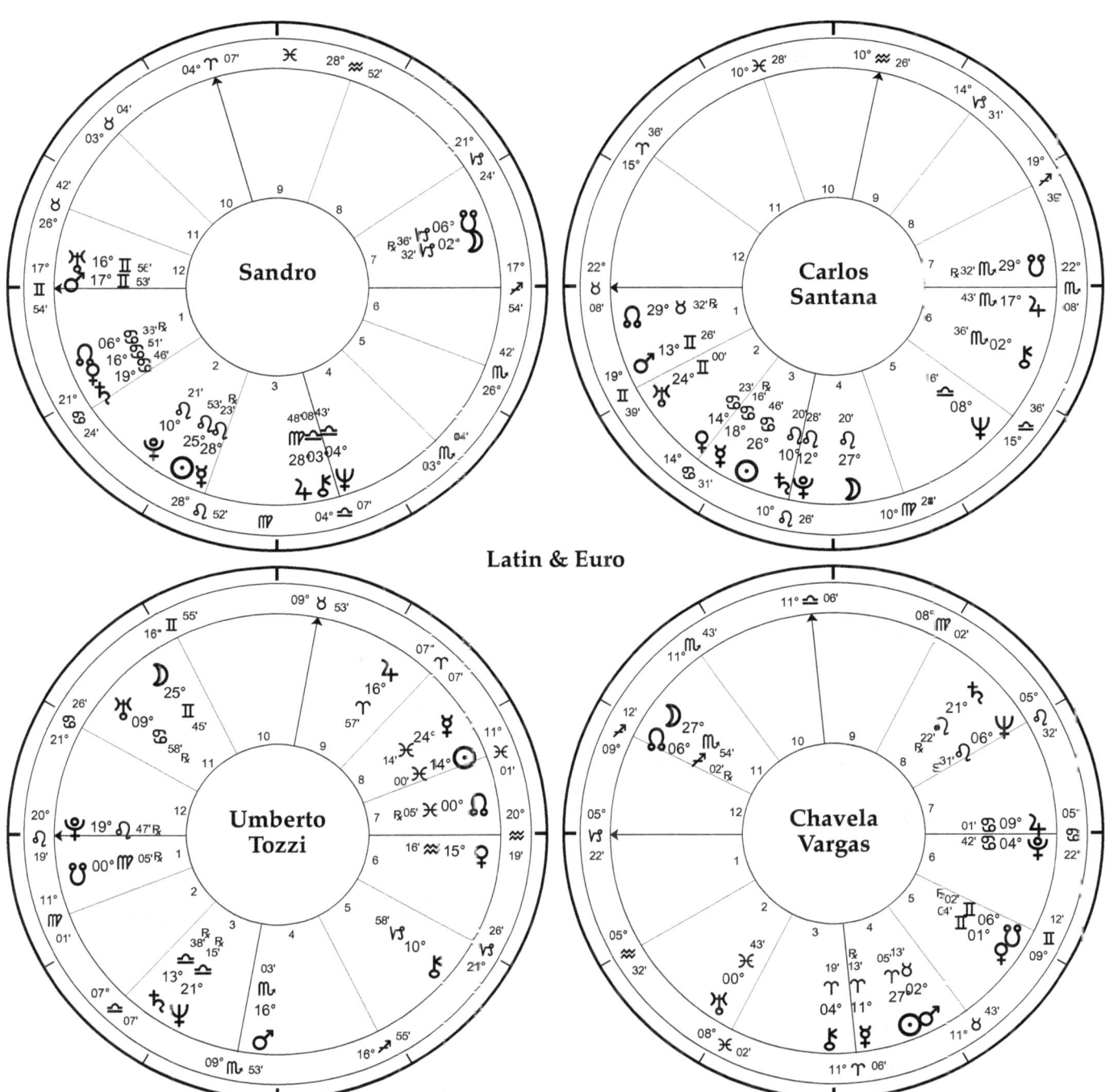

Latin & Euro

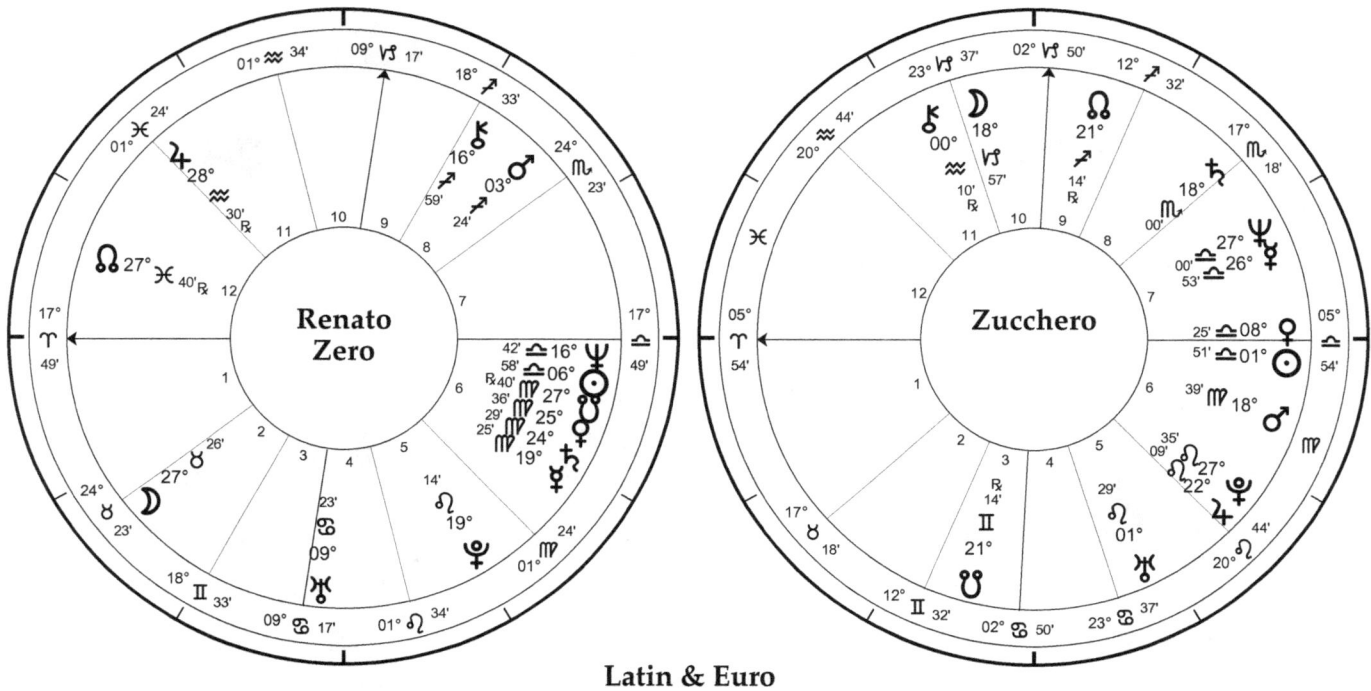

Latin & Euro

Global Reach: Neptune in Sagittarius
Franco

When the slow-moving outer planets enter a zodiac sign, they tend to bring about changes to society that relate to that planet and sign. Neptune, for instance, is a planet that rules music as well as poetry, drugs and alcohol, and fashion. Scorpio is a sign that deals with taboos, sex, power and transformation. Neptune was in Scorpio from 1955 to 1970, a period in which we saw music break down racial barriers in the US (taboos at that time), and songs turned from love and worker tunes to dark and forbidden Scorpionic topics such as sex and drugs.

In 1947, Billboard's top song was Francis Craig's 'Near You'. In 1957, Billboard's top song was Elvis Presley's 'All Shook Up' and, later, in 1967, The Rolling Stones released 'Let's Spend the Night Together', a song title which Ed Sullivan forced them to change on his show to 'Let's Spend Some Time Together'. This song can be considered a nursery rhyme compared to the 1967 Velvet Underground's release 'Venus in Furs', a tune about sadomasochism. After studying this Scorpionic period in music, I was naturally curious as to what occurred when Neptune moved into Sagittarius.

Neptune in Sagittarius: Praise the Lord

Neptune entered Sagittarius, initially from January 1970 until May 1970. It returned in November 1970 and stayed until January 1984, and then had a final stint from June 1984 to November 1984. Sagittarius is the sign of religion, philosophy and foreign lands.

As we approached the new decade the theme of religion was entering the mainstream. Gospel music heavily influenced the African-American singers who gave us all the Motown hits of the 1960s, but it was not until Andrew Lloyd Webber and Tim Rice released *Jesus Christ Superstar* in 1970, a rock opera portraying the Passion of the Christ, that Neptune hit the religious vein. First it was a concept album, then a stage production and later a movie. This was followed by the 1971 Stephen Schwartz's Broadway release of the musical *Godspell* by John-Michael Tebelak, which was based on the Gospel of St Matthew.

The Hare Krishna movement influenced Beatle George Harrison, and he released his hit 'My Sweet Lord' in November 1970. In the US, a new Jesus movement was starting which was led by the Maranatha! Music label, a Christian record label that opened for business in 1971. Canadian song writer Gene MacLellan wrote 'Put Your Hand in the Hand', which was covered by Ocean and reached number two in the Billboard charts. Neptune also 'rules' fashion and this period saw a lot of 'Jesus-like' long hair and sandals. (When I was a child growing up in Toronto, we referred to sandals as 'Jesus boots', which is a term that I have not heard as often since that time.)

The progressive rock band Genesis formed in the late 1960s with their first album, *From Genesis to Revelation*, released in March 1969. In their 1972 release *Foxtrot*, they had a song based on the Book of Revelation called 'Supper's Ready', an obvious play on The Last Supper. The heavy metal band Black Sabbath – which most people associate with demonic dove-biting Ozzy Osbourne – actually started off with religious overtones ('Is God just a thought within your head or is he a part of you?'). And although the hit album *Chant* by the Benedictine Monks of Santo Domingo de Silos did not become famous until 1994, it was originally recorded between 1973 and 1982, while Neptune journeyed through Sagittarius.

While these are one side of the coin, the other side had progressive rockers, Jethro Tull, with their 1971 album *Aqualung*, which openly criticized organized religion in the songs 'My God', 'Hymn 43' and 'Wind-Up', all of which would never have been released in the 1950s.

Music of the World
Jupiter, the planetary ruler of Sagittarius, is associated with expansiveness and its sign is associated with expanding horizons and themes such as foreign lands, a worldly view and an international flavour. As a precursor to Neptune entering the sign of Sagittarius, the western world was introduced to international superstar Ravi Shankar. He was a renowned sitar player in his native India when he met Beatle George Harrison in the mid-1960s. Shankar made his foray into pop culture by playing at the Monterey Pop Festival in 1967 and Woodstock in 1969, just prior to Neptune entering Sagittarius.

In the 1960s, Jamaica's answer to rock 'n' roll was a type of up-tempo music called ska, which features guitars and keyboards that emphasize the offbeat or the 'and' beat (1 & 2 & 3 & 4 &). Musicologists call this the First Wave of Ska. In the 1950s and 1960s, the UK had an influx of immigrants from Jamaica, who brought their music with them. In the 1970s, British teenagers got exposed to ska by hanging out with their Jamaican friends. It was during the punk movement of the late 1970s that several UK ska bands were formed, such as The Beat, The Specials, The Selecter and Madness, who formed the Second Wave of Ska. The Third Wave was in the US in the 1980s.

In 1973, the world was introduced to reggae. Its influence was quickly felt around the world, thanks to its ambassador Bob Marley. Not only did his music influence British and North American pop stars, but he was embraced in Africa. King Sunny Adé started the world fusion beat along with Fela Kuti, who started the Afrobeat sound. The latter grew in popularity, bringing African music genres such as high life, juju and soukous to western ears.

In 1971, the Irish Rovers, a Celtic band comprised of Canadian and Northern Irish performers, were given a television show on the Canadian Broadcasting Corporation. Canada at the time predominantly consisted of people of Irish and Scottish descent, so the Celtic style of music was widely accepted by the 'older' audience. However, a London-based Irish band formed in 1982 called The Pogues went on to become widely popular in the 1980s and 1990s. This trend continued in Canada with bands such as Great Big Sea, Spirit of the West and the Mahones.

In 1982 the Soca tune 'Hot, Hot, Hot' made its way into every wedding conga line, replacing Little Eva's

'Locomotion' for those of you old enough to remember that ditty.

Algerian raï was a music form that started in the 1930s, but in the 1970s it was influenced by Bob Marley and western sounds and transformed into pop raï. Raï music was quite provocative as Islamic fundamentalists would persecute raï stars because they would sing about sex and alcohol.

Ex-Genesis singer, Peter Gabriel, along with a few others, created WOMAD in 1980. It is an acronym for World of Music, Arts and Dance and its mandate was to bring global performers together in one music festival. The first concert took place in the UK in 1982 but was not financially successful. The festival is still active today.

Embracing the world vision, a Japanese taiko drum band was formed in 1971 but played only in Japan under the name Sado no Kuni Ondekoza. They were revamped and renamed Kodo in 1981 and their performances moved outside the country. Their first tour encompassed Italy, San Marino and West Germany in 1981, followed by a North American tour in 1982, and now they even hold workshops in foreign countries.

The exposure of music styles from other countries has continued, thanks to these pioneers during Neptune's time in Sagittarius. Once the world was transformed by sex and drugs and rock 'n' roll. When Neptune left Scorpio, it moved on with spiritual music and then to a global Sagittarian view.

Mercury: The Transgender Singer
Sy Scholfield

Mercury is the transgender singer of the planetary pantheon because it rules both the mutable Air sign Gemini (associated with the changeable sounds of the singing voice as generated by the lungs, the vocal cords and parts of the mouth) and the mutable Earth sign Virgo (associated with the variations of the physical body and its appearance required to change sex or gender). I've found that Mercury is prominent in the charts of vocalists who are, or who play the role of, transgender people, including androgynous-looking folk, gender illusionists (drag queens and drag kings) and transsexuals. As we shall see below, the signature song(s), style and imagery of the transgender singer are influenced by Mercury's natal placement in a particular sign.

Actor and singer Tim Curry embodied the in-your-face, pioneering and aggressive side of the Mercury in Aries archetype through his portrayal of Dr Frank-N-Furter in the 1975 musical film, *The Rocky Horror Picture Show*. Curry's Mercury conjuncts his MC and trines his dramatic Leo Ascendant: his role as the self-proclaimed 'sweet transvestite from Transsexual, Transylvania' (who seduces both Brad and Janet) broke the mould for representations of cross-dressers in popular culture, making him both an international star and a cult figure synonymous with openly brash, carnal transvestism.

The pianist and entertainer Liberace, the world's highest-paid performer from the 1950s to the 1970s, had Mercury in money-making and vain-as-a-peacock Taurus (on his IC and trine his Ascendant in reputation-sensitive Capricorn). 'Stare as long as you like,' he would tell his audiences while parading in one of his trademark sequinned tuxedo-gowns. 'You paid for it!' A 1956 article in the UK's *Daily Mirror* described him as 'the summit of sex – the pinnacle of masculine, feminine, and neuter ... scent-impregnated, luminous, quivering, giggling, fruit-flavoured, mincing', and so on. Liberace sued for libel and won, famously remarking about his settlement, 'I cried all the way to the bank!'

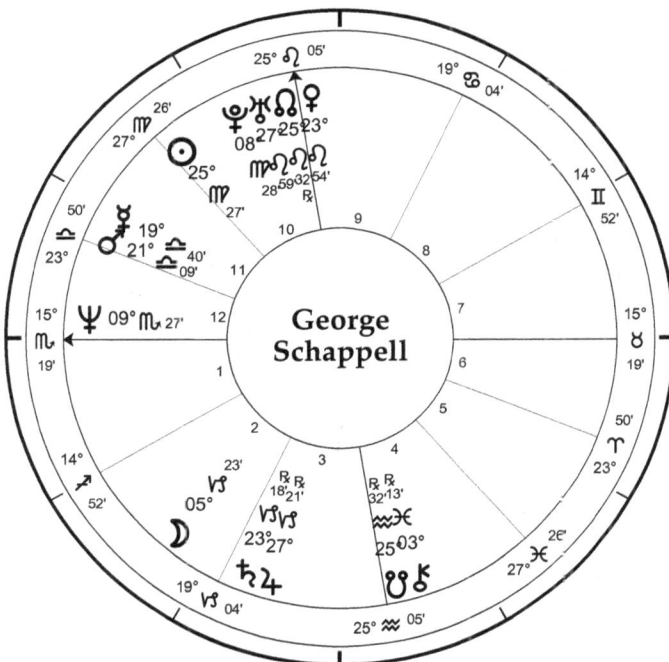

Mercury in its own sign Gemini is final dispositor in the charts of 'the First Lady of country music' Tammy Wynette and 'pop princess' Kylie Minogue. Wynette has Mercury in the first degree: the lyrics to her signature tune 'Stand by Your Man' are so open to interpretation that many high-camp drag queens have claimed it as their lip-synching anthem. Also often imitated by drag queens, Minogue has Mercury sextile Jupiter in audience-loving Leo. She performed at the closing ceremony of the Sydney 2000 Olympics while *Priscilla*-inspired drag queens proudly marched and danced, all telecast to 2.4 billion viewers.

The most famous female impersonator in the world, Danny La Rue, had Mercury in ultra-feminine Cancer unaspected except for a conjunction with Pluto. Famed for his dead-on celebrity impersonations of sex symbols like Elizabeth Taylor and Zsa Zsa Gabor, he performed as the sultry Marlene Dietrich, singing 'Falling in Love Again' in the 1972 comedy *Our Miss Fred*, his only starring role in a feature film. Boy George, lead singer of pop band Culture Club, became the most famous gender-bender of the 1980s. Mercury conjuncts his IC and its dispositor Moon (all in Cancer): his androgynous look harmonizes with his soulful voice.

Pete Burns, vocalist for the band Dead or Alive, was known for his ever-changing, androgynous appearance, greatly modified by facial cosmetic surgery. His Mercury is conjunct the Sun (its dispositor) and Uranus (keywords: oddness, individuality), all three in regal Leo. He appeared on Facebook as Queen Cleopatra; his autobiography is titled *Freak Unique*. Mercury in Leo also likes to show off its butch side, revelling in camp, hyper-masculinity. Lily Tomlin, one of the first female comedians to don male drag, created characters like the lounge-singer Tommy Velour (a cross between Tom Jones and Wayne Newton, complete with a 'rug' of chest hair). Tomlin's Leo Mercury is unaspected except for a close square from Uranus, highlighting the originality of her dramatic male impersonations.

One of the greatest singers in the history of pop music, Freddie Mercury, lead vocalist and lyricist of the rock band Queen, named himself after his ruling planet. With Mercury in flexible Virgo widely conjunct (and, indeed, ruling) his Sun in the same sign, he was a natural, untrained singer and performer whose vocal range extended from the masculine bass low F2 to the feminine soprano high F6. He wrote songs in a wide range of genres: rockabilly, heavy metal, gospel and disco. In the controversial music video for the 1984 Queen song, 'I Want to Break Free', the band members dress as women, but maverick Freddie steals the show, wearing his trademark moustache while playing a housewife (doing the Virgo house-cleaning) in bouffant wig, black miniskirt and pale pink top.

Country singer and transgender conjoined twin George Schappell was named Dori when he was born in a female body – joined at the head with his sister Lori. By 2007 he preferred to be known as George, having self-identified as male from a young age. George and Lori's Mercury in Libra (partnership) is conjunct their Mars, the co-ruler of their Scorpio Ascendant (intimacy, privacy). Physically inseparable, these siblings must share far more than most people and respect each other's individuality. George won an LA Music Award for Best

New Country Artist in 1997. Lori, a trophy-winning bowler, facilitates George's career, and vice versa.

Mercury rising in hyper-sexual Scorpio made 'trashy' disco diva Divine hard to ignore. Described by *People* magazine as the 'drag queen of the century', Divine had a hit in 1984 with a song about unquenchable trans/gay desire: 'You think you're a man (… but you're only a boy/toy … you weren't man enough to satisfy me!)'. In the song's video clip, the plus-size Divine pokes her tongue and rolls her eyes, simulating orgasm while strutting in a teased blonde wig and figure-hugging frock. Julie Andrews (Scorpio Mercury ruling a Virgo Ascendant and Gemini MC) earned a Best Actress Golden Globe for playing Victoria Grant, a soprano who masquerades as Count Victor Grazinski, a gay Polish female impersonator, in *Victor/Victoria* (1982). In 2014, Conchita Wurst (Mercury in the first degree of Scorpio), a drag queen noted for her beard, rose to prominence by winning the Eurovision Song Contest with the very Plutonic track 'Rise Like a Phoenix'.

Mercury in equine Sagittarius rides on Patti Smith's Ascendant, so it comes as no surprise that this rock poet-singer's debut studio album was titled *Horses*. In the album cover photo (shot by her friend Robert Mapplethorpe), Smith wears a man's shirt and braces with a man's jacket over her shoulder. The first woman to cover Van Morrison's 'Gloria', Smith defiantly thrusts herself into the male role of the song. 'Gloria' is the first track on *Horses*, an album that was a major influence not only on the New York punk rock scene but also on female androgyny in the music world.

Marlene Dietrich and Annie Lennox both have Mercury in conservative Capricorn, and each shot to fame attired in a formal suit. Dietrich (Mercury conjunct the Sun and trine the Virgo Ascendant it rules) earned her only Oscar nomination for playing a cabaret singer in *Morocco* (1930), a film best remembered for the sequence in which she sings 'Give Me the Man', dressed in a black tuxedo and white tie, and kisses another woman. Five decades later, in 1983, the Eurythmics skyrocketed to stardom on the back of Lennox's strikingly androgynous look – close-cropped 'buzz cut' orange hair, dark suit, grey tie, black gloves and cane – as featured in the music video for 'Sweet Dreams (Are Made of This)'. In the video for 'Love Is a Stranger', she plays a high-class prostitute who removes a curly blonde wig to reveal her slicked-back hair, which caused some viewers to believe Lennox was a drag queen. Her Mercury conjoins her Sun, Moon and North Node.

Mercury in Aquarius celebrates gender rebellion and sexual non-conformity. Lou Reed's solo hit, 'Walk on the Wild Side', appears on *Transformer*, his 1972 album produced by David Bowie (whose Ascendant conjuncts Reed's Aquarian Mercury, while Reed's Pluto is exactly on Bowie's Moon). Each of the song's five verses poignantly describes one of the misfit 'superstars' at Andy Warhol's Factory: four drag queens (Holly Woodlawn, Candy Darling, 'Sugar Plum Fairy' Joe Campbell and Jackie Curtis, whose Moon conjuncts Reed's Mercury) and hustler Joe Dallesandro who slept and/or co-starred with them in Warhol's films.

Mercury in Pisces confuses or transcends conventional gender boundaries. The 1953 Oscar for Best Original Song was awarded to the writers of 'Secret Love', sung by Doris Day in the title role of the comedic Western musical film *Calamity Jane*. This was the closest Day came to an Oscar. *Calamity Jane* is often cited for its cross-dressing and lesbian overtones (Calamity is a cowgirl tomboy who temporarily shacks up with another woman). Day performs 'Secret Love' wearing a girly blouse and butch buckskins while on horseback (switching from feminine side-saddle pose to riding masculinely astride). Mercury in Pisces (in the secretive Scorpio decan) straddles Day's Descendant while ruling (and in hard aspect to) her Virgo Ascendant and Gemini MC.

The birth data for those listed above (who are not included in the data section of this book) can be found at www.astrodatabank.com

ROCK

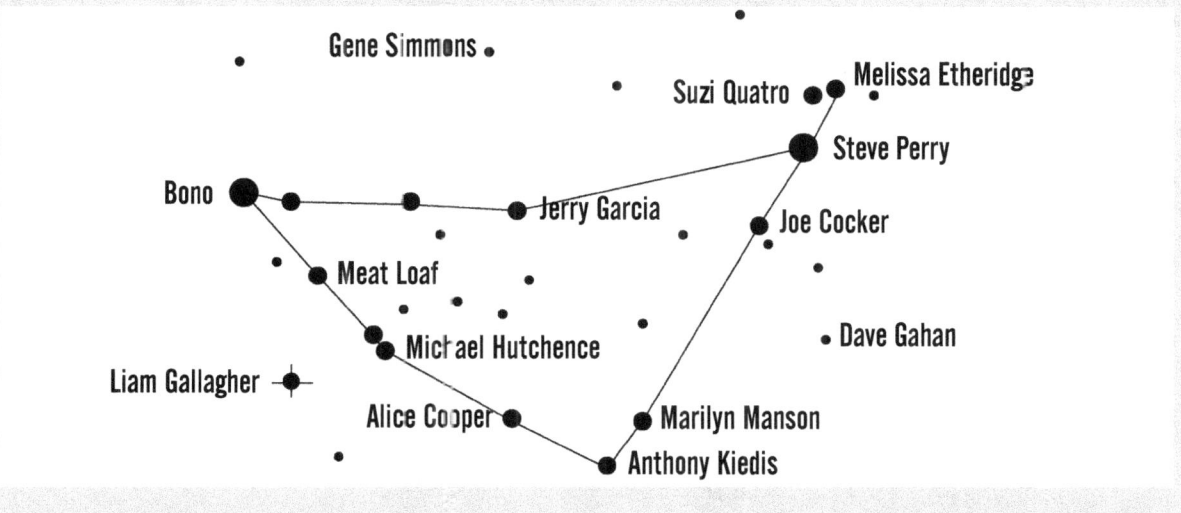

Signatures of Rock

Notes by Frank Clifford

Wild, raucous rock 'n' roll energy, Stadium Rock, raw sexuality and magnetism, groupies – this is the stuff of Scorpio, Mars and Pluto. Examining dozens of rock stars – the frontmen and women – we can throw in a few further ingredients:

- Neptune for stage presence and inspiring crowd euphoria;
- A helping of Jupiter (and its signs) for hedonism, excess and god-like adulation;
- A jolt of dynamic Uranus for shock value and explosive anarchy;
- A predominance of the sensual, pagan Earth signs (particularly rock-like Capricorn);
- And finally, Leo or Sagittarius for charisma and performance exhibitionism.

Here are a few examples:

- Black leather rock mystic Jim Morrison: Moon in Taurus square Pluto setting (on the Descendant), Sun in Sagittarius opposite Mars–Uranus, Jupiter in Leo square MC in Scorpio.
- Wild woman and leather-clad Suzi Quatro: Mars rising square Uranus–MC, Moon in Capricorn plus four planets and Ascendant in Earth signs
- INXS bad-boy Michael Hutchence: Moon–Neptune in Scorpio, Venus–Jupiter in Sagittarius.
- Oasis lead singer Liam Gallagher: Sun–Mercury–Mars in late Virgo (and Pluto in early Libra) on the MC square Jupiter in Sagittarius, Neptune rising, Venus in Leo.
- Ozzy Osbourne: Moon in Capricorn, Mars–Jupiter in Capricorn (opposite Uranus), Moon square Neptune, Sun–Mercury in Sagittarius, Venus in Scorpio square Pluto.

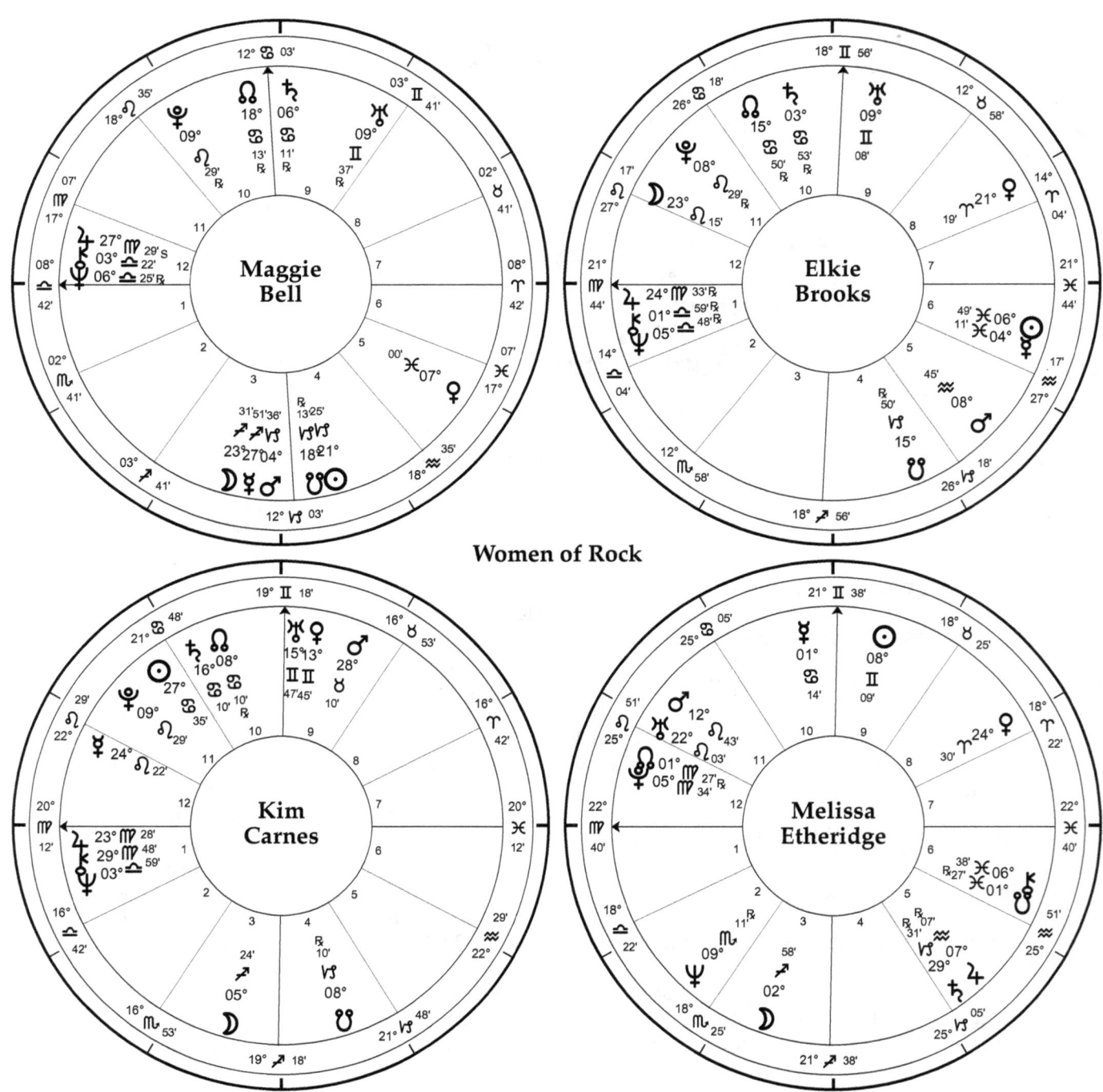

Women of Rock

Rock 193

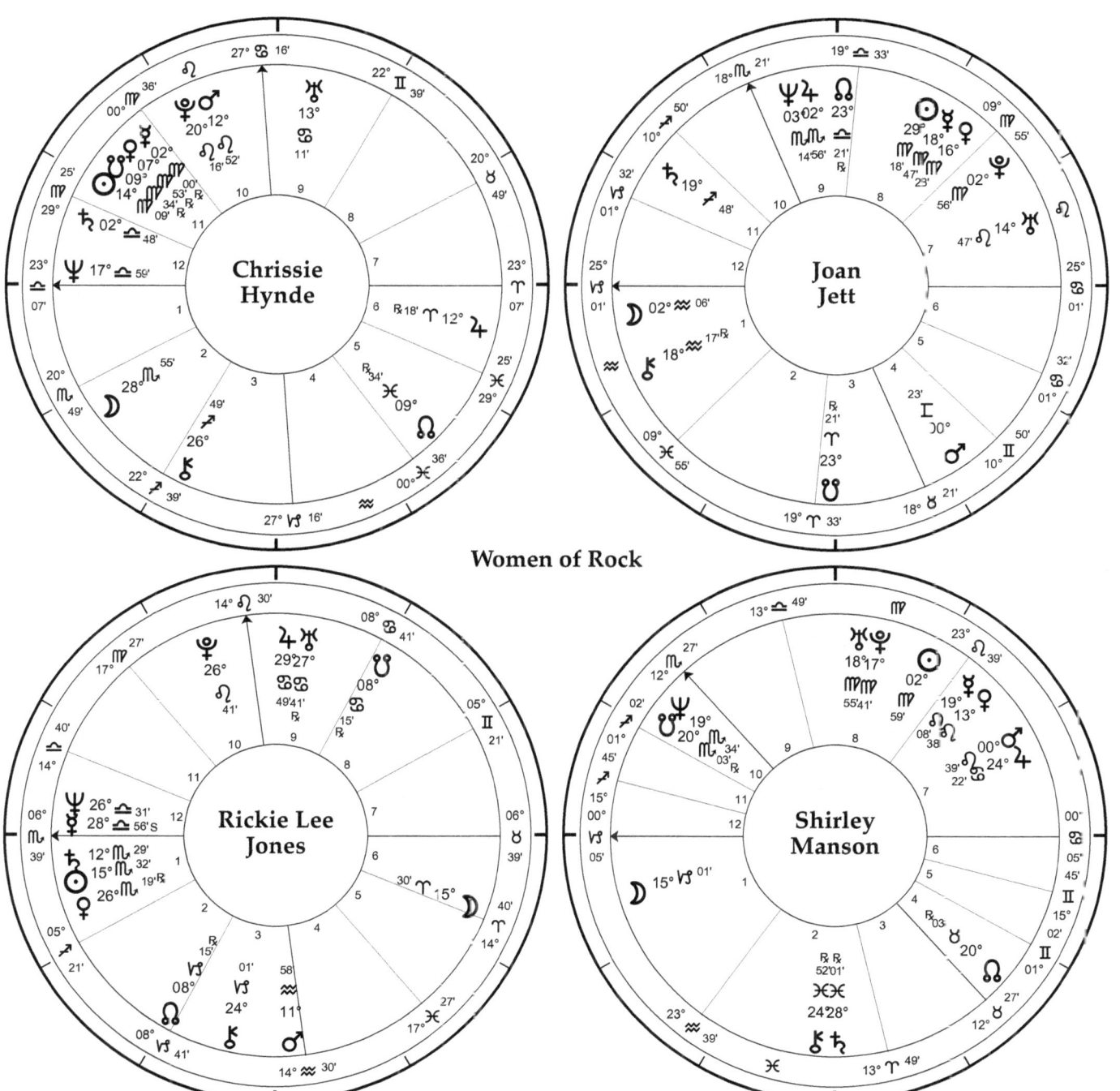

Women of Rock

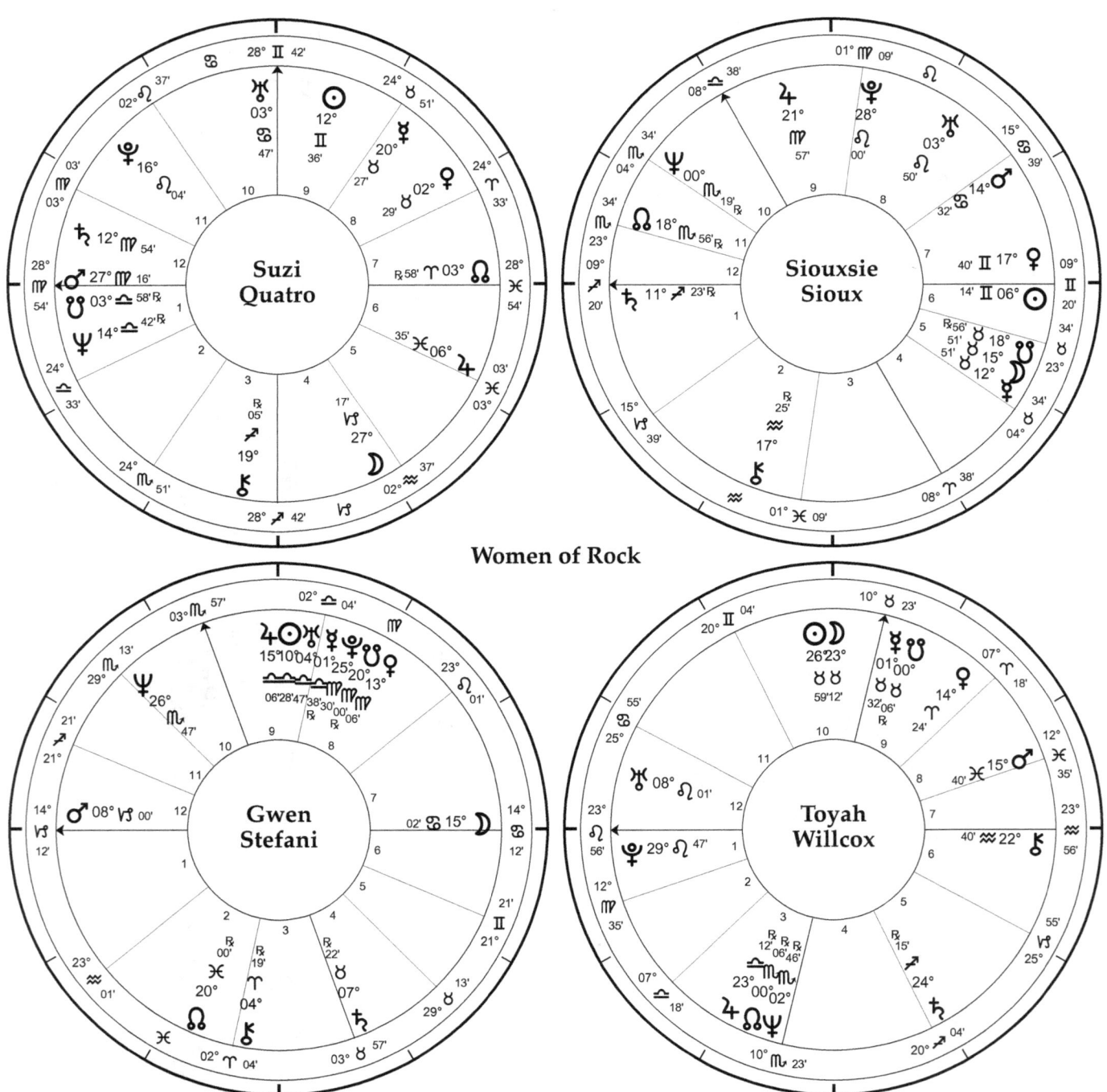

Women of Rock

Women Who Rock

Tony Howard

Our culture's imbalanced gender bias filters into every aspect of human experience. So it's no surprise that women are grossly under-represented in the male-dominated rock scene. Because of the intense barrier to entry, those women who make it in the field stand apart from the crowd.

Once rock was established as a new genre it was quickly dominated and shaped by men who combined the raw sound of electric guitars with varying levels of Mars-fuelled angst, aggression and sex appeal. Rock became so synonymous with the male gender that it would take the Uranus–Pluto conjunction of the 60s to begin to break up the status quo enough that women could start playing more formative roles. As that powerful and world-changing configuration began to square her natal Mars, the fireball powerhouse Janis Joplin was the first woman to successfully embody the rock ethos, rightfully claiming her spot on that stage and in history.

Astrologically it took some powerful chart dynamics to help a woman break through the obstacles into the rock world. We'd expect to see the potential for raw talent and a dynamic physical presence and solar ego – and enough grit and ferocity to embody the rock mystique, be taken seriously and to win over the audience. In fact, the Sun, Mars, Uranus and Pluto combine to make up the strongest planetary signatures in the charts of such iconic women.

I narrowed down a list of successful female rock performers to look at the charts of 51 women whose music could be categorized according to a narrow definition of 'rock' that does not include folk and pop singers or avant-garde artists. To evaluate planetary strength and importance, I used the major Ptolemaic aspects, and also considered parallels and contraparallels of declination, as well as high and low declinations.

In his book *Declination in Astrology* (Wessex, 2006, pp. 12–13), Paul F Newman suggests that the midline, or 'zero line', of the equator is 'one of the most critical positions in declination'. Interpretively, the idea is that planets within a couple of degrees of crossing zero carry enhanced strength or presence.

Planets near the outer limits of declination, including the Sun, also take on a heightened importance. And as planets move beyond the Sun's declination limit of 23°26' North or South, we call them 'out of bounds'. At the centre of our solar system, the Sun metaphorically determines the limits of 'normal', and when a planet moves beyond that limit we think of it as operating outside the Sun's jurisdiction.

Out of bounds planets are said to behave in unusual ways, without limits and potentially unbounded by mainstream rules of appropriate behaviour. In a natal chart they carry the potential for enhanced freedom of expression, or a desire to innovate, to forge new territory and/or an unchecked or unbalanced expression of the planet in question.

My sample confirmed that women who succeed in the rock business have strong Mars placements, strong solar (Sun) energy and important outer planet configurations, especially with Uranus and Pluto. Nearly every woman in my sample has strong Mars, Uranus and Pluto aspects, even taking into account that the majority have charts without birth times, and therefore some potentially strong aspects to the Moon and angles are unaccounted for. With exact birth times, we would surely be near 100% on this count.

Of the charts with no birth times:

- Only five have a potentially unaspected Mars
- 25% have a Mars–Uranus aspect
- 22% have a Sun–Mars aspect
- 18% have a Mercury–Mars aspect
- 22% have a Sun–Pluto aspect
- 24% have a Mercury–Uranus aspect

When we look at declination, we find additional correlations. Of the 51 women, 25 have at least one planet (the Moon, Venus, Mercury or Mars) out of bounds. That's 49% of my sample. Of these, the most common planets at high declination are the Moon (20%)

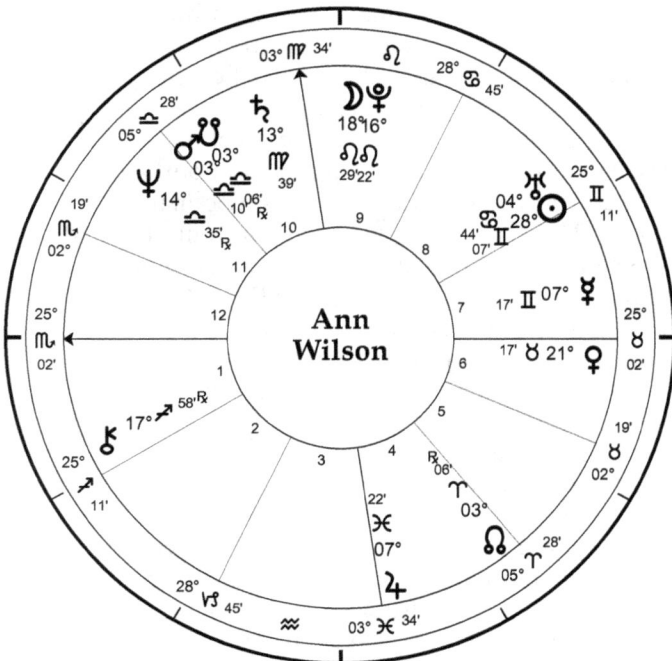

and Mercury (20%), followed closely by Mars (16%). Women from this sample include Stevie Nicks, Chrissie Hynde and Florence Welch, to name a few. In further studies, I've found the Moon out of bounds to correlate with male musicians, such as Jeff Buckley, who make a deep emotional impact with their audience.

Early on, I expected to find Mars out of bounds strongly represented because the out of bounds signature can potentially accentuate Mars's trailblazing and assertive qualities. But I found an even stronger testimony for female rock greatness: the Sun strongly placed by declination. I found that 55% of these women have the Sun either within 2° of the midline, or at high declination above 20° N or S. Thinking of ego strength, consider the following quote from Joan Jett (who has the natal Sun in Virgo at 0°17'N declination): 'Female guitarists have long been forced to navigate an obstacle course that includes morons, hecklers and skeptics. A lot of girls just say "[The heck with] this. I'll just do something that doesn't take such a toll on my self-esteem."' It has taken a robust sense of ego, of solar presence, to push through the many obstacles women in rock have had to face in the male-dominated field, regardless of whether they were graced with natural raw talent.

Now let's take a look at a couple of stand-out charts from my sample that highlight the important role that planetary declination can play in chart expression.

With her natal Mars out of bounds combined with a strong Mercury–Pluto opposition, Janis Joplin's raspy, unmistakable voice set her apart. Pluto imparts depth to whatever it touches and, as Reuters notes, 'Janis Joplin sang with more than her voice. Her involvement was total.'

The out of bounds signature seems to be associated with important cultural figureheads who move things forward, propelling the collective head-first into the future whether we're ready or not. Joplin was a singular force whose cultural impact and style hasn't been duplicated since.

UK bassist Suzi Quatro may be best known in the USA for her breakout pop duet 'Stumblin' In', which doesn't exactly qualify her for rock goddess status. But what you might not know is that she was also the first female bass player to become a major rock star. With her debut album *Suzi Quatro*, she became the first woman to both front a rock band and also play an instrument. To say that Mars is important in her chart is an understatement. With Mars on her Ascendant, square the MC and trine her out of bounds Moon, we have a strong testimony for a trailblazer or leader. That energy is further enhanced by Mars's declination at 1°N44', very close to its crossing at the midline.

Another rock legend with Mars near the zero crossing is the legendary Ann Wilson (chart above), lead singer of Heart. Her natal Mars at 1°S02' by declination is also square Uranus and the Sun, and rules her Scorpio Ascendant. With the additional rare occurrence of both Uranus and Pluto out of bounds (the only woman in my sample with that configuration), she has contributed something truly unique to rock and roll history.

With Wilson's natal Moon in Leo conjunct Pluto out of bounds, she conveys her emotional message with unforgettable power and depth. With her Sun near its peak of declination at 23°N26', she also had the ego strength to back it up onstage, even if she sometimes faltered with characteristic Moon in Leo stage fright. And although her natal Moon is in bounds at 18°N39', her chart-topping and timeless single 'Crazy on You' was fittingly released while her natal Moon had progressed out of bounds.

We can't mention Ann without thinking of her sister Nancy, whose memorable guitar licks helped songs like 'Magic Man' claim a permanent place in rock history. In his 2012 UAC lecture on 'The History of Rock and Roll', Richard Tarnas associated electric guitars with the planet Uranus. In Nancy's chart Uranus is not only sesquiquadrate fast-fingered Mercury, but is also trine her MC and in a tight quincunx with her high declination Mars at 22°N30'. With her Sun also near the midline at 1°S43', like her sister, she had sufficient ego presence to shine onstage as part of one of the most memorable rock duos in history.

Trailblazing rock legend Patti Smith has natal Mars out of bounds, conjunct the Sun and square Neptune. Her natal Mercury out of bounds squares her Moon and sits just 5° below the Ascendant. Today she is as well revered for her poetry and prose as she is for a string ofrock anthems including *Gloria*, *Because the Night* and *People Have the Power* (she has natal Uranus on the Descendant). With a deep love for the rock and roll ethos, she claimed this energy for herself from the very start, gracing her first album cover, *Horses*, in full Mercurial androgyny and rock attitude, donning classic black and white men's attire with a blazer casually slung over her shoulder.

Many of the great women in this sample paved the way for a younger generation to find more doors open to them in the rock world, even though we're still a long way from true gender equality in this field, as in so many others.

List of Women in the Sample
I don't claim this to be the most definitive list of female rock musicians to date. I tried to offer a broad enough sample to allow trends and patterns to emerge in the research without watering down the list with other genres. In my sample, a wide range of rock styles is represented, from more accessible radio-friendly rock to hardcore punk. I suspect that if I narrowed down the list by genre, trends would emerge. The problem is that because women are grossly under-represented in rock, my samples would then be too small to analyse.

Aimee Mann
Amy Lee
  (Evanescence)
Ani DiFranco
Ann Wilson
Ari Up (Slits)
Carrie Brownstein
  (Sleater-Kinney)
Chan Marshall (Cat Power)
Charlotte Caffey
  (the Go-Go's)
Cherie Currie
Chrissie Hynde
Christina Amphlett
Corin Tucker
  (Sleater-Kinney)
Courtney Love
Debbie Harry
Donita Sparks (L7)
Exene Cervenka
Florence Welch
  (Florence and the Machine)

Grace Slick
Heather Nova
Janis Joplin
Joan Jett
Johnette Napolitano

Juliette Lewis
Justine Frischmann (Elastica)
Karen O. (Yeah Yeah Yeahs)

Kate Bush
Kathleen Hanna
  (Bikini Kill)
Kathy Valentine
  (the Go-Go's)
Kim Deal
Kim Gordon
Kristin Hersh
Linda Perry
Lita Ford
Liz Phair
Marianne Faithfull
Martha Davis
Melissa Etheridge
Meredith Brooks
Nancy Wilson
Nico
Nina Hagen
Pat Benatar
Patti Smith
P.J. Harvey
Sarah Barthel
  (Phantogram)
Siouxsie Sioux
Stevie Nicks
Susanna Hoffs
Suzi Quatro
Tina Weymouth
  (Talking Heads)
Wendy O. Williams
  (Plasmatics)

198 The Book of Music Horoscopes

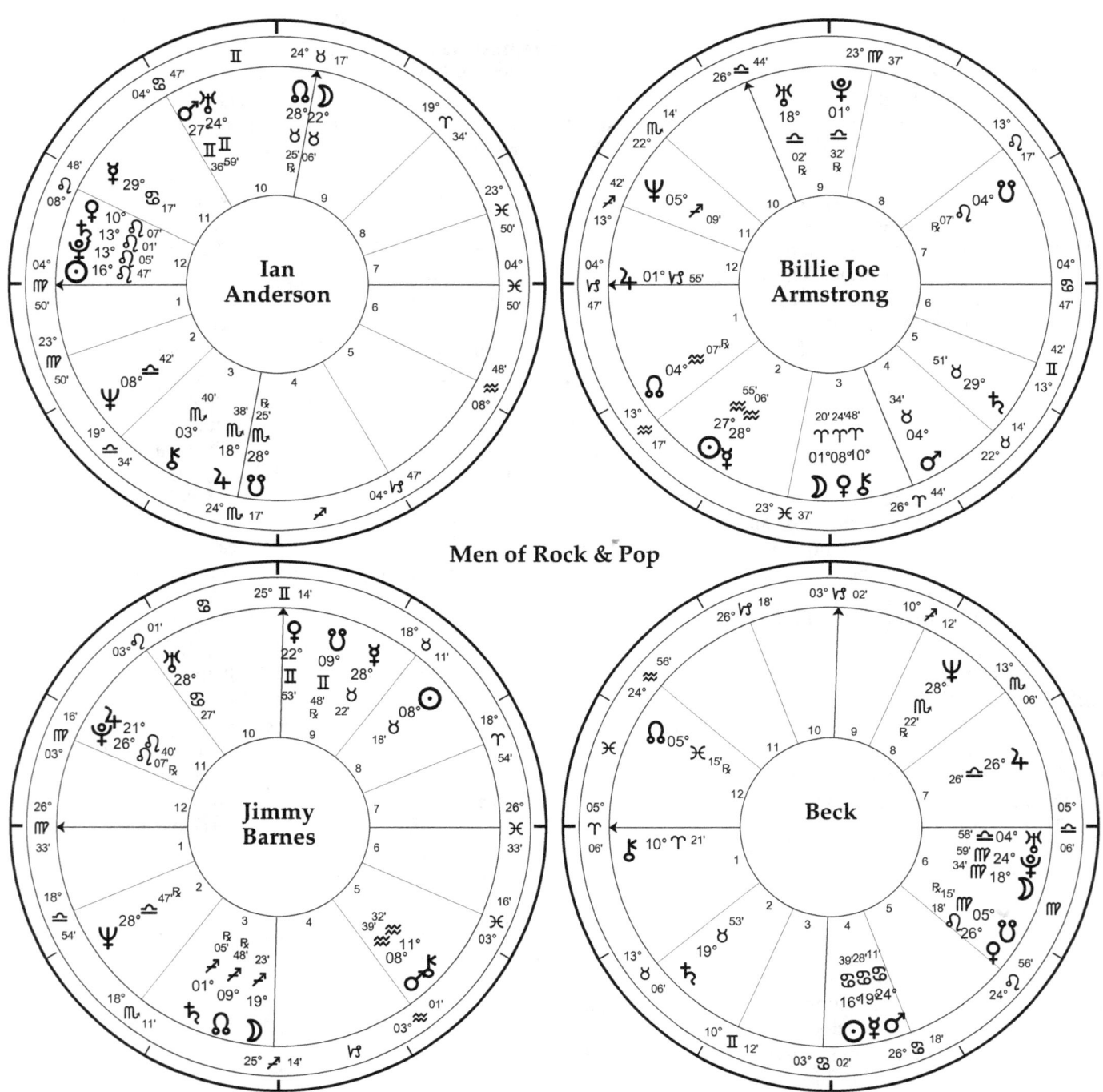

Men of Rock & Pop

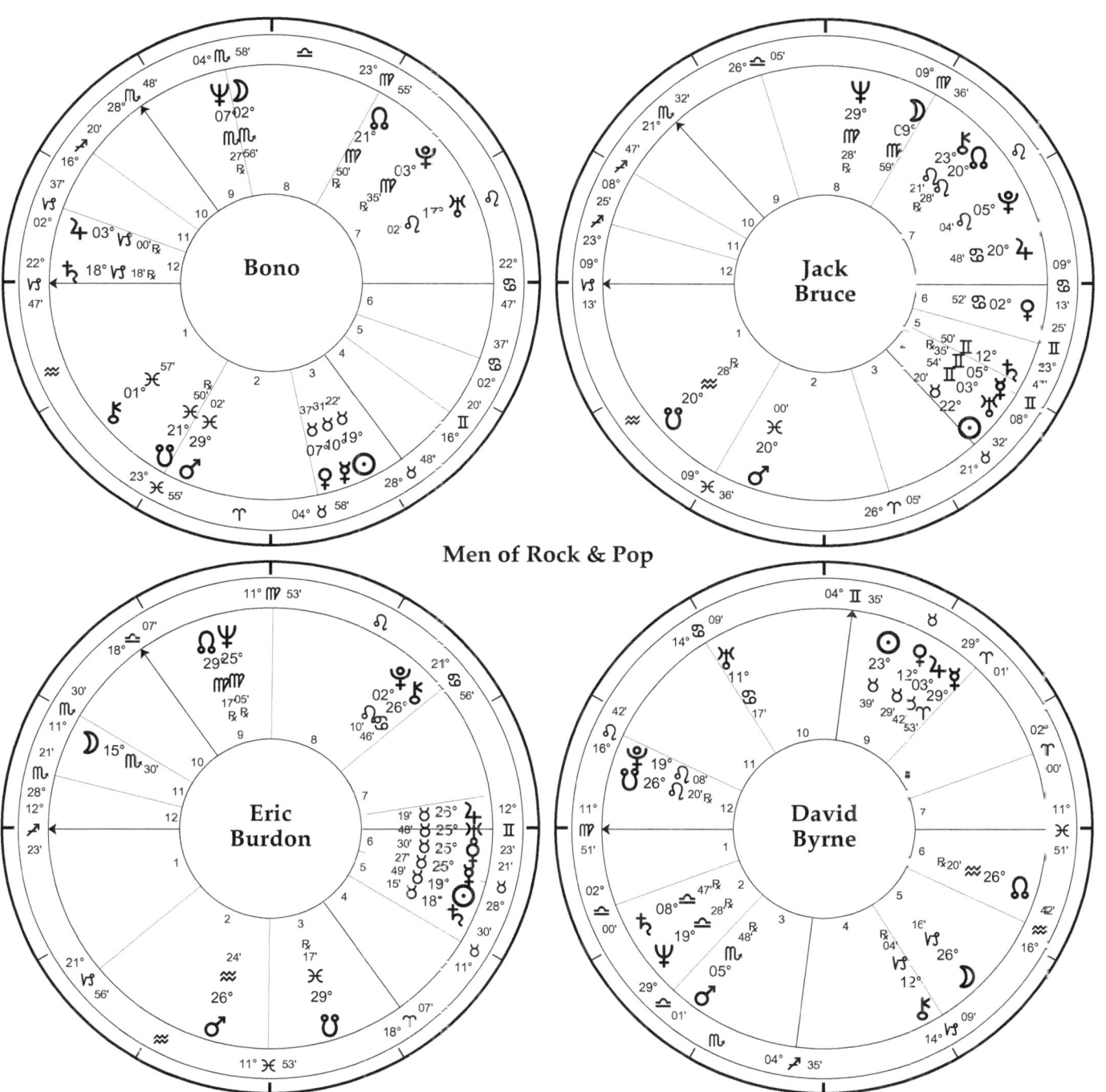

Men of Rock & Pop

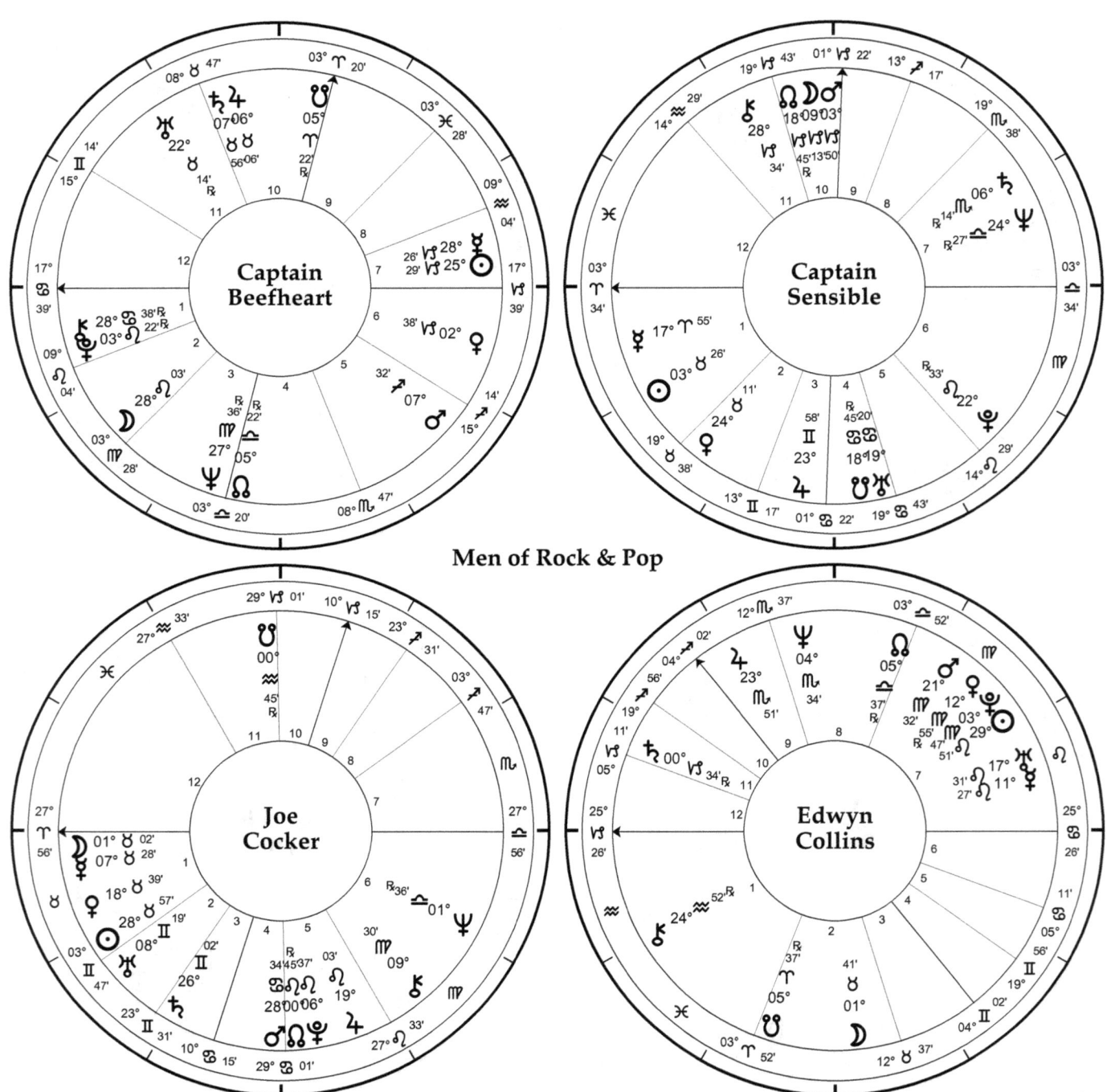

Men of Rock & Pop

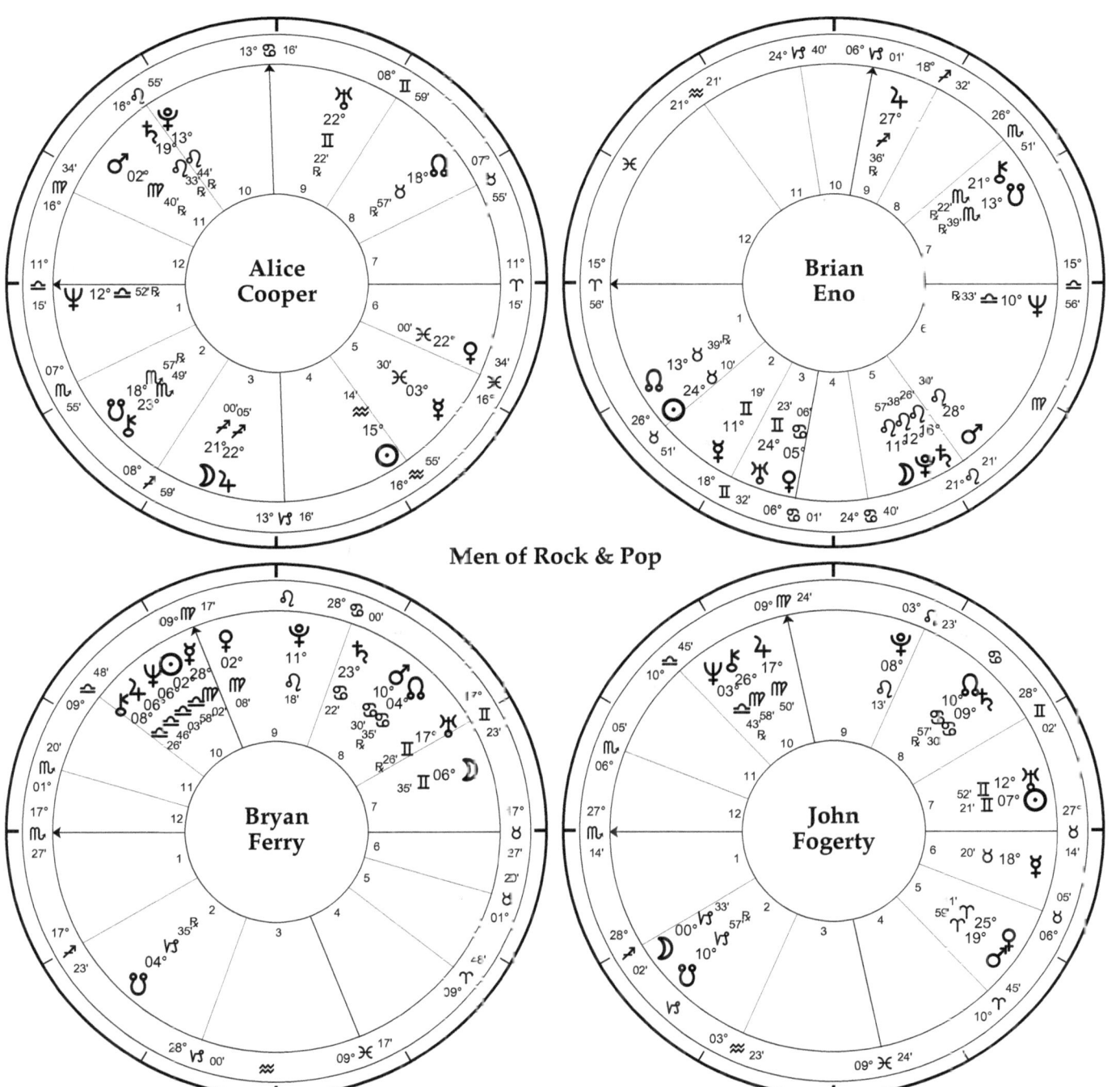

Men of Rock & Pop

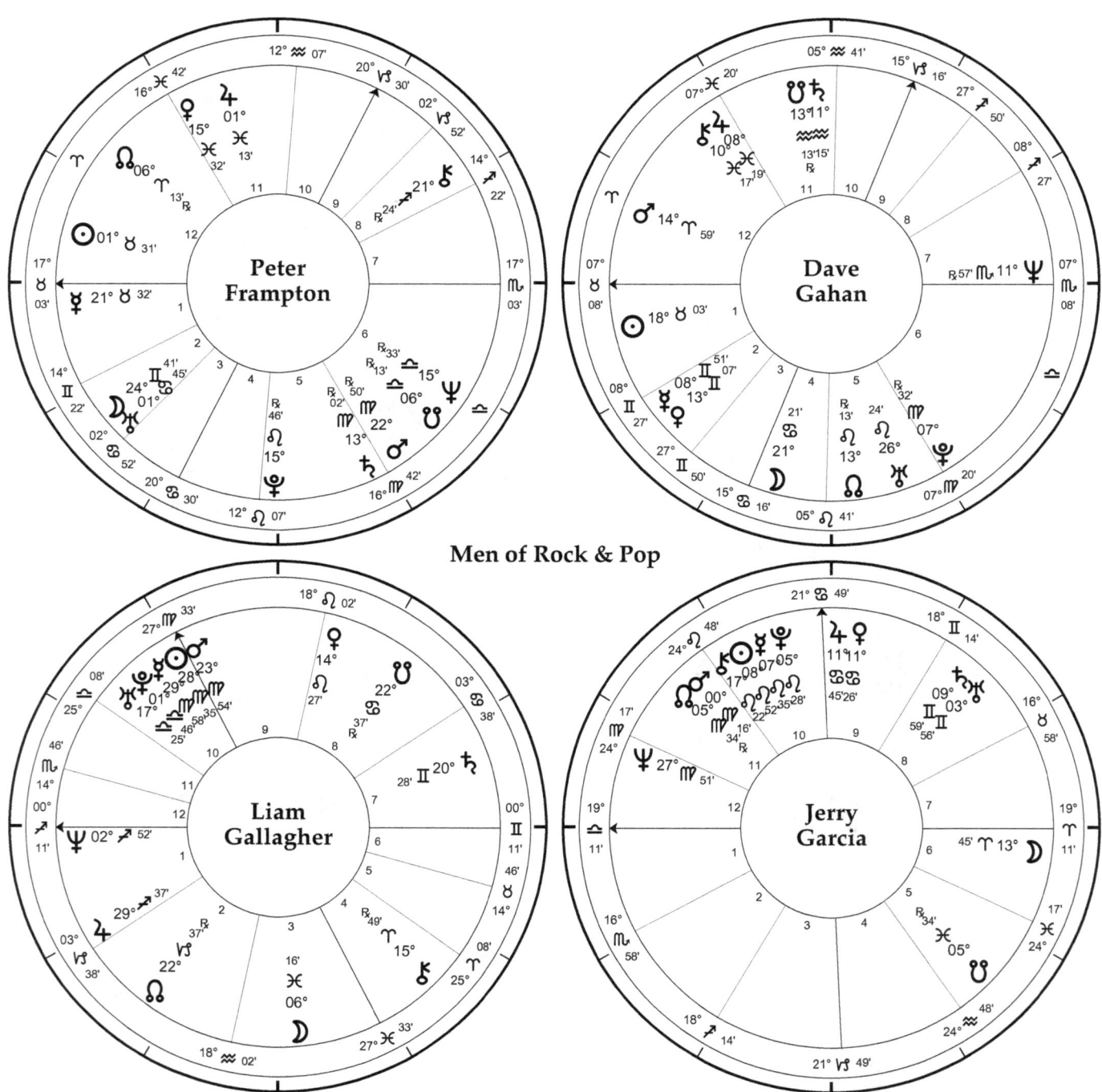

Men of Rock & Pop

Rock

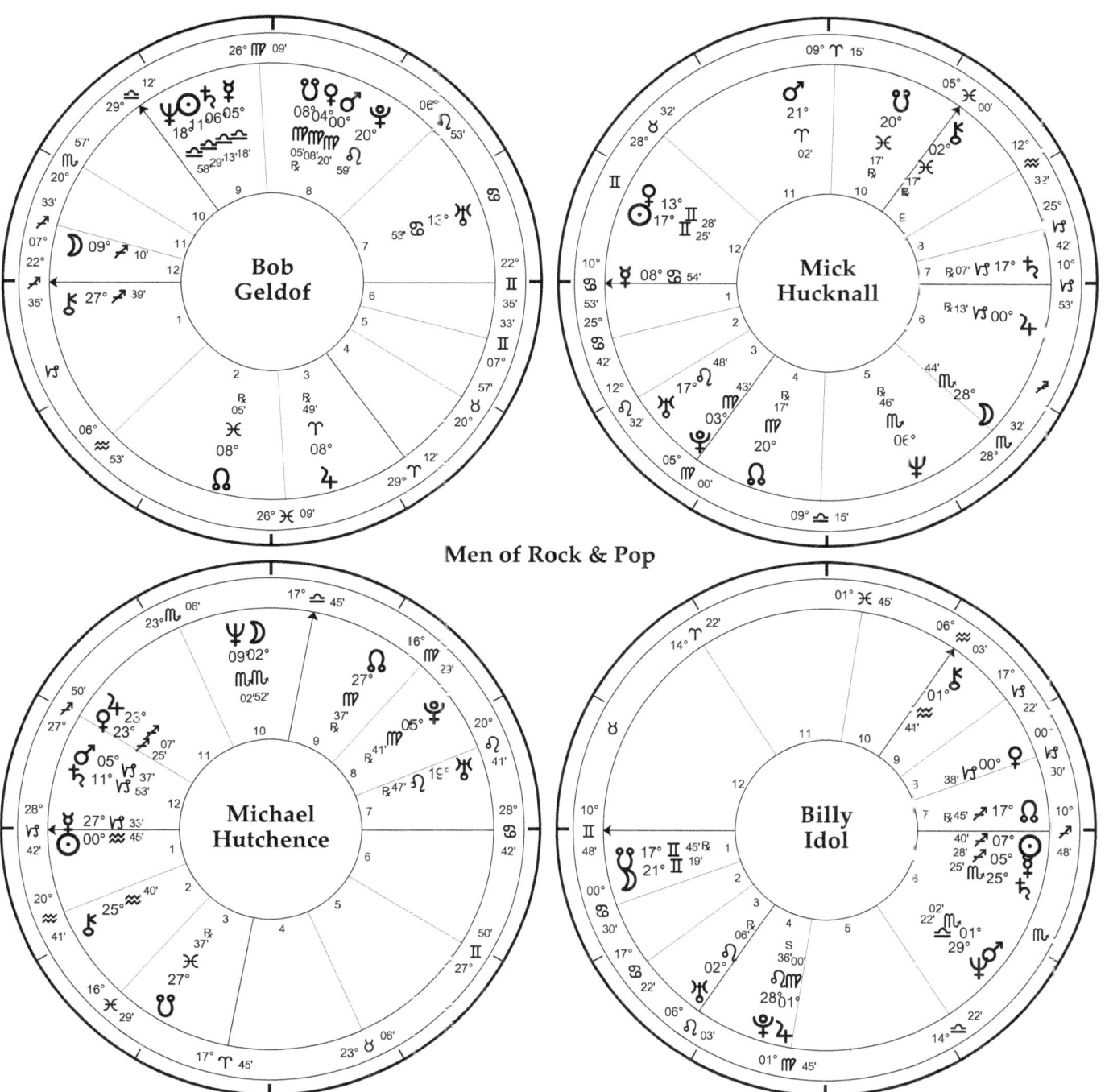

Men of Rock & Pop

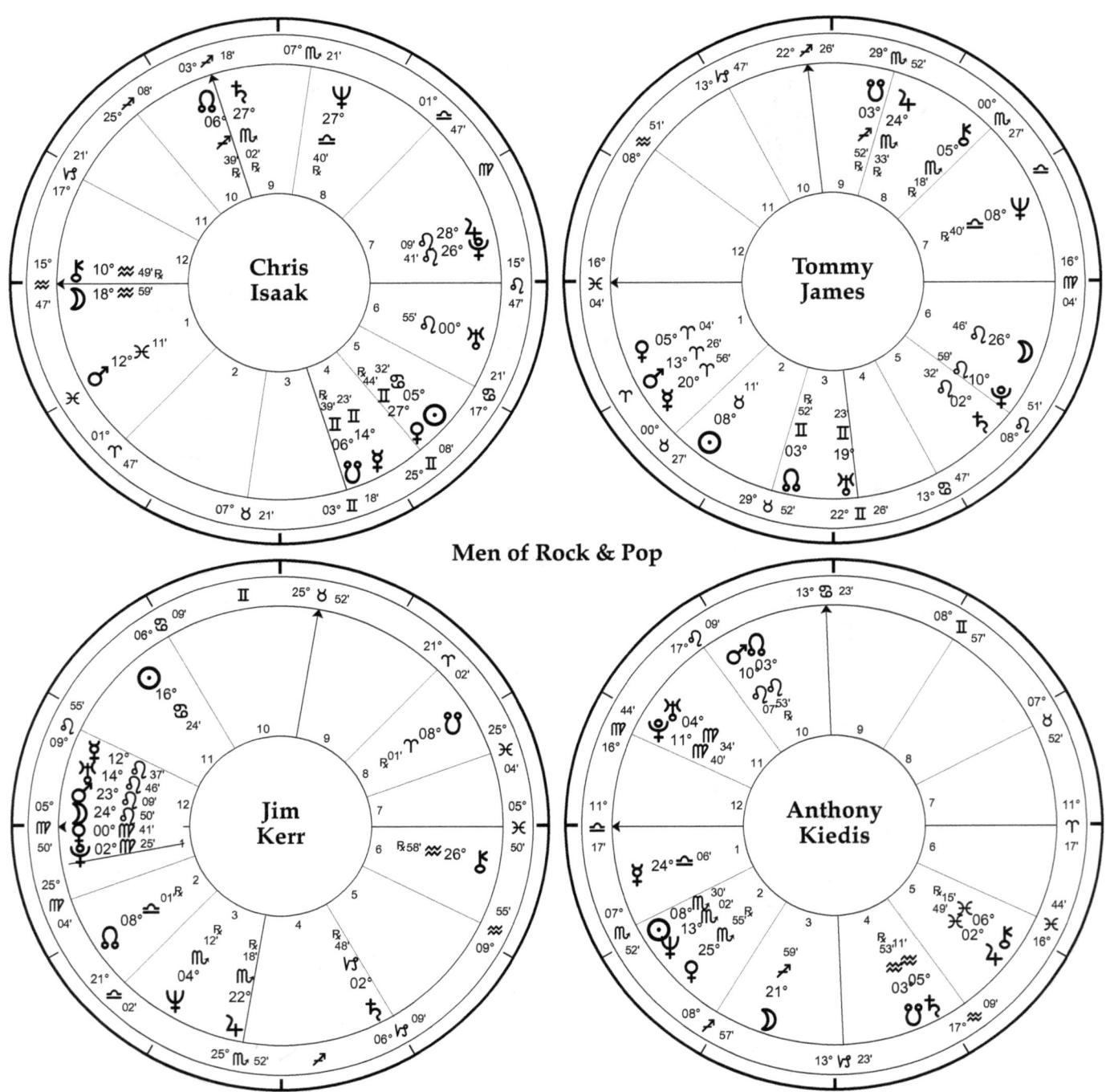

Men of Rock & Pop

Rock 205

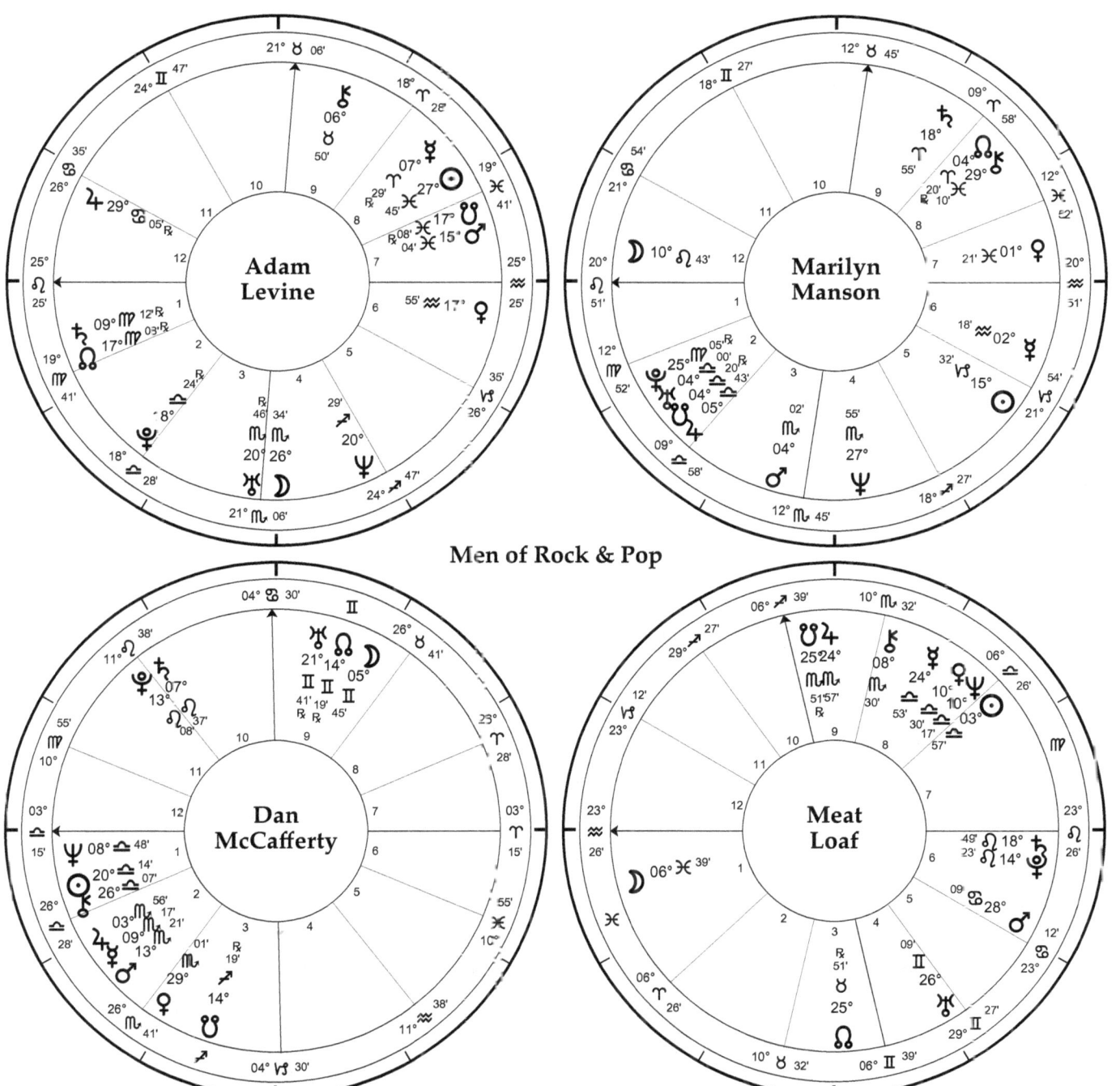

Men of Rock & Pop

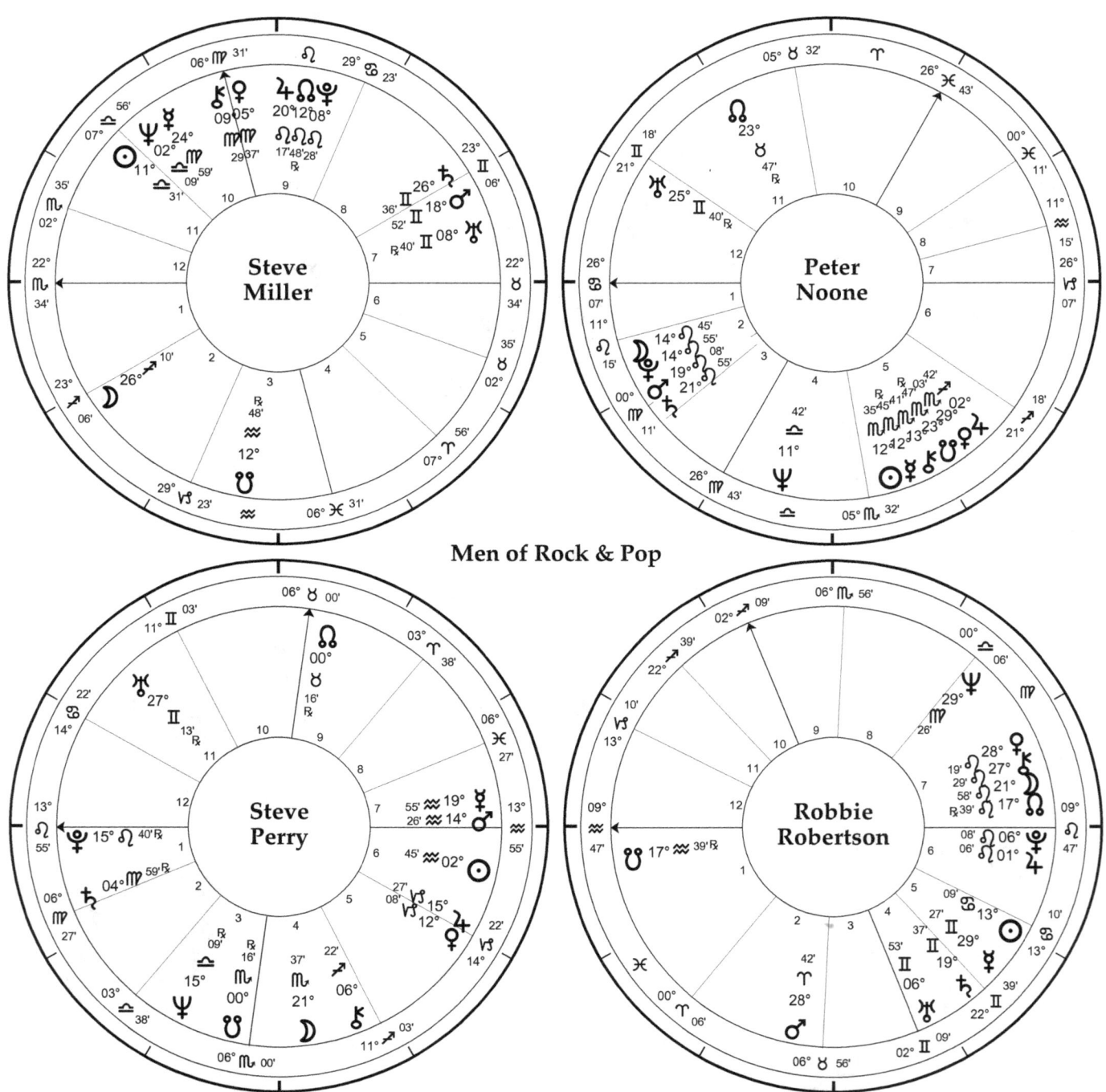

Men of Rock & Pop

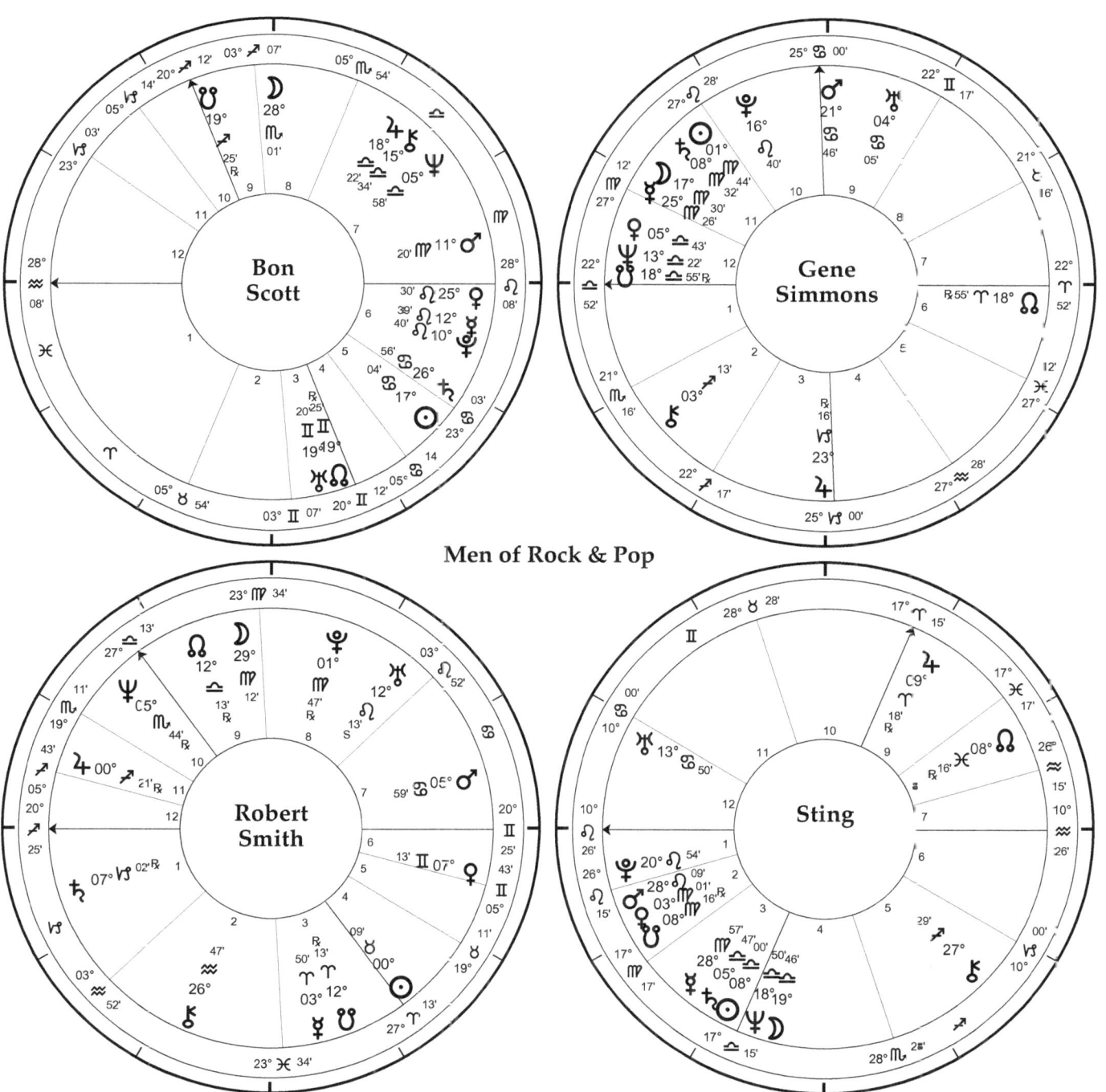

Men of Rock & Pop

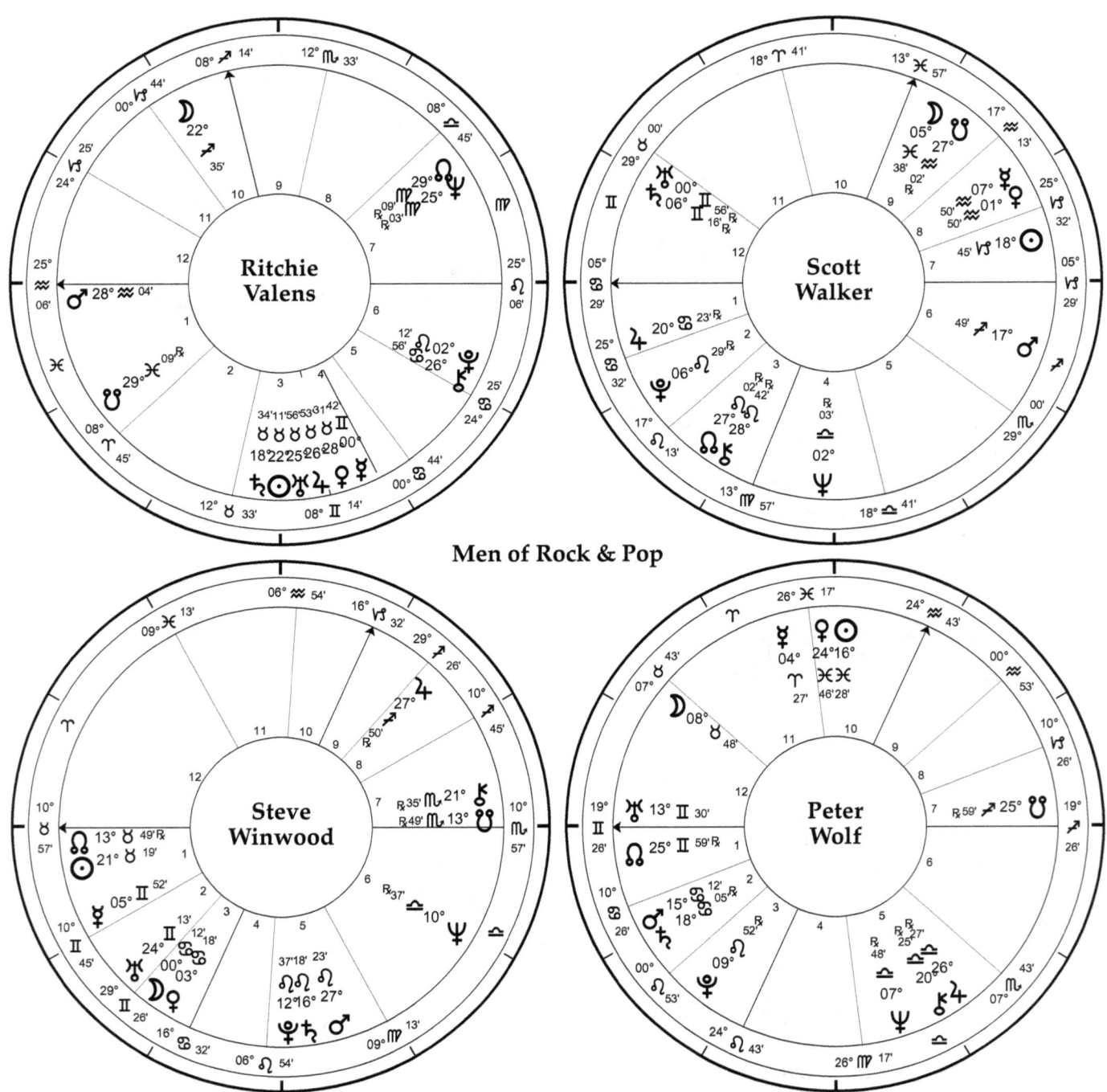

Men of Rock & Pop

The Aquarian, Uranian Nature of Progressive Rock

Tim Burness

As both a fan and musician, I have had more than a passing interest in progressive rock (prog rock or prog) for the last forty years. As an astrologer for the last thirty years or so, I noticed some time ago that Aquarian and Uranian themes are very common in the charts of many progressive rock musicians and that the whole musical genre is essentially Aquarian and Uranian in nature: from the often original and experimental nature of the music, to the frequently intellectual lyrics in search of the truth, to the eccentric personalities of many of the musicians.

Progressive rock gradually evolved out of the late 1960s, beginning with the more experimental sides of the likes of the Beatles, Jimi Hendrix, the Beach Boys and others. 'Progressive' and 'experimental' are of course words that are frequently associated with the astrological symbolism of Aquarius and its ruling planet Uranus, both being concerned with challenging existing conventions and exploring new territory. It has been suggested that *Sergeant Pepper's Lonely Hearts Club Band* (1967) by The Beatles was the first progressive rock album, and it certainly has many features that have come to be recognized as prog rock trademarks: an overall concept, a colourful album cover – a piece of art in itself – and an extraordinarily wide range of musical and lyrical influences. Others have suggested that *In the Court of the Crimson King* (1969) by King Crimson was the beginning of progressive rock. By the 1970s and with the likes of Pink Floyd, Genesis and Yes having established themselves, progressive rock had emerged as a sub-genre in its own right. The term 'prog', sometimes used in a jokey or derogatory sense, appeared much later.

Unusual and quirky time signatures and unconventional song structures are often a feature of progressive rock. Rather than conforming to the more typical 4/4 rock and pop beat, artists such as King Crimson, Pink Floyd and Porcupine Tree often use alternatives such as 7/4 or 13/8. Pink Floyd's 'Money' on *The Dark Side Of The Moon* and Peter Gabriel's 'Solsbury Hill' are examples of using a 7/4 time signature. Aquarian prog rock often breaks the musical rules in all sorts of ways; the traditional verse and chorus structures are frequently avoided in favour of extended instrumental sections or other alternatives. Unpredictability is the name of the game, although critics have observed that this can seem musically pretentious, sometimes appearing to sound different for the sake of it. Such criticism is of course unlikely to bother a musician with several planets in Aquarius or a strong Uranus in their birth chart, who will follow their own path regardless.

A quick look at the astrological charts of famous progressive rock musicians confirms the prominence of either Aquarius or many close aspects between Uranus and the personal planets. Guitarist Dave Gilmour of Pink Floyd was born a Pisces Sun with a square to Uranus. In an October 2014 *Prog* magazine interview promoting Floyd's *The Endless River* album, producer Youth gave a perfect Sun–Uranus description when commenting on his experience of working with Gilmour: 'It's funny with David, you think he's going to be one way and then he goes completely the other. He's unpredictable like that, and that's good.'

Keyboard player Rick Wakeman of Yes has the Moon and Jupiter in Aquarius; flautist and singer Ian Anderson of Jethro Tull (a brilliant eccentric if ever there was one!) has Mars conjunct Uranus in the 10th House. The extraordinarily gifted and uniquely intelligent guitarist Robert Fripp (King Crimson) was born with a close Venus conjunct Uranus trine Jupiter; and the multi-talented guitarist and musician Steve Hillage (originally with crazy but often brilliant Gong) was born with a Mars–Uranus conjunction at the apex of a cardinal T-square. Kate Bush, who made her spectacular live comeback in 2014, has pretty much transcended all genres but the strong prog leanings are there. She has a natal Sun–Uranus conjunction and almost certainly, depending on the time of birth, the Moon in Aquarius.

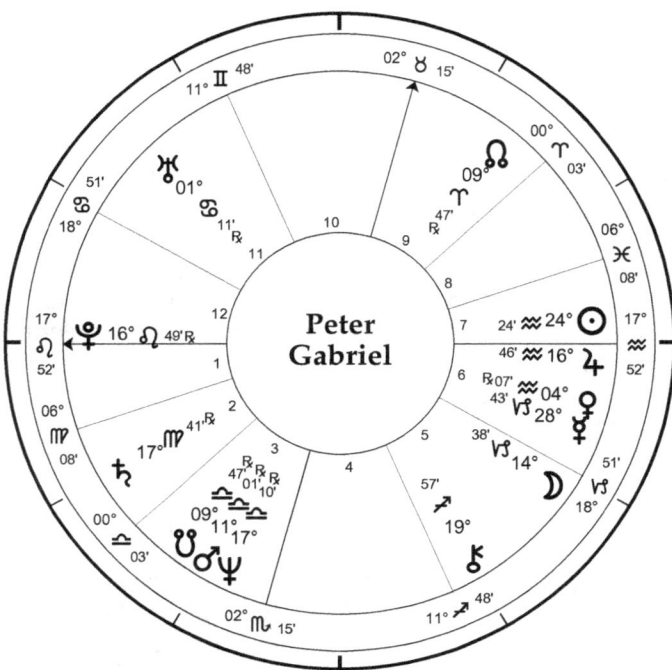

At their 1970s peak, Genesis were one of the most interesting and innovative progressive rock bands. A very English group of musicians making clever and eccentric (Aquarius) music, fronted by Peter Gabriel's clever and eccentric theatrical performances. Although Genesis became more commercially successful after Phil Collins took over as singer, most prog fans consider that the more interesting and original ideas started to run out after Gabriel and then Steve Hackett left the band. Both Hackett and Gabriel have natal Sun, Venus and Jupiter in Aquarius, being born one day apart (12 and 13 February 1950 respectively). The Aquarian urge for freedom and independence would have played its part in their branching out to pursue extremely successful solo careers, each achieving substantial international recognition for their artistic brilliance across a number of musical genres.

With his 7th House Aquarian Sun on display to the public, Peter Gabriel is the living embodiment of the most highly evolved Air sign. A major feature of Gabriel's birth chart is a powerful close opposition between Pluto in Leo on the Ascendant and Jupiter in Aquarius on the Descendant. Gabriel has achieved huge recognition and success as both a Pluto in Leo rock musician and a Jupiter in Aquarius visionary humanitarian. The tension between these two planets is mediated by a gifted and magical conjunction between Mars and Neptune in Libra, a perfect combination for a socially conscious artist and musician. He has often been years ahead of his time, from his founding of the Womad festival to his support for world music through his record label and recording studio, to his involvement with one of the first music download services, OD2. Receiving the Prog God award at the annual Progressive Music Awards in London, September 2014, from comedian and prog fan Bill Bailey (there's a fair bit of Aquarius in his chart too), Gabriel said: 'Despite prog probably being the most derided musical genre of all time there were – as today – a lot of extraordinary musicians trying to break down the barriers to reject the rules of music … We didn't always get it right, but when it did work we could move people and get some magic happening.'

Mainstream progressive rock was carried into the 1980s by Marillion, who are still going strong today. Both the original Marillion singer Fish and new boy Steve Hogarth (who has actually been with the band since 1990) have the planet Mars in Aquarius. It has often been said that guitarist Steve Rothery is Marillion's greatest musical asset, and Rothery was born with an almost exactly stationary Uranus in Leo. Marillion were years ahead of everyone when they famously used crowdfunding to raise money for an American tour in 1997. As with many newer and lesser known 21st century prog acts, the Aquarian Internet has always been important to the band, enabling them to build a worldwide fanbase while remaining largely independent of the music industry – it's that Aquarian freedom thing again.

Although progressive rock has always survived and thrived underground, it was uncool for many years. Since Radiohead's *OK Computer* in the late 1990s, prog rock's influence has become increasingly acceptable in the mainstream again – prog is no longer a dirty word. Nowadays, progressive influences can be heard in the songs of many younger, hipper bands. In new forms, the Aquarian Age of progressive rock continues.

Last Style: The Fender Stratocaster

Armand Diaz

Recall, if you can, what the typical telephone looked like in 1954, and consider the many changes in design that have occurred since then. Do the same thing with automobiles, lamps, refrigerators or just about anything else you care to think about. The changes are sure to be substantial in both style and technology. By contrast, the Stratocaster is an electric guitar with exactly the same style and substantially the same inner workings today as it had when it first appeared in the April 1954 catalogue of the Fender Electric Instrument Company.[1] More than that, the Stratocaster remains contemporary – it is not a retro artefact to be appreciated for its nostalgic value but a continuing leader among electric guitars, influencing the design of instruments to this day.

Music is such a deeply personal and emotional art form that we almost immediately turn our focus to the individuals who create it. We cannot help but stand in awe of those people who somehow – through individual genius or perhaps channelling – bring us the soundtrack of our lives. Our tendency to emphasize the role of these individuals often overlooks the cultural and social milieux in which they create – although we know that some places and times (Vienna in the 18th century, London in the 1980s) are especially rich in creative energy. We also tend to overlook the role of technology in musical innovation, and perhaps even view it askance. Queen's 1976 album *A Night at The Opera* proudly declared 'No Synthesizers!' on its jacket, although most of the instruments the band was playing had in fact been around for less than three decades.

With technological innovation, too, we tend to focus on individuals and their achievements as though new creations suddenly emerge from the ether, with no precedent, via some genius. In truth, most inventions and innovations are part of a collective effort: the Wright brothers were successful in varying the design ideas of their predecessors. Among musicians, legend has it that guitarist Les Paul invented the solid body electric guitar but he was one of many people who worked on the idea (and the guitar that bears his name was designed by others at the Gibson company). The Fender Stratocaster was not even the first solid-body electric guitar designed and marketed by Fender, but it has become one of the most iconic and influential instruments in music history.

The influence of the solid-body electric guitar cannot be underemphasized in the history of music since the middle of the 20th century. Electric guitars had become popular in the 1930s, but these early models were hollow-bodied, much like acoustic guitars. The problem with hollow-body electric guitars is that they are prone to feedback when played loudly. As a result, the guitars used in jazz from the Big Band era into the bebop age tended to have a mellow, laidback sound. In jazz bands, guitars were mostly rhythm instruments, and it fell to the horns – primarily trumpet and saxophone – to provide the soaring leads and stabbing melody lines. Guitars simply could not compete with horns because they lacked the necessary technology.

The advent of the solid-body electric guitar coincided with the emergence of rock and roll music and resulted in a reconfiguration of bands, so that by the 1960s the typical rock band was composed of one or two guitars, bass and drums (think of the Beatles and Rolling Stones, for example). A mere fifteen years earlier, that configuration would have been impossible – there would have been no lead instrument.

Clarence Leonidas 'Leo' Fender was born on 10 August 1909 in a suburb of Los Angeles, California (time unknown). He was a member of the inventive Pluto in Gemini generation, and grew up with such new inventions as the telephone, automobile and radio. By all accounts, Leo was interested in perfecting the style and performance of electronics from an early age. A T-square is quite prominent in his chart, with a very tight opposition of Uranus in Capricorn to Neptune in Cancer, both of which are square to Saturn in Aries. This configuration is an indication of Leo's willingness and ability to go beyond the boundaries in the search for technological innovation, and it was activated by transit at important points in his career. The role of Uranus – the planet associated with innovation – is key to the astrology of both Fender and his creations.

In 1938, just before his Saturn Return and at the square of transiting Uranus to his Sun, Fender lost his day job in accounting and decided to take his moonlighting venture – repairing radios – full time. His knowledge of electronics extended beyond radios and, in 1941, as transiting Uranus squared his Mercury, he developed a new kind of pickup (magnetic coils that register the frequency of the string vibration) for use on electric guitars. In time, Fender gravitated towards working on musical instruments and, by 1946, at the opening transit of Saturn square its natal position and at its conjunction with his natal Neptune and opposition to his natal Uranus, he founded the Fender Electric Instrument Company.

Interestingly, Leo Fender himself never learned to play the guitar and his interest in music tended more towards country music. The earliest Fender guitars were the lap steel guitars used with a slide in country music, and Leo intended his earliest guitars for country musicians. Ironically, his most famous product, the Stratocaster, is most closely associated with rock music, which held little fascination for Fender.

It was at Fender's Uranus opposition to its natal position, a time often associated with innovation and asserting individuality in one's chosen field, that the Stratocaster was introduced. The very name Stratocaster suggests the stratosphere, the layer of the Earth's atmosphere just below outer space. It conveys a sense of pushing beyond the limits and boundaries of the terrestrial – a very Uranian notion. The futuristic, space-age design of the guitar was truly innovative for 1954, perhaps a reflection of the transits to Leo Fender's chart. Keeping in mind that transiting Uranus was not only opposing its natal position but also squaring Fender's natal Saturn and conjuncting his Neptune, we can see that this was a time when the potential of the natal T-square would likely manifest. That is made all the more likely with the transiting North Node of the Moon conjuncting Leo's natal Uranus. Truly he was tapping into the future, bringing a design that would remain innovative (Uranus) through the decades that followed.

The guitar was in design for some time and prototypes were made. The Stratocaster did not have a single designer but was a collaborative effort between several people at the company, including Leo Fender himself. The design of the guitar's body was strongly influenced by Freddie Tavares, a guitarist whose prior claim to fame was that he played the 'WHA!' that began the Warner Brothers's *Looney Tunes* cartoons. Although the Stratocaster passed its second Saturn Return in 2013, the instrument has changed very little since its beginnings. A wide variety of woods has been used and colour variations have always been part of the Stratocaster's history, but the instrument is easily recognizable today as the same guitar it was in 1954.

Although the Stratocaster has changed minimally over the years, no one (or no thing) gets past the Saturn Return without a bump in the road. For the Stratocaster, it was the introduction in 1982 of a lower-priced and ostensibly lower-quality model that Fender (now owned by CBS) markets under the Squire brand name. The main problem for the Fender Stratocaster is that its design – nearly thirty years old at the time – was so functional and fashionable that its junior Squire model is in many respects just as good as the original. While lacking some bells and whistles, it turned out to be a popular alternative to the original, placing the Stratocaster in competition with its progeny.

Leo eventually sold his company to CBS. He went on to found two more successful instrument companies that designed and manufactured electric guitars – Music Man and G&L. Like many other designers, in his newer creations Fender often found himself imitating his most iconic design.

1 I owe the insightful comparison of the Stratocaster to phones and autos to Leonardo Lospennato, in his book *Electric Guitar and Bass Design*, LL Publishing, 2010

Further reading: *Fender: The Golden Age 1946–1970* by Martin Kelly, Terry Foster and Paul Kelly, 2010.

DUOS, GROUPS & BANDS

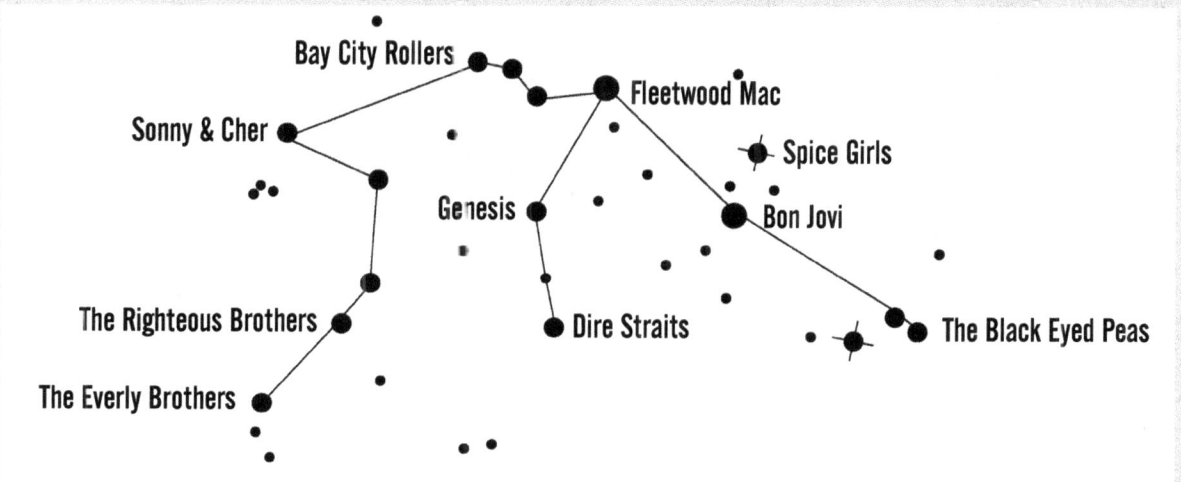

The Everly Brothers

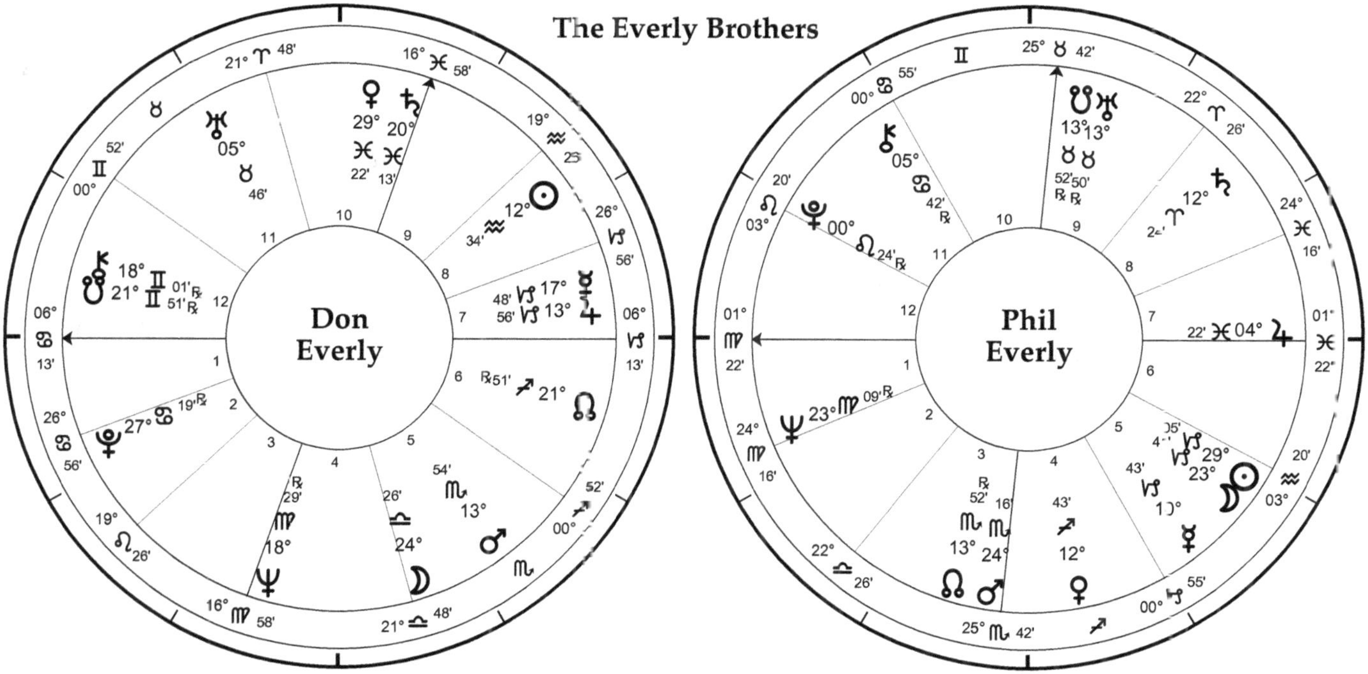

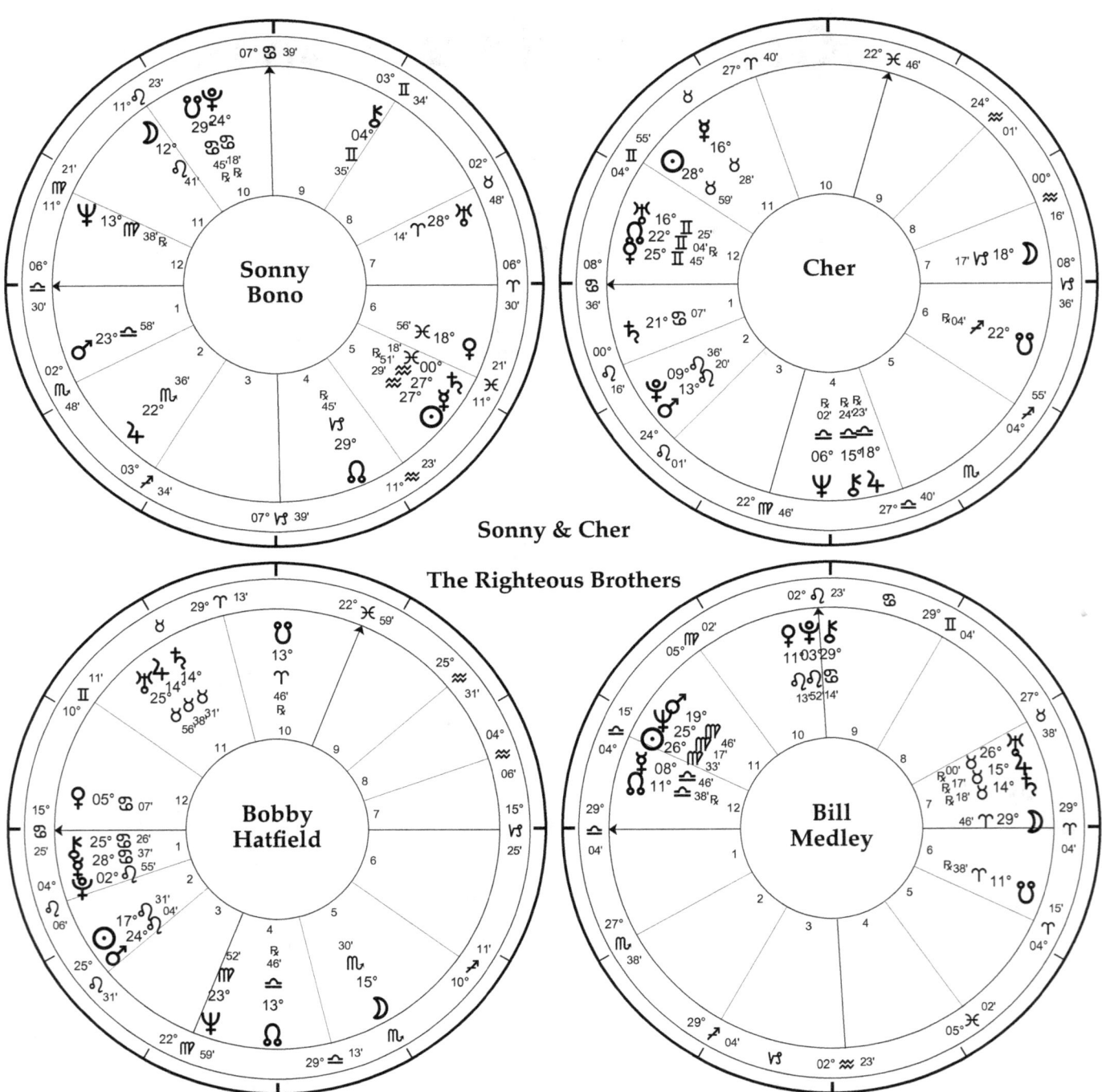

Sonny & Cher

The Righteous Brothers

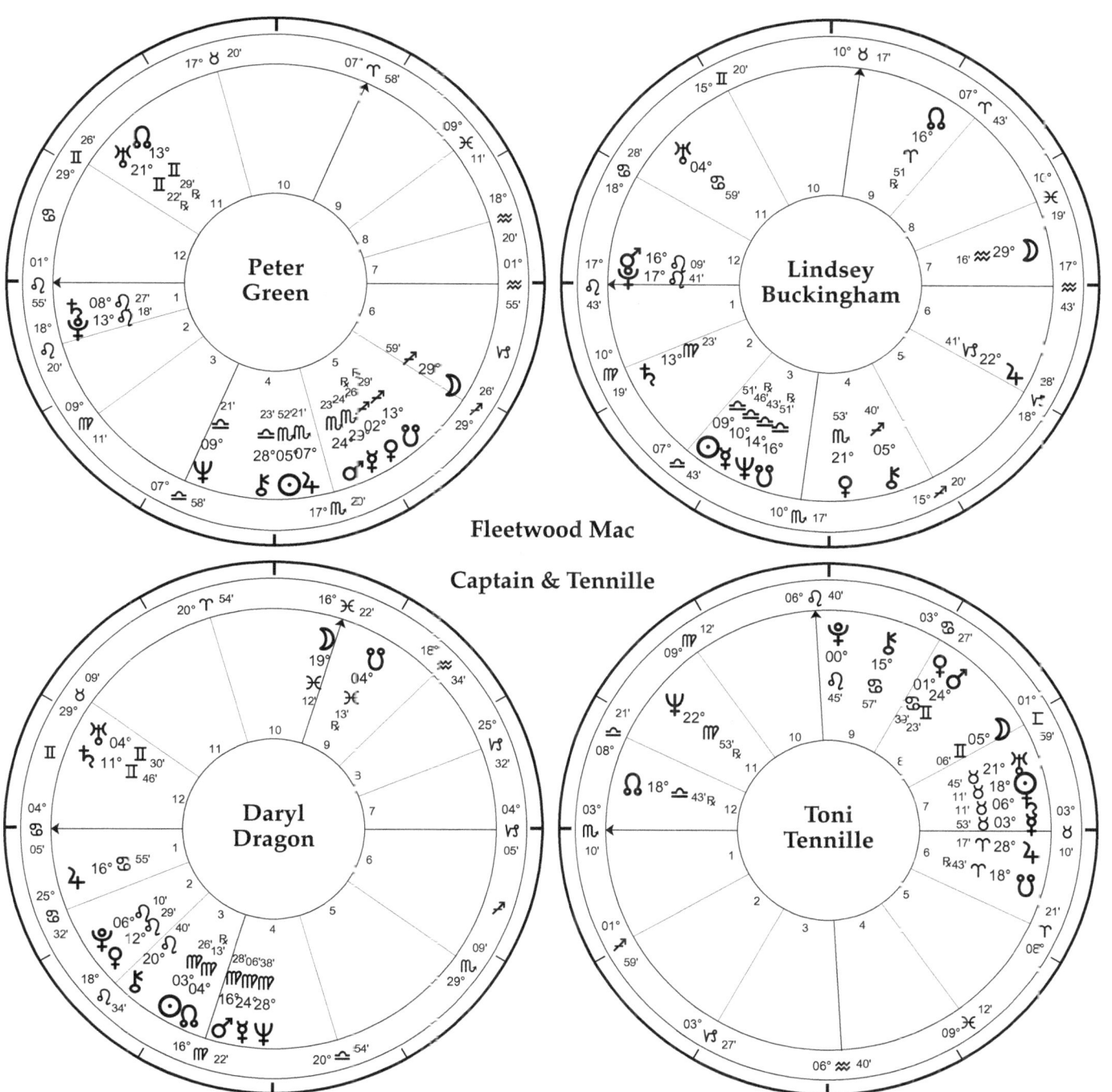

Fleetwood Mac

Captain & Tennille

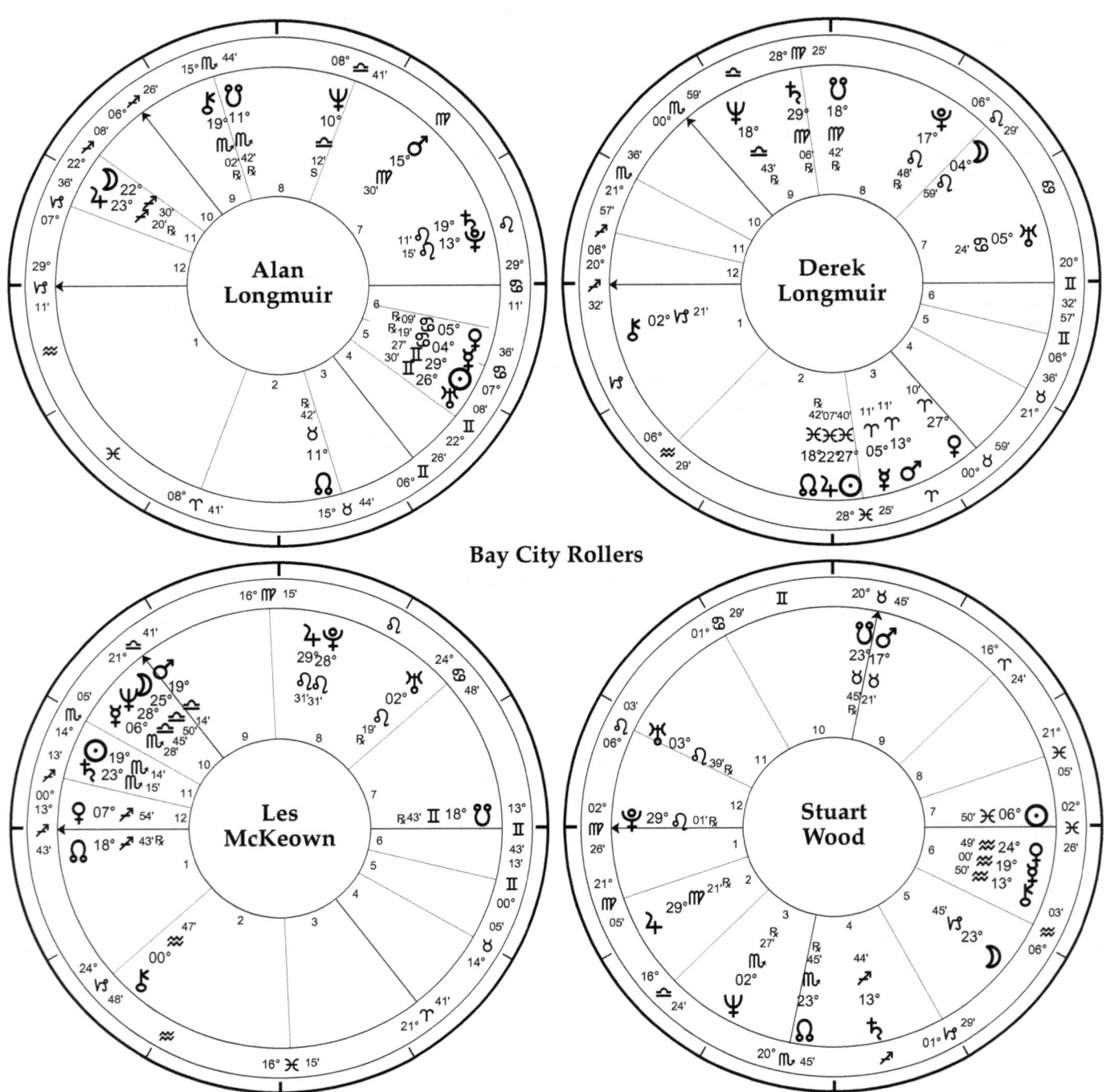

Bay City Rollers

Duos, Groups & Bands

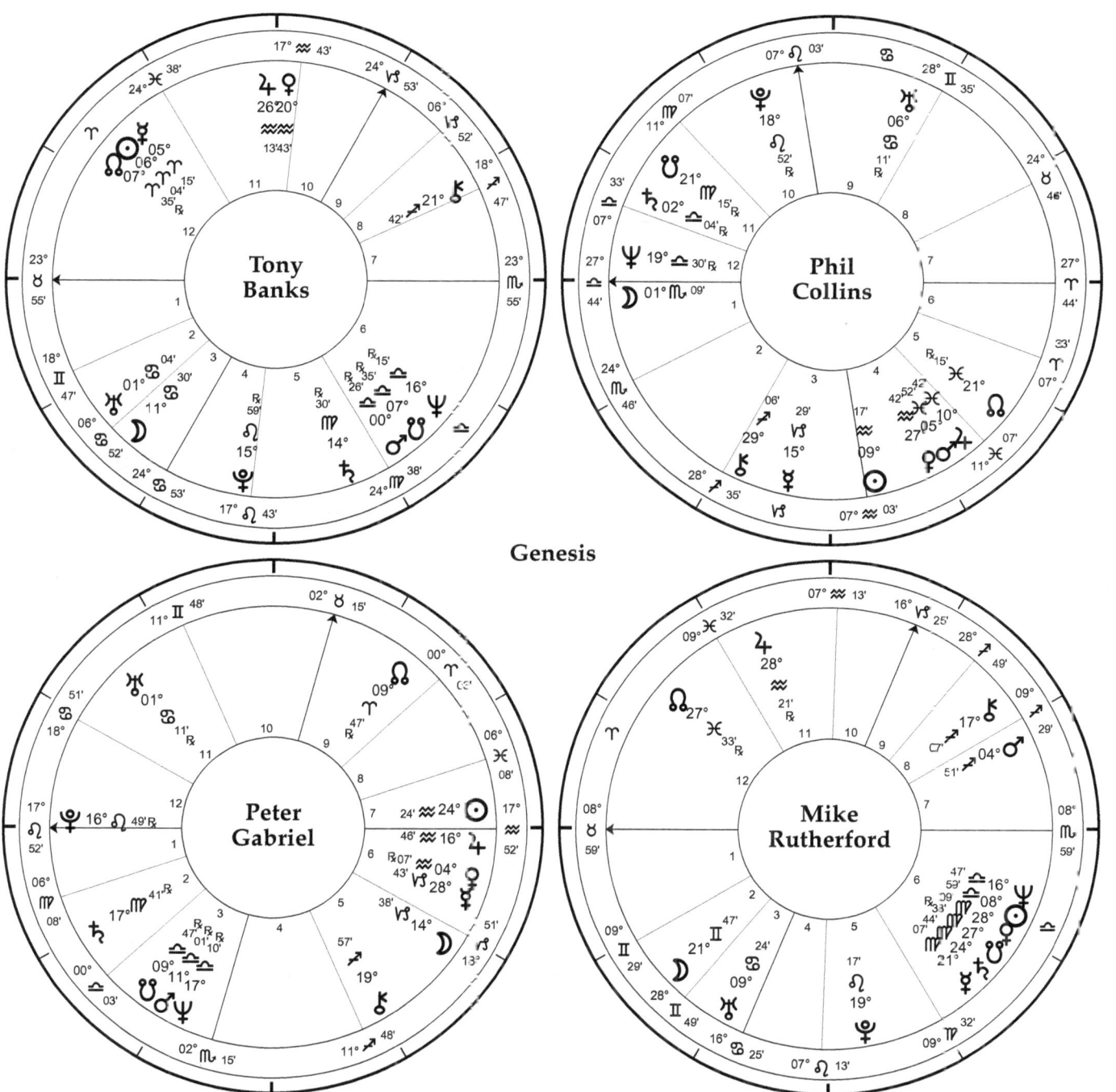

Genesis

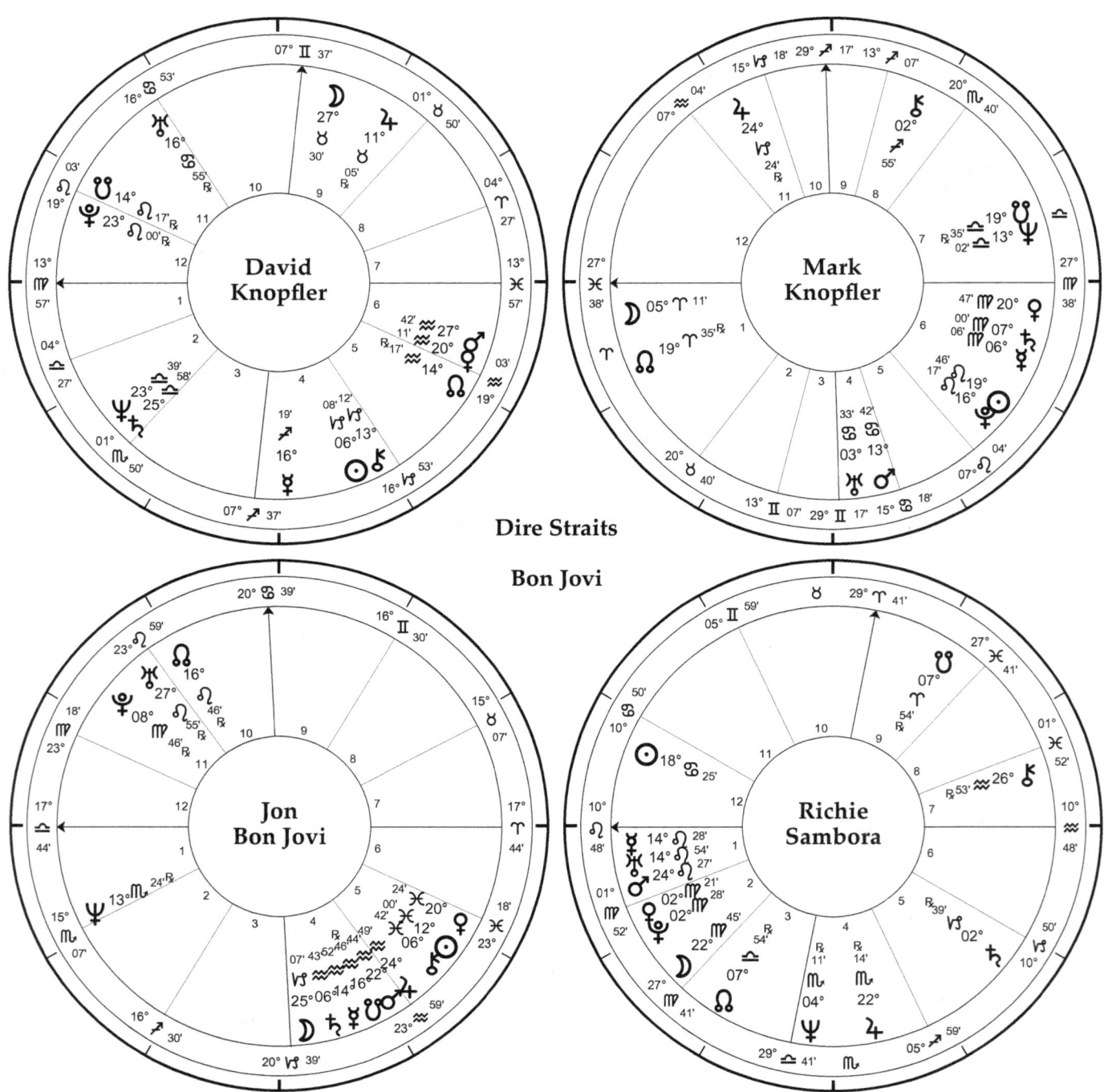

Dire Straits

Bon Jovi

Duos, Groups & Bands 219

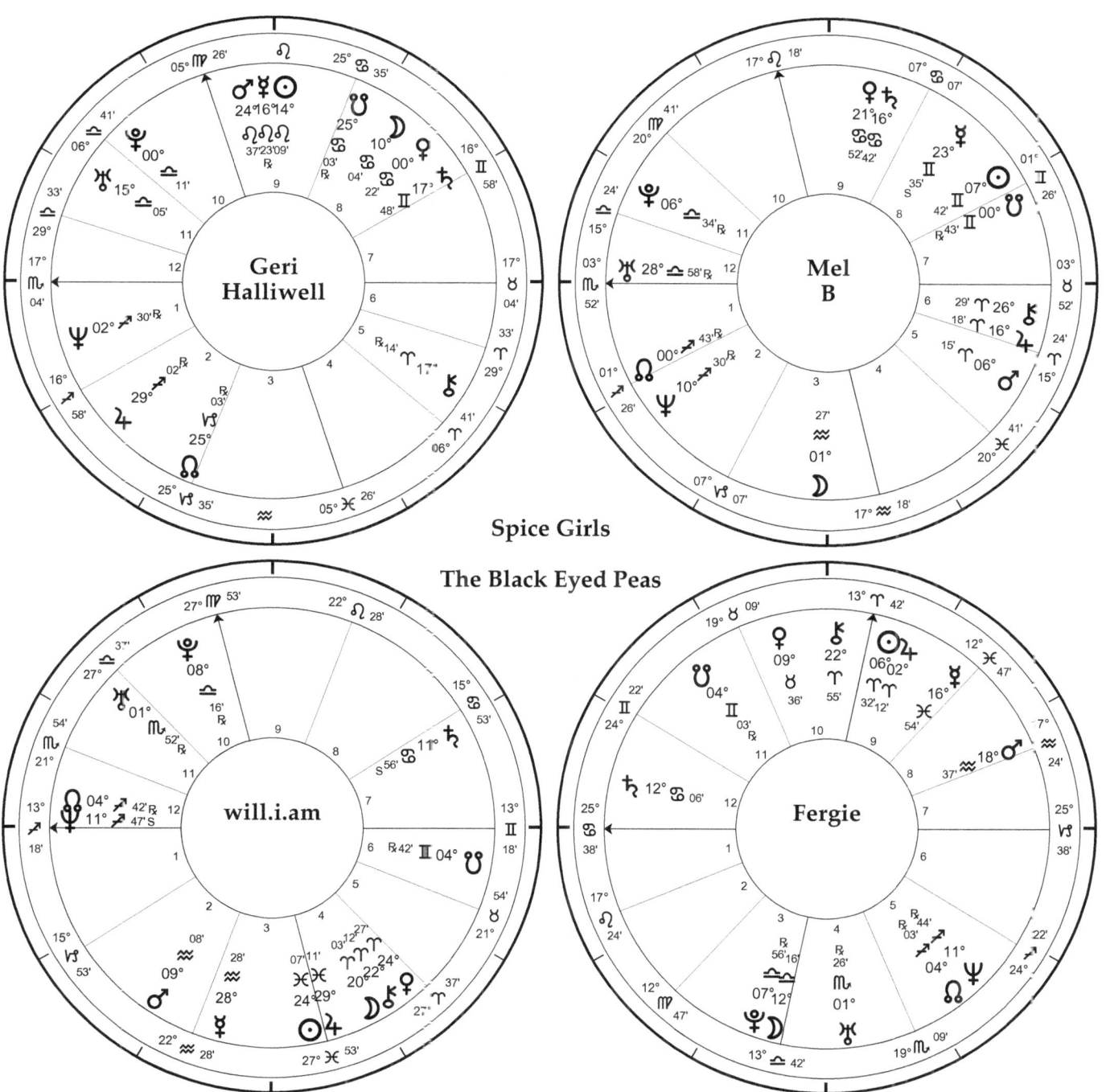

Spice Girls

The Black Eyed Peas

Portrait of a Jam Band: Phish

Kathy Rose

Over the past few years, I have become a big fan of the American rock jam band Phish. My interest in the band and their music has inspired a fascinating astrological exploration and exercise. Let me share my experience, starting with a little background.

I enjoy the practice of 'anticipating astrological patterns'. Instead of immediately looking at the chart for a person or an event, I like first to sit and ponder what I would anticipate seeing in their horoscope. Rather than automatically engaging the rote and mechanical pathways in my brain – associating certain keywords with the planets and zodiac signs – I prefer to access my intuition and reach out with my senses. I search and feel for the elemental, intrinsic energy patterns being radiated – and then convert them to planetary patterns and dominant signs that I assume may be present.

I used this process of anticipation with Phish, and the signatures of particular energy patterns became incredibly clear as I listened to their music and watched them in live performance. It was amazing to simply observe, sense and ponder the potential interplay of planetary connections that I assumed would be present in the band members' charts – before I ever looked at their horoscopes. I'd like to share the process with you and invite you to play along with me in the anticipation analysis as I describe the band.

First, let me give you a clue that I wasn't aware of when I started this process: all four band members were born within two years of each other. Knowing this keys you into the fact that similar outer planet patterns will be present in their charts.

As I mentioned, Phish is a jam band, which is simply a musical group whose performances include long, unscripted, improvised segments. When this band starts a jam, they step into the moment – exhibiting spontaneous creation. This requires the musicians to suspend normal thinking and move into quick, if not instant, intuitive responses to each other. They release control and joyfully embrace the now. The band's musical style is also highly diverse and spans numerous genres. Phish consistently and courageously experiments with many different types of sound and song structure.

So, think about which planet you associate with spontaneity, instant reaction to the moment and experimentation. What dominant planetary energy would you expect for the process of jamming?

Phish also occasionally engages in quirky, silly stunts. For instance, the members have made their entrance into a few of their concerts suspended above the crowd in a flying hotdog! The drummer (Jon Fishman) has a signature look – wearing a big, sleeveless, polka-dot (in doughnut shapes) dress while he plays. He has been quoted as saying, 'I remember I just tried it on, stood in front of the mirror, laughed and thought I looked like Barney Rubble or something. Then I wore it that night onstage for a joke … and then I just wore it every night for the next 15 years.'[1] The musicians in the band are light-hearted, fun-loving, eccentric nonconformists. The energy of strong individualism is palpably projected by each one of them. Are you sensing a particular planetary energy starting to emerge?

The band's talent for creating cohesive, coherent music on the spot through jamming kept leading me to Uranus energy. When I saw Phish in concert – and witnessed the childlike playfulness and their powerfully individualistic expression – the Uranian flavour became clear to me. In addition to the playful spirit that the band demonstrates, there is also a serious dedication to rehearsal and practising. Trey Anastasio (lead guitarist) has mentioned in interviews that there's a lot more discipline and precision required in jamming than most people realize.

The band has improv exercises that help them to stay in the moment and step into the jam with ease. They practise listening – really listening – to each other in a jam. Trey acknowledges that Phish is probably among the most analytical of American bands. They see improvisation as both an art and a craft requiring a lot of preparation and discipline, so that when you're in the moment, you're not really thinking so much as *allowing*.

There is also a powerful energy of humility with these four men. Trey has shared, 'Musicians need to get the hell out of the way. The less you notice them, the better the music sounds.' He also has mentioned that for him the highest level of art in music was 'performed by people who had spent countless hours of work just to be invisible.'[2]

This is certainly not your typical performance band, with theatrical rock star ego-driven behaviour. These guys come on stage, silently step up to their instruments … and play. They may do playful and silly things from time to time, but the energy is all about serving – helping people have a momentary escape from the drudgery, even the chaos, of life, through music.

Phish has been largely ignored by the mass media, most likely because they have not exhibited the flashy, flamboyant practices and protocols that help most bands gain visibility. They have never played the marketing game. Instead, they have forged their own independent and unique path, creating a loyal, faithful following on their own terms.

One more 'indicator': Phish music is often very intricate, requiring high technical skill and technique. Many of their pieces are incredibly complex with multi-layered rhythms, melody lines and voices. Quite frequently a fugue-like structure weaves in and out, and variations on themes exhaust every possibility. Their music embodies an incredible intelligence, even a certain genius. It's not just basic, driving, rock 'n' roll rhythms and licks. Instead, it actively engages the nerve centre of the listener.

So, which zodiac sign comes to mind when you think about humility and service? How about absolute dedication to rehearsal and musical compositions that are technically difficult and complex? What about the analytical approach Phish has? Doesn't that sound like a Virgo signature?

One last 'colour' to fill out the picture: many Phish lyrics are smart, witty, satirical and even delightfully nonsensical. However, much of what they sing is profound, insightful and poetically beautiful. Frequently Phish music rides on waves of deep feeling, with themes that explore contradictions in life. At other times they poke fun at social norms or probe powerful emotions and perspectives connected to life's lessons. I recall that a particular phrase in one Phish song instantly, powerfully, struck me because it describes what I do as an astrologer. The song begins, 'In and out of focus, time turns elastic.' I relate to this because my eyes do indeed go in and out of focus as my gaze stretches forward in the ephemeris, looking at future planetary cycles, then going back in time to trace past astrological patterns. As that poetic lyric so beautifully captures, time does indeed feel elastic when I engage in astrology!

The effect that Phish's music has on their fans is intense. It's normal to see the audience moved to deep emotion at the peak of a jam. Fans often describe on blogs that there is a moment of empowerment and personal transformation that ripples through the entire crowd as the audience blends and energetically participates with the spontaneous expression of music. Interestingly, as the energy of this music flows through the speakers – powerfully projected out to the audience – many begin to dance with abandon! I was happy and surprised to see people completely surrendering to the music and allowing their entire bodies to be moved. I have never before witnessed such a pure, uninhibited response to a band.

What planetary energy comes to mind when you think about deep, profound lyrics, and the audience feeling a sense of empowerment and transformation because of the music? I think of Pluto!

OK – time to reveal the pattern! The dominant planetary statement in the horoscopes of the band members is Uranus and Pluto conjunct in Virgo. All four musicians were born between the spring of 1963 and the spring of 1965 when the individualistic energy of Uranus linked up with the transformational and empowering energy of Pluto in the precise and humble sign of Virgo.

I call this signature 'empowered individualism' or 'controlled chaos'. When you combine this powerful conjunction with gifted, highly intelligent musicians – who then project these vibes out through amplifiers and loudspeakers – you get the phenomenal Phish experience.

The Uranus–Pluto conjunction in Virgo is unique and special because the wild electrical innovation (Uranus) and profound, raw power (Pluto) of these two outer planets are funnelled through a precise and detailed Earth sign (Virgo), which helps to anchor and ground the energy in physical (Earth) form. It's fascinating to observe this band from an astrological perspective because this allows us to experience the planets through our senses, rather than just through our minds.

The fact that all four members of the band were born during the special period in the 1960s – when Uranus and Pluto were conjunct – amplifies the exceptional signature energy of these two outer planets and makes a strong statement about how their music needs to flow. Obviously, not everyone who has this unique and powerful astrological aspect in their chart is a talented jam-band musician. However, we so often see an amazing manifestation of 'edgy brilliance' expressed and exhibited by people with this configuration.

Music offers us an unparalleled richness of opportunity to go beyond dry intellect and strict analysis and, instead, to feel and integrate the intrinsic energy signatures of the planets. All we need to do is to let go and listen.

1. Jon Fishman, as quoted in Spin, July 2000, p. 113.
2. http://www.believermag.com/
issues/201107/?read=interview_anastasio

Here's the band's current line-up (with birth data):

- Trey Anastasio, 30 September 1964, 06:32 CST, Fort Worth, Texas, USA. Source: from Trey's father, as quoted in the Phish Google forum
- Mike Gordon, 3 June 1965, 11:32 EDT, Sudbury, Massachusetts, USA . Source: Birth certificate.
- Jon Fishman, 19 February 1965, Philadelphia, Pennsylvania, USA
- Page McConnell, 17 May 1963, Philadelphia, Pennsylvania, USA

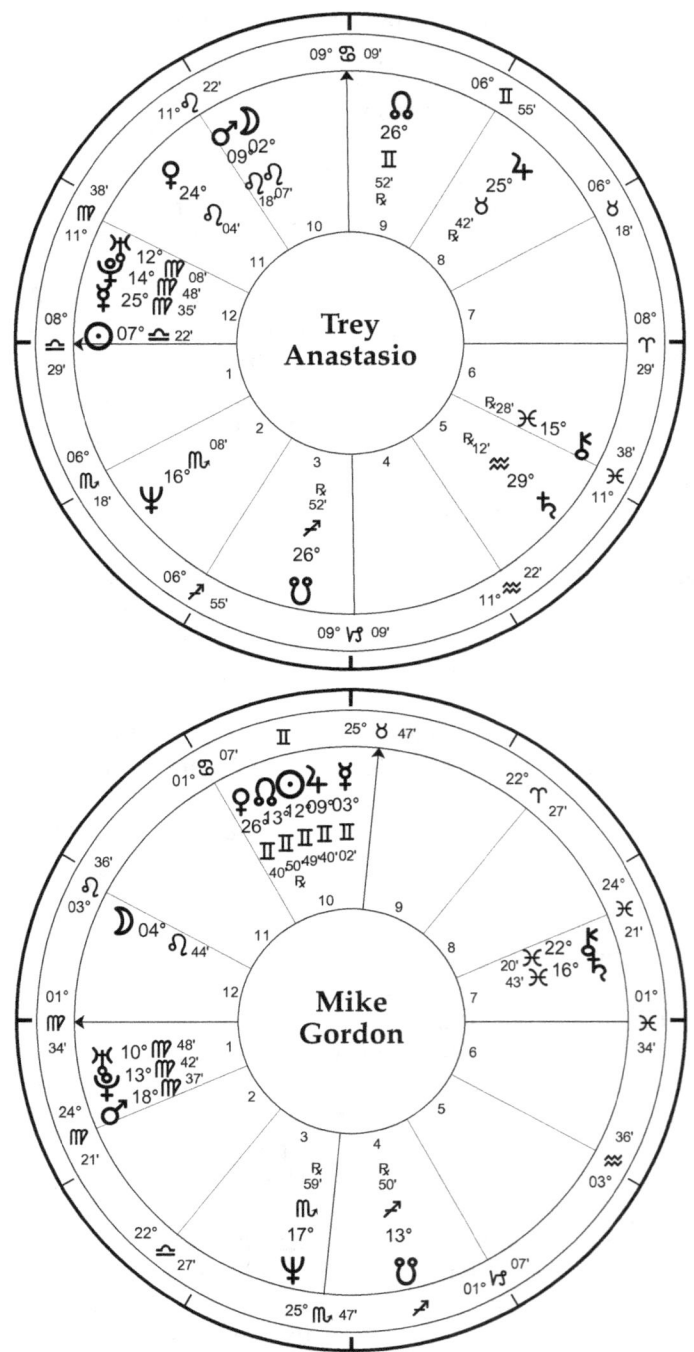

Further Observations

Notes by Frank Clifford

On Stage
Together, the Ascendant and the MC form the public persona. The Ascendant complex (its sign, hard aspects and ruler) comes to the fore when a singer is out in front, centre stage, whereas the MC is a collection of aspirations and attributes that forms the reputation. And the 5th and 7th Houses can provide clues about a singer's following, feelings about performing, their fan base and critics.

Sometimes a singer acts as a spokesperson for a new wave of music and embodies the outer planets which are personalized in their horoscopes: Kurt Cobain reluctantly carried the pressure and angst of the Uranus–Pluto in Virgo of Generation X on his Ascendant, while soulful iconoclast Erykah Badu has the Jupiter–Neptune conjunction of 1971 (which chanted in a new era of spiritual consciousness in music) on her Sagittarius Ascendant.

Musical Notes on Pluto
Pluto is evident in the big business of music — the entrepreneurs/men in suits/plutocrats who entered the scene in the late 1970s; those who shape their generation and 'push buttons'; era-defining artists who wrest control from the moguls and mass-market their product (e.g., Madonna: Pluto conjunct Sun, Ascendant and chart ruler Mercury; Michael Jackson: Pluto conjunct Sun and Mercury; and Prince: Pluto–MC opposite the Moon, square Mercury); those who reinvent themselves, manipulate their image, exploit sex and bring taboos into the musical mainstream; the obsessive side of fame and fandom.

The Disco Era
If Neptune relates to -isms that permeate popular culture, then new musical forms (such as jazz) or fads that revolutionize music and divide public opinion are undoubtedly Uranian in nature. None more so than disco, which gave Middle America three excuses to condemn it, emerging as it did from the gay, Hispanic and black subcultures. The notorious Studio 54 nightclub opened its doors during a T-square of Sun–Mercury opposite Uranus–Ascendant in Scorpio, both square Moon–MC in Leo. Astrologer and musician Jenni Dean Harte was there that night and described the club as a 'Mecca for the new music aristocracy ... the spotlight was on youthful partying, psychoactive drugs and sexual abandon.'

Protest Singers
Where does the protest singer fit into the astrological pantheon? Taking an individual, sometimes risky stand is a principle of Mars and its signs. The countercultural impulse to shake up existing societal structures is Uranian, while the urge to speak out and shoot down hypocrisy – to have one's voice not simply heard (Gemini) but believed – is Sagittarian in nature. And Saturn or Capricorn (more so than Aquarius) features strongly in those who address society's ills and (with Uranus or Mars) rattle the Establishment's cage.

Grassroots activist Billy Bragg created waves in Margaret Thatcher's Britain during the 1980s. He has the Sun and Moon in Sagittarius, Venus opposite Uranus both squaring a Scorpio Ascendant, and Mars in Scorpio in the 1st House square Pluto–MC.

Odetta (31 Dec 1930, 09:20 CST, Birmingham, AL, USA – from birth certificate) was a folk hero ahead of her time and instrumental in lending music's support to the civil rights movement. She had Mars on the Descendant square the Moon, Sagittarius on the MC, and Sun–Saturn in Capricorn square Uranus.

Odetta turned Bob Dylan on to folksinging (their Moons are conjunct, and his Sun is opposite her MC). Dylan's chart has Jupiter and Mercury signatures (plus a strongly aspected Uranus). Heralded as a musical prophet and revolutionary poet of his times, Dylan has Sagittarius rising, the Sun square Mars, and the Moon conjunct Saturn–Uranus

STAGE & SCREEN

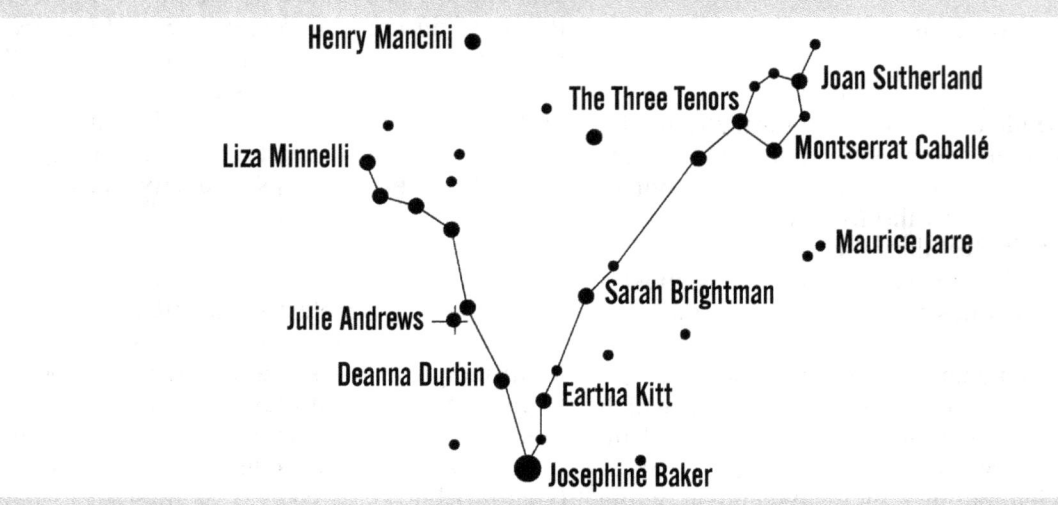

Film Score Composers

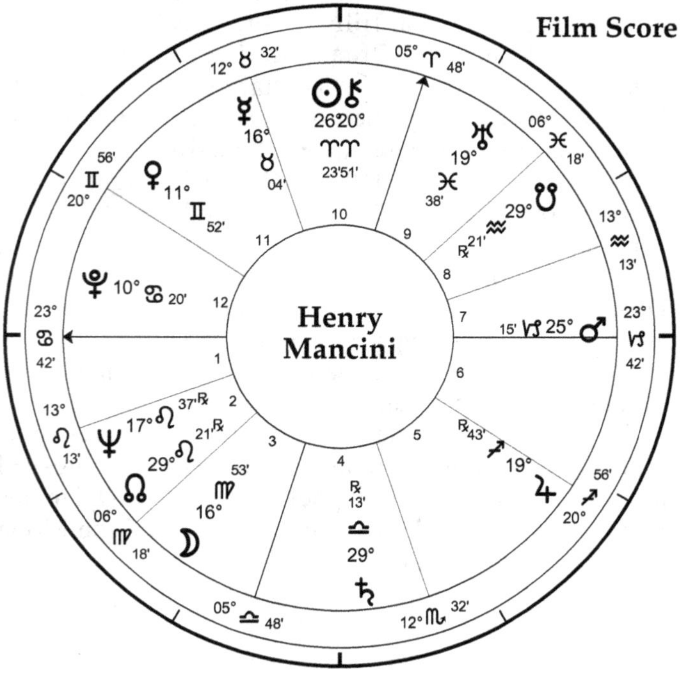

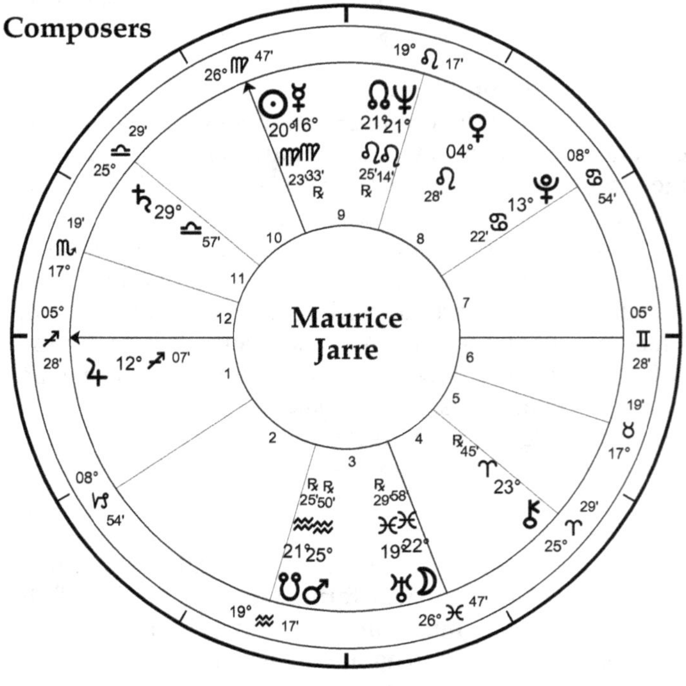

Stage & Screen

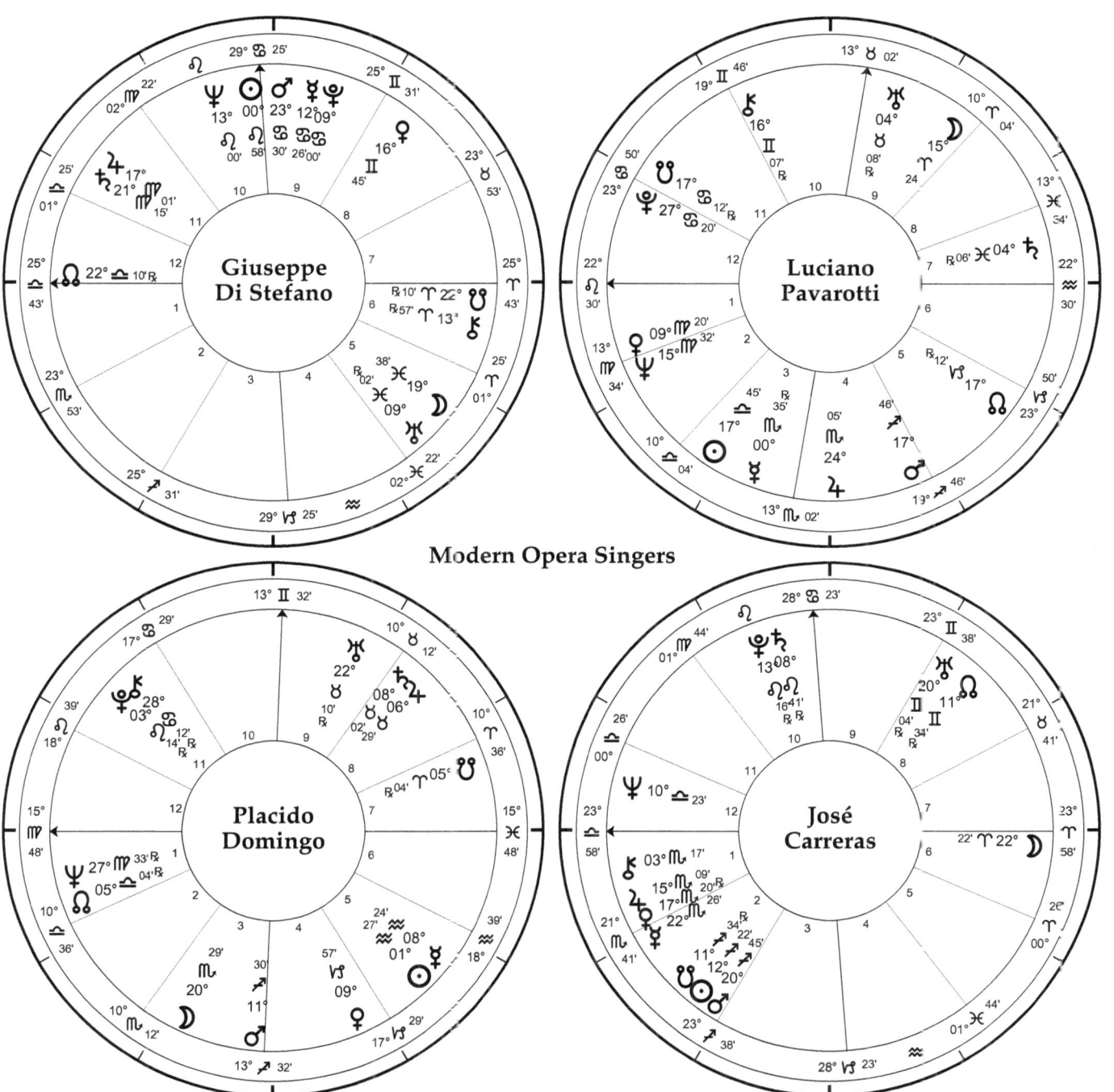

Modern Opera Singers

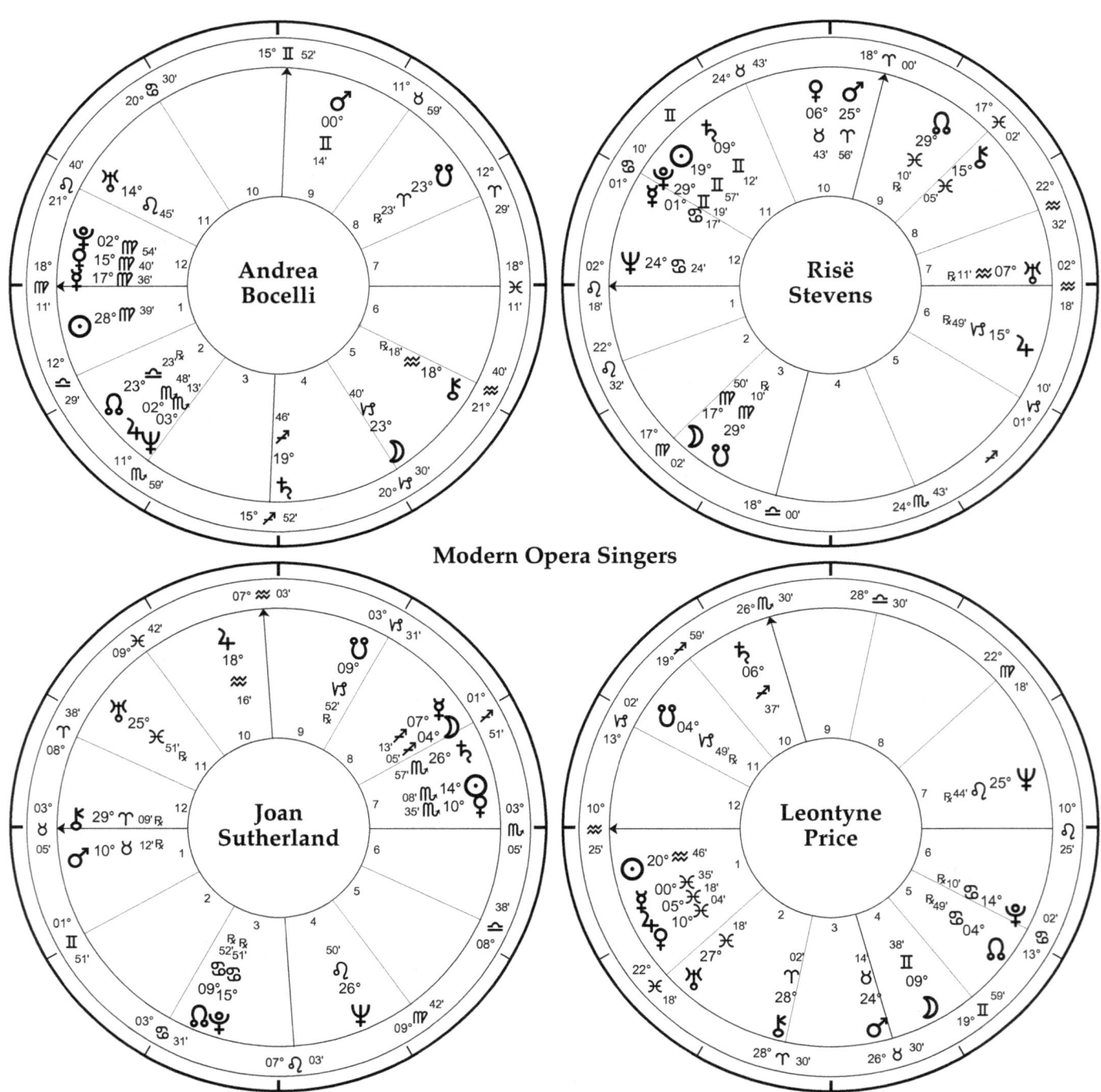

Modern Opera Singers

Stage & Screen

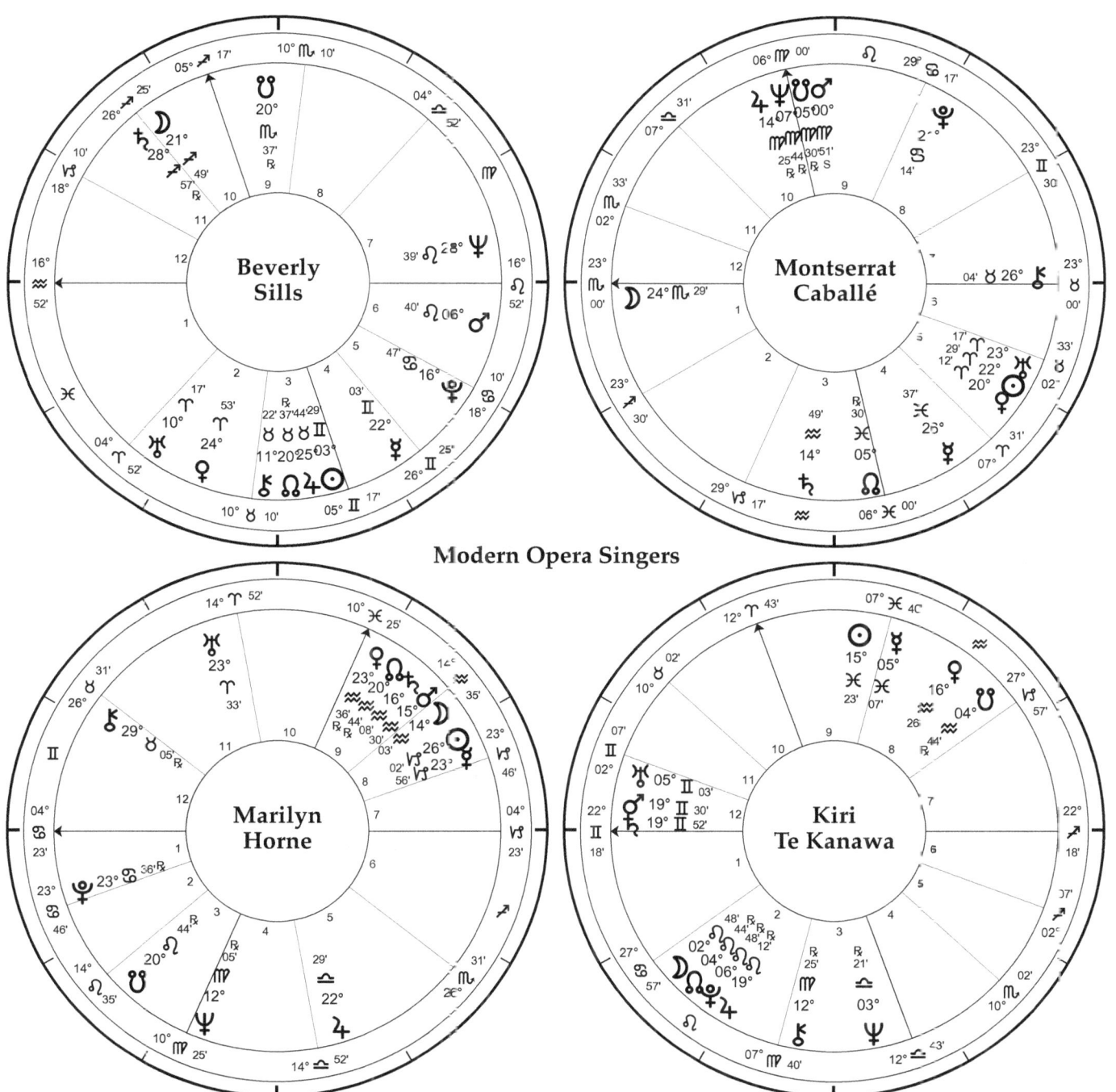

Modern Opera Singers

228 *The Book of Music Horoscopes*

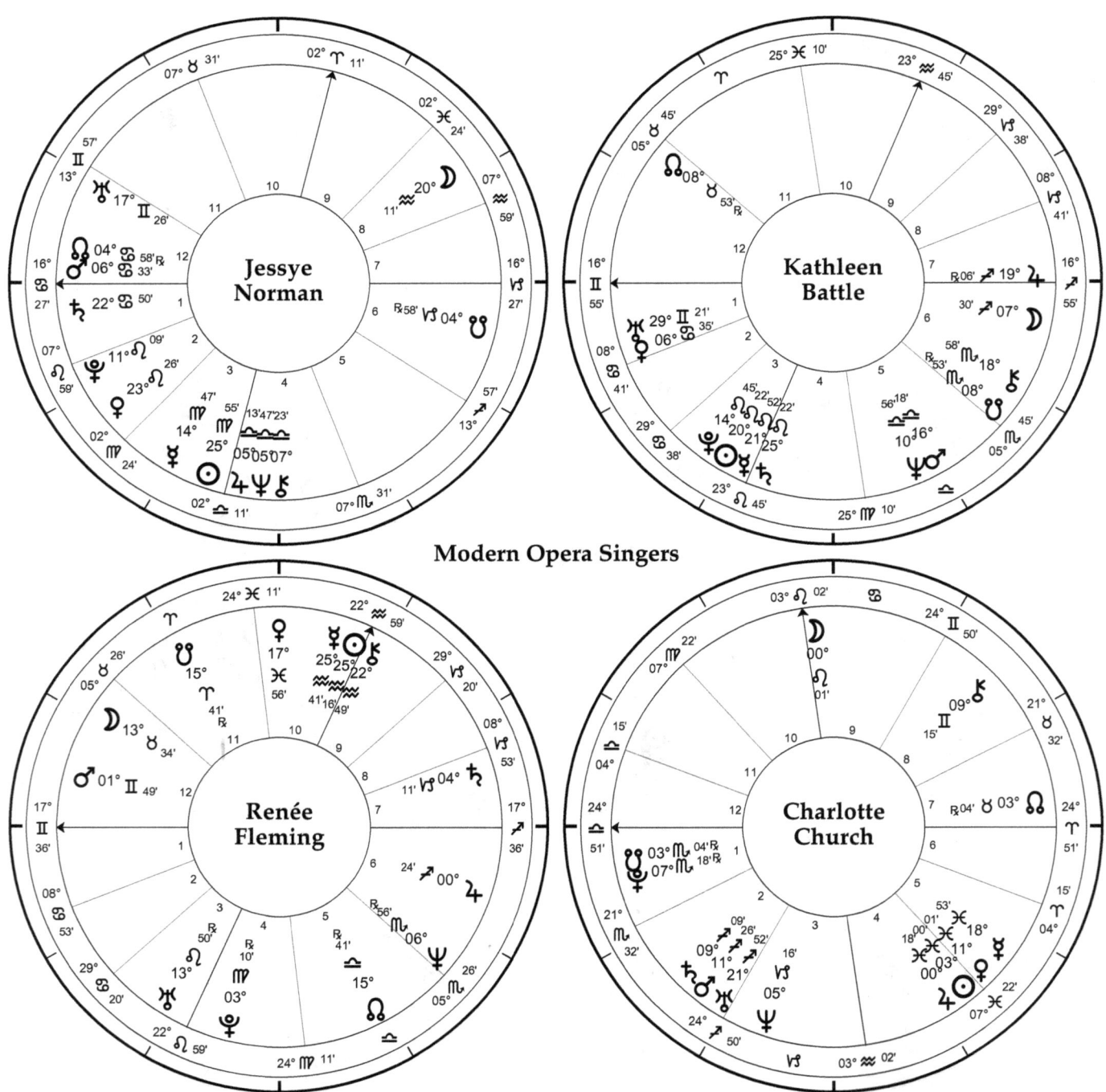

Modern Opera Singers

Stage & Screen

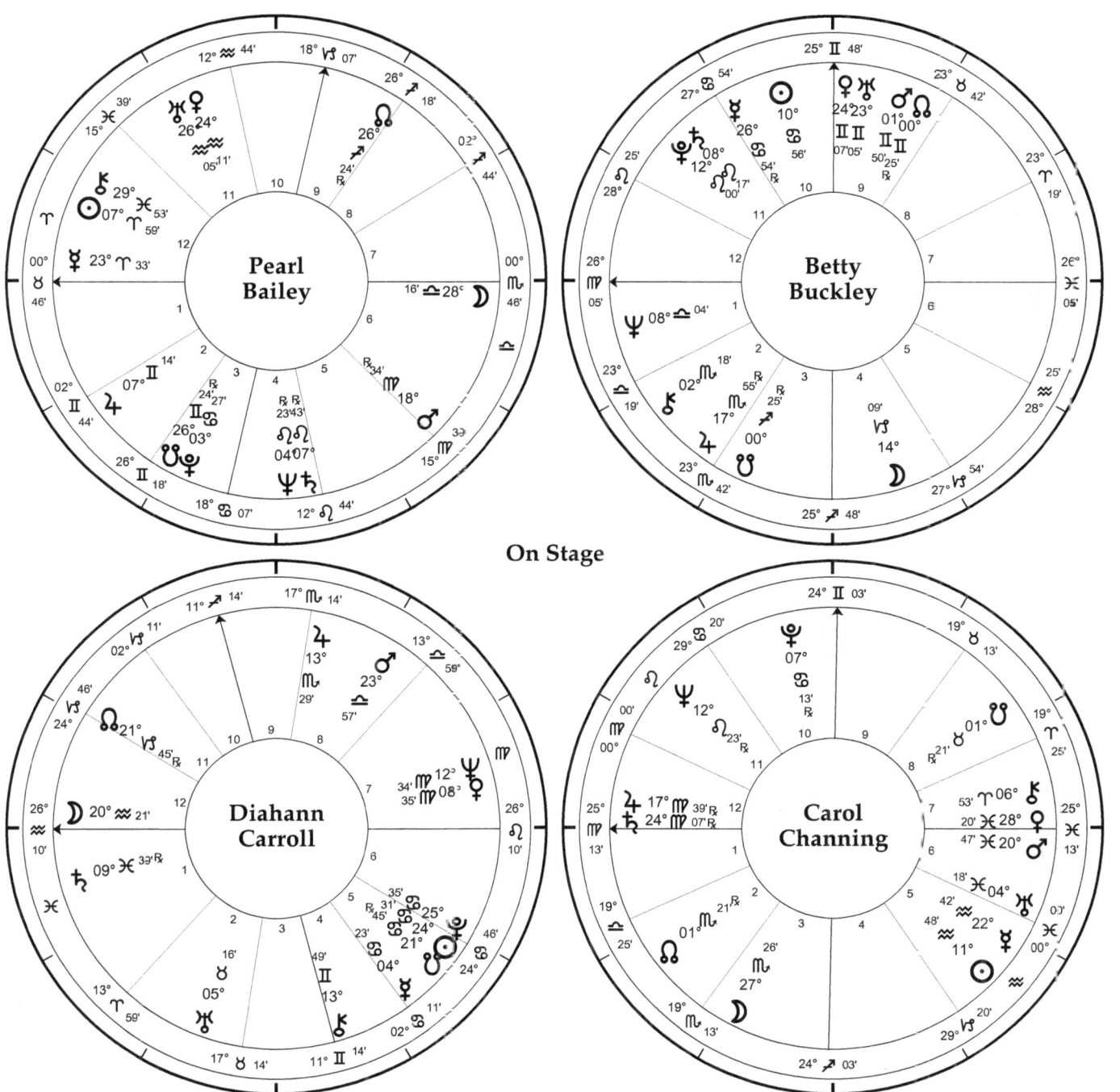

On Stage

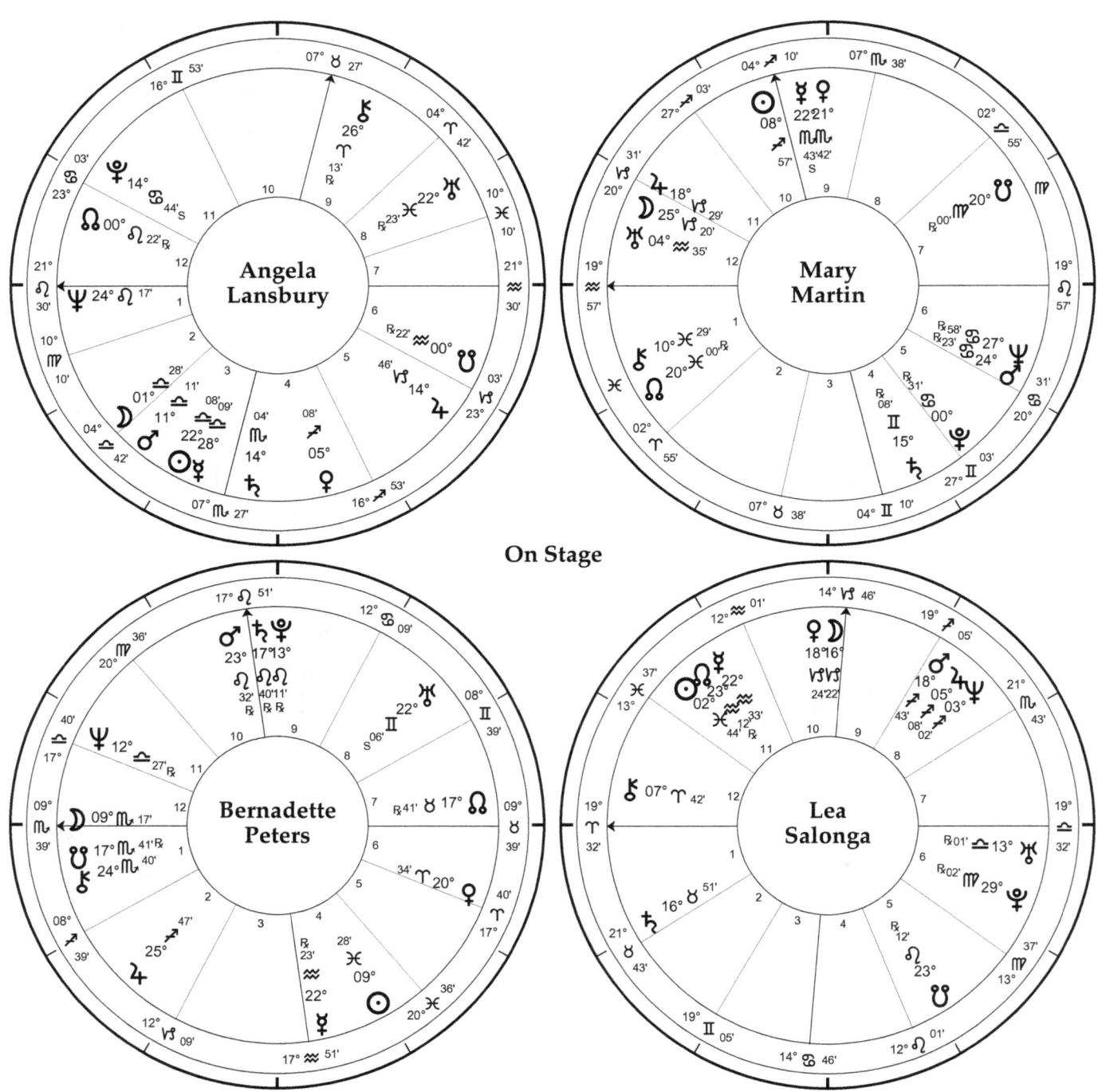

On Stage

Sarah Brightman: An Eclectic Angel

Shawn Nygaard

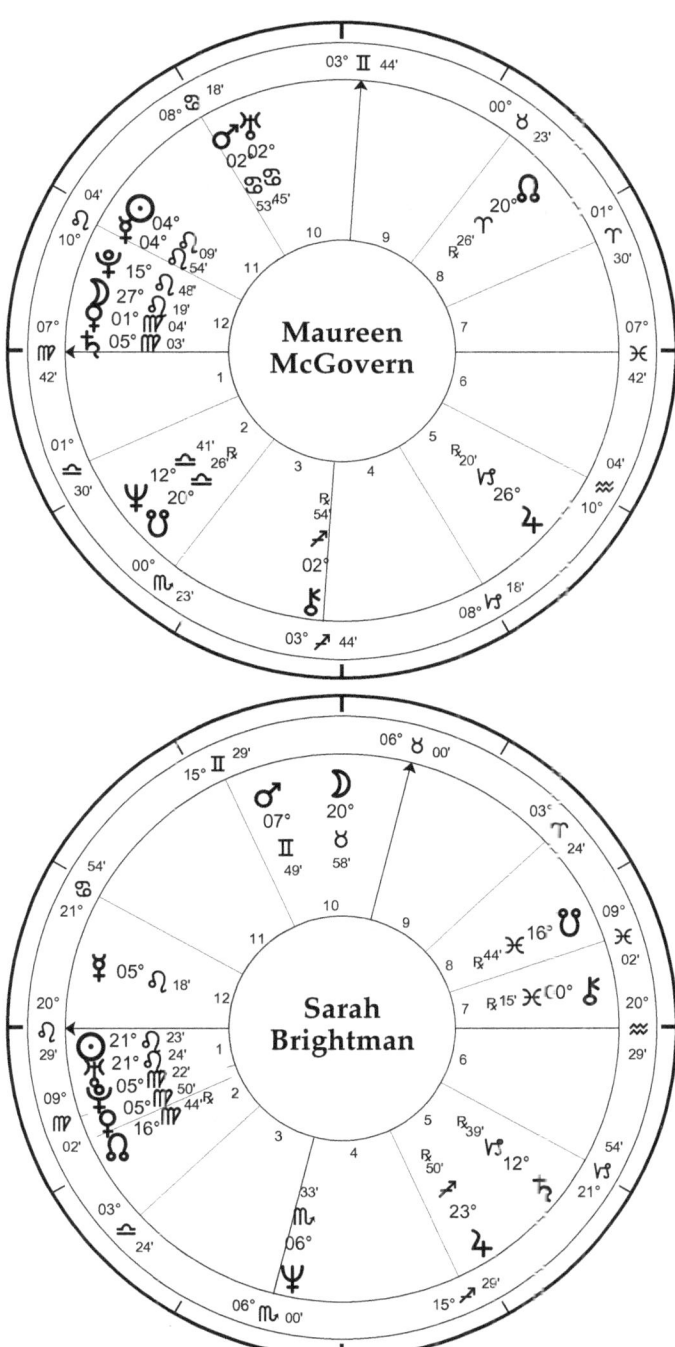

British soprano Sarah Brightman has captivated audiences around the globe for over three decades, from her early hit, 'I Lost My Heart to a Starship Trooper', to her starring role as ingénue Christine Daaé in *The Phantom of the Opera*, which earned her the nickname 'Angel of Music'. Brightman went on to sing the international hit 'Time to Say Goodbye', which identified her as a creative pioneer of the music genre known as 'classical crossover', named for its combinations of pop, rock, opera and other classical motifs.

Appropriately for someone named Brightman, the light in her chart shines luminously bright, with her Leo Sun rising in the 1st House and squaring an exalted Moon in Taurus in the 10th House. The Sun is also conjunct Uranus in Leo and a Leo Ascendant. These strong placements are made even stronger by close orbs, all within 1° of each other.

The Sun represents the individual self and, in Leo, a sense of identity emerges through creative expression. For Brightman, the Sun's tight conjunction with Uranus – arguably the strongest factor in her chart – emphasizes the uniqueness of her creativity and talent, casts her as an innovator, and reveals a woman born with enormous freedom from traditional constraints. After working with Brightman, choreographer Arlene Phillips noted, 'Sarah will never be one of a crowd. She'll never be one of a group.' In fact, Brightman's innate free spirit was established and encouraged early on in her life. Says her mother, Paula Fernyhough, 'I'm not a disciplinarian at all. So I let the children pretty well do everything that they wanted to do.' Brightman credits the 1969 Moon landing as particularly inspiring to her nine-year-old self. 'I started to actually understand at that point that human beings could do amazing things in their life, and think out of the box.'

Brightman's uniqueness showed itself early on when in 1978, at age eighteen, she sang lead on Hot Gossip's science-fiction-themed hit single, 'I Lost My Heart to a Starship Trooper'. Interestingly, the song includes hints of Sarah's future career, by bringing classical music into the pop charts (via a brief sample of Richard Strauss's *Thus Spoke Zarathustra*) and including a plethora of synthesized special effects only possible through the technology (Uranus rules technology) of modern studio production.

In 1981, Brightman auditioned for the West End musical Cats, written by theatre composer Andrew Lloyd Webber. Immediately taken with Brightman and her voice, he gave her a small role in the original cast. Brightman's relationship with Lloyd Webber would prove to be one of the most significant of her life, as the two later became romantically involved, married in 1984, and he began to compose music specifically for her voice.

What is it about that voice? The sign Taurus rules the throat and voice. In Brightman's chart, her exalted Taurus Moon is ruled by Venus (in exact conjunction with Pluto in Virgo). While Venus in Virgo brings to Brightman's soprano the angelic purity and beauty that inspired Lloyd Webber, Venus in fall in Virgo also gives the voice a delicate quality that requires great care. The voice is high-maintenance. 'I have to make my life quite a simple life because of it,' says Brightman, 'because I'm always having to look after it. It's my livelihood, and without it I can't work. I have to go to bed early, I have to eat the right things … I can't party all night after concerts. It's quite a delicate throat. I just have to be really careful.'

Venus is the planet of love, sensual desire, pleasure and fun. In her fall in Virgo, Venus requires more from Brightman than a life of partying. This Venus is more suited to practising scales and Virgo's capacity for repetition – meticulously going over something again and again, practising to get it right.

Following the death of his father in 1982, Lloyd Webber composed a Requiem Mass ('Mass for the Dead'), a piece well suited for the archetypal nature of Brightman's natal Venus–Pluto conjunction. At the time, Pluto, the Lord of the Underworld (the realm of the dead), was squaring Brightman's Mercury – the ruler of her Venus–Pluto conjunction and the only god (Mercury) in myth free to come and go between the heights of Mount Olympus and the depths of the Underworld, not unlike Brightman's voice itself. 'Pie Jesu' from *Requiem* was released as a single in 1985 and became an unlikely chart hit. Singing about death, Brightman brought classical music into the pop charts, in Latin no less.

Brightman is probably best known for her role in Lloyd Webber's musical *The Phantom of the Opera*, based on the classic gothic novel of the same name. The role embodies the Venus–Pluto theme, with Brightman cast as Christine Daaé, the young ingénue aspiring to sing opera, who becomes the object of the obsessive desires of the mysterious masked Phantom who lurks underneath the opera house. With archetypal precision, the story evokes the myth of Hades (Pluto) and Persephone (Venus in Virgo), in which the dark Lord of the Underworld abducts the young, innocent maiden down into his lair. With Pluto still squaring Brightman's Mercury, lyrics such as 'The phantom of the opera is there inside my mind' took on eerie realism. Likewise, during her time in *Phantom*, Pluto in Scorpio was transiting Brightman's 4th House, known in classical astrology as the Underworld. On stage every evening as Christine, Brightman was led by the mysterious Phantom down into his dark, labyrinthine lair where he teaches her to sing.

Brightman's Saturn Return marked most of 1989 and the end of her work with Lloyd Webber, as the couple divorced shortly thereafter. Brightman refers to this time of her life as 'rock bottom'. Transiting Neptune in Capricorn was approaching her Saturn, beginning to dissolve the life she had known, both professionally and personally, allowing her to redefine her career. The next three years included a series of powerful transits, including Pluto opposing Brightman's Moon and squaring her Sun–Uranus conjunction, calling for a profound change to Brightman's core sense of herself and how she shines in the world.

In early 1991, Brightman teamed up with German music producer Frank Peterson, an original member of the group Enigma. His work appealed to her with its unusual combination of Gregorian chant and European dance-floor beats. Together, Brightman and Peterson would forge a path that would become the new 'classical crossover' genre of music. The term 'crossover' points towards Brightman's Mercury, which is rising in the 1st House (by Whole Signs).

In myth, Mercury is the god of the crossroads, a crosser of boundaries. Mercury is also the guide of souls whose joy is in the 1st House, the helm of the ship (the chart). Mercury's clever hands grip the steering wheel of Brightman's ship, casting her whole life as a crossroads in and of itself, neither solidly here nor there, always in between one way of doing and seeing and being (and singing) and another, removing hardline and rigid definitions in favour of the grey areas from which new perspectives, styles and ideas can emerge.

Brightman brings special care and attention to her album covers, mini arenas for Mercury in Leo's creative merchandising and marketing. The covers make full use of ever-adaptable Mercury's joy in the 1st House, the house of appearances. Brightman practically re-invents herself on each album cover, appropriately evoking the unique theme and feel of each album. On the cover of *Eden*, for example, Brightman rests serenely amid lushly sensuous, deep red drapery – much like the peaceful and paradisiacal beauty of the album's music. Conversely, for *Fly*, Brightman is dressed completely in black leather with gloved hands posing *Vogue*-like, all in front of what looks to be the pattern from insect wings. The cover evokes the harder-edged techno feel and darker themes of the album's music. On the cover of *As I Came of Age*, Brightman playfully inserts herself into Arthur Hughes's c.1858 Pre-Raphaelite painting *The King's Orchard*. And recently on *Dreamchaser*, an album of space-themed songs, Brightman wears a gossamer dress, standing in front of a giant Moon, recalling the Moon landing that originally inspired the young Brightman to chase her own dreams.

Mercury also gives Brightman her profound ability to move with tremendous versatility and dexterity between musical styles, not just over the course of her career but often on the same album. She moves freely from popular disco to musical theatre to opera, from singing Latin in a pristine classical voice to belting out the angst-ridden rock-techno gothic fury of 'How Can Heaven Love Me?' She's both the pure and sweet 'Angel of Music' and the seductive siren who sings 'Let me dive in to pools of sin, wet black leather on my skin.' She is equally at home with the gentle lyricism of the Bee Gees' tender 'First of May' as she is with the epic loneliness of 'Only an Ocean Away'. And she can spin the gloriously dignified and stately 'In Pace' ('At Peace') as easily as she can sing of a stalker in the chilling 'Murder in Mairyland Park'.

In perhaps the kind of scenario only possible in a border-crossing Mercurial life, on 23 November 1996 Brightman entered the boxing ring. In fact, she opened the final match of German boxing champion Henry Maske by singing the Italian pop aria 'Time to Say Goodbye' with blind tenor Andrea Bocelli. It was originally a hit by Bocelli, and Brightman's producer Frank Peterson gave the piece a new arrangement and an English title (while retaining the Italian lyrics) and the song was heard by 21 million people watching the televised match. The song – essentially the theme for a boxing match – went on to become the biggest-selling single in Germany's history and one of the best-selling singles in the world.

Brightman embodies the meaning of the word 'eclectic' as both her life and her music resist being confined to any singular model or system. Her music often defies categorization. This has allowed her to essentially create her own genre of music in true Uranian fashion, by breaking open the deeply-rooted traditional styling of classical music, merging it with pop and world music sensibilities, adding modern recording studio technology, and somehow making the whole unlikely combination accessible to a global audience.

Chanteuses

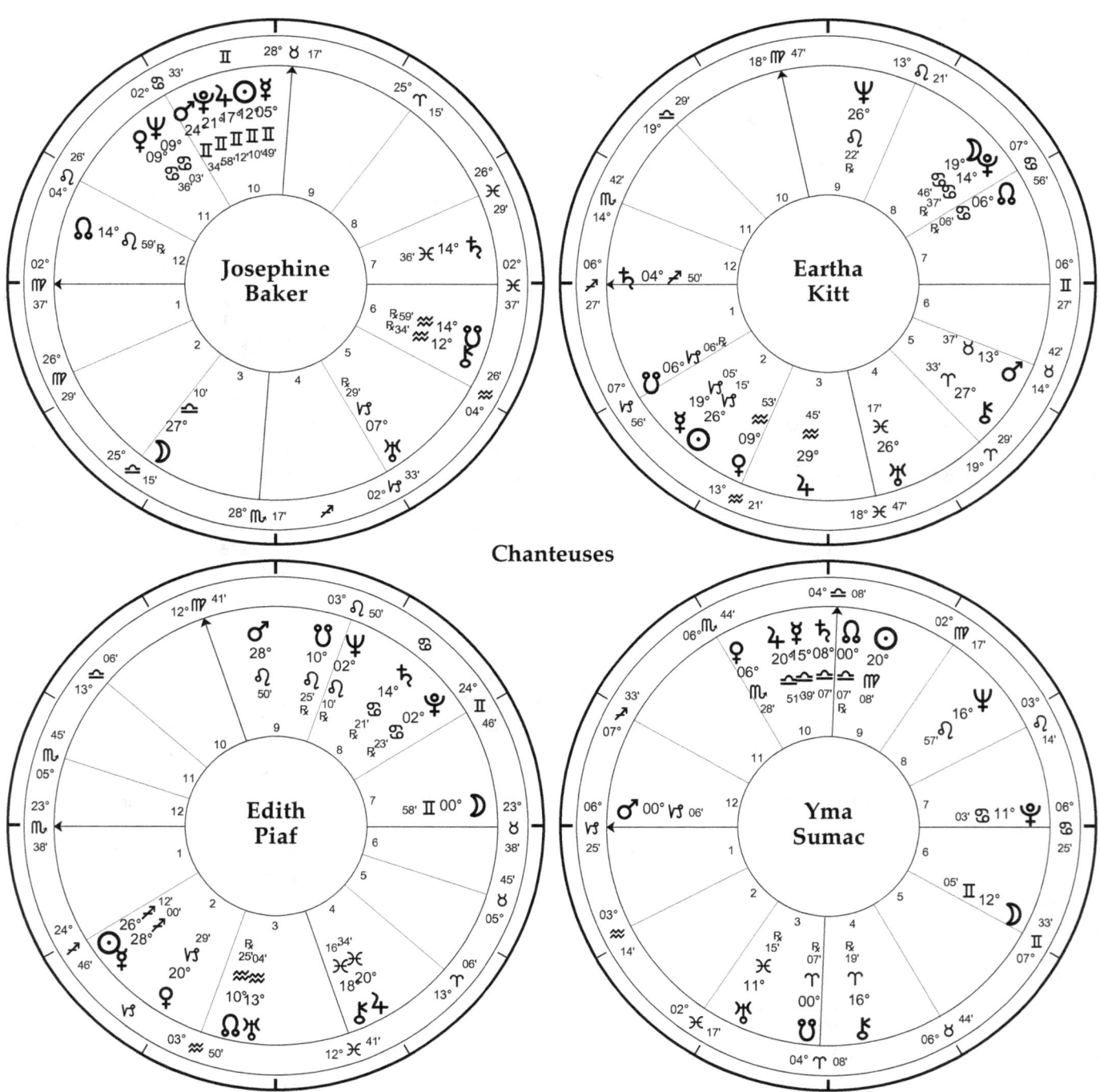

Stage & Screen

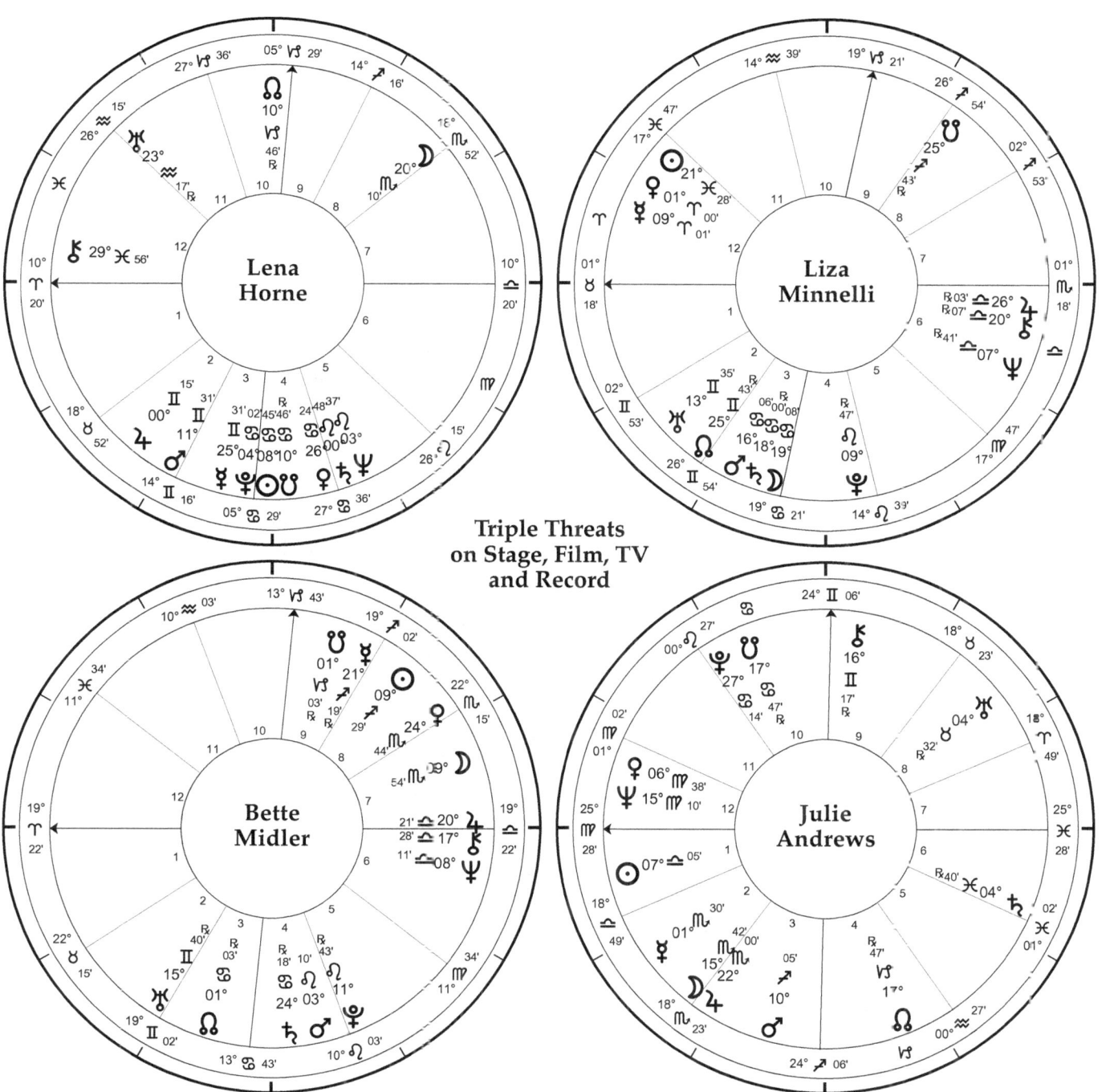

Triple Threats on Stage, Film, TV and Record

The Voice: Julie Andrews

Mari Garcia

Julie Andrews is best known for her singing roles in a variety of musicals both on Broadway and in films. These have included such blockbusters as *The Sound of Music*, *Mary Poppins* and *My Fair Lady*. With the gift of her voice, Andrews has collected multiple awards and gained international recognition for her stage, film and television appearances spanning six decades.

Astrologer Al-biruni tells us that Mercury signifies 'eloquence, fine voice, good memory for stories'. Julie's Mercury is in the Whole Sign 3rd House in the sign of Scorpio. Mercury also makes an applying opposition to Uranus and an applying trine to Saturn. As a child, Julie Andrews was diagnosed as having an adult larynx, echoing Mercury's aspects to both Uranus and Saturn: her unusual (Uranus) voice (Mercury) at such a young age together with its maturity (Saturn).

Mercury plays an important role because it rules both the Virgo Ascendant and the Gemini MC, holding sway over Julie's primary motivation (Ascendant) and is the vehicle through which she would achieve fame and recognition (MC).

With the Virgo Ascendant, Julie's primary motivation is driven by material need. Growing up in a poor part of London, both her parents were vaudeville entertainers. Through hard work the family eventually moved to a better area. Julie sang and performed sporadically with her parents but in 1945 she started to become part of the main act, standing on a milk crate to reach the microphone.

In astrology, the realization of the primary motivation (Ascendant) is the key to a person's happiness and for Julie, with Mercury, the lord of the Ascendant, situated in the 3rd House, the expression and articulation of her ideas and perceptions were done with her voice – in her case through song. The opposition to Uranus colours this expression as being out of the ordinary and non-conformist and yet the aspect to Saturn provides structure, discipline and commitment.

We see the Uranian expression in her vocal ability, which she discovered when she was only seven years old. 'I was a real child prodigy. I had like four octaves, and I could sing cadenzas like crazy. When I went up really high, the dogs from miles around would howl,' she says. 'I was very quickly taken to a specialist to be sure I wasn't doing any harm to my cords, and he said, "You do have an adult larynx, so you're going to be okay, but go to a good teacher."' This occurred at the first Saturn square, and Saturn manifested in the guise of her stepfather who arranged for tuition at the Cone-Ripman School, an independent arts school in London, and later with concert soprano and voice instructor Madame Lilian Stiles-Allen.

Madame Stiles-Allen was so taken with Andrews' voice that in her memoir *Julie Andrews – My Star Pupil* she writes, 'The range, accuracy and tone of Julie's voice amazed me ... she had possessed the rare gift of absolute pitch.' Again, a very Uranian quality, which stood Julie in good stead and enabled her to forge a career which earned her multiple awards for a variety of roles on the stage, in film and on television.

Julie gained her first big opportunity in October 1947 at her first Jupiter Return, when she sang the difficult aria 'Je suis Titania' from *Mignon* as part of a musical revue called *Starlight Roof*. A year later at the first Saturn opposition, she became, on 1 November 1948 at the London Palladium, the youngest solo performer ever to appear in a Royal Command Variety Performance. By the time Saturn transited over her Ascendant at 25° Virgo, Julie Andrews had followed her parents into radio and television, and from 1950–2 she was a regular cast member of *Educating Archie*, a popular Sunday comedy show which boasted a quarter of a million fans.

On the eve of her nineteenth birthday, as the North Node completed its first cycle (the Nodal Return), Julie Andrews made her Broadway debut in *The Boyfriend*. Jupiter had recently transited over the MC and Saturn had just passed over natal Mercury. She made a big impression and, as transiting Jupiter was conjunct her Ascendant in November 1956 and Neptune conjoined natal Mercury, Andrews was cast as Eliza Doolittle in the Broadway production of *My Fair Lady* opposite Rex Harrison.

Julie's North Node sits in the 5th House in the sign of Capricorn. The Nodal axis is the 'internal map' of the life, where the person blends the instinctual with the learned processes (the South Node being the instinctual and the North Node being the learned). In Andrews' case, the North Node in the Whole Sign 5th House signifies that she must learn to develop personal creativity and pleasure versus relying on the collective or group (South Node in the 11th). Additionally, the planets ruling the Nodal axis, which is at Capricorn–Cancer, are Saturn and the Moon. Hence, the journey of her life centres on dealing with emotional insecurity and isolation in order to achieve personal creativity. Here is where Saturn plays such a crucial role in both the definition of the journey and its realization.

We have seen how important both Mercury and Saturn are in the chart. By the time transiting Saturn trined natal Mercury and came back to its natal position (the Saturn Return, in May and July 1964 and February 1965), Julie Andrews was starring in *Mary Poppins*, which became the biggest box-office film in the history of Walt Disney Productions. She won both the 1964 Best Actress Academy Award and Golden Globe Award, as well as a 1965 Grammy Award for Best Album for Children. The following year, 1965, with transiting Jupiter conjunct the MC and transiting Saturn conjunct her Descendant, she starred in *The Sound of Music*, which was the highest-grossing film of the year and the biggest hit in the history of 20th Century Fox Studios. For her performance as Maria Von Trapp, Andrews won her second Golden Globe Award for Best Actress – Motion Picture Musical or Comedy, and was also nominated for the Academy Award for Best Actress. Together Jupiter and Saturn bring the rewards of adulation and hard work.

Both Mercury and Saturn have been instrumental in Julie Andrews' rise. At her second Saturn Return in 1995, Andrews returned to Broadway, after a 35-year absence, in the stage musical version of *Victor/Victoria*, which won huge acclaim. Later, she went on the road in a world tour.

In 1997, while still performing in *Victor/Victoria* she developed vocal problems. She sought treatment through surgery the following year, but the operation damaged her larynx irreparably, presumably ending her singing career, but left her speaking voice unimpaired. From 1997–9, Saturn squared the Nodal axis, signalling a period of crisis and then, together with transiting Jupiter, opposed her natal Mercury. At the same time, transiting Neptune also squared natal Mercury in Scorpio, and transiting Mars became the symbol of the botched surgery, as it too opposed the natal Mercury from the sign of its detriment in Taurus (which rules the throat). In 1999, Andrews filed a malpractice suit against the doctors. The last hit of transiting Jupiter opposite natal Mercury was in February 2000 and the lawsuit was settled in September of that year.

Andrews continued her acting career and new audiences discovered her through other forms of Mercurial expression. She gave voice to the animated characters in films such as *The Princess Diaries* and its sequel, the animated *Shrek* films and *Despicable Me*. She has also written 23 books, some in collaboration with her daughter.

Now in the seventh decade of her career, Julie Andrews is involved in a variety of performing arts, including directing a successful revival of *The Boy Friend*, the show that first brought her to America as a teenager. She continues to act, direct, write and contribute to her favourite causes. In 2008, as Saturn transited the Whole Sign 1st and made an opposition to its natal placement, Andrews published the first volume of her autobiography, *Home: A Memoir of My Early Years*, recounting her life up until her departure for Hollywood to star in *Mary Poppins*. The same year, she made a cautious return to singing in a touring concert performance, *Julie Andrews: The Gift of Music*. In 2010, as Jupiter transited her Whole Sign 7th, conjuncted natal Saturn and then went on to conjunct her Descendant, Julie Andrews marked her return to the London stage for the first time in 21 years with a concert performance at the O2 Arena before 20,000 adoring fans. Julie Andrews has come full circle as her Mercury continues to be a star performer in a stellar nativity.

238 The Book of Music Horoscopes

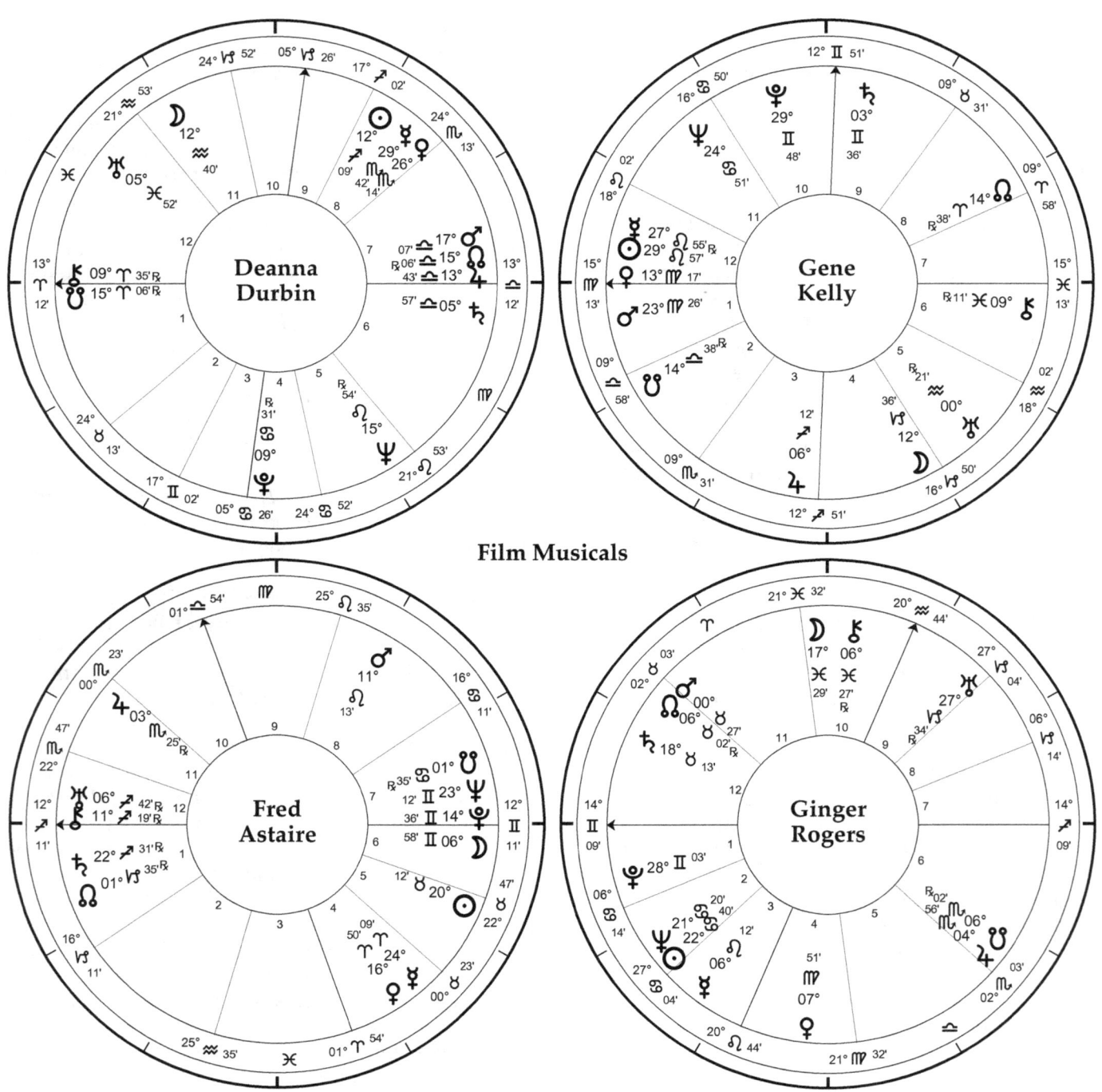

Film Musicals

www.ingramcontent.com/pod-product-compliance
Lightning Source LLC
Chambersburg PA
CBHW080351170426
43194CB00014B/2755